Stress, Coping,
and Cardiovascular Disease

Stress, Coping,
and Cardiovascular Disease

Edited by

Philip M. McCabe
Neil Schneiderman
University of Miami
Tiffany Field
Nova Southeastern University
A. Rodney Wellens
University of Miami

LEA LAWRENCE ERLBAUM ASSOCIATES, PUBLISHERS
2000   Mahwah, New Jersey   London

Lawrence Erlbaum Associates, Inc., Publishers
10 Industrial Avenue
Mahwah, New Jersey 07430-2262

Cover design by Kathryn Houghtaling Lacey

Library of Congress Cataloging-in-Publication Data

Stress, coping, and cardiovascular disease / edited by Philip M. McCabe, Neil Schneiderman, Tiffany Field, and A. Rodney Wellens.
      p. cm. — (Stress and coping)
    Includes bibliographical references and index.
    ISBN 0-8058-3419-2 (c : alk. paper)
    1. Cardiovascular system—Disease—Psychosomatic aspects Congresses. 2. Stress (Psychology) Congresses. I. McCabe, Philip M. II. Field, Tiffany. III. University of Miami Symposia on Stress and Coping. IV. Series: Stress and coping (Unnumbered)
       [DNLM: 1. Cardiovascular Diseases—etiology Congresses. 2. Cardiovascular Diseases—epidemiology Congresses. 3. Cardiovascular Diseases—psychology Congresses. 4. Social Support Congresses. 5. Stress, Psychological Congresses. WG 120S915 1999]
    RC669.S823 1999
    616.1'071—dc21
    DNLM/DLC
    for Library of Congress   99-23561
                                   CIP

Books published by Lawrence Erlbaum Associates are printed on acid-free paper, and their bindings are chosen for strength and durability

Printed in the United States of America
10 9 8 7 6 5 4 3 2 1

Contents

Preface

Stress, Coping, and Cardiovascular Disease is part of a continuing series of volumes based on the annual University of Miami Symposia on Stress and Coping. These symposia focus on important contemporary research topics related to the basic physiological mechanisms, psychosocial factors, developmental aspects, and mental health factors in the relationship between stress and disease. Previous volumes have included a general discussion of the concept of stress, the psychophysiological processes involved in stress and coping, the interaction of behavior with biological processes, the role of stress in the development of disease and mental disorders during different stages of life, and the role of biopsychosocial factors in four of the most common health problems: cardiovascular disease, diabetes, cancer, and the AIDS epidemic.

This volume is focused on the role of biobehavioral and social factors in the leading cause of death in industrialized countries (i.e., cardiovascular disease). Although previous volumes have dealt with these issues in individual chapters, this volume provides an in-depth look at current research dealing with the nervous system and hormonal regulation of cardiovascular function, behavioral–cardiovascular interactions, ethnic differences in cardiovascular regulation, psychosocial influences on cardiovascular systems, and behavioral interventions designed to treat patients following myocardial infarction.

Chapter 1, by Winters, McCabe, Green, and Schneiderman, explores the brain mechanisms involved in emotional responses to stressful stimuli. The authors present an extensive literature review, in addition to describing their own research program, that describes the central nervous system (CNS) circuitry underlying unlearned and learned cardiovascular and behavioral patterns of response in aversive situations. Following a brief tutorial on central autonomic control, the chapter examines the neurobiology of two specific patterns of response seen in animal models: the defense reaction and the vigilance reaction. It has been pointed out that these response patterns are similar to patterns observed in human psychophysiological studies and are consistent with the concept of "go" and "no-go" systems described in the literature. The authors point out the importance of sensory feedback (e.g., baroreceptor, chemoreceptor) in these regulatory processes, and they describe a hierarchical model of control involving cortical, limbic, diencephalic, and brainstem regions. The second part of this chapter explores the CNS circuitry underlying learned affective responses involving stressful stimuli. In particular, the neurobiological mechanisms in classical fear conditioning are discussed. Using this model, researchers have determined that thalamic, cortical, and limbic structures are critical for the neuronal plasticity and expression of emotional behavior seen in the fear conditioning paradigm. The final portion the this chapter provides a synthesis of this large body of literature and presents a model for how the brain integrates learned and unlearned affective responses to stressful stimuli. This model is seen as a neurobiological framework for studying CNS mechanisms in cardiovascular reactivity.

In chapter 2, Dworkin, Elbert, and Rau examine the role of barosensory feedback as a coping mechanism in aversive situations. Although the role of the arterial baroreceptors in buffering blood pressure changes has been well-established, the authors provide evidence that activation of baroafferent pathways leads to a general inhibition of CNS processes. More specifically, it has been shown that following acute blood pressure elevations somatic muscle tone and spinal somatic reflexes are inhibited, anxiety is reduced, cortical electroencephalographic (EEG) activity is synchronized, and sleep can be induced. The authors also propose that during emotionally arousing or painful stimuli, the CNS inhibitory effects of barostimulation provides supplementary homeostatic feedback that helps the organism cope with the aversive situation. This chapter provides evidence that it is the activation of the barosensory pathways, independent of blood pressure elevations, that is critical for these general inhibitory processes to occur. It is also proposed that such mechanisms could contribute to the pathophysiology of essential hypertension by reinforcing blood pressure elevations as a coping response in emotion-arousing situations.

Animal models of coronary heart disease (CHD) are useful because risk factors and pathophysiological mechanisms, that are not easily studied in humans, can be addressed in a well-controlled fashion. In chapter 3, Shively, Adams, Kaplan, and Williams examine how social stress and gender can influence the development of CHD in cynomolgus monkeys. Data presented in this chapter suggest a biological basis for gender differences in the effects of social stress on CHD. Specifically, it is argued that ovarian hormones may influence atherosclerosis, CHD risk, and perhaps plasma cholesterol levels. Furthermore, it was found that female monkeys with more severe CHD are socially subordinate and stressed, whereas males with severe CHD respond to unstable social groupings by being more hostile or aggressive. It is suggested that males and females occupy different positions in society, whether they are human or nonhuman primates, and thus it is not surprising that the effects of psychosocial stressors may be gender-specific.

Hurwitz, Goldstein, Massie, Llabre, and Schneiderman then describe, in chapter 4, a model of the pathogenesis of CHD in humans. The low-flow circulatory model is based on a positive-feedback loop where behavioral factors (e.g., emotional stress), high-fat diet, and sedentary lifestyle exacerbate the progression of insulin resistance, hyperinsulinemia, and an imbalance in sympathetic nervous system drive. As these conditions worsen there is a cascading series of pathophysiological events that may facilate atherogenesis, diminish left ventricular function, and lead to the development of a low-flow circulatory state with elevated blood pressure. The authors describe the use of noninvasive, quantitative methodology to assess hemodynamic and autonomic variables. Furthermore, they suggest that this methodology may be valuable in the detection, prediction, and prevention of CHD.

In chapter 5, Nyklicek, Vingerhoets, and Van Heck explore the dynamic relations between hypertension in humans and various psychological and physiological factors. Specifically, the authors provide a review of studies that have examined the relation between hypertension and objectively derived measures of real-life stressors. In addition, the chapter addresses the relationship between blood pressure and self-reports of exposure to psychosocial stressors. On synthesizing this body of research, the authors propose defensive coping style as an underlying putative psychological mechanism for the association between hypertension and stressor appraisal. Based on this literature review and their own data, several recommendations are made for future studies examining blood pressure and psychosocial variables.

Although hypertension is a major health concern for all Americans, there is a greater prevalence of this disorder in Black Americans than in White Americans. In chapter 6, Saab and colleagues address this ethnic difference in hypertension and examine the factors thought to influence blood pressure regulation that may differ among ethnic groups. The chapter discusses hypertension prevalence rates, comorbidities and mortalities, salt sensitivity, sodium metabolism, and insulin resistance. In addition, the contributions of social, environmental, and psychological factors on blood pressure regulation are explored, and stress-induced responsivity of the different ethnic groups is compared. The chapter concludes with a discussion of the effectiveness of pharmacological and behavioral interventions in treating hypertension among ethnic groups.

In chapter 7, Schneiderman and his colleagues examine the relationship of cardiovascular reactivity to hypertension. The chapter begins with a definition of reactivity and a discussion of the so-called "reactivity hypothesis," including the potential utility of using laboratory studies of reactivity to understand the relationship of stressful events to the pathobiology of cardiovascular disease. Reactivity is then discussed in terms of its usefulness as a predictor of future hypertension, as well as its potential role as a risk factor in the pathogenesis of this disorder. The chapter reviews much of the cardiovascular reactivity literature and makes a strong case for the study of reactivity in controlled laboratory settings.

Several of the chapters in this volume describe the importance of psychosocial factors in the pathogenesis of CHD and hypertension. Of equal interest, however, is the observation that psychological variables influence the prognosis following myocardial infarction (MI). Life stress, anxiety, depressive symptoms, anger and hostility, and social isolation have all been linked to poor outcomes following MI. Frasure-Smith, Lesperance, and Talajic discuss the relationship of these variables to mortality after a heart attack. Chapter 8 describes the Emotions and Prognosis Post-Infarction Project (EPPI), a prospective study designed to examine the prognostic importance of a variety of psychosocial factors, including depression, following MI. The identification of important psychological variables after a heart attack facilitates the development of therapeutic interventions to improve the prognosis following MI.

In chapter 8, Orth-Gomer discusses the role of social networks and social support in promoting host resistance to cardiovascular disease. Social support is viewed as acting as a stress buffer against harmful health effects and as a means of enhancing the health and well-being of the host by itself. The chapter examines epidemiological data from Sweden, and demonstrates the important relation between social isolation and mortality risk in the general population and in a subpopulation of cardiac patients. Finally, the author proposes specific physiological mechanisms to account for the relationship between social support and cardiovascular disease.

The contributions of this volume are not intended to be a comprehensive review of the field of cardiovascular behavioral medicine. Instead, these chapters are representative of recent research in the basic physiological processes in cardiovascular reactivity to stress, pathophysiological mechanisms in cardiovascular disease, psychosocial influence on cardiovascular function and disease, and potential therapeutic strategies to treat cardiovascular disorders. The role of stress in cardiovascular disease is seen as a contributing factor that interacts with other variables such as genetic or constitutional factors. Behavioral interventions used in patients who are at risk for cardiovascular disease, or who exhibit cardiovascular disease, are often designed to change lifestyle, reduce stress, or improve adherence to therapeutic regimens. The contents of this volume provide a solid empirical foundation into the relationship of stress and cardiovascular disease, and will hopefully stimulate further research into the pathophysiology and treatment of the leading cause of death in industrialized countries.

ACKNOWLEDGMENTS

Several individuals, groups, and organizations helped make this symposium and volume possible. First, we thank the participants, who gave freely of themselves and helped carry out the symposium on a rather modest budget. Second, we thank our postdoctoral fellows, graduate students, and staff, whose efforts attentuated the stress associated with the symposium and helped us cope with problems as they arose. Third, we thank Ellie Schneiderman for her gracious hospitality during the conference. Fourth, we thank Brian Dursam and his staff for allowing us to use the magnificent surrounds of the Lowe Art Museum for one day of the symposium. Fifth, we thank Rod Wellens, Chair of the Department of Psychology, for financial support and encouragement. We would also like to thank Sandra Racoobian for her help with travel arrangements, symposium logistics, and in preparing this volume. We also gratefully acknowledge financial support from the National Heart, Lung, and Blood Institute Training Grant (HL07426), and the National Institute Mental Health Training Grant (MH18917).

—Philip M. McCabe
—Neil Schneiderman
—Tiffany Field
—A. Rodney Wellens

1

Stress Responses, Coping, and Cardiovascular Neurobiology: Central Nervous System Circuitry Underlying Learned and Unlearned Affective Responses to Stressful Stimuli

Ray W. Winters
Philip M. McCabe
Edward J. Green
Neil Schneiderman
University of Miami

Affective behaviors are evoked when environmental circumstances pose a threat or challenge to an organism. These integrated somatic and visceral response patterns to emotionally significant stimuli allow an organism to adapt to its environment during stressful situations. Our research program has focused on the central nervous system (CNS) mechanisms that underlie the expression of integrated response patterns to environmental stressors and to the sensory mechanisms that mediate learned emotional responses to these environmental challenges. Several working hypothesizes serve as heuristic guides for our studies. One hypothesis is that the autonomic components of learned affective behaviors are mediated by the neuronal circuitry that subserves hard-wired, unlearned responses to emotional stressors, such as the defense reaction. The autonomic components of the defense reaction serve to prepare the organism for "fight or flight." *Fight or flight* behaviors are not appropriate for the psychosocial stressors that humans face, and although humans do not typically engage in these behaviors, the response patterns of the autonomic nervous system associated with them are still evoked by psychosocial stressors. As a case in point, the cardiovascular responses elicited during the preparation for a stressful speech task are the same ones evoked during the defense reaction, although they clearly exceed the metabolic demands of the task. In general, the autonomic responses elicited to psychosocial stressors are the same ones evoked during unlearned responses to emotional stressors, although they are not always the ones associated with the defense reaction. The observation that these responses exceed the metabolic demands of the task has led a number of investigators to suggest that this is a factor in the etiology of stress-related diseases.

What types of studies must the behavioral neuroscientist conduct to advance the understanding of the CNS mechanisms that underlie emotional responses to psychosocial stimuli? We believe that four types of studies must be conducted. First, it is necessary to delineate the functional pathways in the brain that subserve hard-wired affective behaviors, such as the defense reaction. One of our goals since the late1970s has been to chart the CNS pathway of the defense reaction, using the rabbit as an animal model. We have also mapped many of the elements of a pathway associated with a second type of autonomic–behavioral response pattern to emotional stressors, referred to as the vigilance reaction.

A second type of question that emerges concerns how an event or a set of circumstances (e.g., the preparation for a speech, a job interview) that initially is emotionally neutral becomes affectively significant to the individual so that it evokes an emotional reaction. This, of course, concerns mechanisms of appraisal, learning, and memory. A second goal of our research program has been to delineate the sensory pathways that allow a neutral stimulus to evoke an affective response.

Two other questions are important to the understanding of the brain mechanisms that mediate affective behaviors. As suggested by numerous students of emotions, there must be mechanisms in the brain that allow the organism to appraise the emotional significance of stimuli, whether they are unconditioned or conditioned stimuli. That is, the relevance of an event to one's well-being must be determined before an emotional reaction can occur. In this chapter, we present evidence that the amygdala is a part of the neuronal circuitry necessary for the assignment of emotional significance to sensory events and linking these stimuli to appropriate behaviors. Also presented is evidence that the amygdala is a nodal structure for feedback signals evoked by emotional responses, particularly those sent by baroreceptors and chemoreceptors. Feedback signals from baroreceptors and chemoreceptors are thought to modulate the intensity and duration of an affective behavior and may do so, at least in part, by their effects upon the neuronal circuitry involved in appraisal. Because the feedback signals from baroreceptors attenuate affective responses, the increases in blood pressure that generate these signals may become a conditioned response in stressful situations in which coping responses are not available, thereby attenuating the emotional reaction by their effects on the appraisal mechanism. Also presented is evidence that the effects of peripheral feedback on the strength of the memory trace, developed during experiences that have emotional significance, are mediated by the amygdala. In this way, the intensity of an emotional reaction to various events becomes a factor in determining the strength of memory traces that might be stored. Once again, these effects are thought to be mediated by a nodal structure involved in appraisal, the amygdala.

Finally, in order to understand the brain mechanisms involved in learned affective behaviors, the investigator must determine the CNS structures that form the bridge between the circuitry underlying conditioning and learning, as well as the circuitry that mediates the autonomic components of preprogrammed responses, such as the defense reaction. In this chapter, we present evidence that the hypothalamus is essential to the circuitry that mediates the expression of the autonomic components of affective behaviors in response to conditioned stimuli.

Clinical Significance

Pharmacological treatments and clinical interventions such as neuromuscular relaxation techniques, paced respiration, and exercise are believed to attenuate general arousal (Taylor, 1978), or sensitivity at specific CNS sites, such as the hypothalamus or amygdala, which are nodal structures in the integration and regulation of responses to emotional stressors (Benson, 1983; Gellhorn & Kiely, 1972). These interventions have been found to lead to changes in sympathetic tone (Benson, 1983), cardiovascular reactivity (Allen, 1981), or the recovery rate of cardiovascular responses to a stressor (English & Baker, 1983; Goleman & Schwartz, 1975). Accordingly, one objective of our research program is to provide a neurobiological framework to study human cardiovascular reactivity and to provide an empirical foundation for the development of pharmacological and behavioral interventions that may be employed in the prevention and treatment of cardiovascular disease.

Integrated Coping Responses to Emotional Stressors

Human psychophysiology studies reveal at least two distinct cardiovascular response patterns to laboratory stressors. The first response pattern, that is seen during stressful speech preparation, for example, is characterized by increased cardiac output and a small decrement, or no change, in total peripheral resistance (Hurwitz, Nelesen, Saab, Nagel, Spitzer, Gellman, McCabe, Phillips, & Schneiderman, 1993; Saab, Llabre, Hurwitz, Frame, Fins, McCalla, Cieply, & Schneiderman, 1992). The second pattern of response, seen during the mirror star-tracing task or during the cold pressor task, is characterized by increases in total peripheral resistance with a decrease in cardiac output (Hurwitz et al., 1993; Saab et al., 1992). Interestingly, the same two response patterns have been observed by investigators who use animal models to assess cardiovascular responses to stress (Schneiderman & McCabe, 1985) and are referred to as the defense reaction and vigilance reaction, respectively. Moreover, there is convincing evidence that the pattern of cardiorespiratory activity elicited by stressful or threatening situations in animals is dependent on the availability of a coping response. The behavioral–cardiorespiratory pattern of activity shown when a coping response is available to the animal, the defense reaction, is characterized by cardiovascular and respiratory changes that serve to prepare the animal for fight or flight, that is, increases in cardiac output, heart rate, blood pressure, and hindlimb blood flow, coupled with hyperventilation (Abrahams, Hilton, & Zbrozyna, 1960, 1964; Bolme, Ngai, Uvnas, & Wallenberg, 1967; Smith, Astley, DeVita, Stein, & Walsh, 1980) and inhibition of the cardiomotor component of the baroreceptor reflex. If a coping response is unavailable, the animal shows a behavioral–cardiorespiratory response pattern associated with the inhibition of movement and hypervigilance. This pattern, referred to as the vigilance reaction, is characterized by a pressor response that results from an increase in the total peripheral resistance, but not an increase in cardiac output, bradycardia, the facilitation of the baroreceptor reflex, and inspiratory apnea (Duan et al., 1996b; McCabe et al., 1994). A major objective of our research program is to chart the functional neuroanatomical pathways that mediate the cardiovascular components of these two responses to emotional stressors, using the rabbit as an animal model.

Because the stimuli that elicit emotional behaviors in humans are usually the result of learning experiences, it is also important to understand how coping responses are elicited by conditioned stimuli. A second objective of research from our laboratory, therefore, is to further the understanding of the CNS mechanisms that mediate learned emotional responses. We also use the rabbit as an animal model for these experiments. This chapter provides a summary of what we have learned from our efforts since the 1970s and the relation that our findings bear to research from other laboratories that seek to advance our understanding of the CNS substrates of emotional behavior. The conceptual framework used is primarily based on feedback control theory (Powers, Clark, & McFarland, 1960). CNS structures are examined in terms of their roles in the mediation and modulation of affective behavior and how their activity is modified by sensory feedback from visceral afferents. Similarly, learned emotional responses are assessed in terms of their regulatory functions.

Overview of the Nervous System

The *nervous system* can be defined as a complex network of billions of neurons that regulate internal bodily functions and provides a means for an organism to adapt to the external environment. In order for an organism to regulate interactions with the external environment and maintain a stable internal milieu, information must flow to and from the brain and spinal cord. The brain and spinal cord communicate with the body's muscles and glands via the cranial and spinal nerves. These nerves, are part of the peripheral nervous system, convey sensory information to the CNS and send messages from the CNS to the muscle tissue and glands. Neurons within the cranial and spinal nerves that transmit information to the CNS are referred to as *afferent neurons*; they are activated by receptors located in sense organs, such as the eye, or within the body itself, such as the baroreceptors and chemoreceptors located in the blood vessels. These neurons provide the CNS with information regarding changes in the internal and external environment and with feedback signals to apprise the CNS of the consequences of its command to change the organism's behavior or activity in an internal organ. *Efferent neurons* in the cranial and spinal nerves transmit information from the CNS to striated (skeletal) muscles in order to move the limbs, to the smooth muscle of internal organs, to glandular tissue, and to cardiac muscle. The target organ of efferent neurons of the somatic motor system is striated muscle. The target organs of the efferent neurons of the autonomic nervous system are the smooth muscle of internal organs, the glands, and the heart. The primary function of the autonomic nervous system is the regulation of internal body functions; it is particularly important to behavioral scientists because of its involvement in the expression of emotions.

The nervous system is composed of numerous interconnected subsystems of neurons involved in the regulation of various behaviors and physiological functions. In this context, a *neuronal subsystem* is defined as a network of nuclei and axonal pathways serving a common function. For example, there are separate networks of neurons concerned with movement, emotions, motivation, attention, arousal, cognition, and various sensory functions, such as vision, hearing, taste, and smell. The characterization of the CNS neuronal subsystems involved in the regulation of learned and unlearned emotional behaviors is the focus of our research program.

Organization of the CNS

Superficially, the brain looks like a mushroom. It has a stem, referred to as the brainstem, and an overlying cap, the cerebral hemispheres; the cerebellum lies between the brainstem and the posterior portion of the cerebral hemispheres. The spinal cord is a caudal extension of the brainstem. Information about the external environment and feedback about a person's behavioral and internal bodily responses are sent to the spinal cord, brainstem, cerebellum, and cerebral hemispheres to activate various subsystems of neurons, such as those concerned with memory, attention, control of movement, and emotion.

The brain is usually discussed in terms of three neuroanatomical subdivisions: the forebrain, midbrain, and hindbrain. The *hindbrain* consists of two major divisions, the medulla (myelencephalon) and the pons and cerebellum (metencephalon). The medulla, which is the most caudal portion of the brainstem, contains nuclei that are involved in the control of vital functions such as regulation of the cardiovascular and respiratory systems, the maintenance of skeletal muscle tone, and arousal. The cerebellum receives information from several sensory modalities and integrates this information to allow for smooth, coordinated movements. Damage to this area leads to jerky movements and can impair the ability to walk or even stand. The pons is considered to be the bridge between the cerebellum and the structures in the midbrain, forebrain, and medulla. It also contains nuclei that are part of neural subsystems involved in the regulation of arousal and sleep.

Some of the most complex functions of the brainstem are mediated by neurons in the midbrain. The *midbrain* contains nuclei that are part of neural subsystems that mediate fixed, stereotyped, ritualistic behaviors that are essential for survival and reproduction. As a case in point, both the defense and vigilance reactions can be elicited by electrical or chemical stimulation of the *periaqueductal gray* (PAG), a central structure in the midbrain.

The *forebrain* plays a major role in behaviors that require complex processing (e.g., the storage and retrieval of memories, the integration of emotional experiences and coping behaviors, the coordination of complex movements, and the cognitive processing of information). Affective behaviors, such as the defense and vigilance reactions, are modulated by forebrain structures, and the acquisition of learned affective behaviors require the activation of neuronal subsystems in the forebrain.

CNS Structures Involved
in Affective Behaviors

The basic organizational plan of the brain and spinal cord is a network of neuronal cell body clusters (nuclei or gray matter) interconnected by bundles of neuronal axons (tracts or white matter) and organized into neuronal subsystems that have separate functions. Our research program seeks to map the neuronal subsystems that mediate the cardiovascular components

of the defense and vigilance reactions and those that underlie learned emotional responses. This section of the chapter provides a brief review of what
is known about the CNS regions we have encountered in our studies of affective behavior.

Spinal Cord Structures

Intermediolateral Cell Column (IML). The cell bodies of the
preganglionic neurons of the sympathetic division of the autonomic nervous system are located in the intermediolateral cell column of the thoracic
and lumbar portions of the spinal cord. The axons of these efferent neurons
connect to postganglionic neurons of the sympathetic nervous system located in either the sympathetic trunks, adjacent to the spinal cord, or to
ganglia located near internal organs. These neurons are particularly important to cardiovascular regulation because they connect to the heart and the
smooth muscle of blood vessels.

Hindbrain Structures

The Rostral Ventrolateral Medulla (RVLM). The RVLM is a clus-
ter of cell bodies in the medulla that plays a central role in setting the resting
level of blood pressure by influencing the tonic contractile state of blood
vessels (vasomotor tone). This structure is also involved in the mediation of
phasic changes in blood pressure and heart rate. The RVLM is also a part of
the neuronal subsystem that regulates blood pressure, known as the
baroreceptor reflex.

Dorsal Motor Nucleus of X (Dvn) and Nucleus Ambiguus. The
cell bodies of the preganglionic neurons of the parasympathetic division of the
autonomic nervous system are located in the brainstem and the sacral portion
of the spinal cord. The axons of these efferent neurons, therefore, are found in
cranial nerves and spinal nerves. The tenth cranial nerve, the vagus nerve, is
particularly important to cardiovascular regulation because many of its axons
connect to the heart. The cell bodies of these efferent neurons are found in
nucleus ambiguus and the dorsal motor nucleus of the vagus nerve (DVN).
They are a component of the reflex arc that mediates the cardiomotor component of the baroreceptor reflex. The vagus nerve also contains afferents that
provide visceral sensory information to the CNS, thereby providing feedback
about visceral responses that occur during affective behavior.

Nucleus of the Solitary Tract (NTS).   This cluster of cell bodies receives sensory information from visceral organs. As discussed later in this chapter, there is evidence that visceral sensory information conveyed to the NTS modulates the storage of memories that have emotional significance to the organism. The NTS is also a part of the baroreceptor reflex arc, receiving information from baroreceptors located in blood vessels and sending information to CNS structures that lead to changes in vasomotor tone and cardiac output, to regulate blood pressure.

Medullary Raphe.   The neurons situated along the midline of the medulla, pons, and midbrain are collectively referred to as the *raphe nuclei*. A substantial number of the raphe neurons secrete the synaptic transmitter serotonin. The raphe neurons in the medulla project to the spinal cord and are best known for their role in the modulation of neurons that transmit pain information. Electrical stimulation of medullary raphe also inhibits the activity of sympathetic preganglionic neurons located in the IML of the spinal cord.

Lateral Tegmental Field of the Medulla (LTFM).   Although the LTFM is believed to be involved in cardiovascular regulation, its exact role is unknown. One view is that these neurons are a source of excitatory input to RVLM neurons, that in turn, connect to preganglionic neurons of the sympathetic nervous system located in the spinal cord.

Midbrain Structures

Periaqueductal Gray.   This region embodies neural subsystems that control complex species-specific behaviors such as aggression, flight, and mating. For example, a rabbit's freezing response that leads to sustained immobility appears to be organized in the PAG. The PAG also contains neurons that are part of a brainstem neuronal subsystem that modulates pain.

Inferior Colliculus.   This nucleus is a part of the auditory pathway. The axons of these neurons project to the medial geniculate nucleus of the thalamus via the brachium of the inferior colliculus.

Forebrain Structures

Hypothalamus.   This structure, located at the base of the forebrain, is involved in the organization and regulation of a number of behaviors that are essential to survival such as mating, flight, feeding, drinking, and aggression. This structure also secretes hormones that regulate the activity of the pituitary gland, which is attached to the base of the hypothalamus. The pituitary gland is often referred to as the "master gland" because it secretes essential hormones such as vasopressin, which influences kidney function, and it exerts control over other glands of the endocrine system, such as the adrenal gland and thyroid gland.

Medial Geniculate Nucleus. This structure, that receives input from the inferior colliculus via the brachium of the inferior colliculus, is a part of the auditory pathway. It is located in the thalamus, a region in the core of the forebrain that provides most of the projections to the cerebral cortex.

Amygdala. This structure appears to be critical in linking stimuli to appropriate emotional responses. Damage to restricted regions of the amygdala can abolish a wide range of learned or unlearned affective behaviors. The Kluver-Bucy syndrome results from removal of the entire amygdala and adjacent structures. This syndrome is characterized by a reduction in aggression and an inability to distinguish between appetitive stimuli, such as food and potentially dangerous objects. The animal becomes hypersexual but, more importantly, perhaps, is not able to make the appropriate discriminations regarding the gender and species of the sex partner. Thus, it appears that the amygdala is involved in assessing the emotional significance of stimuli. This important function of this structure is discussed in greater detail later in the chapter.

Both the amygdala and hypothalamus are among a set of forebrain structures referred to as the *limbic system.* Many investigators believe that these interconnected structures work as a whole in regulating motivated and emotional behaviors.

Overview of Research Strategy

The research strategy that we use to trace the descending pathways that mediate the defense reaction and vigilance reaction is referred to as a retrograde analysis. The *retrograde analysis* is a seven stage program that begins at a cardiovascular structure in the lower brain stem (e.g., the rostral ventrolateral medulla) or spinal cord (e.g., the IML) and ends at a neuroanatomical site, (e.g., the hypothalamus or PAG), that yields an affective behavior when stimulated electrically. Suppose, for example, that we wanted to trace the pathway from the hypothalamic defense area to the preganglionic neurons of the sympathetic nervous system located in IML of the spinal cord. The first experiment we would conduct would be a retrograde neuroanatomical tracing study. We would inject a retrograde tracer, such as horseradish peroxidase (HRP) or fluorogold, into the IML of the spinal cord. The tracer would enter axon terminal endines in the region and would be transported back to the cell bodies of these axons located in the brainstem. Histochemical techniques would be used to determine the location of cell bodies that showed retrograde labeling. We know from previous studies from our laboratory that two such regions are the RVLM and the medullary raphe. The fact that the cell bodies in the RVLM and medullary raphe show labeling does not prove, however, that they are part of the pathway from the hypothalamus to the IML. Positive results must be obtained on six additional types of experiments to establish that these neurons are part of the descending pathway. First, the structure must yield one or more components of the defense reaction when stimulated electrically. We know from our studies that electrical stimulation of the RVLM and one portion of the medullary raphe leads to an increase in heart rate and blood pressure. These cardiovascular changes, however, could have resulted from electrical stimulation of axons passing through the region, so we stimulate the same site chemically with L-glutamate; L-glutamate stimulates neuronal cell bodies but not axons. The next set of studies use electrophysiological techniques to help establish that the structure is a part of the descending pathway. One criterion that must be met is that the cell bodies of neurons at the site in question can be activated antidromically, that is, the stimulation (axon) and the recording (cell body) sites are from the same neuron. We know from our studies that cell bodies in the RVLM and medullary raphe can be activated antidromically by stimulating their axon terminals in the IML. In addition, electrical stimulation of the structure that showed retrograde labeling (the RVLM and medullary raphe in the example) must alter the discharge rate of single cells at the site at which the retrograde tracer was injected (IML in our example). Next, single cell recordings are made from cell bodies at the labeling site (RVLM and medullary raphe) during electrical stimulation of the hypothalamic defense area. If hypothalamic stimulation changes the firing rate of these neurons, we determine the effect of reversible lidocaine lesions at the site on the response elicited by electrical stimulation of the hypothalamic defense area. If positive results are obtained in all of these studies, the entire procedure is repeated, beginning at the brainstem nucleus that was being tested. Thus, once we established that the RVLM was part of the descending pathway from the hypothalamic defense area, we injected the retrograde tracer horseradish peroxidase in the RVLM and looked for retrograde cell body labeling in structures that were neuroanatomically closer to the hypothalamic defense area. This procedure is repeated until all of the retrograde tracer experiments lead to labeling the hypothalamic defense area

CNS Sites That Yield Integrated Stress Responses

Hypothalamus. We observed that the behavioral and cardiorespiratory components of the defense reaction and vigilance reaction can be elicited from the PAG in the midbrain (Duan et al., 1993, 1997) and the hypothalamus (Duan et al., 1996a; McCabe et al., 1994) in the rabbit. Studies from our laboratory reveal that electrical stimulation of the ventromedial portion of the posterior hypothalamus elicits tachycardia, a pressor response, and hyperventilation in anesthetized rabbits (Duan et al., 1994; McCabe et al., 1994). Because electrical stimulation of the same site in conscious rabbits was observed to evoke escape behaviors, we referred to this region as the hypothalamic defense area for the rabbit (Duan et al., 1996a). Our studies of affective behavior in conscious rabbits also revealed that electrical stimulation of the mediolateral hypothalamus leads to phasic immobility and signs of increased vigilance, including exophthalmos and mydriasis (Duan et al., 1996a). Electrical stimulation of this region in anesthetized rabbits elicits a profound bradycardia, a pressor response, and inspiratory apnea (Duan et al., 1994; Duan et al., 1993; McCabe et al., 1994). This response pattern, which we have referred to as the vigilance reaction, appears to correspond to the one reported by Evans (1976, 1978, 1980) in his studies of affective behavior in rabbits. It bears many similarities to affective behaviors reported by other investigators including immobile confrontation (Zanchetti, Baccelli, & Mancia, 1976), attentive immobility (Marks, 1987), and alert immobility (Sudre, de Barros, Sudre, & Schenberg, 1993).

In a study conducted several years ago, we compared the skeletal muscle and the visceral blood flow patterns elicited by the electrical stimulation of the hypothalamic defense area (HDA) and the hypothalamic vigilance area (HVA) of the rabbit (McCabe et al., 1994). Electrical stimulation of the HDA evoked a pressor response, tachycardia, hyperventilation, an increase in blood flow to the skeletal muscles, and decreased blood flow to the visceral organs. Stimulation of the HVA yielded a pressor response, bradycardia, inspiratory apnea, and decreased blood flow to both the skeletal muscles and the viscera. Preliminary observations were indications that, in conscious rabbits, escape behaviors were associated with the site that yielded the cardiovascular components of the defense reaction in the anesthetized animal, and that the inhibition of movement was linked to the vigilance site. Subsequently, we sought to fully characterize the behavioral responses associated with these two sites in the hypothalamus (Duan et al., 1996a). Individual rabbits were implanted with stimulating electrodes at both hypothalamic locations, and after recovery from surgery, the hypothalamic sites were stimulated, and the behavioral responses were observed and quantified using a computer tracking system. HDA stimulation at moderate intensities evoked agitated running; the amount of running was proportional to stimulus intensity. Stimulation of the HVA at moderate intensities elicited phasic immobility, increased extensor muscle tension, and created head tremors. The behavioral changes elicited by HDA and HVA stimulation were accompanied by pupillary dilation and exophthalmos. Thus, it appears that these two behavioral response patterns (i.e., defense and vigilance) are mediated by distinct populations of cells in the hypothalamus.

The findings from our hypothalamic studies, for the most part, are consistent with those reported from other species; although as of this writing, hypothalamic sites associated with the vigilance reaction have not been reported for species other than the rabbit. The defense reaction can be elicited by electrical stimulation of the ventral perifornical region of the hypothalamus of the cat (Abrahams et al., 1960; Brown, Hunsperger, & Rusuold, 1969; Hess & Brugger, 1943; Hilton & Smith, 1984) and the posterior hypothalamus of the rat (DiMicco & Abshire, 1987; Shekhar & DiMicco, 1987). The behaviors displayed by the animal from stimulating the hypothalamus appears to be species-specific, with the cat showing affective attack, quiet biting, or flight (Abrahams et al., 1960; Bandler & Carrive, 1988; Blanchard & Blanchard, 1987) and the rat showing escape behaviors or aggression (Brown et al., 1969; DiMicco & Abshire, 1987). The neuroanatomical site in the hypothalamus that yields the defense reaction in the rabbit appears to overlap the site that produces escape behaviors in the rat.

As discussed earlier, responses evoked by electrical stimulation may be due to activation of axons passing through the stimulation site rather than cell bodies of neurons in the region. Attempts by investigators to elicit the defense reaction by injecting excitatory amino acids into the hypothalamus have not been successful (Gelsema, Roe, & Calaresu, 1989; Hilton & Redfern, 1983; Spencer, Sawyer, & Lowey, 1990). In contrast, microinjections of gamma-aminobutyric acid (GABA) antagonists into the posterior hypothalamus of the rat (Abshire, Hankins, Roehr, & DiMicco, 1988; DiMicco & Abshire, 1987) and the cat (Bauer, Vela, Simon, & Waldrop, 1988; Waldrop & Bauer, 1989; Waldrop, Bauer, & Iwamoto, 1988) elicit the cardiorespiratory changes characteristic of the defense reaction; escape behaviors are elicited when GABA antagonists are injected at the same site in conscious animals (DiScala, Schmitt, & Karli, 1984; Milani & Graeff, 1987; Shekhar & DiMicco, 1987). GABA is an inhibitory transmitter, so activation of the defense reaction with a GABA antagonist would be the result of releasing inhibitory constraint on hypothalamus imposed by another region in the CNS. One reasonable possibility is that the neurons in the amygdala inhibit neurons in the hypothalamic defense area. As discussed later, there is evidence that the amygdala is part of the neuronal circuitry involved in the assignment of emotional significance to a stimulus. If the defense reaction is not appropriate for a particular set of stimulus conditions, neurons in the hypothalamus may be inhibited by neurons in the amygdala.

Amygdala. The cardiorespiratory components of the defense reaction can be elicited by electrical stimulation of the central nucleus of the amygdala (ACe) and from the magnocellular portion of the basal nucleus in the anesthetized cat (Stock, Schlor, & Buss, 1978; Timms, 1981); the behavioral components of the response can be elicited from the same regions (Hilton & Zbrozyna, 1963) in the cat. Kapp and co-workers (Applegate, Kapp, Underwood, & McNall, 1983) were able to elicit the defense reaction by high intensity electrical stimulation of the ACe in the rabbit. They suggested, however, that this finding was due to the current spread to adjacent areas because low intensity stimulation in the ACe produced inhibition of movement and bradycardia. The effect of excitatory amino acids or GABA antagonists on neurons in the amygdala has not been investigated extensively. Gelsema and colleagues (Gelsema, McKitrick, & Calaresu, 1987) were not able to elicit the autonomic or behavioral components of the defense reaction by stimulating the amygdala with the excitatory amino acid DL-homocysteic acid in rats. Clearly, more work needs to be done on the neuroanatomy of the amygdaloid defense area. One of the goals of our research program is to investigate the role of the amygdala in the organization and regulation of the defense reaction and the vigilance reaction.

Periaqueductal Gray (PAG). Both the defense reaction and vigilance reaction can be elicited by stimulating the PAG. Several laboratories, including our own, have presented evidence that the dorsal PAG is associated with the defense reaction, and the ventrolateral PAG (vlPAG) is part of the neuronal circuitry, underlying the vigilance reaction. We were able to elicit the cardiorespiratory components of the defense reaction when we electrically stimulated the dorsal PAG but not the ventral vlPAG (Markgraf et al., 1991). Moreover, we observed that electrical stimulation of the vlPAG in anesthetized rabbits evokes a cardiorespiratory response pattern that is nearly identical to the one elicited by stimulating the hypothalamic vigilance area (Duan et al., 1993, 1997). Although we have not examined the behavioral changes elicited by electrical stimulation of the vlPAG in conscious rabbits in detail, preliminary observations indicate that motor activity is inhibited. Stimulation of the vlPAG has also been reported to elicit immobility in the cat and the rat (Bandler, Carrive & Zhang, 1991; Carrive, 1993).

Stimulation of the PAG with electrical stimuli, excitatory amino acids, or GABA antagonists has been found to elicit the defense reaction in the cat and the rat (Bandler & Carrive, 1988; Carrive, Bandler, & Dampney, 1989; Hilton & Redfern, 1983; Schmitt, Di Scala, Brandao, & Karli, 1986; Yardley & Hilton, 1986). Several investigators have presented evidence for differences in the responses elicited from the dorsal and ventral PAG of the rat. Electrical stimulation (Fardin, Oliveras, & Besson, 1984; Shaikh, Barrett, & Siegel, 1987; Yardley & Hilton, 1986), chemical stimulation with DL-homocysteic acid (Hilton & Redfern, 1989; Shaik et al., 1987), or GABA antagonists (Schmitt et al., 1986) elicited the defense reaction in the rat when the stimulation site was the dorsal PAG but not when it was the vlPAG.

Medial Prefrontal Cortex (mPFC).   It has been observed that electrical stimulation of the mPFC elicits autonomic responses (Cechetto & Saper, 1990; Neafsey, Terreberry, Hurley, Ruit, & Frystzak, 1993; Buchanan, Valentine, & Powell, 1985). Furthermore, it has been demonstrated that lesions in this region interfere with conditioned autonomic responses (Frysztak & Neafsey, 1994; Powell, Watson, & Maxwell, 1994). These observations have led some researchers to label the mPFC as the visceral motor cortex (Hurley, Herbert, Moga, & Saper, 1991; Neafsey et al., 1993). The mPFC is a region on the anterior medial surface of the cerebral cortex and typically includes the anterior cingulate cortex, the infralimbic cortex, and the prelimbic cortex. Using neuroanatomical tracing techniques it has been demonstrated that the mPFC can be subdivided into a dorsal system and a ventral system, each with its own unique projection fields (Buchanan, Thompson, Maxwell, & Powell, 1994; Hurley et al., 1991; Neafsey et al., 1993). The dorsal system primarily projects to other cortical structures (Hurley et al., 1991), however it also projects to the dorsomedial PAG (Neafsey et al., 1993). The ventral pathway projects extensively to the thalamus, hypothalamus, amygdala, and brainstem autonomic regulatory nuclei such as the vlPAG, parabrachial nucleus of the pons, nucleus tractus solitarius, dorsal vagal nucleus, nucleus ambiguus, median raphe, RVLM, and IML in the spinal cord (Hurley et al., 1991; Neafsey, et al., 1993; Buchanan et al., 1994). Recently, it has been reported in the macaque monkey that there are parallel, descending projections from the mPFC to the medial and lateral hypothalamus (Ongur, An, & Price, 1996) as well as a strong projection to vlPAG (Bandler & Price, 1996). It has been suggested that the mPFC receives a variety of sensory information, including visceral sensory information, and helps the organism to select appropriate behavioral and autonomic responses for those stimuli and the emotional requirements of the situation (Carmichael & Price, 1996; Hurley et al., 1991; Neafsey et al. 1993).

CNS Pathways That Mediate the Defense Reaction and Vigilance Reaction

Changes in Peripheral Resistance and Cardiac Output.   T h e intermediolateral nucleus (IML) of the spinal cord is the final common pathway for many of the cardiovascular components of the defense reaction and vigilance reaction. Our initial studies determined the location of the cell bodies of the sympathetic preganglionic neurons that project to the superior ganglion of the sympathetic trunk. Injections of the retrograde tracer, HRP, led to retrograde cell body labeling in the intermediolateral nucleus (IML) at the T1–T8 segments of the spinal cord, with most of the labeling in the T2–T4 segments (Vera, Ellenberger, Haselton, Haselton, & Schneiderman, 1986). We then identified descending projections from the medulla to sympathetic preganglionic neurons in the IML by injecting HRP in the IML at the T2–T4 level (Haselton et al., 1985). One site that showed retrograde labeling was the RVLM. Injections of HRP into the RVLM produced anterograde labeling bilaterally in the IML. Pressure injections of glutamate, an excitatory amino acid that does not activate fibers of passage, into the RVLM elicited profound increases of arterial blood pressure. These findings are similar to those reported by other laboratories, and they suggest that the RVLM contains neurons that project monosynaptically to the preganglionic sympathetic neurons located in the IML.

There is ample evidence from studies in cats and rats that the RVLM plays a key role in setting the resting level of vasomotor tone and in the mediation of phasic changes in blood pressure and heart rate. Electrical stimulation of the RVLM leads to increases in blood pressure (Dampney, Goodchild, Robertson, & Montgomery, 1982; Ross, Ruggiero, Park, Joh, & Sved, 1984) and heart rate (Gong, Huangfu, & Li, 1987; Ross et al., 1984), and these changes appear to be the result of the stimulation of cell bodies in the region because the application of the excitatory amino acid L-glutamate or D,L-homocysteic acid also produces pressor responses (Dampney et al., 1982; Haselton et al., 1985; Ross et al., 1984).

We also observed that HRP injections in the IML lead to retrograde label-ing of neurons in the medullary raphe (Haselton, Winters, Haselton, McCabe, & Schneiderman, 1988b). Electrical stimulation of the ventral portions of the medullary raphe was observed to evoke a pressor response ac-companied by bradycardia (Haselton, Winters, Haselton, McCabe, & Schneiderman, 1988a), whereas stimulation of the most dorsal portion of the medullary raphe evoked a pressor response and tachycardia, two compo-nents of the defense reaction. Chemical stimulation of the medullary raphe with glutamate also led to a pressor–tachycardia response at the dorsal sites and a pressor–bradycardia response at the ventral sites.

The injection of the retrograde tracer Fluorogold, or the retrograde and anterograde tracer HRP, into RVLM produced retrograde and anterograde labeling in midbrain and forebrain regions (Markgraf et al., 1991). Dense retrograde labeling was observed in the hypothalamic defense area. In the midbrain, retrograde labeling was seen in the PAG, with one group of cells located in the dorsal portion of PAG and a second group of labeled cells lo-cated in the vlPAG. The results of electrical stimulation studies (Duan et al., 1993, 1997; Markgraf et al., 1991) provide evidence that these sites corre-spond to the PAG defense areas and the vigilance areas, respectively.

HRP injections into medullary raphe produced cell body labeling in both the dorsal and ventrolateral regions of PAG (Haselton et al., 1988). Cells in medullary raphe could be orthodromically activated by electrical stimula-tion of the PAG defense area.

There is considerable evidence that neurons in the lateral tegmental field of the medulla (LTFM) are involved in cardiovascular regulation. We ob-served that electrical stimulation of the dorsomedial portion of the LTFM elicited a pressor–tachycardia response (Winters, McCabe, Green, Duan, & Schneiderman, 1991) and that single unit activity in the LTFM was altered by electrical stimulation of the hypothalamic defense area. A substantial number of cells that were affected by hypothalamic stimulation were phasically modulated within the cardiac cycle and responded to transient increases in blood pressure, thereby indicating that they received input from baroreceptors. Injections of HRP or Fluorogold into the LTFM led to retro-grade labeling in the medullary raphe and the RVLM but not the PAG or hy-pothalamic defense areas (Winters et al., 1991). Anterograde HRP labeling was observed in the RVLM and the medullary raphe, suggesting the pres-ence of reciprocal connections between these two regions and the LTFM. Taken together, the data suggest that, although cells in the LTFM can be driven by stimulating of the HDA, this input is not monosynaptic but in-stead may be mediated through the hypothalamic projection to the RVLM or via the hypothalamic-PAG-raphe projection. The precise role of the LTFM in the regulation of affective behavior is not clear, but there is evidence that LTFM cells are a source of the basal discharge of the RVLM neurons that provide excitatory drive to cardiovascular preganglionic neurons in the IML portion of the spinal cord (Barman & Gebber, 1987). Barman and Gebber, 1989, suggested that LTFM neurons may be a part of a network in the brainstem reticular formation that selects between various programmed patterns of sympathetic outflow that would be appropriate for a particular behavior pattern. For example, it may be involved in selecting between the outflow pattern associated with the defense reaction and vigilance reaction.

Modulation of the Baroreceptor Reflex.   The baroreceptor reflex is a negative feedback mechanism that plays an important role in circulatory homeostasis. Rapid changes in blood pressure are detected by baroreceptors located primarily in the arterial walls of the aortic arch and the carotid sinuses. Afferent information from baroreceptors is sent to the CNS structures that modulate cardiac output (the cardiomotor component of the reflex) and peripheral resistance (the vasomotor component of the reflex) so that blood pressure returns to the steady state level.

When the demands on the cardiovascular system are increased by environmental stressors, baroreceptor reflex mechanisms are often abrogated, and homeostasis within the circulatory system is no longer maintained. Indeed, in order to increase cardiac output during the defense reaction, it would be necessary to suppress the cardiomotor or vasomotor component of this homeostatic reflex. Similarly, in order to maintain the increase in peripheral resistance associated with the vigilance reaction, characterized by inhibition of movement and hence reduced venous return to the heart, it may be necessary to facilitate the cardiomotor component of the reflex. We tested these ideas by assessing the effects of electrical stimulation of the HDA and the HVA on the bradycardia–depressor response elicited by the stimulation of baroreceptor afferent axons, the aortic nerve (AN). Concurrent HDA and AN stimulation was observed to attenuate the AN-elicited bradycardia but enhanced the depressor response elicited by AN stimulation (Duan et al., 1996b). In contrast, concurrent stimulation of the HVA and AN enhanced the bradycardia elicited by AN stimulation but reduced the magnitude of the AN-elicited depressor response. These results provide evidence for differential modulation of the baroreceptor reflex during the defense and vigilance reactions.

The results of single cell recording studies conducted in our laboratory (Duan et al., 1994) are consistent with the view that baroreflex modulation, resulting from hypothalamic stimulation, occurs in the medullary solitary complex (nucleus of the solitary tract and DVN). Electrical stimulation of the hypothalamic defense area was found to inhibit most solitary complex neurons that received excitatory input from baroreceptors, thereby providing a means to suppress the cardiomotor component of the reflex during the defense reaction. Similarly, facilitation of the cardiomotor component of the reflex during stimulation of the HVA could occur at solitary complex neurons that receive HVA input and baroreceptor input of the same polarity. Accordingly, we observed (Duan et al., 1994) that 48% of the solitary complex neurons that received excitatory input from the HVA were also excited by baroreceptor activation and that 36% of the solitary complex neurons that were inhibited by HVA stimulation were also inhibited by baroreceptor activation.

Summary of the CNS Circuitry Involved in the Mediation of the Defense Reaction and the Vigilance Reaction

Figure 1.1 provides a summary of what we have learned about the CNS pathways involved in the mediation of the defense and vigilance reactions. Taken collectively, our observations indicate that these two response patterns are mediated by two separate efferent pathways in the CNS. The pathway that subserves the defense reaction mediates an active coping response (i.e., a "go response"), that leads to an increase in cardiac output, shunting of blood flow to the muscle beds, inhibition of the baroreceptor reflex, and, for the rabbit, the initiation of flight behavior.

The second pathway mediates a coping response that is characterized by the inhibition of movement (i.e., a "no-go coping pattern"). The autonomic components of this response are consistent with behavioral inhibition and include an increase in peripheral resistance, a decrease in cardiac output, and a facilitation of the cardiac component of the baroreceptor reflex. Though these coping patterns are "unlearned," there is evidence, as discussed in subsequent sections, that these pathways are also involved in the mediation of learned, active coping and inhibitory coping responses to stressors.

Role of Feedback Signals From Visceral Sensory Afferents

One observation that we routinely made in our single-cell-recording studies was that electrical stimulation of affective response-producing sites in the hypothalamus or PAG often led to an excitatory or inhibitory response from neurons after the stimulus was terminated, if the stimulus was strong enough to elicit an increase in blood pressure. For example, the discharge

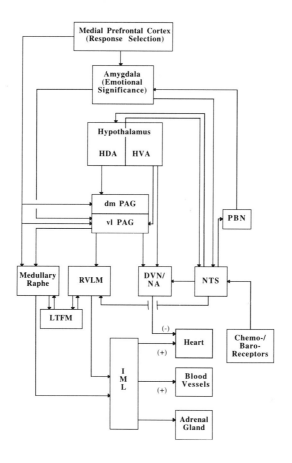

FIG. 1.1 Summary of the proposed CNS circuitry involved in the defense and vigilance
reactions. This hierarchical model suggests that several parallel projections mediate different aspects of the integrated responses including: response selection (i.e., "go" vs. "no-go")
mediated by the medial prefrontal cortex, emotional significance of the situation mediated
by the amygdala and its cortical connections, and autonomic–endrocrine integration mediated by the hypothalamus. The PAG is viewed as a nodal point that is modulated by these
higher pathways. In turn, the PAG projects to several brainstem regulatory regions, that
mediate stress responses. Note that most regions receive feedback information (i.e.,
barosensory, chemosensory), that modulates the control system. A break in a line indicates
that two lines are crossing. Abbreviations: hypothalamic defense area (HDA); hypothalamic vigilance area (HVA); dorsomedial periaqueductal grey (dm PAG); ventromedial
periaqueductal grey (vl PAG); parabrachial nucleus of the pons (PBN); rostral
ventrolateral medulla (RVLM);dorsal vagal nucleus (DVN); nucleus ambiguus (NA); nucleus tractus solitarius (NTS); lateral tegmental field of the medulla (LTFM);
intermediolateral cell column of the spinal cord (IML).

rate of a neuron in the medullary raphe might decrease in response to electrical stimulation of the hypothalamic defense area and show an increase in the firing rate at stimulus offset. When we tested these neurons for baroreceptor input, we found that the polarity of the discharge at the termination of the stimulus, either excitatory or inhibitory, was the same polarity as that of the baroreceptor input. Thus, if the neuron received excitatory input from baroreceptors, the poststimulus response was an increase in the firing rate. The poststimulus response could be eliminated by lowering stimulus intensity so that the neuron could still be driven by electrical stimulation but low enough to eliminate the pressor response. Taken together, these observations indicated to us that the response observed at the termination of the stimulus was due to feedback from baroreceptors that were activated by the small pressor response elicited. We observed this phenomenon in the raphe (Haselton et al., 1988b), lateral tegmental field of the medulla (Winters et al., 1991), the PAG (Liskowsky, Winters, McCabe, & Schneiderman, 1987), and the medullary solitary complex (Duan et al., 1994). There is also evidence for feedback signals to the amygdala (Cechetto & Calaresu, 1983, 1984).

Hypothesized Roles of Feedback From Visceral Afferents. The elicitation of the autonomic and behavioral components of affective behaviors leads to the activation of sensory receptors located in the muscles and in the target organs of the autonomic nervous system, thereby providing feedback signals to the CNS. In regards to the role of feedback in affective behavior, three views have emerged. One idea is that feedback information is a part of a mechanism that serves to modulate the intensity and duration of an affective behavior by altering the gain of the response system. *Gain* is defined in this context as the ratio of response magnitude to stimulus magnitude. It is a measure of the sensitivity of the response system and is thought to be modulated by the effect of feedback on the neuronal circuitry (i.e., the amygdala) involved in determining the emotional significance of the stimulus (i.e., the appraisal mechanism). Another idea is that feedback generated by the affective behavior mitigates the physiological impact of noxious sensory stimulation that occur during stressful situations (Dworkin et al., 1994). A third view is that feedback from the periphery regulates the storage of the memory trace associated with the event or set of circumstances, which elicited the affective response (Williams & McGaugh, 1992, 1993). As in the case of gain changes, these effects are thought to be mediated by the effects of feedback on the appraisal mechanism (the amygdala).

Evidence for Hypothesized Roles of Feedback From Visceral Sensory Afferents

If feedback signals alter the intensity and duration of affective response systems, it should be possible to modulate one or more components of an affective response pattern by stimulating receptors in autonomic or somatic structures that are activated during the response. Indeed, studies of defensive behaviors in decorticate cats (Baccelli, Guazzi, Libretti, & Zanchetti, 1964; Bizzi, Libretti, Malliani, & Zanchetti, 1961; Marshall, 1981) demonstrate that an integrated affective response pattern, *sham rage*, can be elicited by stimulating peripheral chemoreceptors. Sham rage is a sterotyped response pattern that is similar to the defense reaction but is produced in decorticate animals. Arterial chemoreceptors help regulate blood gas composition, particularly $pO2$, by modifying respiratory drive. The somatic and autonomic responses observed in the sham rage of decorticate cats are similar to those associated with the defense reaction in the same species so it comes as no surprise that autonomic components of the defense reaction can be elicited by the activation of chemoreceptors in anesthetized cats (Marshall, 1981).

Defensive behaviors, such as sham rage, can also be modulated by stimulating peripheral baroreceptors. Activation of baroreceptors by pharmacological agents, carotid occlusion, or by low-intensity electrical stimulation of the aortic nerve inhibits both the somatic and autonomic components of this type of affective behavior (Baccelli et al., 1964; Bartorelli, Bizzi, Libretti, & Zanchetti, 1960). Studies conducted by Cechetto and Calaresu (1983, 1984) provide evidence for separate feedback pathways for these two receptor populations. They contended that baroreceptor information is conveyed to the ventrolateral amygdala and chemoreceptors connect to the dorsomedial amygdala. Electrical stimulation of the ventrolateral amygdala inhibits the expression of defensive behaviors, and the defense reaction is elicited by electrical stimulation of the dorsomedial amygdala (Hilton & Zbrozyna, 1963; Stock, Rupprecht, Stumpf, & Schlor 1981).

The prevailing view among investigators who study human emotions is that there must be mechanisms in the brain that allow an individual to appraise the significance of events, in terms of the organism's well-being, before an emotional reaction can occur. As will be discussed later in the chapter, there is substantial evidence that the amygdala is a nodal structure in the appraisal process. Thus, because baroreceptors and chemoreceptors send signals to the amygdala, one way that reactivity may be attenuated is by the effect of these signals on the appraisal mechanism.

In addition to its putative effects on the gain of the affective response system, feedback signals may attenuate the impact of aversive stimulation occurring during the affective behavior. This view of the function of feedback information is based on a considerable body of literature that indicates that feedback from baroreceptors has a general inhibitory effect on central nervous system activity (see Dworkin et al., 1994). Activating the baroreceptors by elevations of blood pressure, mechanical stretch, or electrical stimulation lead to the attenuation of pain sensations, a reduction in anxiety, synchrony in the electroencephalogram (that signifies a decrease in general arousal), or possibly the inducement of sleep (see Basbaum & Fields, 1984; Dworkin, Filewich, Miller, & Craigmyle, 1979; Dworkin et al., 1994; Zamir & Shuber, 1980). Arousing emotional and noxious stimuli leads to elevations in blood pressure and, in many cases, hypoalgesia. As a case in point, pain sensitivity is known to be reduced during the defense reaction. As suggested elsewhere (Basbaum & Fields, 1984), most so-called stress-induced reductions in pain sensitivity may be secondary to the elevations in blood pressure that occur during stressful situations.

Because the feedback signals from baroreceptors attenuate affective responses, they may be important signals in stressful situations in which coping responses are not available. More specifically, the increase in blood pressure that generates these signals may become a conditioned response in stressful situations where coping responses are not available. The signal from the baroreceptors would serve as a mechanism to attenuate reactivity. This effect may be mediated by feedback signals sent to a key structure involved in determining the emotional significance of the stimulus (i.e., appraisal), the amygdala.

Feedback from visceral afferents may also modulate memory storage. According to this view, the strength of a memory trace is related to the emotional significance of the experience that generated the memory (Williams & McGaugh, 1992, 1993). The relative importance of a particular experience is thought to be reflected primarily by the intensity of the responses at effector organs of the autonomic nervous system. Response intensity is monitored by receptors in peripheral tissues and signaled as visceral sensory information to CNS structures involved in the modulation of memory.

The activation of the autonomic nervous system that occurs during affective behaviors often leads to the release of one or more hormones from the adrenal glands. One of the adrenal hormones, epinephrine, has been the focus of studies that seek to assess the memory-modulating effects of peripherally-acting agents. There is abundant evidence that the peripheral administration of epinephrine in low to moderate doses immediately after training improves retention performance involving a wide variety of learning tasks (Gold & van Buskirk, 1978; Sternberg, Isaacs, Gold, & McGaugh,

1985). Moreover, drugs that stimulate epinephrine released by the adrenal glands, such as tyramine, 4-OH amphetamine, or d-amphetamine also enhance retention performance if they are administered systemically immediately after training (Packard, Williams, & McGaugh, 1992; Williams, & Jensen, 1991). These effects are attenuated by adrenal demedullation (Liang, Bennette, & McGaugh, 1985).

Studies by McGaugh and colleagues (Gold & van Buskirk, 1978; Sternberg et al., 1985) provide evidence that the memory modulating effects of peripherally administered agents such as epinephrine, which does not cross the blood–brain barrier, are mediated by afferents in the vagus nerve that connect to the NTS. If afferent feedback from the vagus nerve provides a signal about the emotional significance of an event or a set of circumstances that evoked affective behavior, this information must be sent to CNS structures involved in the processing and storage of affective information. One CNS structure that appears to be particularly important in this regard is the amygdala. Indeed, there is substantial evidence that the amygdala is sensitive to the memory modulating effects of various chemical substances (Packard et al., 1992; Williams & Jensen, 1991), including those that are administered systemically. These effects could be mediated by afferents of the vagus nerve that connect to the nucleus of the solitary tract, that, in turn, connects (polysynaptically) to the amygdala (Williams & McGaugh, 1993).

As discussed previously, students of emotions generally agree that there must be neuronal circuitry that assesses the significance of events with respect to an organism's well-being. As will be discussed in the last part of the chapter, the amygdala appears to be a key structure in this circuitry. Thus, one implication of the work of McGaugh and coworkers, is that the intensity of an emotional reaction is an important factor in determining the strength of memory traces associated with various experiences. These effects are mediated, at least in part, by feedback signals sent to a nodal structure involved in appraisal, the amygdala.

Clinical Significance of Feedback Information

Clinical interventions seek to attenuate integrated emotional responses, such as the defense and vigilance reactions, to stimuli with affective significance. The CNS mechanisms that alter the reactivity of affective response systems are poorly understood, but several techniques, such as exercise, paced respiration, and progressive neuromuscular relaxation, utilize feedback signals from peripheral organs to alter the gain of integrated response systems or general arousal. In view of this observation, one of the goals of our research program is to expand our understanding of how signals from visceral sensory afferents modulate the gain of the defense reaction and vigilance reaction by feedback signals sent to nodal integrative sites in the CNS, such as the amygdala, PAG, and hypothalamus.

CNS Circuitry Underlying Learned Responses to Emotional Stressors

Although organisms respond to a variety of emotional stressors in a reflexive, or unlearned manner (i.e., defense reaction or vigilance reaction), they also possess the ability to learn emotional responses to stimuli. The functional significance of these learned emotional responses has been debated (see discussion that follows), however, more than likely, they play an important role in adaptive preparation for an impending aversive event. One important model for studying learned responses to emotional stressors is aversive classical conditioning, more commonly referred to as fear conditioning (Davis, 1992; Fanselow & Kim, 1994; Kapp, Pascoe, & Bixler, 1984; LeDoux, 1995). In the fear conditioning model, a neutral auditory-conditioned stimulus (CS) is repeatedly paired with an aversive somatosensory unconditioned stimulus (US). In relatively few pairings of the CS and US, the organism began to exhibit a variety of autonomic and behavioral conditioned responses (CRs) including changes in heart rate (Cohen, 1969; Kapp, Frysinger, Gallager, & Haselton, 1979; Powell, Lipkin, & Milligan, 1974; Schneiderman, Smith, Smith, & Gormezano, 1966; Supple & Leaton, 1990), blood pressure (LeDoux, Sakaguchi, & Reis, 1984), pupillary responses (Oleson, Ashe, & Weinberger, 1975), behavioral suppression of operant responses (DeToledo & Black, 1966; LeDoux et al., 1984; Swadlow, Hosking, & Schneiderman, 1971), and potentiated startle responses (Davis, Gendelman, Tischler, & Gendelman, 1982). Because this constellation of CRs is similar to human responses during fear, and because some of these CRs can be attenuated by the administration of anxiolytic drugs, it has been suggested that these CRs are indicative of a conditioned fear state (Davis, 1992; LeDoux, 1995).

Using this paradigm, these rapidly acquired CRs typically occur together, and therefore, are most likely integrated at critical sites in the CNS. In our laboratory we have chosen to focus on one aspect of fear conditioning (i.e., the conditioned heart rate response). It is reasoned that aspects of the CNS circuitry underlying HR conditioning, that pertain to sensory processing and emotional significance, will overlap with other fear conditioned responses. At some point in the circuitry, after the association between the CS and US has been formed and emotional significance, has been assigned, individual pathways mediating each CR diverge and project separately to the different effector systems (e.g., HR vs. pupillary responses). In the rabbit, the HR CR is a deceleration, or bradycardia, which has been shown to be expressed via the vagus nerve (Schneiderman et al., 1969), (i.e., a parasympathetic response). By viewing the vagus nerve as an anchor point in the nervous system, we used a retrograde approach to trace the CNS circuitry underlying classically conditioned bradycardia.

HR Conditioned Response Pathway

In the rabbit, it has been demonstrated that the cells of origin of the vagus nerve are found in the DVN and nucleus ambiguus (NA) of the medulla (Ellenberger, Haselton, Liskowsky, & Sneiderman, 1983; Jordan, Khalid, Schneiderman, & Spyer, 1982; Schwaber & Schneiderman, 1975). Through the use of retrograde neuroanatomical tracers, it has been shown that the ACe projects monosynaptically to the dorsal medulla (Hopkins & Holstege, 1978; Price & Amaral, 1981; Schwaber, Kapp, & Higgins, 1980, 1982), most likely influencing cells in the nucleus tractus solitarius (Pascoe, Bradley, & Spyer, 1989), that then projects to DVN and NA. In addition to this monosynaptic link, it has been demonstrated that an oligosynaptic pathway connects ACe and the medulla (McCabe, Gentile, Markgraf, Teich, & Schneiderman, 1992). This pathway descends through the lateral hypothalamus, lateral zona incerta (Kaufman, Hamilton, Wallach, Petrik, & Schneiderman, 1979), and lateral parabrachial nucleus (Hamilton, Elle berger, Liskowsky, & Schneiderman, 1981) before terminating in the medulla. Electrical stimulation of ACe (Kapp, Gallager, Underwood, McNall, & Whitehorn, 1982) or along the amygdaloid-vagal pathway (Ellenberger et al., 1983; Kaufman et al., 1979; Hamilton et al., 1981) elicits a short-latency, primary bradycardia (or heart rate slowing) of as much as 100 beats per minute.

The amygdala is an important structure in learning and emotional behavior (e.g., Blanchard & Blanchard, 1972; Davis, 1992; Kapp et al., 1984; LeDoux, 1995). Given the existence of a descending bradycardia pathway originating in the amygdala, it was hypothesized that cells in ACe might play a role in the expression of fear conditioning, and more specifically the HR CR (Gentile, Jarrell, Teich, McCabe, & Schneiderman, 1986; Kapp et al., 1979; McCabe et al., 1992). Electrolytic or chemical lesions in ACe prevented the acquisition of the HR CR (Kapp et al., 1979; McCabe et al., 1992) and abolished the retention of the HR CR (Gentile et al., 1986). These effects were specific to the HR CR because ACe lesions did not affect the HR orienting response, HR unconditioned response, baseline HR, or simultaneously conditioned eye-blink responses. Interestingly, in fear-conditioning paradigms examining other CRs (e.g., blood pressure, suppression of behavior, potentiated startle), ACe lesions also prevented the fear-conditioned CR (Hitchcock & Davis, 1986; Iwata, LeDoux, Meely, Armeric, & Reis, 1986).

Single ACe neurons exhibit associative electrophysiological activity during the acquisition of the HR CR (McEchron, McCabe, Green, Llabre, & Schneiderman, 1995), the retention of a previously conditioned CR (Pascoe & Kapp, 1985; McEchron et al., 1995), and the extinction of the CR (McEchron et al., 1995). These single unit responses occur at a fairly long latency (i.e., 30–60 msec), suggesting that many synapses precede the associative neuronal responses in ACe. Interestingly, McEchron and colleagues (1995) reported that the unit response latency decreased as a function of conditioning, which suggests that synaptic plasticity or rerouting of information may be occurring within the conditioning circuitry. LeDoux and colleagues have reported that lesions of the lateral amygdaloid nucleus (AL) prevent the acquisition of fear conditioned responses (LeDoux, Cicchetti, Xagoranis, & Ronanski, 1990). It has been proposed that sensory information (i.e., US) accesses the amygdala through AL, which then relays the information to other amygdaloid structures, such as ACe (LeDoux, 1995). In support of this notion, associative neuronal activity occurs at a shorter latency in AL than in ACe during a fear-conditioning paradigm (Clugnet & LeDoux, 1990). In this model, AL is seen as a critical site for the convergence of sensory information and synaptic plasticity underlying fear-conditioned responses (LeDoux, 1995).

Taken together, these findings suggest that neurons in the amygdala are involved in fear-conditioned responses. More specifically, the data suggest that HR CRs are expressed via a short-latency descending pathway from the ACe to the cells of origin of the vagus nerve in the medulla. Although cells in the amygdala exhibit associative changes in firing rate and latency due to conditioning, it is not clear whether synaptic plasticity underlying the associative learning occurs within the amygdala.

Conditioned Stimulus Pathway

As originally described by Pavlov (1927) and Hebb (1949), a prerequisite for associative learning is the convergence of sensory information. In the classical conditioning paradigm, it is necessary for neurons conveying the CS and US information to converge at some point or points for associative activity to occur. If the amygdala is viewed as a potential site for associative plasticity in the fear conditioning paradigm then CS and US information must project to amygdaloid neurons in the conditioning circuitry. Because the CS in the fear conditioning paradigm is typically an acoustic stimulus, it was hypothesized that structures in the CNS auditory pathway must relay CS information to the amygdala.

Injections of retrograde neuroanatomical tracers into the amygdala labeled cell bodies in the medial subnucleus of the medial geniculate nucleus (mMG); (Jarrell et al, 1986; LeDoux, Ruggiero, & Reis, 1985; Ottersen & Ben-Ari, 1979; & Veening, 1978). Although the ventrolateral portion of the medial geniculate nucleus is an important thalamic structure in auditory perception, the mMG receives inputs from many sensory systems (auditory, visual, somatosensory) and is viewed as part of a "secondary lemniscal" system involved in other aspects of sensory processing, such as polymodal associations (Weinberger & Diamond, 1987). LeDoux and colleagues have performed a careful neuroanatomical analysis in the rat, and they have found that the mMG and an additional adjacent region, the posterior intralaminar nucleus (PIN), relay acoustic information to the AL but not directly to the ACe (LeDoux, Farbb, & Buggiero, 1990). This is consistent with a model in which the AL serves as the sensory interface for CS–US information, which is then relayed to other amygdaloid nuclei, such as ACe.

Electrolytic or chemical lesions of the mMG–PIN prevent the acquisition of fear-conditioned responses (Jarrell & Gentile, 1986, Jarrell, McCabe, et al., 1986; LeDoux et al., 1984; & McCabe, McEchron, Green, & Schneiderman, 1993) and abolish the retention of previously conditioned CRs (Jarrell, Gentile, Romanski, McCabem & Schneider, 1987). Similar to the amygdaloid lesion experiments, the mMG–PIN lesions did not affect other HR responses or simultaneous eye blink conditioning (Jarrell & Gentile, 1986, Jarrell, Romanowski, Gentile, McCabe, & Schneiderman 1986, 1987; McCabe et al., 1993), suggesting that these thalamic neurons relay information specifically to the HR CR and other fear-conditioned responses. Electrophysiological recordings from single mMG–PIN neurons have shown that these cells exhibit associative activity during the acquisition (McEchron et al., 1995), retention (Gabriel, Saltwick, & Miller, 1975; Gabriel, Miller, & Saltwick, 1976; McEchron et al., 1995; Ryugo & Weinberger, 1978; Supple & Kapp, 1989), and extinction (McEchron et al., 1995), phases of conditioning. Following the CS onset, the mMG–PIN neurons fire at a shorter latency than amygdaloid neurons, providing evidence that CS information is processed in the thalamus before being relayed to the amygdala (McEchron et al., 1995). Furthermore, the latencies of these mMG–PIN neurons decrease as a function of conditioning, suggesting synaptic plasticity or rerouting of information occurs at or before this level of the conditioning circuitry. Edeline and Weinberger (1992) and his colleagues have provided evidence that neurons in the mMG exhibit sensory plasticity as a result of classical conditioning. Individual cells in the mMG showed associative retuning of auditory receptive fields, such that the tuning curve of the mMG neuron shifted toward the CS frequency following conditioning.

The cellular mechanism for CNS plasticity underlying associative learning may be a result of changes in synaptic efficacy at critical points within the conditioning circuit (Hebb, 1949). Within the fear-conditioning circuit, it is likely that the convergence of CS and US inputs leads to changes in the synaptic strength of the CS inputs, such that, following training, presentation of the CS allows these inputs to activate the neuronal circuitry involved in the expression of a CR. In our laboratory, we have hypothesized that the CS inputs to cells in the mMG, which project to the amygdala, strengthen during conditioning. This neuronal plasticity is seen as part of the biological substrate for associative learning in the fear-conditioning paradigm. In a recent experiment, it was found that auditory (CS) synaptic inputs to mMG neurons strengthen electrophysiologically as a result of conditioning, whereas non-CS synaptic inputs (from the superior colliculus) to the same mMG cells did not strengthen (McEchron, Greene, et al., 1996). The increase in synaptic strength did not occur in pseudoconditioned controls, suggesting that the changes in synaptic efficacy in the CS inputs were associative in nature. These data represent the first evidence of a specific site of neuronal plasticity within the fear-conditioning circuit, however, they do not rule out the possibility that changes in synaptic efficacy are occurring in other CNS structures as well (e.g., amygdala).

Unconditioned Stimulus Pathways

The presence of associative neuronal responses in mMG–PIN and in the amygdala suggests that US information (nocioceptive stimuli), in addition to CS information (auditory stimuli), is conveyed to these regions. In a recent experiment, it was demonstrated that single neurons in mMG and in ACe exhibit short latency responses to the presentation of the US alone (McEchron et al., 1995). It has been shown that auditory and somatosensory projection fields overlap within mMG–PIN (LeDoux, Ruggerio, Forest, Stornetta, & Reis, 1987) and that neurons in this region respond to polymodal stimulation (Love & Scott, 1969; Wepsic, 1966). In the rabbit HR conditioning paradigm, the US is a corneal airpuff which is conveyed to the CNS via the infraorbital branch of the trigeminal nerve (McEchron, McCabe, et al., 1996). It was demonstrated that the presentation of the corneal airpuff US leads to expression of the c-Fos protein, a cellular marker of functional activity, in the ventral portion of the ipsilateral spinal trigeminal subnuclei caudalis and interpolaris. Interestingly, these spinal trigeminal subnuclei also project monosynaptically to mMG (McEchron, McCabe, et al., 1996), thereby providing a potentially direct US input to the CS pathway.

Although there is neuroanatomical and electrophysiological evidence for a direct trigeminal-mMG pathway, it is not clear that this pathway is necessary and sufficient to support HR conditioning. The classic somatosensory pathway that relays tactile and nociceptive information from the face involves trigeminal nuclei projections to the ventral posterior medial nucleus of the thalamus (VPM). Recently, we have shown that lesions of the VPM prevent the acquisition of the HR CR and alter the unconditioned response to the corneal airpuff US (McCabe, McEchon, Green, & Schneiderman, et al., 1995). These findings are consistent with the notion that the VPM is a component of a circuit that relays trigeminal US information to the mMG and, perhaps, to the amygdala. Although amygdaloid neurons respond electrophysiologically to somatosensory stimuli, there is little evidence that somatosensory inputs that access amygdala are independent of mMG–PIN. Turner and Herkenham (1991) proposed that the amygdaloid somatosensory inputs project via the mMG–PIN pathway to the amygdala. In this model, auditory-CS and somatosensory-US information converges and is integrated within mMG–PIN before being sent to the amygdala.

Role of the Cerebral Cortex in Conditioned Emotional Responses

Although subcortical circuitry, including the acoustic thalamus, amygdala, and brainstem regulatory nuclei, is sufficient for the acquisition and expression of simple fear conditioning, the cerebral cortex plays an important role in learned emotional responses. Auditory-CS and somatosensory-US information project to sensory cortical regions, such as the primary and secondary auditory cortices (Anderson, Knight, & Merzenich, 1980; Weinberger & Diamond, 1987; Winer, Diamond, & Raczowski, 1977) and the primary and secondary somatosensory cortices, respectively. Individual neurons in the auditory cortex exhibit associative changes in firing rate (Diamond & Weinberger, 1984; Weinberger & Diamond, 1987; Weinberger, Hopkins, & Diamond, 1984; Weinberger, Javich, & Lepan, 1995) and the retuning of auditory receptive fields (Diamond & Weinberger, 1989; Edeline, Pham, & Weinberg, 1993; Edeline & Weinberger, 1993; Weinberger, Javid, & Lepan, 1993) as a result of conditioning. Lesions in the auditory cortex interfere with the acquisition (Teich et al., 1988), retention (Jarrell et al., 1987), and extinction (Teich et al., 1989) of HR conditioning. It has been proposed (Jarrell et al., 1987; Teich et al., 1989) that the auditory cortex, through descending connections to the mMG, may be involved in inhibitory responses seen in extinction training or differential conditioning (i.e., involving inhibition of response to a CS-).

LeDoux and colleagues have described a cortical pathway by which CS and US information reaches the amygdala (LeDoux, Farb, & Romanski, 1991; Romanski & LeDoux, 1993). It was demonstrated that either the subcortical or cortical pathway to the amygdala was sufficient to support fear conditioning (Romanski & LeDoux, 1992). It has also been shown that contextual fear conditioning can be prevented by lesioning the amygdala or the hippocampus (Kim, Rison, & Fanselow, 1993; Phillips & LeDoux, 1992; Selden et al., 1991). Based on these findings, LeDoux (1995) has proposed a multistage model of fear conditioning in which cognitive aspects of conditioning (e.g., context, explicit memories) may be mediated by a pathway involving interactions among cortical association areas, the hippocampus, and the amygdala.

Role of Other CNS Regions in Conditioned Emotional Responses

Although the acoustic thalamus, auditory cortex, and amygdala have received a great deal of attention in regard to fear conditioning, several other CNS regions have been implicated in this model of associative learning. It has been reported that the cerebellum (Supple & Kapp, 1993; Supple & Leaton, 1990), medial dorsal thalamus (Powell et al., 1990), prefrontal cortex (Powell et al., 1994), cingulate cortex (Buchanan & Powell, 1982), septal nucleus (Sparks & LeDoux, 1995), and perirhinal cortex (Campeau & Davis, 1995) play a role in some aspects of fear conditioning. In our model of emotional conditioning, which is shared by many others, conditioning is viewed in a multiple trace context, in which there may be several sites of synaptic modification for each learned response. Therefore, the presence of plasticity in mMG–PIN, the auditory cortex, or the amygdala does not preclude the possibility that other CNS regions also exhibit plasticity and are important for the acquisition and expression of conditioned fear responses.

Summary of the CNS Circuitry for Learned Emotional Responses

Based on the findings from several laboratories, a proposed outline of the CNS circuitry underlying conditioned fear responses is presented in Fig. 1.2. Auditory-CS information ascends via the primary and secondary lemniscal systems to cells in the medial geniculate, which then projects to the auditory cortex. A subset of medial geniculate neurons in mMG–PIN also receive somatosensory-US information (spinothalamic or trigeminal), and an association is then formed between the CS and US. This associative

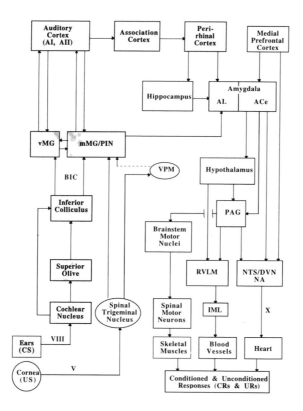

FIG. 1.2 Summary of the proposed CNS circuitry involved in classically conditioned emotional responses in the fear conditioning paradigm. The model consists of a subcortical pathway involving the association of the CS auditory information and the US nocioceptive information at the medial subnucleus of the medial geniculate. This region is concerned primarily with stimulus characteristics and associations in and between sensory modalities. The information is then relayed subcortically to the amygdala, that has efferent projections to diencephalic and brainstem regions that control unconditioned and conditioned autonomic and somatomotor responses (URs and CRs). It has been suggested that the amygdala is involved in determining the emotional significance of the situation and that this subcortical circuit may be involved in subconscious emotional learning. The model also includes a cortical loop whereby CS and US information is relayed to the auditory cortex, and through a multisynaptic pathway, this information ultimately reaches the amygdala. It has been proposed that this loop also carries associative information but is concerned with response inhibition (e.g., extinction) and more cognitive aspects of learning, such as stimulus perception, polymodal representations, and contextual learning. A break in a line indicates that two lines are crossing. Abbreviations: primary auditory cortex (AI); secondary auditory cortex (AII); lateral amygdaloid nucleus (AL); central amygdaloid nucleus (ACe); ventral subnucleus of the medial geniculate (vMG); medial subnucleus of the medial geniculate (mMG); posterior interlaminar nucleus (PIN); brachium of the inferior colliculus (BIC); ventral posterior medial nucleus of the thalamus (VPM); periaqueductal grey (PAG); rostral ventrolateral medulla (RVLM); nucleus tractus solitarius (NTS); dorsal vagal nucleus (DVN); nucleus ambiguus (NA); intermediolateral cell column of the spinal cord (IML); vagus nerve (X); acoustic-vestibular nerve (VIII); trigeminal nerve (V).

information is relayed subcortically to the amygdala via cells in the mMG–PIN region and to the auditory cortex. The auditory cortex processes the associative information, as well as CS information alone, and through multisynaptic cortico-cortical connections, projects to the amygdala. In addition, the auditory cortex reciprocally influences cells in the mMG, in part through inhibitory connections, which may play a role in extinction and differential conditioning. CS–US inputs access the amygdala subcortically via AL, that then projects to the ACe. It is not clear whether US information projects independently to the amygdala or whether it accesses the amygdala via mMG–PIN. Through widespread descending projections to diencephalic and brainstem regulatory nuclei, the ACe modulates the constellation of autonomic and behavioral CRs indicative of fear conditioning (e.g., bradycardia, blood pressure responses, behavioral inhibition, potentiated startle, pupillary responses).

In this model of learned emotional behavior, the initial associative process occurs in mMG–PIN. It has been proposed, however, that important neuronal plasticity also occurs at other sites in the conditioning circuitry. Using this "multiple trace" idea of conditioning, different aspects of the conditioned emotional behavior are processed at critical sites in the circuit. For example, aspects pertaining to stimulus significance may be processed in the acoustic thalamus; higher order auditory processing (e.g., extinction and inhibitory processes) may occur in the auditory cortex; contextual learning may be processed in association cortices, and the hippocampus, the assignment of emotional significance (e.g., fear) may occur in the amygdala, and the appropriate autonomic–behavioral responses may be determined by diencephalic and brainstem regulatory nuclei.

Functional Significance of Conditioned Emotional Responses

Although the observed relationships among the stimuli and responses in the fear conditioning paradigm are well established, there has been some debate concerning the functional significance of these CRs. It has been proposed, for example, that the bradycardiac CR observed in the rabbit HR conditioning paradigm represents an anticipatory parasympathetic response, which serves to attenuate an eventual sympathetic response (i.e., the UR) elicited by the aversive US in a restrained animal (Schneiderman, 1974). Thus, the bradycardiac CR in the rabbit is viewed as a homeostatic, regulatory response designed to buffer the physiological impact of stressful environmental stimuli in the absence of an adaptive somatomotor response.

Dworkin (1993) also views conditioning as a regulatory process. In this model, the CR serves as a negative feedback mechanism that attenuates the physiological impact of the US, and thereby the amplitude of the UR. As an example, during Pavlovian conditioning of a salivary response, the saliva produced during conditioning reduces irritation of the mucosa by diluting the acid injected into the mouth. The CR anticipates the noxious US, and in theory, will grow in magnitude until it completely neutralizes the effects of the US. This negative feedback mechanism may become particularly important in stressful situations when active coping responses are not available. If increases in blood pressures become CRs in these situations, the feedback signals, particularly to the amygdala, which is involved in appraisal, may attenuate the emotional reaction.

Another view of the significance of this class of CRs has been proposed by Kapp (Kapp, Wilson, Pascoe, Supple, & Whalen, 1990; Kapp, Supple, & Whalen, 1994; Whalen & Kapp, 1991) and Gallagher and Holland (1994). They suggested that the CRs reflect learned arousal or attention, which is defined as a behavioral state characterized by an enhanced readiness to process information. The conditioning circuitry and, in particular ACe, is thought to be responsible for facilitating the detection and processing of certain types of sensory information. Thus, after the emotional significance of a stimulus is determined, CNS structures involved in arousal and attention would be activated; among these would be the cholinergic system (in the dorsal tegmentum and parabrachial area), the noradrenergic system (of the locus coeruleus), and the serotonergic system (of the dorsal raphe). These systems make widespread connections to forebrain structures and their activation is thought to allow the organism to focus its attention to stimuli that have adaptive relevance. Indeed, the amygdala, a region involved in appraising the emotional significance of stimuli yields increases in vigilance when stimulated electrically, and the amygdala projects to the cholinergic system (Hobson & Steriade, 1986). Although this idea is not incompatible with the "stress regulatory" model described previously, it views emotional conditioning as a sensory–attentional process rather than an autonomic behavioral process.

Another interesting possibility is that by accessing neurons involved in the integration of autonomic–behavioral responses (e.g., vigilance reaction), the conditioning circuitry can elicit a conditioned integrated pattern of response (i.e., a conditioned vigilance response). As mentioned previously, CRs that have been observed during fear conditioning include bradycardia, pressor responses, and behavioral inhibition, that are responses seen during the stimulation of vigilance regions in the brain. Therefore, sensory neurons conveying the CS and US participate in associative events, and then access neurons in the ACe that may be part of a CNS network which regulates the vigilance reaction. This model is compatible with those presented by Schneiderman (1974), Dworkin (1993), Kapp et al. (1990), and Gallagher (Gallagher & Holland, 1994) in that it involves conditioned vigilance (i.e., arousal or attention) and it leads to autonomic and behavioral CRs that are regulatory.

Conceptual Model for the Mediation and Modulation of Learned and Unlearned Affective Behaviors

Function of the PAG. Because affective behaviors such as the defense reaction and vigilance reaction can be elicited by localized stimulation in the amygdala, hypothalamus, and PAG, a question arises concerning the functional significance of this redundant organization. One possibility is that the three regions constitute an interdependent integrated neural system that is responsible for the expression of a particular affective behavior, such as the defense reaction or the vigilance reaction. The more plausible view, we believe, is that unlearned affective behaviors are integrated in the PAG and modulated by the amygdala and hypothalamus. This working hypothesis is based primarily on studies of the defense reaction. The defense reaction can be elicited by electrical stimulation of the PAG or with natural stimuli when the PAG has been isolated from rostral structures, such as the hypothalamus and amygdala (Ellison & Flynn, 1968; Fernandez de Molina & Hunsperger, 1962; Gellen, Gyorgy, & Doda, 1972; Keller, 1932; Kelly, Beaton, & Magoun, 1946).

Beitz (1982), in his review of the organization of the afferent projections to the PAG, argued that the neuroanatomical data provide convincing evidence that the PAG serves as an interface between the limbic system, autonomic nervous system, and the somatic motor system. A comparison of the afferent and efferent projections of the PAG shows that many of the CNS structures involved in the regulation of the autonomic nervous system and somatic motor system are reciprocally connected with the PAG. These reciprocal projections may provide a basis for the feedforward and feedback mechanisms that allows these structures to modify the output of the PAG.

Carrive's (1993) view of the PAG is certainly consistent with the one expressed by Beitz. He suggested that the principle function of the PAG is somatosensory integration. It receives direct projections from somatosensory neurons in the spinal cord and the spinal trigeminal nucleus, and the PAG does not receive second order afferents associated other senses such as vision, olfaction and audition. According to this view, the defense reaction mediated by the PAG, without involvement of rostral structures such as the amygdala and hypothalamus, is elicited by noxious cutaneous stimuli.

Function of the Hypothalamus.   In contrast to the PAG, it appears that the hypothalamus and amygdala are involved in higher order processing of stimuli that have affective significance. According to our working hypothesis, the autonomic components of learned affective behaviors are mediated by the hypothalamic sites that yield an unlearned pattern when stimulated electrically (e.g., the hypothalamic defense area and the hypothalamic vigilance area). If this view is valid, the autonomic components of unlearned affective responses (e.g., the defense reaction and vigilance reaction) may be coupled with a wide variety of learned coping behaviors. Indeed, as previously discussed, human psychophysiology studies provide evidence that the autonomic components of the defense reaction are evoked during a variety of situations involving active coping, such as preparation for public speaking. Similarly, the autonomic components of the vigilance reaction may be evoked during a variety of tasks involving inhibitory coping, such as the cold pressor task, where the subject must inhibit the tendency to remove a head or foot from a painful, icy-cold stimulus.

The results of studies by Smith and colleagues (Smith et al., 1980) provide evidence that the hypothalamus is involved in the mediation of autonomic responses to conditioned stimuli that elicit affective responses. Operant conditioning techniques were used to train conscious baboons to respond to colored lights by either executing a mild dynamic leg exercise response or pressing a lever, depending on the color of the light. After learning these tasks, classical conditioning techniques were used to develop a conditioned emotional response to a tonal stimulus that was paired with an electric shock to the abdominal skin. Colored lights were used during these sessions as signals for feeding or lever pressing. The CS (tone) for the conditioned emotional response was only presented during lever pressing. The CR to the tonal stimulus was a tachycardia, a pressor response, increased aortic blood flow, and secretion of catecholamines by the adrenal glands; the tonal stimulus also led to suppression of lever pressing. Bilateral lesions of the perifornical hypothalamic region, the hypothalamic defense area for this species (see Smith, DeVito, & Astley, 1990), abolished or severely attenuated the conditioned cardiovascular response to the tonal stimulus. The tonal stimulus, however, still led to suppression of lever pressing. Apparently, this area of the hypothalamus, in addition to modulation of the defense reaction, is involved in the mediation of learned cardiovascular responses specifically associated with emotional behavior because the cardiovascular responses associated with exercise, feeding, and lever pressing were unaffected by these lesions. One might argue that this region of the hypothalamus is associated with assessing the emotional significance of stimuli, but this, clearly, is not the case because lever pressing was still

suppressed when the tonal stimulus was presented to animals with hypothalamic lesions.

Studies of classically conditioned affective behavior, referred to by some
authors as fear, in the rat are consistent with the view that the hypothalamus
is an essential structure in the neuronal circuitry that mediates the autonomic components of emotional responses to higher order stimuli (LeDoux,
Iwata, Cicchetti, & Reis, 1988). Lesions of the medial part of the medial
geniculate or the amygdala were found to abolish both the autonomic (an
increase in blood pressure) and behavioral (inhibition of somatic motor activity) components of the affective response to a conditioned acoustic stimulus, whereas lesions in the lateral hypothalamus were observed to abolish
the cardiovascular component of response but not the somatic motor component of the response. Lesions of the PAG were found to disrupt the somatic motor component of the affective behavior but did not affect the
conditioned change in blood pressure.

Function of the Amygdala.   The amygdala also appears to be involved in the higher order processing of stimuli that have affective significance. More specifically, the amygdala appears to be a part of the neuronal
circuitry necessary for the assignment of emotional significance to sensory
events and linking those stimuli to appropriate behaviors (see Aggleton &
Mishkin, 1986; LeDoux, 1994, for reviews). Chemical lesions of the ACe
prevent the acquisition of a conditioned bradycardiac response (McCabe et
al., 1992). Similarly, radio frequency lesions of the ACe attenuate the conditioned bradycardia response to an acoustic stimulus but does not affect
baseline heart rate or the heart rate orienting response to the CS (Kapp et
al., 1979). A number of studies have shown that the amygdala is a key structure in assigning reward value to stimuli in operant conditioning paradigms
(Gaffan, Gaffan, & Harrison, 1988; Gaffan & Harrison, 1987; Jones &
Mishkin, 1972) and in the elicitation, by stimulation of the CNS, of behavioral and autonomic responses associated with affective behaviors
(Fernandez de Molina & Hunsperger, 1962; Hilton & Zbrozyna, 1963). The
Kluver–Bucy syndrome reflects a diminished ability to ascribe affective significance to sensory events. Several studies provide evidence that discon-
nection of the amygdala from modality-specific sensory areas of the CNS
produce Kluver–Bucy symptoms specific to the disconnected modality
(Dowener 1961; Horel, Keating, & Misantone, 1975).

The amygdala, thus, is a nodal structure in the CNS mechanisms that underlie learned and unlearned affective behaviors. Its integrity is essential in
the determination of the adaptive relevance (emotional significance) of the
USs that elicit the defense and vigilance reactions, and the CSs that evoke

the conditioned autonomic and behavioral responses in conditioning studies. The amygdala serves as a bridge in learning paradigms where the response to the CS is mediated by structures in the efferent pathway for the defense and vigilance reactions. Indeed, the synaptic plasticity underlying associative learning, may take place in the amygdala.

Because of its role in appraisal, the amygdala may also mediate the effects of baroreceptor and chemoreceptor feedback on affective behavior and the effects of peripheral feedback on the strength of the memory trace developed during experiences that have emotional significance. Thus, for example, feedback signals generated by conditioned increases in blood pressure in stressful situations where coping responses are not available, would attenuate emotional reactions to the stressor. Similarly, the strength of memory traces associated with events that elicited strong emotional reactions would be greater than those where there was a weak emotional reaction, or none at all. This difference would be due to the differences in the feedback signals sent to the amygdala and, hence, the appraised significance.

The view that the amygdala is a key structure in the modulation of emotional reactivity is not a new one. As a case in point, there is evidence the anxiolytic effect of benzodiazepines such as diazepam (Valium) are mediated primarily by their effects upon benzodiazepine receptors located in the amygdala (Davis, 1992). Both benzodiazepines and opiates decrease the learning and expression of conditioned emotional responses (Davis, 1992).

Summary: Function of the Amygdala, PAG, and Hypothalamus in Affective Behavior

The conceptual model that emerges from studies of the PAG, hypothalamus, and amygdala is that the PAG is a part of the final common pathway for the mediation of unlearned affective behavior. The types of stimuli that this structure processes directly are unlearned ones mediated by somatic sensory afferents. The amygdala is viewed as a structure that modulates unlearned affective behaviors, particularly in regards to assessing the affective significance of the US that elicited the response.

According to this model, neurons in the amygdala and the hypothalamus must be activated in order for higher order stimuli, such as CS, to evoke affective behaviors. The amygdala is viewed as a part of the neuronal circuitry involved in the assignment of emotional significance to learned or unlearned stimuli. The amygdala also appears to be involved in the mediation of the effects of feedback from visceral receptors on the intensity and duration of an affective behavior and the mediation of the effects of feedback on the strength of the memory trace developed during the learning of an affective behavior. The hypothalamus is seen as essential to the circuitry mediating the expression of the autonomic components of affective behaviors in response to the CS. The sites in the hypothalamus that are a part of this circuitry may also be involved in the regulation of unlearned affective responses, such as the defense reaction. Although the integrity of the PAG appears to be essential to the expression of the somatic motor components of learned affective behavior to CS, its exact role in the expression of the autonomic components of the response to these stimuli remains to be determined. Notwithstanding, it appears that the mediation of the somatic components of CRs requires the activation of PAG neurons that mediate unlearned affective behaviors.

Function of Conditioned Emotional Responses

Conditioned emotional responses, in our view, have several functions. Most stressors lead to the activation of the sympathetic nervous system. Conditioning in a constrained individual is seen as a way to buffer the physiological impact of this sympathetic response by the development of an anticipatory parasympathetic response (the CR) (Schneiderman, 1974). The CR may also attenuate the physiological impact of stressful stimuli by serving as a negative feedback mechanism (Dworkin et al., 1994). This may be mediated by effects on sensory processing mechanisms or by brain mechanisms involved in determining the emotional significance of stimuli. Notwithstanding, the CR leads to a decrease in the magnitude of the unconditioned response by mitigating the impact of the US (i.e., the stressor). Finally, conditioned emotional responses may lead to changes in arousal and attention that facilitate the processing of some types of sensory information.

REFERENCES

Abrahams, V. C., Hilton, S. M., & Zbrozyna, A. W. (1960). Active muscle vasodilatation produced by stimulation of the brain stem: Its significance in the defence reaction. *Journal of Physiology (London)*, *154*, 491–513.

Abrahams, V. C., Hilton, S. M., & Zbrozyna, A. W. (1964). The role of active muscle vasodilatation in the alerting stage of the defence reaction. *Journal of Physiology (London)*, *171*, 89–202.

Abshire, V. M., Hankins, K. D., Roehr, K. E., & DiMicco, J. A. (1988). Injections of 1-Allyglycine into the posterior hypothalamus in rats causes decreases in local GABA which correlate with increases in heart rate. *Neuropharmacology*, *27*, 1171–1177.

Aggleton, J. P., & Mishkin, M. (1986). The amygdala: Sensory gateway to the emotions. In R. Plutchik, & H. Kellerman (Eds.), *Emotion: Theory, research and experience, Vol. 3. Biological foundations of emotions* (pp. 281–299). New York: Academic Press.

Allen, R. (1981). Controlling stress and tension. *Journal of School Health*, *17*, 360–364.

Anderson, R. A., Knight, P. I., & Merzenich, M. M. (1980). The thalamocortical and corticothalamic connections of AI, AII, and the anterior auditory field (AAF) in the cat:

Evidence for two largely segregated systems of connections. *Journal of Comparative Neurology, 194*, 663–701.

Applegate, C. D., Kapp, B. S., Underwood, M. D., & McNall, C. C. (1983). Autonomic and somatomotor affect of amygdala central nucleus stimulation in awake rabbits. *Physiology and Behavior, 31*, 353–360.

Baccelli, G., Guazzi, M., Libretti, A., & Zanchetti, A. (1964). Pressoceptive and chemoceptive aortic reflexes in decorticate and in decerebrate cats. *American Journal of Physiology, 208*(4), 708–714.

Bandler, R., & Carrive, P. (1988). Integrated defense reaction elicited by excitatory amino acid microinjection in the midbrain periaqueductal gray region of the unrestrained cat. *Brain Research, 439*, 95–106.

Bandler, R., & Price, J. L. (1996). Medial and orbital prefrontal connections of the midbrain periaqueductal gray of the macaque. *Society for Neuroscience, 22*, 671.

Bandler, R., Carrive, P., & Zhang, S. P. (1991). Integration of somatic and autonomic reactions within the midbrain periaqueductal gray: Viscerotopic, somatotopic and functional organization. In G. Holstege (Ed.), *Role of the forebrain in sensation and behavior. Progress in brain research, Vol. 87* (pp. 269–305). Amsterdam: Elsevier Science.

Barman, G. L., & Gebber, S. M. (1989). A physiologically-based model of the brain stem generator of sympathetic nerve discharge. In J. Ciriello, M. M. Caverson & C. Polosa (Eds.), *Progress in Brain Research* (pp. 131–139).

Barman, S. M., & Gebber, G. L. (1987). Lateral tegmental field neurons of cat medulla: A source of basal activity of ventrolateral medullospinal sympathoexcitatory neurons. *Journal of Neurophysiology, 57*, 1410–1424.

Bartorelli, C., Bizzi, E., Libretti, A., & Zanchetti, A. (1960). Inhibitory control of sinoarotic pressoceptive afferents on hypothalamic autonomic activity and sham rage behavior. *Archives of Italian Biology, 98*, 308–326.

Basbaum, A. I., & Fields, H. L. (1984). Endogenous pain control systems: Brainstem spinal pathways and endorphin circuitry. *Annual Review of Neuroscience, 7*, 309–338.

Bauer, R. M., Vela, M. B., Simon, T., & Waldrop, T. G. (1988). A GABAergic mechanism in the posterior hypothalamus modulates baroreflex bradycardia. *Brain Research Bulletin, 20*, 633–642.

Beitz, A. J. (1982). The organization of afferent projections to the midbrain periaqueductal gray of rat. *Neuroscience, 7*(1), 133–159.

Benson, H. (1983). The relaxation response: Its subjective and objective historical precedents and physiology. *Trends in Neuroscience, 6*, 281–284.

Bizzi, E., Libretti, A., Malliani, A., & Zanchetti, A. (1961). Reflex chemoceptive excitation of diencephalic sham rage behavior. *American Journal of Physiology, 200*(5), 923–926.

Blanchard, D. C., & Blanchard, R. J. (1972). Innate and conditioned reactions to threat in rats with amygdaloid lesions. *Journal of Comparative and Physiological Psychology, 81*, 281–290.

Blanchard, R. J., & Blanchard, D. C. (1987). Ethoexperimental approach to the study of fear. *The Psychology Record, 37*, 305–316.

Bolme, P., Ngai. S. H., Uvnas, B., & Wallenberg, L. R. (1967). Circulatory and behavioural effects on electrical stimulation of the sympathetic vasodilator areas in the hypothalamus arid the mesencephalon in unanaesthetized dogs. *Acta Physiology Scandinavia, 70*, 334–346.

Brown, J. L., Hunsperger R. W., & Rusuold, H. E. (1969). Defence attack and night elicited by electrical stimulation of the hypothalamus of the cat. *Experimental Brain Research, 8*, 113–124.

Buchanan, S. L., & Powell, D. A. (1982). Cingulate cortex: Its role in Pavlovian conditioning. *Journal of Comparative Physiological Psychology, 96*, 755–774.

Buchanan, S. L., Thompson, R. H., Maxwell, B. L., & Powell, D. A. (1994). Efferent connections of the medial prefrontal cortex in the rabbit. *Experimental Brain Research, 100,* 469–483.

Buchanan, S. L., Valentine, J., & Powell, D. A. (1985). Autonomic responses are elicited by electrical stimulation of the medial but not lateral frontal cortex in rabbits. *Behavioral Brain Research, 18,* 51–62.

Campeau, S. & Davis, M. (1995). Involvement of subcortical and cortical afferents to the lateral nucleus of the amygdala in fear conditioning measured with fear-potentiated startle in rats trained concurrently with auditory and visual conditioned stimuli. *Journal of Neuroscience, 15*(3), 2312–2317.

Carmichael, S. T., & Price, J. L. (1996). Connectional networks within the orbital and medial prefrontal cortex of macaque monkeys. *Journal of Comparative Neurology, 371,* 179–207.

Carrive, P. (1993). The periaqueductal gray and defensive behavior: Functional representation and neuronal organization. *Behavior Brain Research, 58,* 27–24.

Carrive, P., Bandler, R., & Dampney, R. A. L. (1989). Viscerotopic control of regional vascular beds by discrete groups of neurons within the midbrain periaqueductal gray. *Brain Research, 493,* 385–390.

Cechetto, D. F., & Calaresu, F. R. (1984). Units in the amygdala responding to activation of carotid baro- and chemoreceptors. *American Journal of Physiology, 246 (Regulatory Integrative Comp. Physiology), 15,* R832–R836.

Cechetto, D. F., & Saper,C. B. (1990). Role of the cerebral cortex in autonomic function. In A. Loewy, & K. M. Spyer (Eds.), *Central regulation of autonomic function* (pp. 209–223). New York: Oxford University Press.

Cechetto, D. G., & Calaresu, F. R. (1983). Response of single units in the amygdala to stimulation of buffer nerves in cat. *American Journal of Physiology, 244 (Regulatory Integrative Comp. Physiology, 13,* R646–R651.

Clugnet, M. C., & LeDoux, J. E. (1990). Synaptic plasticity in fear conditioning circuits: Induction of LTP in the lateral nucleus of the amygdala by stimulation of the medial geniculate body. *Journal of Neuroscience, 10,* 2812–2824.

Cohen, D. H. (1969). Development of a vertebrate experimental model for cellular neurophysiologic studies of learning. *Conditioned Reflexes, 4,* 61–80.

Dampney, R. A. L, Goodchild, A. K., Robertson, L. G., & Montgomery, W. (1982). Role of ventrolateral medulla in vasomotor regulation: A correlative anatomical and physiological study. *Brain Research, 249,* 223–235.

Davis, M. (1992). The role of the amygdala in fear and anxiety. *Annual Review of Neuroscience, 15,* 353–375.

Davis, M., Gendelman, D. S., Tischler, M. D., & Gendelman, P. M. (1982). A primary acoustic startle circuit: Lesion and stimulation studies. *Journal of Neuroscience, 6,* 791–805.

DeToledo, L., & Black, A. H. (1966). Heart rate: Change during conditioned suppression in rats. *Science, 152,* 1404–1460.

Diamond, D. M., & Weinberger, N. M. (1989). Role of context in the expression of learning-induced plasticity of single neurons in auditory cortex. *Behavioral Neuroscience, 103,* 471–494.

Diamond, D. M., & Weinberger, N. M. (1984). Physiological plasticity of single neurons in auditory cortex of the cat during acquisition of the pupillary conditioned response: II. Secondary field (AII). *Behavioral Neuroscience, 98,* 189–210.

DiMicco, J. A., & Abshire. V. M. (1987). Evidence for GABAergic inhibition of a hypothlamic sympathoexcitatory mechanism in anesthetized rats. *Brain Research, 402,* 1–10.

DiScala, G., Schmitt, P., & Karli, P. (1984). Flight induced by infusion of Bicuculline into periventricular structures. *Brain Research, 309*, 199–208.

Dowener, J. D. C. (1961). Changes in visual gnostic function and emotional behavior following unilateral temporal lobe damage in the split-brain monkey. *Nature, 119*, 50–51.

Duan, Y.-F., Winters, R., McCabe, P.M., Green, E. J., Huang, Y., & Schneiderman, N. (1997). Functional relationship between the hypothalamic vigilance area and PAG vigilance area. *Physiology & Behavior, 62*(3), 675–679.

Duan, Y.-F., Winters, R., McCabe, P. M., Green, E. J., Huang Y., & Scheiderman, N. (1996a). Behavioral characteristics of defense and vigilance reactions elicited by electrical stimulation of the hypothalamus in rabbits. *Behavioral Brain Research, 81*, 33–41.

Duan, Y.-F., Winters, R. W., McCabe, P. M., Green, E. J., Huang, Y., & Schneiderman, N. (1996b). Modulation of the baroreceptor reflex by stimulation of the hypothalamic defense and vigilance areas. *Physiology and Behavior, 59*, 1093–1098.

Duan, Y.-F., Winters, R., McCabe, P. M., Green, E. J., Huang, Y., & Schneiderman, N. (1994). Modulation of neuronal firing in the medullary solitary complex by electrical stimulation of the hypothalamic defense and vigilance areas in rabbits. *Brain Research, 643*, 218–226.

Duan, Y.-F., McCabe, P. M., Winters, R. W., Green E. J., Huang, Y., & Schneiderman, N. (1993). Vigilance reaction elicited by electrical stimulation of the midbrain periaqueductal gray and the hypothalamus may involve separate neural pathways in rabbits. *Society of Neuroscience Abstracts, 19*, 947.

Dworkin, B. R. (1993). *Learning and Physiological Regulation*. Chicago: University of Chicago Press.

Dworkin, B. R., Elbert, T., Rau, H., Birbaumer, N., Pauli, P., Droste, C., & Brunia, C. H. M. (1994). Central effects of baroreceptor activation in humans: Attenuation of skeletal reflexes and pain perception. *Proceedings of the National Academy of Sciences, 91*, 6329–6333.

Dworkin, B. R., Filewich, R. J., Miller, N. E., & Craigmyle, N. (1979). Baroreceptor activation reduces reactivity to noxious stimulation: Implications for hypertension. *Science, 205*, 1299–1301.

Edeline, J. -M., & Weinberger, N. M. (1993). Receptive field plasticity in the auditory cortex during frequency discrimination training; selective retuning independent of task difficulty. *Behavioral Neuroscience, 107*, 82–103.

Edeline, J. -M., & Weinberger, N. M. (1992). Associative retuning in the thalamic source of input to the amygdala and auditory cortex: receptive field plasticity in the medial division of the medial geniculate body. *Behavioral Neuroscience, 106*, 81–105.

Edeline, J. -M., Pham, P., & Weinberger, N. M. (1993). Rapid development of learning-induced receptive field plasticity in the auditory cortex. *Behavioral Neuroscience, 107*, 539–551.

Ellenberger, H. H., Haselton, J. R., Liskowsky, D. R., & Schneiderman, N. (1983). The location of chronotrophic cardioinhibitory vagal motorneurons in the medulla of the rabbit. *Journal of the Autonomic Nervous System, 9*, 513–529.

Ellison, G. D., & Flynn, J. P. (1968). Organized aggressive behavior in cats after surgical isolation of the hypothalamus. *Archives of Italian Biology, 106*, 1–20.

English, E., & Baker, T. (1983). Relaxation training and cardiovascular response to experimental stressors. *Health Psychology, 2*, 239–259.

Evans, M. H. (1976). Stimulation of the rabbit hypothalamus: Caudal projections to respiratory and cardiovascular center. *Journal of Physiology, 269*, 205–222.

Evans, M. H. (1978). Potentiation of cardioinhibitory reflex by hypothalamic stimulation in the rabbit. *Brain Research, 154*, 331–343.

Evans, M. H. (1980). Vasoactive sites in the diencephalon of the rabbit. *Brain Research, 183,* 329–340.

Fanselow, M. S., & Kim, J. J. (1994). Acquisition of contextual Pavlovian fear conditioning is blocked by application of an NMDA receptor antagonist D,L-2-amino-5-phosphonovaleric acid to the basolateral amygdala. *Behavioral Neuroscience, 108,* 210–212.

Fardin, V., Oliveras, J. -L., & Besson, J. -M. (1984). A reinvestigation of the analgesic effects induced by stimulation of the periaqueductal gray matter in the rat I. The production of behavioral side effects together with analgesia. *Brain Research, 306,* 105–123.

Fernandez de Molina, A., & Hunsperger, R. W. (1962). Organization of the subcortical system governing defense and flight reactions in the cat. *Journal of Physiology (London), 160,* 200–213.

Frysztak, R. J., & Neafsey, E. J. (1994). The effect of medial frontal cortex lesions on cardiovascular conditioned emotional responses in the rat. *Brain Research, 643,* 181–193.

Gabriel, M., Miller, J. D., & Saltwick, S. E. (1976). Multiple-unit activity of the rabbit medial geniculate nucleus in conditioning, extinction, and reversal. *Physiological Psychology, 4,* 124–134.

Gaffan, D., & Harrison, S. (1987). Amygdalectomy and disconnection in visual learning for auditory secondary reinforcement by monkeys. *Journal of Neuroscience, 7,* 2285–2292.

Gaffan, E. A., Gaffan, D., & Harrison, S. (1988). Disconnection of the amygdala from visual association cortex impairs visual reward–association learning in monkeys. *Journal of Neuroscience, 8*(9), 3144–3150.

Gallagher, M., & Holland, P. C. (1994). The amygdala complex: Multiple roles in associative learning and attention. *Proceedings of the National Academy of Science, 91,* 11771–11776.

Gellen, B., Gyorgy, L., & Doda, M. (1972). Influence of surgical isolation of the hypothalamus on oxotremorin-induced rage reaction and sympathetic response in the cat. *Acta Physiological Science Hung, 42,* 195–202.

Gellhorn, E., & Kiely, W. (1972). Mystical states of consciousness. *Journal of Nervous and Mental Disease, 154,* 399–405.

Gelsema, A. J., McKitrick D. J., & Calaresu, F. R. (1987). Cardiovascular response to chemical and electrical stimulation of amygdala in rats. *American Journal of Physiology, 253,* 712–718.

Gelsema, A. J., Roe, M. J., & Calaresu, F. R. (1989). Neurally mediated cardiovascular responses to stimulation of cell bodies in the hypothalamus of the rat. *Brain Research, 482,* 67–77.

Gentile, C. G., Jarrell, T. W., Teich, A. H., McCabe, P. M., & Schneiderman, N. (1986). The role of amygdaloid central nucleus in differential Pavlovian conditioning of bradycardia in rabbits. *Behavioral Brain Research, 20,* 263–273.

Gold, P. E., & van Buskirk, R. B. (1978). Posttraining brain norepinephrine concentrations: Correlation with retention performance of avoidance training with peripheral epinephrine modulation of memory processing. *Behavioral Biology, 23,* 5092520.

Goleman, D., & Schwartz, G. (1975). Meditation as an intervention in stress reactivity. *Journal of Consulting and Clinical Psychology, 15,* 110–111.

Gong, Q. L., Huangfu, D. H, & Li, P. (1987). Exploration of cardiovascular and respiratory neuron groups in the ventrolateral medulla in the rabbit. *Chinese Journal of Physiological Science, 3,* 149–156.

Hamilton, R. B., Ellenberger, H., Liskowsky, D., & Schneiderman, N. (1981). Parabrachial area as mediator of bradycardia in rabbits. *Journal of the Autonomic Nervous System, 4,* 261–281.

Haselton, J. R., Winters, R. W., Haselton C. L., McCabe. P. M., & Schneiderman, N. (1988b). Anatomical and functional connections for neurons of the rostral medullary raphe of the rabbit. *Brain Research, 453,* 171–182.

Haselton, J. R., Haselton, C. L., Vera, P. L., Ellenberger, H. H., LeBlanc, W. G. Schneiderman, N., & McCabe, P. M. (1985). Nucleus reticularis lateralis involvement in the pressor component of the cerebral ischemic response. *Brain Research, 335,* 315–320.

Haselton, J. R., Winters, R. W., Haselton, C. L., McCabe, P. M., & Schneiderman, N. (1988a). Cardiovascular responses elicited by chemical stimulation of the rostral medullary raphe of the rabbit. *Brain Research, 453,* 167–175.

Hebb, D.O. (1949). *The Organization of Behavior.* New York: Wiley.

Hess. W. R., & Brugger, M. (1943). Das subkortikale Zentrum der affektiven Abwehrreaktion. *Helv. Physiol. Pharmacol. Acta, 1,* 33–52.

Hilton, S. M., & Redfern, W. S. (1983). Exploration of the brain stem defense areas with a synaptic excitant in the rat. *Journal of Physiology, 345,* 134. London.

Hilton, S. M., & Redfern, W. S. (1989). A search for brainstem cell groups integrating the defence reaction in the rat. *Journal of Physiology (London), 278,* 213–228.

Hilton, S. M., & Smith, P. R. (1984). Ventral medullary neurons excited from the hypothalamic and mid-brain defence areas. *Journal of the Autonomic Nervous System, 11,* 35–42.

Hilton, S. M., & Zbrozyna, A. W. (1963). Amygdaloid region for defence reactions and its efferent pathway to the brain stem. *Journal of Physiology, 165,* 160–173.

Hitchcock, J. M., & Davis, M. (1986). Lesions of the amygdala, but not of the cerebellum of red nucleus, block conditioned fear as measured with the potentiated startle paradigm. *Behavioral Neuroscience, 100,* 11–22.

Hobson, J. A., & Steriade, M. (1986). Neuronal basis of behavioral state control. In V. B. Mountcastle (Ed.), *Handbook of physiology: Section 1. The nervous system. Vol. 4. Intrinsic regulatory systems of the brain* (pp. 701–823). Bethesda, MD: American Physiological Society.

Hopkins, D. A., & Holstege, G. (1978). Amygdaloid projections to the mesencephalon, pons, and medulla oblongata in the cat. *Experimental Brain Research, 32,* 529–547.

Horel, I. A., Keating, E. G., & Misantone, L. J. (1975). Partial Kluver-Bucy syndrome produced by destroying temporal neocortex or amygdala. *Brain Research, 94,* 347–359.

Hurley, K. M., Herbert, H., Moga, M. M., & Saper, C. B. (1991). Efferent projections of the infralimbic cortex of the rat. *Journal of Comparative Neurology, 308,* 249–276.

Hurwitz, B. E., Nelesen, R. A., Saab, P. G., Nagel, J. H., Spitzer, S. B., Gellman, M. D., McCabe, P. M., Phillips, D. J., & Schneiderman, N. (1993). Differential patterns of dynamic cardiovascular regulation as a function of task. *Biological Psychology, 36,* 75–95.

Iwata, J., LeDoux, J. E., Meely, M. P., Arneric, S., & Reis, D. J. (1986). Intrinsic neurons in the amygdaloid field projected to by the medial geniculate body mediate emotional responses conditioned to acoustic stimuli. *Brain Research, 383,* 195–214.

Jarrell, T. W., Gentile, C. G., McCabe, P. M., & Schneiderman, N. (1986a). The role of medial geniculate nucleus in differential Pavlovian conditioning of bradycardia in rabbits. *Brain Research, 374,* 126–136.

Jarrell, T. W., McCabe, P. M., Teich. A., Gentile, C. G., VanDercar, D., & Schneiderman, N. (1986b). Lateral subthalamus area as mediator of classically conditioned bradycardia in rabbits. *Behavioral Neuroscience, 100,* 3–10.

Jarrell, T. W., Romanski, L. M., Gentile, C. G., McCabe, P. M., & Schneiderman, N. (1986). Ibotenic acid lesions in the medical geniculate region prevent the acquisition of differential Pavlovian conditioning of bradycardia to acoustic stimuli in rabbits. *Brain Research, 382,* 199–203.

Jarrell, T. W., Gentile, C. G., Romanski, L. M., McCabe, P. M., & Schneiderman, N. (1987). Involvement of cortical and thalamic auditory regions in retention of differential bradycardia conditioning to acoustic conditioned stimuli in rabbits. *Brain Research*, *412*, 285–294.

Jones, B., & Mishkin, M. (1972). Limbic lesions and the problem of stimulus-reinforcement associations. *Experimental Neurology*, *36*, 362–377.

Jordan, D., Kalid, M. E. M., Schneiderman, N., & Spryer, K. M. (1982). Localization and properties of ganglionic cardiomotor neurons in rabbits. *Pflugers Archiv-European Journal of Psyiology*, *395*, 244–250.

Kapp, B. S., Frysinger, R. C., Gallagher, M., & Haselton, J. R. (1979). Amygdala central nucleus lesions: Effect on heart rate conditioning in the rabbit. *Physiology and Behavior*, *23*, 1109–1117.

Kapp, B. S., Gallagher, M., Underwood, M. D., McNall, C. C., & Whitehorn, D. (1982). Cardiovascular responses elicited by electrical stimulation of the amygdala central nucleus in the rabbit. *Brain Research*, *234*, 251–262.

Kapp, B. S., Pascoe, J. P., & Bixler, M. A. (1984). The amygdala: A neuroanatomical systems approach to its contribution to aversive conditioning. In L. R. Squire (Ed.), *Neuropsychology of memory* (pp. 473–488). New York: Guilford.

Kapp, B. S., Supple, W. F., & Whalen, P. J. (1994). Effects of electrical stimulation of the amygdaloid central nucleus on neocortical arousal in the rabbit. *Behavioral Neuroscience*, *108*, 81–93.

Kapp, B. S., Wilson, A., Pascoe, J. P., Supple, W., & Whalen, P. J. (1990). A neuroanatomical systems analysis of conditioned bradycardia in the rabbit. In M. Gabriel, & J. W. Moore (Eds.), *Neurocomputation and Learning: Foundations of Adaptive Networks*. Cambridge, MA: Bradford Books, The MIT Press.

Kaufman, M. P., Hamilton, R. B., Wallach, J. H., Petrik, G. K., & Schneiderman, N. (1979). Lateral subthalamic area as mediator of bradycardia responses in rabbits. *American Journal of Physiology*, *236*, H471–H479.

Keller, A. D. (1932). Autonomic discharges elicited by physiological stimuli in mid-brain preparations. *American Journal of Physiology*, *100*, 576586.

Kelly, A. H, Beaton, L. E., & Magoun, H. W. (1946). A midbrain mechanism for facio–vocal activity. *Journal of Neurophysiology*, *9*, 181–189.

Kim, J. J., Rison, R. A., & Fanselow, M. S. (1993). Effects of amygdala, hippocampus, and periacqueductal gray lesions on short- and long-term contextual fear. *Behavioral Neuroscience*, *107*, 1093–1098.

LeDoux, J. E. (1994). Cognitive emotional interactions in the brain. In P. Ekman, & R. J. Davidson (Eds.), *The nature of emotions* (pp. 216–223). Oxford University Press.

LeDoux, J. E. (1995). Emotion: Clues from the brain. *Annual Review of Psychology*, *46*, 209–235.

LeDoux, J. E., Cicchetti, P., Xagoraris, A., & Romanski, L. (1990). The lateral amygdaloid nucleus: Sensory interface of the amygdala in fear conditioning. *Journal of Neuroscience*, *10*, 1062–1069.

LeDoux, J. E., Farb, C., & Ruggiero, D. A. (1990). Topographic organization of neurons in the acoustic thalamus that project to the amygdala. *Journal of Neuroscience*, *10*, 1043–1054.

LeDoux, J. E., Iwata, J., Cicchetti, P., & Reis, D. J. (1988). Different projections of the central amygdala and nucleus mediate autonomic and behavioral correlates of conditioned fear. *Journal of Neuroscience*, *8*, 2517–2529.

LeDoux, J. E., Ruggiero, D. A., & Reis, D. J. (1985). Projections of the subcortical forebrain from anatomically defined regions of the medial geniculate body in the rat. *Journal of Comparative Neurology*, *242*, 182–213.

LeDoux, J. E., Ruggiero, D. A., Forest, R., Stornetta, R., & Reis, D. J. (1987). Topographic organization of convergent projections to the thalamus from the inferior colliculus and spinal cord in the rat. *Journal of Comparative Neurology, 264,* 123–146.

LeDoux, J. E., Sakaguchi, A., & Reis, D. J. (1984). Subcortical efferent projections of the medial geniculate nucleus mediate emotional responses conditioned to acoustic stimuli. *Journal of Neuroscience, 4,* 683–698.

LeDoux, J. R., Farb, C. R., & Romanski, L. M. (1991). Overlapping projections to the amygdala
and striatum from auditory processing areas of the thalamus and cortex. *Neuroscience Letters, 134,* 139–144.

Liang, K. C., Bennette, C., & McGaugh, J. L. (1985). Peripheral epinephrine modulates the effects of posttraining amygdala stimulation on memory. *Behavioural Brain Research, 15,* 93–100.

Liskowsky, D. R, Winters, R. W., McCabe, P. M., & Schneiderman, N. (1987). Connections between cardiovascular related areas in the hypothalamus and the periaqueductal gray region in rabbits. *Society for Neuroscience Abstracts, 13.*

Love, J. A., & Scott, J. W. (1969). Some response characteristics of cells of the magnocellular division of the medial geniculate body of the cat. *Canadian Journal of Physiology and Pharmacology, 47,* 881–888.

Markgraf, C. G., Liskowsky, D. R., Winters, R. W., McCabe, P. M., Green, E. J., & Schneiderman, N. (1991). Hypothalamic, midbrain, and bulbar areas involved in the defense reaction in rabbits. *Physiology and Behavior, 49,* 493–500.

Marks, I. M. (1987). Fear behaviors: The four strategies. In I. M. Marks, (Ed.), *Fears, phobias, and rituals* (pp. 53–82). New York: Oxford University Press.

Marshall, J. M. (1981). Interaction between the responses to stimulation of peripheral chemoreceptors and baroreceptors: The importance of chemoreceptor activation of the defence areas. *Journal of the Autonomic Nervous System, 3,* 389–400.

McCabe, P. M., Duan, Y. -F., Winters, R. W., Green, E. J., Huang, Y., & Schneiderman, N. (1994). Comparison of peripheral blood flow patterns associated with the defense reaction and vigilance reaction in rabbits. *Physiology and Behavior, 56*(5), 1101–1106.

McCabe, P. M., Gentile, C. G., Markgraf, C. G., Teich, A. H., & Schneiderman, N. (1992). Ibotenic acid lesions in the amygdaloid central nucleus but not in the lateral subthalamic area prevent the acquisition of differential Pavlovian conditioning of bradycardia in rabbits. *Brain Research, 580,* 155–163.

McCabe, P. M., McEchron, M. D., Green, E. J., & Schneiderman, N. (1993). Effects of electrolytic and ibotenic acid lesions of the medial nucleus of the medial geniculate nucleus on single tone heart rate conditioning. *Brain Research, 619,* 291–298.

McCabe, P. M., McEchron, M. D., Green, E. J., & Schneiderman, N. (1995). Destruction of neurons in the VPM thalamus prevents rabbit heart rate conditioning. *Physiology & Behavior, 57,* 159–163.

McEchron, M. D., Green, E. J., Winters, R. W., Nolen, T. G., Schneiderman, N., & McCabe, P. M. (1996). Changes of synaptic efficacy in the medial geniculate nucleus as a result of auditory classical conditioning. *Journal of Neuroscience, 16,* 1273–1283.

McEchron, M. D., McCabe, P. M., Green, E. J., Hitchcock, J. M., & Schneiderman, N. (1996). Immunohistochemical expression of the c-FOS protein in the spinal trigeminal nucleus following presentation of a corneal airpuff stimulus. *Brain Research, 710,* 112–120.

McEchron, M. D., McCabe, P. M., Green, E. J., Llabre, M. M., & Schneiderman, N. (1995). Simultaneous single unit recording in the medial nucleus of the medial geniculate nucleus and amygdaloid central nucleus throughout habituation, acquisition, and extinction of the rabbit's classically conditioned heart rate. *Brain Research, 682,* 157–166.

Milani, H., & Graeff, F. G. (1987). GABA-benzodiazepine modulation of aversion in the medial hypothalamus of the rat. *Pharmacology, Biochemistry, and Behavior, 28,* 21–27.

Neafsey, E. J., Terreberry, R. R., Hurley, K. M., Ruit, K. G., & Frystzak, R. J. (1993). Anterior cingulate cortex in rodents: Connections, visceral control functions, and implications for emotion. In B. A. Vogt & M. Gabriel (Eds.), *Neurobiology of cingulate cortex and limbic thalamus: A comprehensive* handbook (pp. 206–223). Boston: Birkhauser.

Oleson, T. D., Ashe, J. H., & Weinberger, N. M. (1975). Modification of auditory and somatosensory system activity during pupillary conditioning in the paralyzed cat. *Journal of Neurophysiology, 38,* 1114–1139.

Ongur, D., An, X., & Price, J. L. (1996). Orbital and medial prefrontal cortical projections to the hypothalamus in macaque monkeys. *Society for Neuroscience Abstracts, 22,* 672.

Ottersen, O. P., & Ben-Ari, Y. (1979). Afferent connections to the amygdaloid complex of the rat and cat. I. Projections of the thalamus. *Journal of Comparative Neurology, 187,* 401–424.

Packard, M. G., Williams, C. L., & McGaugh, J. L. (1992). Enhancement of win-shift radial maze retention by peripheral posttraining administration of d-amphetamine and 4-OH amphetamine. *Psychobiology, 20,* 280–285.

Pascoe, J. D., & Kapp, B. S. (1985). Electrophysiological characteristics of amygdaloid central nucleus neurons during differential Pavlovian conditioned heart rate responding in the rabbit. *Behavioral Brain Research, 16,* 117–133.

Pascoe, J. P., Bradley, D. J., & Spyer, K. M. (1989). Interactive responses to stimulation of the amygdaloid central nucleus and baroreceptor afferents in the rabbit. *Journal of the Autonomic Nervous System, 26,* 157–167.

Pavlov, I. P. (1927). *Conditioned Reflexes.* New York: Dover.

Phillips, R. G., & LeDoux, J. E. (1992). Differential contribution of amygdala and hippocampus to cued and contextual fear conditioning. *Behavioral Neuroscience, 106*(2), 272–285.

Phillips, R. G., & LeDoux, J. E. (1995). Lesions of the fornix but not the entorhinal or perirhinal cortex interfere with contextual fear conditioning. *Journal of Neuroscience, 15,* 5308–5315.

Powell, D. A., Lipkin, M., & Milligan, W. L. (1974). Concomitant changes in classically conditioned heart rate and corneoretinal potential discrimination in the rabbit (oryctolagus cuniculus). *Learning and Motivation, 5,* 532–547.

Powell, D. A., Watson, K. L., & Buchanan, S. L. (1990). Neuronal activity in the mediodorsal and intralaminar nuclei of the dorsal thalamus during classical heart rate conditioning. *Brain Research, 532,* 211–221.

Powell, D. A., Watson, K., & Maxwell, B. (1994). Involvement of subdivisions of the medial prefrontal cortex in learned cardiac adjustments in rabbits. *Behavioral Neuroscience, 108,* 294–307.

Powers, W. T., Clark, R. K., & McFarland, R. L. (1960). A general feedback theory of human behavior. *Perception and Motor Skills (Part I), 11,* 71–88; *Part II,* 309–323. Reprinted in *General Systems, 5,* 66–83.

Price, J. L., & Amaral, D. G. (1981). An autoradiographic study of the projections of the central nucleus of the monkey amygdala. *Journal of Neuroscience, 1,* 1242–1259.

Romanski, L. M., & LeDoux, J. E. (1992). Equipotentiality of thalamo-amygdala and thalamocortico-amygdala projections as auditory conditioned stimulus pathways. *Journal of Neuroscience, 12,* 4501–4509.

Romanski, L. M., & LeDoux, J. E. (1993). Information cascade from primary auditory cortex to the amygdala: Corticocortical and corticoamygdaloid projections of temporal cortex in the rat. *Cerebral Cortex, 3*, 515–532.

Ross, C. A., Ruggiero, D. A., Park, D. H., Joh, T. H., & Sved, A. F. (1984). Tonic vasomotor control of the rostral ventrolateral medulla: Effect of electrical or chemical stimulation of the area containing C1 adrenalin neurons on arterial pressure. Heart rate and plasma catecholamines and vasopressin. *Journal of Neuroscience, 4*, 474–494.

Ryugo, D. K., & Weinberger, N. M. (1978). Differential plasticity of morphologically distinct neuron populations in the medial geniculate body of the cat during classical conditioning. *Behavioral Biology, 22*, 275–301.

Saab,P. G., Llabre, M. M., Hurwitz, B. E., Frame, C. A., Reineke, L. J., Fins, A. I., McCalla, J., Cieply, L. K., & Schneiderman, N. (1992). Myocardial and peripheral vascular responses to behavioral challenges and their stability in black and white Americans. *Psychophysiology, 29*, 384–397.

Schmitt, P. G., Di Scala, M. L., Brandao, M. L., Karli, P. (1986). Behavioral effects of microinjections of SR 95103, a new GABA-A antagonist, into the medical hypothalamus or the mesencephalic central gray. *European Journal of Pharmacology, 117*, 149–158.

Schneiderman, N., VanDercar, D. H., Yehle, A. L., Manning, A. A., Golden, T., & Schneiderman, N. E. (1969). Vagal compensatory adjustment: Relationship to heart-rate classical conditioning in rabbits. *Journal of Comparative and Physiological Psychology, 68*, 176–183.

Schneiderman, N. (1974). The relationship between learned and unlearned cardiovascular responses. In P. A. Obrist, A. H. Black, J. Brenner, & L. V. Dicara (Eds.), Cardiovascular Psychophysiology, pp. 190–210. Chicago: Aldine-Atherton.

Schneiderman, N., & McCabe, P. M. (1985). Biobehavioral responses to stressors. In T. M. Field, P. M. McCabe, & N. Schneiderman (Eds.), *Stress and coping*. Hillsdale, NJ: Lawrence Erlbaum Associates.

Schneiderman, N., Smith, M. C., Smith, A. C., & Gormezano, I. (1966). Heart rate classical conditioning in rabbits. *Psychonomic Science, 6*, 241–242.

Schwaber, J. S., Kapp, B. S., & Higgins, G. (1980). The origin and extent of direct amygdala projections to the region of the dorsal motor nucleus of the vagus and the nucleus of the solitary tract. *Neuroscience Letters, 20*, 15–20.

Schwaber, J. S., Kapp, B. S., Higgins, G. A., & Rapp, P. R. (1982). Amygdaloid and basal forebrain direct connections with the nucleus of the solitary tract and the dorsal motor nucleus. *Journal of Neuroscience, 2*(11), 14141–438.

Schwaber, J., & Schneiderman, N. (1975). Aortic nerve activated cardioinhibitory neurons and interneurons. *American Journal of Physiology, 229*, 783–789.

Selden, N. R. W., Everitt, B. J., Jarrard, L. E., & Robbins, T. W. (1991). Complimentary roles for the amygdala and hippocampus in aversive conditioning to explicit and contextual cues. *Neuroscience, 42*, 335–350.

Shaikh, M. B., Barrett, J. A., & Siegel, A. (1987). The pathways mediating affective defense and quiet biting attack behavior from the midbrain central gray of the cat: An autoradiographic studs. *Brain Research, 437*, 9–25.

Shekhar, A., & DiMicco, J. A. (1987). Defense reaction elicited by injection of GABA antagonists and synthesis inhibitors into the posterior hypothalamus in rats. *Neuropharmacology, 26*, 407–417.

Smith, O. A., Astley, A. C., De Vita, J. L., Stein, J. M., & Walsh, K. E. (1980). Functional analysis of hypothalamic control of the cardiovascular responses accompanying emotional behaviour. *Federation Proceedings, 39*, 2487–2494.

Smith, O. A., DeVito, J. L., & Astley, C. A. (1990). Neurons controlling cardiovascular response to emotion are located in lateral hypothalamus-perifornical region. *American Journal of Physiology, 259,* 943–954.

Sparks, P. D., & LeDoux, J. E. (1995). Septal lesions potentiate freezing to contextual but not to phasic conditioned stimuli in rats. *Behavioral Neuroscience, 109,* 184–188.

Spencer, S. E., Sawyer. W. B., & Lowey, A. D. (1990). L-Glutamate mapping of cardioreactive areas in the rat posterior hypothalamus. *Brain Research, 511,* 149–157.

Sternberg, D. B., Isaacs, K., Gold, P. E., & McGaugh, J. L. (1985). Epinephrine facilitation of appetitive learning: Attenuation with adrenergic receptor antagonists. *Behavioral and Neural Biology, 44,* 447–453.

Stock, G., Rupprecht, U., Stumpf, H., & Schlor, K. H. (1981). Cardiovascular changes during arousal elicited by stimulation of amygdala, hypothalamus and locus coeruleus. *Journal of Autonomic Nervous System, 3,* 503–510.

Stock, G., Schlor, K. H., & Buss, J. (1978). Psychomotor behavior and cardiovascular patterns during stimulation of the amygdala. *Pflugers Archives, 376,* 177–194.

Swadlow, H. A., Hosking, K. E., & Schneiderman, N. (1971). Differential heart rate conditioning and lever lift suppression in restrained rabbits. *Physiology and Behavior, 7,* 257–260.

Sudre, E. C. M., de Barros, M. R., Sudre, G. N., & Schenberg, L. C. (1993). Thresholds of electrically induced defense reaction of the rat: Short and long term adaptation mechanisms. *Behavior, Brain Research, 58,* 141–154.

Supple, W. F., & Kapp, B. S. (1989). Response characteristics of neurons in the medial geniculate nucleus during Pavlovian differential fear conditioning in the rabbit. *Behavioral Neuroscience, 103,* 1276–1286.

Supple, W. F., & Kapp, B. S. (1993). The anterior cerebellar vermis: essential involvement in classically conditioned bradycardia in the rabbit. *Journal of Neuroscience, 13(9),* 3705–3711.

Supple, W. F., & Leaton, R. N. (1990). Lesions of the cerebellar vermis and cerebellar hemispheres: Effects on heart rate conditioning in rats. *Behavioral Neuroscience, 104,* 934–947.

Taylor, C. B. (1978). Relaxation training and related techniques. In W. S. Agras (Ed.), *Behavioral modification* (pp. 30–52). Boston: Little, Brown.

Teich, A. H., McCabe, P. M., Gentile, C. G., Schneiderman, L., Winters, R. W., Liskowsky, D. R., & Schneiderman, N. (1989). Auditory cortex lesions prevent the extinction of Pavlovian differential heart rate conditioning to tonal stimuli in rabbits. *Brain Research, 480,* 210–218.

Teich, A. H., McCabe, P. M., Gentile, C. G., Winters, R. W., Liskowsky, D. R., & Schneiderman, N. (1988). Role of auditory cortex in the acquisition of differential heart rate conditioning. *Physiology and Behavior, 44,* 405–412.

Timms, R. J. (1981). A study of the amygdaloid defense reaction showing the value of althesin anesthesia in studies of the function of the forebrain in cats. *Pflugers Archives, 391,* 49–50.

Turner, B. H., & Herkenham, M. (1991). Thalamoamygdaloid projections in the rat: A test of the amygdala's role in sensory processing. *Journal of Comparative Neurology, 313,* 295–325.

Vera, P. L., Ellenberger, H. H., Haselton, J. R., Haselton, C. L., & Schneiderman, N. (1986). The intermediolateral nucleus: An 'open' or 'closed' nucleus? *Brain Research, 386,* 84–92.

Veening, J. G. (1978). Subcortial afferents of the amygdsloid complex in the rat: An HRP study. *Neuroscience Letters, 8,* 197–202.

Waldrop, T. G., & Bauer, R. M. (1989). Modulation of sympathetic discharge by hypothalamic GABAergic mechanism. *Neuropharmacology, 28,* 263–269.

Waldrop, T. G., Bauer, R. M., & Iwamoto, G. A. (1988). Microinjection of GABA antagonists into the posterior hypothalamus elicits locomotor activity and a cardiorespiratory activation. *Brain Research, 444*, 84–94.

Weinberger, N. M., Hopkins, W., & Diamond, D. M. (1984). Physiological plasticity of single nuerons in auditory cortex of the cat during acquisition of the pupillary conditioned response. I. Primary field (AI). *Behavioral Neuroscience, 98*(2), 171–188.

Weinberger, N. M. (1984). The neurophysiology of learning: A view from the sensory side. In L. R. Squire, & N. Butters (Eds.), *Neuropsychology of memory* (pp. 489–503). New York: Guilford Press.

Weinberger, N. M., & Diamond, D. M. (1987). Physiological plasticity in auditory cortex: Rapid induction by learning. *Progressions in Neurobiology, 29*, 1–55.

Weinberger, N. M., Javid, R., & Lepan, B. (1993). Long term retention of learning-induced receptive field plasticity in the auditory cortex. *Proceedings of the National Academy of Science, 90*, 2394–2398.

Weinberger, N. M., Javid, R., & Lepan, B. (1995). Heterosynaptic long-term facilitation of sensory-evoked responses in the auditory cortex by stimulation of the magnocellular medial geniculate in guinea pigs. *Behavioral Neuroscience, 109*, 10–17.

Wepsic, J. G. (1966). Multimodal sensory activation of cells in the magnocellular medial geniculate nucleus. *Experimental Neurology, 15*, 299–318.

Whalen, P. J., & Kapp, B. S. (1991). Contributions of the amygdaloid central nucleus to the modulation of the nictitating membrane reflex in the rabbit. *Behavioral Neuroscience, 105*, 141–153.

Williams C. L., & Jensen, R. A. (1991). Vagal afferents: A possible mechanism for the modulation of peripherally acting agents. In R. C. A. Frederickson & J. L. McGaugh (Eds.), *Peripheral signaling of the brain in neural-immune and cognitive function* (pp 467–472). Gottingen, FRG: Hogrefe & Huber.

Williams, C. L., & McGaugh, J. L. (1993). Reversible lesions of the nucleus of the solitary tract attenuate the memory-modulating effects of posttraining epinephrine. *Behavioral Neuroscience, 107*(6), 955–962.

Williams, C. L., & McGaugh, J. L. (1992). Reversible inactivation of the nucleus of the solitary tract impairs retention performance in an inhibitory avoidance task. *Behavioral and Neural Biology, 58*, 204–210.

Winer, J. A., Diamond, I. T., & Raczowski, D. (1977). Subdivisions of the auditory cortex of the cat: The retrograde transport of horseradish peroxidase to the medial geniculate body and posterior thalamic nuclei. *Journal of Comparative Neurology, 176*, 387–418.

Winters, R. W., McCabe, P. M., Green, E. J., Duan, Y. -F., & Schneiderman, N. (1991). Electrophysiological evidence for hypothalamic defense area input to cells in the lateral tegmental field of the medulla in rabbits. *Brain Research, 558*, 171.–175.

Yardley, C. P., & Hilton. S. M. (1986). The hypothalamic and brainstem areas from which the cardiovascular and behavioural components of the defence reaction are elicited in the rat. *Journal of the Autonomic Nervous System, 15*, 227–244.

Zamir, N., & Shuber, E. (1980). Altered pain perception in hypertensive humans. *Brain Research, 201*, 471–474.

Zanchetti, A., Baccelli, G., & Mancia, G. (1976). Fighting, emotions, and exercise: Cardiovascular effects in the cat. In G. Onesti & M. Fernandes (Eds.), *Regulation of blood pressure by the central nervous system* (pp. 87–103). New York: Grune & Stratton.

2

Blood Pressure Elevation as a Coping Response

Barry R. Dworkin
Pennsylvania State University College of Medicine
Thomas Elbert
University of Konstanz, Germany
Harald Rau
University of Tübingen, Germany

Mechanoreceptors in the carotid sinus and aortic arch are the afferent limb of reflexes that regulate blood pressure. The vagal cardioinhibitory and sympathoinhibitory vascular effects of these reflexes have been studied for more than 60 years. It is undisputed that the baroreflexes buffer changes in arterial pressure via specific cardiovascular mechanisms; however, in addition to these peripheral effects, mediated by the autonomic efferents, stimulation of the baroreceptors also produces less known, but clearly documented, general inhibition of central nervous processes: Independent of changes in general circulation, the activation of baroafferent pathways by electrical nerve stimulation, mechanical stretch, or elevation of blood pressure will decrease somatic muscle tone, inhibit spinal somatic reflexes, induce synchronization of the electroencephalogram (EEG), increase cortical positivity, blunt pain sensations, reduce anxiety, and induce sleep or even clinically significant syncope (see below). Arousing emotional and pain stimuli elevate blood pressure, (Harshfield, Pickering, James, & Blank, 1990; Harshfield, Pickering, Kleinert, Blank, & Laragh, 1982; James, Yee, Harshfield, Blank, & Pickering, 1986; Jonsson & Hansson, 1977; Peterson, Augenstein, Tanis, & Augenstein, 1981; Pickering & Gerin, 1990; Pickering, Harshfield, Kleinert, Blank, & Laragh, 1982), and the CNS inhibitory effects of barostimulation most simply can be seen to provide supplementary, homeostatic, negative feedback, that along with cardioinhibition and vasodilatation, helps to restore excessively elevated blood pressure to a safer level.

COULD BARORECEPTOR-CNS INHIBITION REWARD LEARNING OF HYPERTENSION?

Unlike the vagal and sympathetic reflexes, which act directly through specific hemodynamic mechanisms, baroreceptor-mediated CNS inhibition has a broad impact on the nervous system, which carries the potential for nonregulatory behavioral consequences: In particular, in stressful situations, prompt alleviation of pain–anxiety by coping behaviors can reward, and through learning, strengthen these behaviors. Thus, it is at least conceivable that pain and anxiety reduction produced by baroreceptor stimulation could similarly reward various behaviors. As with other general reinforcement mechanisms, baroreceptor pain–anxiety reduction could potentially reward a range of learnable behaviors, however, one class of behaviors, those that lead to elevation of blood pressure, is of special interest.

There is, in fact, ample experimental evidence in humans and animals showing that, given appropriate rewards, behaviors that raise blood pressure can be learned. These studies have shown that humans, at least those with spinal injuries, can learn to significantly increase their blood pressure given accurate, contingent reinforcement (Pickering, Brucker, Frankel, Mathias, Dworkin, & Miller, 1977). Similar, more rigorously controlled experiments have been done on intact infrahuman primates: Plumfee (Plumfee, 1969) and Benson (Benson, Herd, Morse, & Kelleher, 1969) trained monkeys and Harris (Harris, Gilliam, Findley, & Brady, 1973) used baboons. When these blood pressure learning findings are combined with the animal results on baroreceptor pain–anxiety inhibition, a somewhat surprising, but nonetheless logically consistent, hypothesis emerges: *Because blood pressure elevation stimulates baroreceptors and barostimulation inhibits pain and anxiety, then, repeated baroactivation could strengthen through learning those behaviors that caused the blood pressure to rise in the first place.*

In certain individuals this kind of learning could have a role in initiating essential hypertension.[1] The hypothesis specifically predicts that individu-

---

[1]Four specific interacting conditions are required: (a) presence of a chronic source of noxious stimulation; (b) perception of this stimulation as aversive; (c) an ability to learn to raise blood pressure; and (d) an individual trait determining the degree of pain inhibition produced by baroreceptor stimulation (see Dworkin, 1991). The baroreceptor reinforcement instrumental learning (BR-IL) model of essential hypertension: Biological data, quantitative mechanisms, and computer modeling. In A. Shapiro, & A. Baum (Eds.), *Perspectives in behavioral medicine: behavioral aspects of cardiovascular disease* (pp. 213–225).

als would be predisposed to "learn hypertension as a coping response" by the conjunction of a strong baroreceptor CNS inhibition trait, and chronic exposure to noxious social or environmental stimuli that are perceived as aversive or "stressful."[2] If either of these factors is absent the response–reinforcement loop required for learning is not completed, and under the hypothesis neither the magnitude of the baroreceptor pain inhibition effect nor the degree of stress would be expected to predict blood pressure.

Next, we describe recently published findings that together, appear to support the above hypothesis. The data are of two kinds: experimental measurements of the inhibitory effects of baroreceptor stimulation in a group of normotensive individuals, and longitudinal changes in blood pressure in these subjects as a function of their preceived level of stress.

CENTRAL NERVOUS SYSTEM INHIBITORY EFFECTS OF BARORECEPTOR STIMULATION

Barostimulation Methods in Animals

Dworkin and colleagues (Dworkin, Filewich, Miller, Craigmyle, & Pickering, 1979) reported that rats escape from, and avoid, a mildly aversive trigeminal nucleus stimulus to a lesser degree when their blood pressure was pharmacologically elevated, and that the effect could be abolished by denervation of the baroreceptors; using different aversive stimuli, Randich and Maixner (1984), replicated and extended these findings, and showed that reflex bradycardia (that could indirectly mediate the perception of anxiety) was not a factor in the altered pain sensitivity. The experimental animal literature on baroreceptor mediated CNS inhibition is quite extensive. Beginning with Koch's (1932) observations, using mechanical stimulation of a carotid cul-de-sac in dogs, and Bonvallet and Dell's analysis (Bonvallet, Dell, & Hiebel, 1954) of the neurophysiology in decerebrate cats, well controlled animal experiments have confirmed that stimulation of the baroreceptors produces many typical manifestations of CNS inhibition.

Hillsdale, NJ: Lawrence Erlbaum Associates (pp. 213–245). It was also pointed out that if there were other more efficient coping responses, which could be learned more easily, they might be learned instead of blood pressure elevation; this provides a mechanism for symptom specificity that most other psychosomatic theories lack.

[2]The blood pressure learning process can be likened to experimental barbiturate addiction, wherein learning of drug self-administration behaviors depends on the chronic presence of background aversive stimulation that is ameliorated by the drug. See Miller, N. E., Davis, J. D., & Lulenski, G. C. (1968). Comparative studies of barbiturate self-administration. *Journal of the Addictions, 3,* 207–214.

Barostimulation Methods in Humans

In humans, baroreceptor CNS inhibition can be pronounced and even have substantial medical consequences: Weiss and Baker's (1933) detailed clinical study showed that certain forms of frank and intractable syncope had a purely neural carotid mechanism that did not depend on compromising circulatory antecedents, and anthropologists Schlager and Meier (1947) described how native practitioners in the Balinese islands routinely used therapeutic carotid massage to induce sleep. Recently, there have been efforts to experimentally evaluate barostimulation effects on pain thresholds, EEG spectra, and cortical slow waves in human subjects (Elbert, Rockstroh, Canavan, Birbaumer, Bülow, & Linden, 1991; Elbert, Tafil-Klawe, Rau, & Lutzenberger, 1991; Rau, Brody, Droste, & Kardos, 1993; Vaitl & Gruppe, 1990, 1991). On the whole, the results of these studies are concordant with the animal results, but the human experiments have not included fully convincing control conditions. The main obstacle has been in devising effective and noninvasive manipulations that unequivocally separate baroreceptor activation from other effects on the CNS. For example, although vasoconstrictive drugs, such as phenylephrine, elevate blood pressure and stimulate the baroreceptors, without the denervation control, that can be used only in animal studies, central and peripheral side effects of the drug that are unrelated to barostimulation could explain their impact on perception and general CNS function.

Balloon distention of a surgically isolated carotid sinus cul-de-sac of a dog is the "gold standard" of experimental barostimulation methods, and a related, but noninvasive, pressure stimulation method can be used in humans. The baroreceptors are actually stretch receptors in the arterial wall, and pressure inside the artery normally *pushes* the wall outward, but the wall also can be artificially *pulled* outward by extravascular suction applied through an pneumatic collar that encircles the neck. In the usual arrangement, a constant or static *negative* pressure in the neck chamber summed with the pulsatile intracarotid *positive* pressure increases the average stretch of the sinus and simulates an elevated mean arterial pressure (MAP). The "static pressure" neck chamber has been used extensively to study the peripheral physiology of the human baroreflex, but the static neck chamber has a serious drawback for behavioral studies: Although not at all painful, neck suction is distracting, and distraction itself could affect perceptual–behavioral results through mechanisms that are unrelated to barostimulation.

Instead of static or constant neck chamber suction, it is possible to use sequences of brief, cardiac cycle-coordinated pressure changes to stimulate or inhibit baroreceptor activity. Eckberg (1976) first observed that brief suction pulses applied randomly during various parts of the cardiac cycle differentially affected subsequent P-P intervals. Dworkin (1988) elaborated on Eckberg's (1976) method by using a cardiac cycle synchronized train of repeatedly alternating pressure and suction pulses to continuously stimulate or inhibit the carotid receptors for as long as several minutes. Alternating suction during systole with positive pressure during diastole increased the carotid sinus pulse pressure (CSPP), whereas the opposite phase relationship decreased the CSPP. With this method, heart rate was 5% to10% lower during stimulation (compared to the control condition), and blood pressure was only slightly affected. Rau (Rau et al., 1993; Rau, Elbert, Geiger, & Lutzenberger, 1992) however, noted that because in humans, diastole is much longer than systole, the control and stimulation conditions in this method were not exactly symmetrical and the discrepancy could, at least in theory, differentially affect the sensory state of a subject, potentially intruding the kind of nonbaroreceptor-mediated perceptual bias that the phase-locked stimulation method was designed to avoid. Rau's revised method incorporated a variable length atmospheric pressure pulse with appropriately phased symmetrical suction and positive pressure pulses, and modulated the CSPP to about the same degree as Dworkin's (1988), but his control and barostimulation conditions had exactly the same mean pressure, and, as is critical for perceptual studies, the control and stimulation phase-related external suction (PRES) conditions are essentially indistinguishable, even to subjects who are specifically instructed to attempt to discriminate them (Furedy, Rau, & Roberts, 1992).

Effects of Barostimulation on Reflexes and Pain Perception

Because the PRES method affects cartoid sinus pulse pressure (CSPP) and not mean cartoid sinus pressure (CSP), it modulates the range, rather than the mean rate of baroreceptor firing over a cardiac cycle,[3] and brief, cardiac cycle coordinated test stimuli[4] can be presented against any of four predict-

---

[3]Stimuli occurring during systole coincide with enhanced baroreceptor activity, but those falling in diastole coincide with lower than normal firing; however some net effect may result from asymmetrical rate sensitivity of the baroreceptors.

[4]The effectiveness of brief sensory stimuli placed in the natural cardiac cycle was studied in the past. Some investigators reported substantial attenuation of stimuli presented during systole; however, others were unable to reproduce their results. See Birren, J. E., Cardon, P. V., Jr., & Phillips, S. L (1963). Reaction

ably graded baroactivity levels (see Fig. 2.1a). Using PRES in this way, we measured the effect of baroreceptor activity on the reported painfulness of discrete electrical stimuli and on the magnitude of the Achilles tendon reflex to a standard hammer blow. Similar procedures were used in both kinds of experiment: Subjects, fitted with a foam-lined malleable-metal neck chamber, reclined in a comfortable chair. Hoses connected the chamber to an electrocardiograph (ECG) triggered, computer switched, pneumatic valve that alternated among sources of *negative, positive* (approximately ± 40 Torr), and *atmospheric* pressure.[5] For the tendon reflex experiment, an electrically operated hammer struck the subject's ankle, while EMG electrodes recorded the reflex response of the soleus muscle.[6] For the pain per-

---

time as a function of the cardiac cycle in young adults. *Science, 140,* 195–196; Callaway, E. I., & Layne, R. S. (1964). Interaction between the visual evoked response and two spontaneous biological rhythms: The EEG alpha cycle and the cardiac arousal cycle. *Annals New York Academy of Sciences, 95,* 421–431; Obrist, P. A., Webb, R. A., Sutterer, J. R., & Howard, J. H. (1970). Cardiac deceleration and reaction time: an evaluation of two hypotheses. *Psychophysiology, 6,* 695–706. The inconsistency in these earlier experiments is understandable: Within a subject there is substantial moment-to-moment variability in both pulse amplitude and MAP, and these factors interact with the individual's baroreceptor adaptation level to affect the degree of modulation of the baroreceptor output over the cardiac cycle and greatly augment the error variance across subjects. The PRES method yields more consistent results by stabilizing the baro stimulus both within and between subjects.

[5]In the PRES condition a pulse of negative pressure (suction) coincided with systole, and positive pressure with diastole. In the control condition positive pressure coincided with systole and negative pressure with diastole. In both conditions the initial pressure pulse commenced 100 msec after the ventricular R-wave, the diastolic pulse was immediately followed by an opposite pulse during systole; both pulses were equal in duration to one half of the mean cardiac interbeat interval less 100 ms, and following the diastolic pulse, the chamber was returned to atmospheric pressure. The same PRES or control sequence was repeated for each heart beat in a 6 s trial; then, the condition was switched. There were a total of 64 trials: 32 PRES and 32 control. In the neck chamber, the typical positive pressure was ~ + 10 Torr and the negative pressure ~ − 30 Torr (the asymmetry and variability result from practical limitations in the pneumatic seal to the neck). For details see Rau, H., Elbert, T., Geiger, B., & Lutzenberger, W. (1992). PRES: The controlled noninvasive stimulation of the carotid baroreceptors in humans. *Psychophysiology, 29*(2), 165–172.

[6]Reflexes were evoked in the right leg by means of a 5 cm long, 2 cm diameter plastic rod, that struck the Achilles tendon at a 90^0 angle. The rod was mounted on a piston, creating a T-shaped hammer. Activation was by a vibration transducer (Bruel & Kjaer), triggered by a 9 ms half wave, produced by a Bruel & Kjaer 2706 power amplifier. Fixation of both the leg and the stimulator assured that the hammer blow was repeatable. The response magnitude was measured from a pair of Ag-AgCl EMG surface electrodes placed 4 cm apart over the distal portion of the right soleus muscle. The signal was amplified by a Hellige EE preamplifier (-3dB band width 0.3-150Hz) and sampled at a rate of 1 kHz. In addition, a rectified EMG was obtained from two adjacent electrodes, amplified through a Beckman type 9852A coupler, and digitized continuously with 1,000 samples/s. This second EMG channel served to control for variations in tonic EMG.

ception experiment,[7] a small gold electrode delivered a constant current stimulus to a finger tip, and at the end of each 6-second, randomized trial, the subjects rated the perceived pain by positioning a computer cursor along an analog scale.

Both the tendon reflexes and pain estimates were attenuated when test stimuli were applied during periods of higher baroreceptor activation. Figure 2.1b summarizes the results for the 12 subjects in the tendon experiment (each bar corresponds to one of the conditions diagrammed in Fig. 2.1a). For the PRES conditions (systolic-suction–diastolic-pressure), the difference between *diastole* (the minimal carotid stretch) and *systole* (the maximal carotid stretch) is in the predicted direction, that is, the reflex was reliably weaker with enhanced baroreceptor input ($t = -5.2$, df $= 11$; $p < 0002$); whereas, for the control conditions (diastolic-suction–systolic-pressure) in which the carotid pulse was partially suppressed, the response magnitudes were similar to one another ($t = 0.22$; $p = .83$), and their absolute strength was between those of the PRES values. In addition to clear group differences, the differences in the PRES condition were reliably in the predicted direction for each of the 12 subjects, thus, the Achilles reflex inhibition by barostimulation is a very robust effect.[8]

Figure 2.1c summarizes the results from a pain perception study in a group of 19 cardiac ischemia patients at the Bad Krozingen Cardiovascular Rehabilitation Center. Similar to the tendon reflex result, the difference between the PRES conditions was reliably in the direction consistent with baroreceptor activation, reducing the painfulness of noxious stimuli ($t = -3.7$, df $= 18$; $p < 001$). Figure 2.1d gives the results of a similar pain percep-

---

[7]The stimuli were bipolar 10 ms pulses delivered by an optically isolated, constant current generator to a intracutaneously applied gold electrode on the tip of the left middle finger. To minimize cutaneous resistance, the epidermis was mildly abraded with a hand-held dental burr (diameter 1 mm). See Bromm, B., & Maier, W. (1984). The intracutaneous stimulus; a new pain model for analgesiometric studies. *Methods and Findings of Experimental and Clinical Pharmacology*, 6, 405–410. To allow time for stabilization, the stimuli were delivered 100 msec after the change in cuff pressure. Several initial practice trials assured that the subjects understood the procedure. At the beginning of the experiment each subject's pain threshold (maximum 1 mA) was determined and the stimulus intensity fixed at 120% of the threshold. The experiment itself consisted of 64 trials, each including a 1 s baseline period, a 6 s baroreceptor manipulation period, and a 1 s post-baseline period. Intertrial intervals varied pseudo-randomly between 5 s and 13 s. The pain stimuli were delivered following the second and fourth heart beat of the baroreceptor manipulation period. At the end of each trial, the subjects were prompted to perform a computerized subjective magnitude estimation of the two stimuli. The visual analog scale ranged from 0, representing no perception, to 24, representing unbearable pain. The entire procedure required approximately 1 hour.

[8]An unlikely but possible source of artifact is that at the moment of stimulus delivery conditions A and D are also differentiated by neck chamber pressure; however, for conditions B and D the pressure is the same at the moment of stimulus delivery and these conditions also reliably differ in the predicted direction (t = 3.02, p < .02).

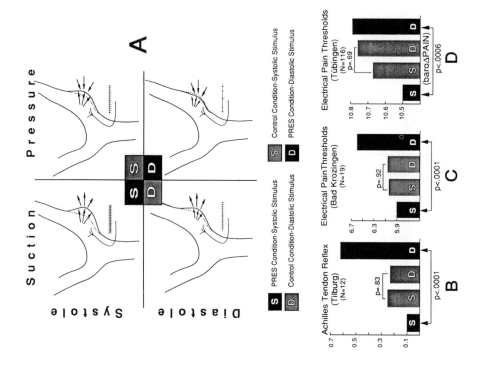

FIG. 2.1a   The PRES technique for stimulating the human carotid baroreceptors. The "extravascular" arrows represent the cardiac cycle synchronized pressure (or suction) levels in the external neck chamber. In the top left the extravascular suction adds to the systolic pressure, maximizing the carotid sinus distention and stimulation of the neural pathway, and in the bottom right the extravascular pressure subtracts from the diastolic level, minimizing the stretch; thus, the largest pulse difference in baroreceptor activity is between these conditions, wherein the internal and external pressure levels are synergistic. In the control condition (top right and bottom left) the natural CSPP is suppressed by opposing it with external pressure in systole and suction in diastole. Because the approximately rectangular waveform of the neck suction attenuates but does not completely obliterate the intraarterial waveform, the control condition is a very conservative estimate of the actual zero-pulse baseline. If sensory test stimuli are either protracted or presented randomly within the cardiac cycle averaging over excitatory and inhibitory phases will weaken the net PRES effect, thus, to use the method to its best advantage, test stimuli must be brief, distinct, and have a constant relationship to the cardiac cycle. (Fig. 2.1b) The mean tendon reflex amplitude (arbitrary electromyographic [EMG] units) of 12 normal subjects: A total of 64 stimuli in an individually pseudo randomized sequence were presented to each subject (16 in each of the 4 conditions). The EMG was scored by averaging peak-to-peak amplitudes in the interval 30 to 80 msec after the stimulus. The scores were averaged across trials and the resulting averages entered into a repeated measures ANOVA. $F(11/3) = 13.073; p < 0001; p$ (Greenhouse-Geisser) $< .0001; \Delta = .701;$ For the contrast between the PRES systolic and diastolic conditions: $F = 35.579; p < 0001; p$ (G-G) $< .0001.$ Figure 2.1c, the mean pain perception of 19 cardiac ischemia patients at Bad Krozingen: 16 stimuli of each condition were applied in pseudo randomized sequence to each subject. Stimuli consisted of biphasic electrical impulses of 10 msec duration each applied intracutaneously to the finger. After each trial, subjects rated the perceived intensity of the pain stimulus on a computer screen. Ratings were averaged across trials, separated by conditions and subjects; means were entered into repeated measures ANOVA: $F(18/3) = 8.859; p < .0001; p$ (G-G) $= .0002; \Delta = .868;$ for the contrast between the PRES conditions: $F = 22.017; p < 0001; p$ (G-G) $< .0001.$ Figure 2.1d, the mean pain perception of 115 normal subjects at Tübingen (same procedures as 2.1c): $F(115/3) = 4.844; p = .0026; p$ (G-G) $= .0031; \Delta = .945;$ for the contrast: $F = 11.951; p = .0006; p$ (G-G) $= .0008.$ (The PRES systolic–diastolic difference is the baroΔPAIN score used in the longitudinal blood pressure study described here.) In all three experiments, the difference between systolic and diastolic stimulus presentation in the control condition is far from significant (the Fs for the contrasts are .042, .009, and .25); whereas the difference in the PRES condition is highly reliable; also, all of the means of the control conditions fall between the corresponding systolic and diastolic PRES means. An alternative and more conservative (because of the limited efficiency of the control condition) analysis is a 2 x 2 ANOVA containing the factors "heart cycle" (presentation during systole vs. presentation during diastole) and "neck chamber phase condition" (PRES stimulation vs. control condition). For the interaction terms with this analysis the F ratios were 37.0, 18.5 and 4.99, with corresponding ps of .0001, .0005, and .03.

tion experiment conducted in Tübingen with a group of 115 normal volunteers[9]; it also showed that the pain rating was reliably ($t = -3.1$, df $= 115$; $p < 003$) lower in the PRES systolic compared to diastolic, stimulation condition; again, the pain ratings in the control conditions fell between those of maximal and minimal baroreceptor activation achieved in the PRES conditions. Taken together these three independent experiments, combining the PRES neck chamber method with brief stimuli differentially positioned in the cardiac cycle, showed that stimulation of the high pressure baroreceptors in humans has general CNS inhibitory effects.

CAN BLOOD PRESSURE PRODUCED BAROSTIMULATION REWARD BLOOD PRESSURE ELEVATING BEHAVIORS?

Humans can learn to elevate blood pressure, and laboratory animals have learned substantial and sustained blood pressure elevations. However, the reward in the animal experiments was avoidance or escape from moderately painful electric shocks, and escaping from shock is an unquestionably dramatic behavioral consequence. Thus, it is reasonable to ask: Is the baroreceptor CNS inhibition effect actually strong enough to reward blood pressure elevation? But first, we must ask: how strong a reinforcement effect is required to effectively modify behavior? It is important to appreciate that with trial and error learning, over sufficient time, responses with comparatively modest, but consistent, behavioral advantage can incrementally accrue considerable strength.[10] The acquisition

---

[9]Subjects were recruited by newspaper announcements and were paid 100 DM for participation in the experiment. Exclusion criteria were any kind of chronic or acute diseases including hypertension. This procedure resulted in a sample of 73 male and 47 female healthy subjects: Wt. $= 69.7 \pm 8.8$ Kg; Ht. $= 173.0 \pm 8.8$ cm; Age $= 31.4 \pm 6.0$ yrs; MBP $= 103.5 \pm 9.5$ mmHg. At the start of the experiment a complete set of data was available for 115 subjects. Informed consent was obtained and all procedures conformed to the Human Subject regulations of Tübingen University.

[10]See Talan, M. I., & Engle, B. T. (1986). Learned control of heart rate during dynamic exercise in nonhuman primates. *Journal of Applied Physiology, 61*, 545–553. However, most laboratory studies of learning intentionally employ easily learned responses and powerful reinforcers to speed the process into a more convenient time scale. Although in principle, direct laboratory demonstrations of blood pressure learning using baroreceptor stimulation as a reward are possible, given the fact that the baroreceptor reward appears to be of moderate strength, and that there is no particular evidence that blood pressure learning is especially easy; they are not likely to succeed. See Dworkin, B. R. (1991). The baroreceptor reinforcement instrumental learning (BR–IL) model of essential hypertension: Biological data, quantitative mechanisms, and computer modeling. In A. Shapiro & A. Baum (Eds.), *Perspectives in behavioral medicine: behavioral aspects of cardiovascular disease* (pp. 213–245). Hillsdale, NJ: Lawrence Erlbaum Associates.

of musical, athletic, or typing skills are good examples of gradual but substantial learning with innumerable small rewards; and, another more medically relevant example is the antalgic gait, or limp, that emerges (frequently without any clear awareness) following a foot injury (Sutherland, 1984). Given this perspective, it is evident that if for certain individuals, increasing blood pressure consistently ameliorates the discomforts of a stressful daily life (in the same sense that learning to limp ameliorates the pain of an injury), some of those individuals might learn to use blood pressure elevating behaviors to help reduce or cope with the aversiveness of events that contributed to their life-stress. Furthermore, it is at least plausible that with sufficient time, for sufficiently sensitive subjects, the learning might eventually cumulate[11] to measurable increases in basal blood pressure.

The Baroreceptor Reinforcement Hypothesis Makes Definite Predictions Other Theories Do Not,and Provides the Basis for an Unusually Strong Inference

For a particular individual, this theory (Dworkin, 1988) predicts a pure interaction between the strength of the baroreceptor CNS inhibition trait and the level of chronic aversiveness. This means that without any aversiveness, even a large baroreceptor inhibition trait should be without detectable consequence, and without an inhibition effect, aversiveness itself, should not influence blood pressure. (To manifest itself inhibition needs something to inhibit.) Quantitatively, the reward and thus, the blood pressure learning effect, are predicted to increase, roughly in proportion to the product of the two factors. This prediction was tested for the 115 subjects of the Tübingen study using the following measures: (a) the baroreceptor inhibition trait (baroΔPAIN) was defined as the difference between the pain responses to stimuli presented in the S and D phases of the PRES condition (see Fig. 2.1d), (b) individual levels of perceived aversiveness, or Stärke Belastung (STRESS), were based on the median of a series of 7 daily at home estimates[12] recorded by the subjects on a standard

---

[11]For a discussion of how baroreceptor adaptation or resetting interacts with the putative blood pressure learning mechanism, see Dworkin (1991).

[12]The term stress, or, Stärke Belastung, was chosen only as a convenient figure of speech to help the subjects identify and estimate the degree of aversiveness that they perceived to characterize their daily lives.

scale of 0 to 10, and (c) for the initial MAP subjects measured and recorded their own blood pressure[13] with an automated monitoring device. This was done each day immediately following the recording of the STRESS estimate. The laboratory sessions were run between February, 1990 and February, 1991. For each subject procedures 2 and 3 were completed in the week immediately following the laboratory barostimulation session. Approximately 18 months later, 107 of the 115 subjects were successfully contacted and of those, 100 agreed to repeat the seven daily blood pressure readings with the same instrument. The difference between the median of these and the median of the initial readings measured the individual's change in blood pressure (ΔMAP) during the ensuing 1 9.7 $\pm$ 3.8 months. The data used in the analyses consists of the 96 completed sets of measurements, and is composed of a laboratory baroreceptor pain inhibition measurement (baroΔPAIN), a median aversiveness estimate (STRESS), and the change[14] in median MAP (ΔMAP). None of the 96 subjects were excluded from any of the analyses.

---

[13]Ambulatory blood pressure recording has revealed the large situational variability of human blood pressure, and has shown that psychosocial factors are an important source of that variability: measures taken in arousing circumstances such as a medical office or laboratory are known to be poorly correlated with resting blood pressure. See Pickering, T. G. (1991). *Ambulatory monitoring and blood pressure variability*. London: Science Press. Obrist, P. A., Light, K. C., James, S. A., & Strogatz, D. S. (1987). Cardiovascular responses to stress: I. Measures of myocardial response and relationship to high resting systolic pressure and parental hypertension. *Psychophysiology*, 24, 65–78, Obrist and colleagues demonstrated a particularly large overestimation of blood pressure during and after laboratory procedures as compared to measurements taken on neutral days. Any laboratory blood pressure measurement is thus confounded with a stress response to the situation; although, such a provoked measurement might be useful for diagnoses of hypertension, it would clearly have been undesirable for the present experiment wherein we sought to independently estimate these variables. Teaching the subjects to use the automated blood pressure recorders and instructing them to use them at home at a quiet time each day provided more appropriate estimates of resting pressure. The use of MAP rather than separate diastolic or systolic pressures simplified the presentation and slightly improved the stability of the blood pressure data (it is effectively a weighted average of the two measures); however, had we instead used either systolic or diastolic separately, the statistical results and conclusions would have been essentially unchanged.

[14]An alternate procedure, which eliminates any contribution to the covariance by the initial score, uses the difference between the observed and regression predicted final MAP, rather than between the initial and final raw ΔMAP. See Cronbach, L. F., & Furby, L. (1970). How we should measure "change"—or should we? *Psychological Bulletin*, 74, 68–80; however, its applicability depends on homogeneity of the regression across the relevant variables, and because of the interaction (see text) these data did not satisfy that requirement for the STRESS variable; notwithstanding, the results and conclusions throughout are essentially the same using either method, and Fig. 2.3 gives several key correlations using both "baseline-free" regression generated and raw difference score estimates of ΔMAP.

BLOOD PRESSURE RISE DEPENDS
ON AN INTERACTION OF BARORECEPTOR
PAIN INHIBITION AND STRESS

For the 96 subjects, there was a reliable positive linear relationship ($r =$ 0.29, $F = 8.8$; $p < .004$) between the pain inhibition score (baroΔPAIN) and the change in blood pressure (ΔMAP). Although baroΔPAIN accounted for only 7.5% of the ΔMAP variance (adjusted for the degrees of freedom of the model, Neter; Wasserman, & Kutner, 1985; [chap. 7]), given the inherent "noisiness" of the ΔMAP and baroΔPAIN measures and the multitude of other factors that could have influenced an individual's blood pressure during 20 months,[15] the correlation clearly showed that a substantial component of the pain inhibition measure impacted in some way on long-term blood pressure regulation. But, how? One possibility is that baroΔPAIN and ΔMAP were independently affected by individual baroreflex sensitivity parameters, which were unrelated to CNS inhibition. This, however, is not very likely, although the baroreceptors are most prominently the receptive field of blood pressure stabilizing reflexes, because of resetting, the buffer reflexes, themselves, are not thought to directly participate in long-term blood pressure regulation. Going beyond speculation about other possible artifacts of this kind, it is clear that if the long-term blood pressure rise in the barosensitive subjects was learned, and if baroreceptor CNS inhibition mediated the reward, then for a given individual, the strength of reward would have to have strongly depended on an interaction between the strength of the inhibition (baroΔPAIN), and the individual's perceived level of aversiveness or STRESS. This in fact is the case.

The graph in Fig. 2.2 is a plot of a least squares regression surface fit to the baroΔPAIN, STRESS and ΔMAP data. Following conventional statistical practice, both the linear terms and the interaction were included in the initial model. The resulting surface accounted for 7% of the model adjusted ΔMAP variance ($r = 0.31$, $F = 3.4$; $p < .02$), which was only slightly greater than barosensitivity alone, however, inspection of Fig. 2.2, shows, more importantly, the actual irrelevance of the linear terms to the analysis. For example, for those subjects reporting zero STRESS, pain inhibition apparently had no influence on ΔMAP, and conversely for subjects with zero baroΔPAIN there was hardly any STRESS effect on ΔMAP. This implied

---

[15]For example, the correlation between the initial and final MAP is only .76; using this to conservatively estimate the ΔMAP reliability and correct for attenuation in the usual manner, the values of accounted for variance would be ~ 30% to 45% larger than those we have presented.

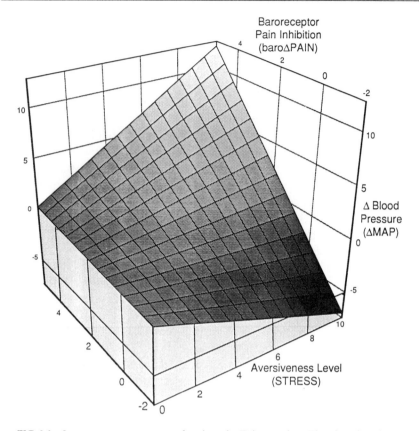

FIG. 2.2   Least squares regression surface fit to the Tübingen data. This plot is based on a
regression model that included the linear terms (baroΔPAIN and STRESS); however, inclusion of these terms did not augment the ΔMAP variance accounted for by the interaction (baroΔPAIN x STRESS) alone. This result, based on data from normotensive
volunteers, is consistent with the hypothesis that blood pressure activated, baroreceptor
mediated, CNS inhibition can reduce the aversiveness of noxious (stressful) stimuli sufficiently to reward and eventually strengthen blood pressure elevating behaviors (see text).

that the linear terms contributed only error variance and that a simpler regression model was more appropriate. In fact, a regression equation containing only the interaction (STRESS x baroΔPAIN) and an intercept term
conformed exactly to the predictions of the baroreceptor reward theory, and
this model accounted for 8.6% of the model adjusted ΔMAP variance ($r =
0.31, F = 9.9; p < .002$). (The plot of the least squares-regression surface for
the pure interaction is nearly identical to Fig. 2.2.)

   Some of the key features of Fig. 2.2 are possibly more easily appreciated by
comparing the baroΔPAIN–ΔMAP correlations in selected subgroups of

subjects who reported different STRESS levels. Arbitrarily splitting the STRESS scale at its center,[16] classified 62 subjects as low stress and 34 as high stress. For the low stress ($<$ 5.5) subjects, only 1% of the variance in MAP was accounted for by baroΔPAIN (r = .11, F = .72; p = .40); whereas, for the 34 subjects whose stress estimate was above mid-scale, 29% of the MAP variance was accounted for by baroΔPAIN (r = .5 6, F = 14.2; $p <$ .001). The surface in Fig. 2.2 is especially steep for the highest stress levels, and this coincided well with the actual correlations. For the 17 subjects with STRESS $>$ 7, approximately 35% of the adjusted ΔMAP variance (r = .63, F = 9.7; $p <$ .01) was accounted for by the baroΔPAIN score, and for the 8 highest stress subjects (approximately the upper decile), who reported median daily STRESS levels of 9 or 10, the laboratory baroΔPAIN accounted for more than 80% of the adjusted ΔMAP variance (r = .93, F = 15.2; $p <$ .01). Figure 2.3 gives additional subgroup correlations, rank order

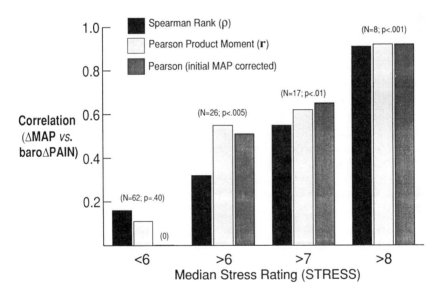

FIG. 2.3   The baroΔPAIN–ΔMAP correlations in subgroups of subjects reporting different median STRESS levels. The similarity between the Pearson Product Moment and Spearman Rank correlations indicates that the effects are not likely; due to a few extreme cases, and comparing the raw and regression corrected difference scores shows that, although initial MAP probably contributed to the weak correlation in the low STRESS subjects, it was not involved in the much larger correlations in high STRESS subjects. Above each group of columns is the reliability for the raw score Pearson r.

[16]Midscale is 5.5. (The rating was on a 0–10 integer scale and scores were approximately normally distributed; thus, an exact median split into two equal groups was not possible.)

statistics, and correlations with the initial baseline ΔMAP controlled by regression.

In conclusion, CNS inhibitory effects of baroreceptor activation have been reported since 1932.[17] More recently, the experimental methods have been refined to eliminate confounding artifacts and confirm that the inhibition is an authentic product of baroreceptor stimulation (Dworkin, 1994; Ghione, 1996). It can now be said that baroreceptor CNS inhibition is a robust physiological mechanism that rests on a broad empirical foundation and that it probably has a unique regulatory function: When acute sensory or emotional excitation raises blood pressure excessively, CNS dampening can augment vagal and sympathoinhibitory negative feedback mechanisms to help restore safer levels.

The additional hypothesis, that baroreceptor CNS inhibition of pain and/or anxiety might reward antecedent blood pressure elevating behaviors, and thus contribute to hypertension, was first proposed in 1977 (Miller & Dworkin, 1977), and animal experiments showing behavioral consequences of baroreceptor activation were reported in 1979 (Dworkin et al., 1979) The longitudinal observations (Elbert et al., 1994) were intended to further evaluate the putative mechanism of that hypothesis in normotensive human volunteers: It found a correlation between baroreceptor pain inhibition and long-term blood pressure changes, which increased in proportion to the amount of perceived life stress. This specific interaction provides additional evidence of the existence of a novel behavioral mechanism by which chronic exigencies from the environment, through the learning of blood pressure elevating behaviors, could gradually raise a sensitive individual's basal blood pressure, and contribute to the development of essential hypertension.

ACKNOWLEDGMENTS

This research was supported by Deutsch Forschungsgerneinshaft Grant EL 10 1/3 to Thomas Elbert, and National Institutes of Health grant R01 HL40837 to B. R. Dworkin.

This summary article combines and interrelates text and figures from two recent publications by the same senior authors. The first article: Dworkin, B. R., Elbert, T., Rau, H., Birbaumer, N., Pauli, P., Droste, C., & Brunia, C. H. M. (1994). Central effects of baroreceptor activation in humans: Attenua-

---

[17]In fact, the root verb of the Greek word *karotides* (karotides) is *karo*, to fall into a deep, heavy sleep. See chapter 2 in the comprehensive monograph by Eckberg, D. L., & Sleight, P. (1992). *Human Baroreflexes in health and disease*. Oxford: Clarendon.

tion of skeletal reflexes and pain perception. *Proceedings of the National Academy of Sciences USA, 91,* 6329–6333, described the experimental procedures, and the second, Elbert, T., Dworkin, B. R., Rau, H., Birbaumer, N., Pauli, P., Droste, C., & Brunia, C. H. M. (1994). Sensory effects of baroreceptor activation and perceived stress predicts long-term blood pressure elevations. *International Journal of Behavioral Medicine, 3,* 215–228, described the longitudinal blood pressure observations.

REFERENCES

Benson, H., Herd, J. A., Morse, W. H., & Kelleher, R. T. (1969). Behavioral induction of arterial hypertension and its reversal. *American Journal of Physiology, 217,* 30–34.

Bonvallet, M., Dell, P., & Hiebel, G. (1954). Tonus sympathique et activite electrique corticale. *Electroencephalography and Clinical Neurophysiblogy, 6,* 119–144.

Dworkin, B. R. (1991), The baroreceptor reinforcement instrumental learning (BR-IL) Model of essential hypertension: Biological data, quantitive mechanisms and computer modeling. In A. Baum & A. Shapiro (Eds.), *Perspectives in behavioral medicine: Behavioral aspects of cardiovascular disease,* pp. 213–245. Hillsdale, NJ: Lawrence Erlbaum Associates.

Dworkin, B. (1988). Hypertension as a learned response. The baroreceptor reinforcement hypothesis. In T. Elbert, W. Langosch, A. Steptoe, & D. Vaitl (Eds.), *Behavioral medicine in cardiovascular disorders* (pp. 17–47). Chichester: Wiley.

Dworkin, B. R., Filewich, R. J., Miller, N. E., Craigmyle, N., & Pickering, T. G. (1979). Baroreceptor activation reduces reactivity to noxious stimulation: Implications for hypertension. *Science 205,* 1299–1301.

Dworkin, B. R., Elbert, T., Rau, H., Birbaumer, N., Pauli, P., Droste, C., & Brunia, C. H. M. (1994). Central effect of baroreceptor activation in humans: Attenuation of skeletal reflexees and pain perception. *Proceedings of the National Academy of Sciences USA, 91,* 6329–6333.

Eckberg, D. L. (1976). Temporal response patterns of the human sinus node to brief carotid baroreceptor stimuli. *Journal of Physiology, 258,* 769–782.

Elbert, T., Dworkin, B. R., Rau, H., Birbaumer, N., Pauli, P., Droste, C., & Brunia, C. H. M. (1994). Sensory effects of baroreceptor activation and perceived stress predicts long-term blood pressure elevations. *International Journal of Behavioral Medicine, 3,* 215–228.

Elbert, T., Rockstroh, B., Canavan, A. G. M., Birbaumer, N., Bülow, V. L., & Linden, A. (1991). Self-regulation of slow cortical potentials and its role in epoileptogenesis. In G. Carslon & R. Seifert (Eds.), *International Perspectives on Self-Regulation and Health* (pp. 65–94). New York: Plenum.

Elbert, T., Tafil-Klawe, M., Rau, H., & Lutzenberger, W. (1991). Cerebral and cardiac responses to unilateral stimulation of carotid sinus baroreceptors. *Journal of Psychophysiology, 5,* 327–335.

Furedy, J., Rau, H., & Roberts, L. (1992). Physiological and psychological differentiation of bidirectional baroreceptor carotid manipulation in humans. *Physiology and Behavior, 52,* 953–958.

Ghione, S. (1996). Hypertension-associated hypalgesia: Evidence in expermental animals and humans, pathopysciological mechanisms, and potential clinical consequences. *Hypertension, 28,* 494–504.

68 DWORKIN, ELBERT, RAU

Harris, A. H., Gilliam, W. J., Findley, J. D., & Brady, J. V. (1973). Instrumental conditioning of large-magnitude, daily, 1 2-hour blood pressure elevations in the baboon. *Science, 182,* 175–177.

Harshfield, G. A., Pickering, T. G., James, G. D., & Blank, S. G. (1990). Blood pressure variability and reactivity in the natural environment. In W. Meyer-Sabellek, M. Anlauf, R. Cotzen, & L. Steinfeld (Eds.), *Blood Pressure Measurements* (pp. 211–216). Darmstadt, Germany: Steinkopff.

Harshfield, G. A., Pickering, T. G., Kleinert, H. D., Blank, S., & Laragh, J. H. (1982). Situation variation of blood pressure in ambulatory hypertensive patients. *Psychosomatic Medicine, 44,* 237–245.

James, G. D., Yee, Y. S., Harshfield, G. A., Blank, S. G., & Pickering, T. G. (1986). The influence of happiness, anger, and anxiety on the blood pressure of borderline hypertensives. *Psychosomatic Medicine, 48,* 502–508.

Jonsson, A., & Hansson, L. (1977). Prolonged exposure to a stressful stimulus (noise) as a cause of raised blood pressure in man. *The Lancet, 1977-i,* 86–87.

Koch, E. B. (1932). Die Irradiation der pressorezeptorischen Kreislaufreflexe. *Kfinische Wochenschrift, 2,* 225–227.

Miller, N. E., & Dworkin, B. R. (1977). Critical issues in therapeutic applications of biofeedback. In G. E. Schwartz & J. Beatty (Eds.), *Biofeedback-theory and research* (pp. 129–161). New York: Academic Press.

Neter, J., Wasserman, W., & Kutner, M. H. (1985). *Applied Linear Statistical Models* (2nd ed.). Homewood, IL: Irwin.

Peterson, E. A., Augenstein, J. S., Tanis, D. C., & Augenstein, D. G. (1981 Noise raises blood pressure without impairing auditory sensitivity. *Science, 217,* 1450–1452.

Pickering, T. G., Brucker, B., Frankel, H. L., Mathias, C. J., Dworkin, B. R., & Miller, N. E. (1977). Mechanisms of learned voluntary control of blood pressure in patients with generalized bodily paralysis. In J. Beatty & H. Legewie (Eds.), *Biofeedback and Behavior* (pp. 225–234). New York: Plenum.

Pickering, T. G., & Gerin, W. (1990). Cardiovascular reactivity in the laboratory and the role of behavioral factors in hypertension: A critical review. *Annals of Behavioral Medicine, 12,* 3–16.

Pickering, T. G., Harshfield, G. A., Kleinert, H. D., Blank, S., & Laragh, J. H. (1982). Blood pressure during normal daily activities, sleep, and exercise. Comparison of values in normal and hypertensive subjects. *Journal of the American Medical Association, 247,* 992–996.

Plumlee, L. (1969). Operant conditioning of increases in blood pressure. *Psychophysiology, 6,* 283–290.

Randich, A., & Maixner, W. (1984). Interactions between cardiovascular and pain regulatory systems. *Neuroscience & Biobehavioral Reviews, 8*(3), 343–367.

Rau, H., Brody, S., Droste, C., & Kardos, A. (1993). Blood pressure changes validate PRES, a controlled human baroreceptor stimulation method. *European Journal of Applied Physiology, 67,* 26–29.

Rau, H., Elbert, T., Geiger, B., & Lutzenberger, W. (1992). PRES: The controlled noninvasive stimulation of the carotid baroreceptors in humans. *Psychophysiology, 29*(2), 165–172.

Schlager, E., & Meier, T. (1947). A strange Balinese method of inducing sleep. *Acta Tropica, 4,* 127–134.

Sutherland, D. H. (1984). *Gait disorders in childhood and adolescence.* Baltimore: Williams & Wilkins.

Vaitl, D., & Gruppe, H. (1990). Changes in hemodynamics modulate electrical brain activity. *Journal of Psychophysiology, 4,* 41–49.

Vaitl, D., & Gruppe, H. (1991). *Baroreceptor stimulation and changes in EEG and vigilance.* In P. B. Persson & H. R. Kirchheim (Eds.), *Baroreceptor Reflexes* (pp. 293–313). Berlin: Springer-Verlag.

Weiss, S., & Baker, J. P. (1933). The carotid sinus reflex in health and disease: its role in the causation of fainting and convulsions. *Medicine, 12,* 297–354.

3

Social Stress, Gender, and Coronary Heart Disease Risk in Monkeys

Carol A. Shively
Michael R. Adams
Jay R. Kaplan
J. Koudy Williams
Wake Forest University School of Medicine

A NONHUMAN PRIMATE MODEL OF CORONARY ARTERY ATHEROSCLEROSIS AND CORONARY HEART DISEASE RISK

Epidemiological and clinical studies of the factors that influence Coronary Heart Disease (CHD) risk invariably raise questions that cannot be answered in studies of human beings because such studies are either unethical, infeasible, or unaffordable. In such cases, experiments using appropriate animal models have traditionally been used to supplement scientific knowledge. Atherosclerosis (an accumulation of fatty, connective, and necrotic tissue) of the coronary arteries is the principal pathological process that causes CHD. Cynomolgus monkeys (*Macaca fascicularis*) are currently the only animal models of gender differences in susceptibility to diet-induced atherogenesis. Among Whites in western society, men have about twice the incidences of CHD and the coronary artery atherosclerosis is twice as extensive as in women (Tejada, Strong, Montenegro, Restropo, & Solberg, 1968; Vanecek 1976; Wingard, Suarez, & Barrett-Connor, 1983). The male to female ratio of coronary artery atherosclerosis extent in cynomolgus monkeys is also a ratio of about 2:1. Like women, female cynomolgus monkeys are protected against atherosclerosis relative to their male counterparts (Hamm, Kaplan, Clarkson, & Bullock, 1983).

Female cynomolgus monkeys have menstrual cycles that are similar to those of women in terms of length and cyclic hormone fluctuations (Jewett & Dukelow, 1972; Mahoney, 1970). Following bilateral ovariectomy, extensive coronary artery atherosclerosis develops in females in amounts that are indistinguishable from those of males (Adams, Kaplan, Clarkson, & Koritnik, 1985). CHD risk is also increased in oophorectomized and postmenopausal women (Kannel, Hjortland, McNamara, & Gordon, 1976). Subcutaneous replacement of estradiol, or estradiol and progesterone in physiological doses, protects against atherosclerosis in female monkeys (Adams et al., 1990), and hormone replacement therapy (HRT) is associated with decreased CHD risk in postmenopausal women (Bush et al., 1987). Thus, ovarian function, and estradiol in particular, is implicated in the phenomenon of female protection, both in women and female cynomolgus macaques.

There are gender differences in plasma lipid profiles in cynomolgus monkeys (Shively, Sherwin, Walsh, Wilson, & Knox, 1993). Like human beings, male cynomolgus monkeys have a more atherogenic lipid profile than their female counterparts, that is, lower High Density Lipoprotein (HDL) cholesterol concentrations and a higher ratio of total to HDL (total/HDL), cholesterol. Also like human beings, the atherogenic lipid profile of male cynomolgus monkeys is believed to be one reason for more extensive coronary artery atherosclerosis in males than females. The protective lipid profile of females is due, at least in part, to the influence of ovarian hormones. Ovariectomy is associated with an increase in the total plasma cholesterol and a modest decline in HDL cholesterol concentrations. These changes result in a total/HDL cholesterol ratio that is significantly higher in ovariectomized versus intact monkeys (Adams et al., 1985).

Endogenous sex-steroid concentrations appear to, also, affect cholesterol concentrations in women, although the available data have not been consistent. Among premenopausal women, increases in very low density lipoprotein cholesterol and total triglyceride concentrations have been observed during the ovulatory phase, and decreases in low density lipoprotein (LDL) cholesterol concentrations have been observed during the luteal phase (Ahumada-Hemer et al., 1985; Kim & Kalkhoff, 1979). No change (Woods et al., 1987), as well as increases in HDL cholesterol concentrations have been observed during the ovulatory phase (Azogui et al., 1992; Barclay, Barclay, Skipski, & Meuller, 1965). No information has been available concerning the relationship between plasma cholesterol concentrations and irregular or anovulatory menstrual cycles or periods of amenorrhea. After menopause, women typically have small decreases in HDL cholesterol, small increases in LDL cholesterol levels, and a tendency to produce smaller, denser LDL cholesterol particles (Campos, McNamara,

Wilson, Ordovas, & Schaefer, 1988; Matthews et al., 1989), all of which suggest that ovarian function influences cholesterol metabolism (Shively et al., 1993) concentrations. These changes result in a total/HDL cholesterol ratio that is significantly higher in ovariectomized versus intact monkeys (Adams et al., 1985).

PSYCHOSOCIAL FACTORS THAT INFLUENCE CORONARY ARTERY ATHEROSCLEROSIS AND CHD RISK IN FEMALE MONKEYS

Cynomolgus monkeys typically live in large social groups that are characterized by complex social relationships. A major social organizing mechanism of monkey society is the social status hierarchy (Shively, 1985). Monkeys with low social status, or subordinates, are behaviorally and physiologically different than dominants. Among females, subordinates receive more aggression and spend more time alone, socially isolated from their dominant counterparts (Shively, Clarkson, & Kaplan, 1989; Shively, Manuck, Kaplan, & Koritnik, 1990). Primates typically communicate nonverbally, by touch, facial expressions, and body language or postures. Although human primates can also communicate with language, they still rely heavily on nonverbal communication. When a female monkey spends time alone, it means that the monkey is not in physical contact or in touching distance of another monkey. Rather, the monkey is socially isolated. This is intriguing, given the observations of human beings that suggest that social support is associated with reduced CHD risk and observations of deleterious effects of social isolation on coronary artery atherosclerosis in monkeys, which is discussed in the following in more detail (Shively et al., 1989; Shumaker & Hill, 1991).

Physiological characteristics of subordinates that distinguish them from dominants include exaggerated adrenocortical function. Following dexamethasone suppression, the adrenal glands of subordinate females hypersecrete cortisol in response to an adrenocorticotropic hormone challenge (Kaplan, Adams, Koritnik, Rose, & Manuck, 1986). Because the hypersecretion of cortisol may be indicative of a stressed individual, this finding implies that, in general, subordinate females are stressed.

Subordinate females also have more abnormal menstrual cycles than dominant females (Adams et al., 1985). Progesterone concentrations are lower during the luteal phase, and estradiol concentrations are lower in the follicular phase of subordinate females. Moderately low luteal-phase progesterone concentrations indicate that, although ovulation may have occurred, the luteal phase was hormonally deficient. Very low luteal-phase

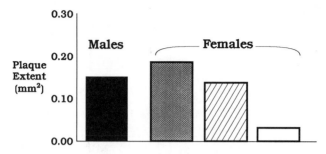

FIG. 3.1 Coronary artery atherosclerosis (measured as plaque extent) in males and in females in different reproductive conditions. Among females: *Shaded bar* = *ovariectomized* females; *striped bar* = *intact* socially subordinate females with poor ovarian function; *white bar* = *intact* socially dominant females with good ovarian function. (Adapted from Adams et al., 1985; Hamm et al., 1983.)

progesterone concentrations indicate an anovulatory cycle (Wilks, Hodgen, & Ross, 1976, 1979). Thus, stressed, subordinate females have poor ovarian function in comparison to dominants.

Subordinate females with impaired ovarian function also have lower HDL cholesterol concentrations and higher total/HDL ratios than dominant females with good ovarian function (Adams et al., 1985). In fact, the lipid profile of subordinate females with impaired ovarian function is indistinguishable from that of ovariectomized females. Notably, subordinate females with poor ovarian function have more coronary artery atherosclerosis than their dominant counterparts (Fig. 3.1). Indeed, the coronary artery atherosclerosis extent in these subordinate, stressed females is comparable to that found in both ovariectomized females and males (Adams et al., 1985; Kaplan, Adams, Clarkson, & Koritnik, 1984;).

The effects of stress on ovarian function in women are difficult to evaluate because of the difficulties in characterizing the quality of a menstrual cycle over long periods of time. However, the results of several studies are consistent with the hypothesis that stress can have a deleterious effect on ovarian function in women (Barnea & Tal, 1991; Gindoff, 1989; Matteo, 1987). Furthermore, mechanistic pathways relating stress to impaired reproductive function in female primates and other mammals have been identified, suggesting that the stress–ovarian function-impairment hypothesis is plausible from a physiological perspective (Abbott, O'Byrne, Sheffield, 1989; Abbott, Saltman, Schultz-Darken, 1992; Biller, Federoff, Koenig, & Klibanski, 1990; Ferin, 1989; Gindoff, & Ferin 1989; Hayashi, & Moberg, 1990). Intriguingly, women with hypothalamic amenorrhea also have increased hypothalamic-pituitary-adrenal activity similar to that observed in subordinate female cynomolgus moneys (Nappi et al., 1993). The relationship between poor ovarian function during the premenopausal years and CHD risk is also difficult to ascertain due to two challenges (i.e., characterizing ovarian function and detecting an adequate number of clinical CHD events in women). However, there is one report that women with a history of irregular menstrual cycles are at increased risk for CHD (La Vecchia et al., 1987).

Ovarian hormones, particularly estradiol, are also associated with the function of the coronary arteries. In response to neuroendocrine signals, coronary arteries either dilate or constrict to modulate the flow of blood to the heart. Inappropriate coronary artery constriction, or vasospasm, early in life may change flow dynamics, injuring the epithelium and exacerbating atherosclerosis. Coronary vasospasm later in life, in the presence of exacerbated atherosclerosis, may increase the risk of myocardial infarction. The coronary arteries of normal cycling females dilate in response to acetylcholine infused directly into the coronary artery, whereas those of ovariectomized females constrict in response to acetylcholine. The dilation response can be restored in ovariectomized females by administering estradiol, that is, estrogen replacement therapy (Williams, Adams, Herrington, & Clarkson, 1992; Williams, Adams, & Klopfenstein, 1990) Furthermore, data from our laboratory suggest that the coronary arteries of dominant females dilate in response to an infusion of acetylcholine, whereas those of subordinate females constrict in response to acetylcholine (Fig. 3.2; Williams, Shively, & Clarkson, 1994). These data suggest that some chest pain in women may be due to coronary vasospasm caused by estrogen deficiency. Thus, female primates with poor ovarian function may be at increased CHD risk for two reasons: impaired coronary artery function and increased atherogenesis.

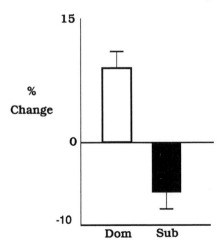

FIG. 3.2 Coronary artery responsivity to intracoronary infusion of acetylcholine (measured as percent change from artery diameter at baseline infusion of saline) in socially dominant (dom) or subordinate (sub) female cynomolgus monkeys with diet-induced atherosclerosis. (Adapted from Williams et al., 1994.)

Ovarian function declines at menopause, particularly the production of estradiol and progesterone. Importantly, clinically detectable events occur most frequently during and after the menopausal decline in ovarian function. Thus, the impact of premenopausal ovarian function on CHD risk may be temporally separate from the clinical manifestation of CHD. However, atherogenesis is a dynamic process that occurs over a lifetime. We hypothesize that atherogenesis, during young and middle adulthood, may be accelerated among socially stressed women. These women enter the menopausal years with exacerbated atherosclerosis. During the estrogen-deficient menopausal years, the combined effect of a more atherogenic lipid profile, exacerbated atherosclerosis, and increased likelihood of coronary vasospasm result in increased CHD among women who experienced excessive premenopausal social stress.

GENDER DIFFERENCES IN PSYCHOSOCIAL STRESS EFFECTS ON ATHEROGENESIS IN MONKEYS

The fact that psychosocial stress acts, at least in part, through ovarian function to exacerbate coronary artery atherosclerosis suggests the possibility of gender differences in psychosocial stress effects on atherogenesis. Comparison of the results of two experiments comprised of 30 male monkeys and 23 female monkeys supports this hypothesis (Kaplan et al., 1984; Kaplan, Manuck, Clarkson, Lusso, & Taub, 1982). Adult monkeys were housed in stable social groups of four to six animals for approximately 2 years, during which they formed social status hierarchies. Adult monkeys were also housed in unstable social groups of four to six animals, in which the constituency of each social group was changed at regular intervals for approximately two years. Thus, at each social reorganization, the animals were challenged by the presence of nongroup members, a potent social stressor for this species. These animals had to form new social status hierarchies each time the members of the group changed, which resulted in extensive social disruption. In the socially unstable groups of males, an estrogen-treated female was also added in order to exacerbate social competition and disruption. A male was present in each of the social groups of females.

Gender differences in the effects of this manipulation are shown in Fig. 3.3. Among males, coronary artery atherosclerosis was significantly greater in those living in the unstable social situation, but only if they were socially dominant (Kaplan et al., 1982). The effects of social status and social instability were different in female monkeys. Social instability did not appear to affect atherogenesis in females. However, social status affected atherogenesis in the opposite direction of that seen in males. Among females, it was the subordinates, irrespective of social stability, that had wors-

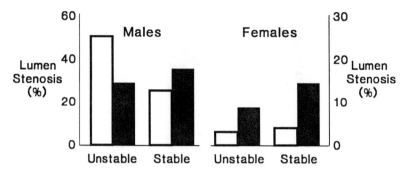

FIG. 3.3 Gender differences in psychosocial effects on coronary artery atherosclerosis. Coronary artery atherosclerosis extent, expressed as percent lumen stenosis that is occupied by plaque. Monkeys were housed in either socially stable or unstable groups, and they were either socially dominant *(white bars)* or subordinate *(black bars)*. (Adapted from Kaplan et al., 1982, 1984.)

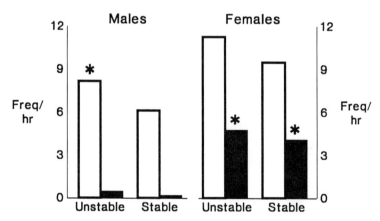

FIG. 3.4 The frequency per hour (freq/hr) of aggressive acts in male and female monkeys housed in socially stable and unstable groups. Monkeys were considered either socially dominant *(white bars)* or subordinate *(black bars)*. Bars that are starred represent treatment groups that had increased coronary artery atherosclerosis (see Fig.3.3). (Adapted from Kaplan et al., 1982, 1984.)

ened coronary artery atherosclerosis (Kaplan et al., 1984). This gender difference in the social status and coronary artery atherosclerosis has since been replicated. Thus, among nonhuman primates, there appear to be gender differences in the effects of psychosocial stressors on coronary artery atherosclerosis.

Because hostility may be associated with greater risk for CHD, the frequency of hostile or aggressive behavior in these monkeys was assessed (Fig. 3.4).

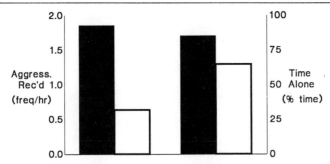

FIG. 3.5   Behavioral characteristics of socially dominant *(white bars)* and subordinate *(black bars)* female monkeys. The freq/hr of aggression received is plotted on the left vertical axis and the percentage of time (% time) spent alone is plotted on the right vertical axis. (Adapted from Shively et al., 1986, 1990.)

Among males, individuals with exacerbated coronary artery atherosclerosis were also aggressive and socially dominant. However, among females, the less aggressive individuals, the subordinates, had the most coronary artery atherosclerosis. Thus, there appear to be gender differences in the behavior of individuals associated with exacerbated coronary artery atherosclerosis (Kaplan et al., 1982, 1984).

The distinguishing behavioral characteristics of females that develop the most coronary artery atherosclerosis are depicted in Fig.3.5. Subordinate females are the recipients of about three times as much hostility or aggression than their dominant counterparts. Furthermore, subordinates spend significantly more time alone than dominant females (Shively, Kaplan, & Adams, 1986; Shively et al., 1990).

SOCIAL ISOLATION: A PSYCHOSOCIAL RISK FACTOR FOR ATHEROSCLEROSIS IN FEMALE MONKEYS

We hypothesized that social isolation was associated with exacerbated coronary artery atherosclerosis in female monkeys. To test this hypothesis, the outcomes of two experiments were compared, in which females consumed the same atherogenic diet for approximately 2 years. In one experiment, they were housed in social groups with other females, and in the other, they were housed individually in single cages. Socially housed females formed social status hierarchies. Single caged females could see, hear, and smell other monkeys, but they could not touch them. Females that were socially isolated in single cages had four times as much coronary artery atherosclerosis as socially housed females (Shively, Clarkson, & Kaplan, 1989).

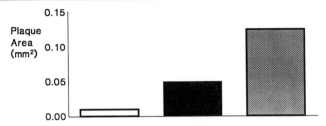

FIG. 3.6   Coronary artery atherosclerosis extent expressed as plaque area (mm²) of socially housed dominant *(white bar)*, subordinate *(black bar)* female monkeys, and female
monkeys housed alone in single cages *(shaded bar)*. (Adapted from Shively et al., 1989.)

Because subordinate females spend more time alone than dominants, we
compared atherosclerosis extent among socially dominant, socially subordinate, and single-caged monkeys. Dominants had the least coronary artery
atherosclerosis, single-caged females had the most, and socially housed subordinate females fell in between two groups (Fig. 3.6). Thus, the most socially isolated females had the most coronary artery atherosclerosis, the least
socially isolated females had the least atherosclerosis, and those that spent
intermediate amounts of time alone, the socially housed subordinates, had
intermediate amounts of coronary artery atherosclerosis. These data suggest
that social isolation may be a behavioral risk factor for coronary artery atherosclerosis in female primates (Shively et al., 1989).

SOCIAL STATUS INCONGRUITY: A PSYCHOSOCIAL RISK FACTOR FOR ATHEROSCLEROSIS IN FEMALE MONKEYS

An interesting aspect of the nature of social status in cynomolgus monkeys
is that females that are dominant in one social group are likely to be dominant in multiple, subsequent social groups. Likewise, females that are socially subordinate in one group are likely to be subordinate in multiple
subsequent social groups. This observation suggests that social status is a reliable characteristic of the individual (Shively & Kaplan, 1991).

It has been appreciated for some years that health quality of life depends,
to a large extent, on individual-environment congruity or fit (Levi, 1981,
1984). Levi suggested that the fit between the individual and the environment included the satisfaction of needs and congruency between abilities
and demands, as well as between expectations and the perception of reality
and proposed that the quality of life was dependent on it (Levi, 1981, 1984).
Other researchers have invoked similar concepts in assessing gender (Davis,
& Matthews, 1996; Matthews, Davis, Stoney, Owens, & Caggiula, 1991)

and cultural (Marmot, 1989; Matsumato, 1970) differences in stress-health relationships. The purpose of the next experiment was to study the effects of the modification of a psychosocial risk factor, social status, on coronary artery atherosclerosis. Because changing the social status of an individual appears to be equivalent to altering a characteristic of the individual, the individual–environment fit may be affected. Forty-eight adult female monkeys were fed an atherogenic diet, housed in small social groups, and social status was altered in half of the animals (subordinates became dominant, and dominants became subordinate). Thus, half of the animals occupied incongruous social positions throughout the majority of the experiment (Fig. 3.7). The manipulation of social status significantly affected coronary artery atherosclerosis, while having minimal effects on risk factors, providing further support for the hypothesis that social status has direct effects on atherogenesis in these females. Additionally, the psychosocial effects on coronary artery atherosclerosis were independent of ovarian function. All animals that occupied incongruous social positions had worsened coronary artery atherosclerosis. The modification of this psychosocial risk factor may

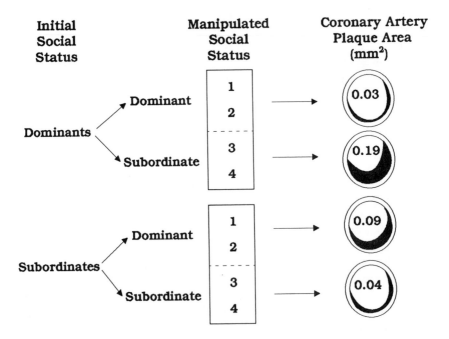

FIG. 3.7   The effects of changing social status on diet-induced coronary artery atherosclerosis extent in female monkeys. Shown are mean values of coronary artery plaque area adjusted for preexperimental predictors of atherosclerosis extent. (Adapted from Shively & Clarkson, 1994.)

have resulted in individual–environment incongruity and exacerbated coronary artery atherosclerosis (Shively & Clarkson, 1994).

SUMMARY AND CONCLUSIONS

In summary, there appear to be gender differences in behavioral risk factors for coronary artery atherosclerosis. Among males, those with the most coronary artery atherosclerosis are dominant animals in unstable social groupings that are constantly being challenged and defending their dominant status. They respond to this social challenge by being more hostile or aggressive. In contrast, females with worsened coronary artery atherosclerosis are socially subordinate and stressed. They are the recipients of aggression, and they are also relatively socially isolated. These findings paint a different picture of the behavioral characteristics of females at risk for coronary artery atherosclerosis as compared to those of males. These gender differences are reminiscent of the observation of Haynes and others (Haynes, Feinleib, & Kannel, 1980) that among men, those employed in white collar positions are disproportionately affected by CHD, whereas among women, those employed in clerical positions are at the greatest risk for CHD. Finally, among females, two psychosocial risk factors for coronary artery atherosclerosis have been identified: social isolation and social status incongruity.

The evidence from studies of cynomolgus monkeys suggests that ovarian hormones influence coronary artery atherosclerosis, CHD risk, and CHD risk factors, such as plasma cholesterol concentrations. Thus, it is likely that there are gender differences in the etiology of CHD. The majority of recommendations given to women about health care and habits with regard to CHD risk are based on the results of studies of men. The single biological factor that best distinguishes women from men is ovarian function. To make recommendations concerning health care and habits that influence CHD risk in women, the role of ovarian function must be considered.

Furthermore, the results of these studies suggest a biological basis for gender differences in the effects of social stress on CHD. Males and females occupy different positions in society, whether they are human or nonhuman primates, and thus, it is not surprising that there are gender differences in the behavioral characteristics of individuals at increased risk for CHD, or that psychosocial stressors may be gender-specific. Some psychosocial stressors may impair ovarian function, increasing the risk of coronary artery atherosclerosis and CHD in females. Thus, to knowledgeably discuss psychosocial factors that influence CHD risk in women, the interrelationships between ovarian function, psychosocial factors, CHD, and CHD risk factors must be understood. Other psychosocial stressors may exacerbate coronary artery atherosclerosis and, thus, increase CHD risk in females, independently of ovarian function. Whether such stressors are gender-specific, and the mechanisms that underlie their relation to coronary artery atherosclerosis, remain to be determined.

ACKNOWLEDGMENTS

This research was supported by grants HL-39789 and HL-14164 from the National Heart, Lung, and Blood Institute.

REFERENCES

Abbott, D. H., O'Byrne, K. T., Sheffield, J. W. (1989). Neuroendocrine suppression of LH secretion in subordinate female marmoset monkeys (Callithrix jacchus). In R. H. Eley (Ed.), *Comparative Reproduction in Mammals and Man: Proceedings of the Conference of the National Center for Research in Reproduction* (pp. 63–67). Nairobi, Kenya: Institute of Primate Research, National Museums of Kenya.

Abbott, D. H., Saltzman, W., & Schultz-Darken, N. J. (1992, June). *Hypothalamic switches regulating fertility in primates.* Paper presented at the XIVth Congress of the International Society of Primatology, Strasbourg, France.

Adams, M. R., Kaplan, J. R., Clarkson, T. B., & Koritnik, D. R. (1985). Ovariectomy, social status, and atherosclerosis in cynomolgus monkeys. *Arteriosclerosis, 5,* 192–200.

Adams, M. R., Kaplan, J. R., Manuck, S. B., Koritnik, D. R., Parks, J. S., Wolfe, M. S., & Clarkson, T. B. (1990). Inhibition of coronary artery atherosclerosis by 17-beta estradiol in ovariectomized monkeys. *Arteriosclerosis, 10,* 1051–1057.

Ahumada-Hemer, H., Valles De Bourges, V., Juarez Ayala, J., Brito, G., Diaz-Sanchez, V., & Garza-Flores, J. (1985). Variations in serum lipids and lipoproteins throughout the menstrual cycle. *Fertility & Sterility, 44,* 80–84.

Azogui, G., Ben-Shlomo, I., Zohar, S., Kook, A., Presser, S., & Aviram, M. (1992). High density lipoprotein concentration is increased during the ovulatory phase of the menstrual cycle in healthy young women. *Gynecological Endocrinology, 6,* 253–257.

Barclay, M., Barclay, R. K., Skipski, V. P., & Meuller, C. H. (1965). Fluctuation in human serum lipoprotein during the normal menstrual cycle. *Biochemical Journal, 96,* 205–209.

Barnea, E. R., & Tal, J. (1991) Stress-related reproductive failure. *Journal of In Vitro Fertilization & Embryo Transfer, 8,* 15–23.

Biller, B. M., Federoff, H. J., Koenig, J. I., & Klibanski, A. (1990). Abnormal cortisol secretion and responses to corticotropin-releasing hormone in women with hypothalamic amenorrhea. *Journal of Clinical Endocrinology & Metabolism, 70,* 311–317.

Bush, T. L., Barrett-Connor, E., Cowan, L. D., Criqui, M. H., Wallace, R. B., Suchindran, C. M., Tyroler, H. A., & Rifkind, B. M. (1987). Cardiovascular mortality and noncontraceptive use of estrogen in women: results from the Lipid Research Clinics Program Follow-up Study. *Circulation, 75,* 1102–1109.

Campos, H., McNamara, J. R., Wilson, P. W. F., Ordovas, J. M., & Schaefer, E. J. (1988). Differences in low density lipoprotein subfractions and apolipoproteins in premenopausal and postmenopausal women. *Journal of Clinical Endocrinology & Metabolism, 67,* 30–35.

Davis, M. C., & Matthews, K. A. (1996). *Do gender relevant characteristics determine cardiovascular reactivity? Match vs. mismatch of traits and situation.* Manuscript submitted for publication.

Ferin, M. (1989). Two instances of impaired GnRH activity in the adult primate: The luteal phase and 'stress'. In H. A. Delemarre-van de Waal (Ed.), *Control of the Onset of Puberty III.* (pp. 265–273). Amsterdam: Elsevier Science Publishers.

Gindoff, P. R. (1989). Menstrual function and its relationship to stress, exercise, and body weight. *Bulletin of the New York Academy of Medicine, 65,* 774–786.

Gindoff, P. R., & Ferin, M. (1989). Endogenous opioid peptides modulate the effect of corticotropin-releasing factor on gonadotropin release in the primate. *Endocrinology, 121,* 837–842.

Hamm, T. E., Jr., Kaplan, J. R., Clarkson, T. B., & Bullock, B. C. (1983). Effects of gender and social behavior on the development of coronary artery atherosclerosis in cynomolgus macaques. *Atherosclerosis, 48, 221–233.*

Hayashi, K. T., & Moberg, G. P. (1990). Influence of the hypothalamic-pituitary-adrenal axis on the menstrual cycle and the pituitary responsiveness to estradiol in the female rhesus monkey (Macaca fascicularis). *Biology of Reproduction 42,* 260–265.

Haynes, S. G., Feinleib, M., & Kannel, W. B. (1980). The relationship of psychosocial factors to coronary heart disease in the Framingham Study, III. Eight-year incidence of coronary heart disease. *American Journal of Epidemiology III,* 37–58.

Jewett, D. A., & Dukelow, W. R. (1972). Cyclicity and gestation length of Macaca fascicularis. *Primates, 13,* 327–330.

Kannel, W. B., Hjortland, M. C., McNamara, P. M., Gordon, T. (1976). Menopause and risk of cardiovascular disease: The Framingham Study. *Annals of Internal Medicine, 85,* 447–452.

Kaplan, J. R., Adams, M. R., Clarkson, T. B., & Koritnik, D. R. (1984). Psychosocial influences on female 'protection' among cynomolgus macaques. *Atherosclerosis, 53,* 283–295.

Kaplan, J. R., Adams, M. R., Koritnik, D. R., Rose, J. C., & Manuck, S. B. (1986). Adrenal responsiveness and social status in intact and ovariectomized Macaca fascicularis. *American Journal of Primatology, 11,* 181–193.

Kaplan, J. R., Manuck, S. B., Clarkson, T. B., Lusso, F. M., & Taub, D. M. (1982). Social status, environment, and atherosclerosis in cynomolgus monkeys. *Arteriosclerosis, 2,* 359–368.

Kim, H. J., & Kalkhoff, R. K. (1979). Change in lipoprotein composition during the menstrual cycle. *Metabolism, 28,* 663–668.

La Vecchia, C., Decarli, A., Franceschi, S., Gentile, A., Negri, E., & Parazzini, F. (1987). Menstrual and reproductive factors and the risk of myocardial infarction in women under fifty-five years of age. *American Journal of Obstetrics Gynecology, 157,* 1108–1112.

Levi, L. (1981). *Society, stress, and disease.* New York: Oxford University Press.

Levi, L. (1984). Work, stress and health. *Scandinavian Journal of Work Environment & Health, 10,* 495–500.

Mahoney, C. J. (1970). A study of the menstrual cycle in Macaca irus with special reference to the detection of ovulation. *Journal of Reproduction & Fertility, 21,* 153–163.

Matteo, S. (1987). The effect of job stress and job interdependency on menstrual cycle length, regularity and synchrony. *Psychoneuroendocrinology, 12,* 467–476.

Matthews, K. A., Davis, M. C., Stoney, C. M., Owens, J. F., & Caggiula, A. R. (1991). Does the gender relevance of the stressor influence sex differences in psychophysiological responses? *Health Psychology, 10,* 112–120.

Matthews, K. A., Meilahn, E., Kuller, L., Kelsey, S. F., Caggivla, A. W., & Wing, R. R. (1989). Menopause and risk factors for coronary heart disease. *New England Journal of Medicine, 321,* 641–646.

Nappi, R. E., Petraglia, F., Genazzani, A. D., D'Ambrogio, G., Zarta, C., & Genazzani, A. R. (1993). Hypothalamic amenorrhea: evidence fora central derangement of hypothalamic-pituitary-adrenal cortex axis activity. *Fertility & Sterility, 59,* 571–576.

Shively, C. A. (1985). The evolution of dominance hierarchies in nonhuman primate society. In S. L. Ellyson, & J. F. Dovidio (Eds.), *Power, dominance, and nonverbal behavior* (pp. 67–88). New York: Springer-Verlag.

Shively, C.A., & Clarkson, T. B. (1994). Social status incongruity and coronary artery atherosclerosis in female monkeys. *Arteriosclerosis & Thrombosis, 14,* 721–726.

Shively, C. A., Clarkson, T. B., & Kaplan, J. R. (1989). Social deprivation and coronary artery atherosclerosis in female cynomolgus monkeys. *Atherosclerosis, 77,* 69–76.

Shively, C. A., & Kaplan, J. R. (1991). Stability of social status rankings of female cynomolgus monkeys, of varying reproductive condition, in different social groups. *American Journal of Primatology, 23,* 239–245.

Shively, C. A., Kaplan, J. R., & Adams, M. R. (1986) Effects of ovariectomy, social instability and social status on female Macaca fascicularis social behavior. *Physiology & Behavior, 36,* 1147–1153.

Shively, C. A., Manuck, S. B., Kaplan, J. R., & Koritnik, D. R. (1990). Oral contraceptive administration, interfemale relationships, and sexual behavior in Macaca fascicularis. *Archives of Sexual Behavior, 19,* 101–117.

Shively, C. A., Knox, S, Sherwin, B. B., Walsh, B. W., & Wilson, P. W. F. (1993). Sex steroids, psychosocial factors, and lipid metabolism. *Metabolism, 42* (Suppl. 1), 16–24.

Shumaker, S. A., & Hill, D. R. (1991). Gender differences in social support and physical health. *Health Psychology, 10,* 102–111.

Tejada, C., Strong, J. P., Montenegro, M. R., Restropo, C., & Solberg, L. A. (1968). Distribution of coronary and aortic atherosclerosis by geographic location, race, and sex. *Laboratory Investigation, 18,* 509–526.

Vanecek, R. (1976). Atherosclerosis of the coronary arteries in five towns. *Bulletin of the World Health Organization, 53,* 509–518.

Wilks, J. W., Hodgen, G. D., & Ross, G. T. (1976). Luteal phase defects in the rhesus monkey: The significance of serum FSH: LH ratios. *Journal of Clinical Endocrinology & Metabolism, 43,* 1261–1267.

Wilks, J. W., Hodgen, G. D., & Ross, G. T. (1979). *Endocrine characteristics of ovulatory and anovulatory menstrual cycles in the rhesus monkey.* In E. S. E. Hafez, (Ed.), Human ovulation (pp. 205–218). Amsterdam: Elsevier/North-Holland Biomedical Press.

Williams, J. K., Adams, M. R., Herrington, D. M., & Clarkson, T. B. (1992). Short-term administration of estrogen and vascular responses of atherosclerotic coronary arteries. *Journal of the American College of Cardiology, 20,* 452–457.

Williams, J. K., Adams, M. R., & Klopfenstein, H. S. (1990). Estrogen modulates responses of atherosclerotic coronary arteries. *Circulation, 81,* 1680–1687.

Williams, J. K., Shively, C. A., & Clarkson, T. B. (1994). Vascular responses of atherosclerotic coronary arteries among premenopausal female monkeys. *Circulation, 90,* 983–987.

Wingard, D. L., Suarez, L., & Barrett-Connor, E. (1983). The sex differential in mortality from all causes and ischemic heart disease. *American Journal of Epidemiology, 117,* 19–26.

Woods, M., Schaefer, E. J., Morrill, A., Goldin, B. R., Longscope, C., Dwyer, J. D., & Gorbach, S. L. (1987). Effect of menstrual cycle phase on plasma lipids. *Journal of Clinical Endocrinology & Metabolism, 65,* 321–323.

4

Low-Flow Circulatory State and the Pathophysiological Development of Cardiovascular Disease: A Model of Autonomic Mediation of Cardiovascular Regulation

Barry E. Hurwitz
Rita Goldstein
Clifford A. Massie
Maria M. Llabre
Neil Schneiderman
Behavioral Research Center, University of Miami

Low-flow circulatory state is a hemodynamic pattern in which there is diminished ejection fraction and cardiac output and is accompanied by diminished parasympathetic cardiac input in addition to elevated systemic vascular resistance (Braunwald & Grossman, 1992). This hemodynamic pattern is highly prevalent in the progression of coronary heart disease (CHD) and hypertension (Braunwald & Grossman, 1992; Messerli, Carvalho, Christie, & Frolich, 1978). In this chapter, literature supporting a model of the pathogenesis of cardiovascular disease is reviewed. The model is based on a positive feedback loop in which behavioral factors, such as emotional stress, high-fat diet, and sedentary lifestyle, exacerbate or promote the progression of insulin resistance, hyperinsulinemia, and an imbalance in autonomic-sympathetic drive. The worsening of these conditions leads to a cascading series of pathophysiological events that may promote or facilitate atherogenesis, diminished left ventricular function, and the development of a low-flow circulatory state with elevated blood pressure. To the extent that the worsening of the low-flow circulatory state is a reflection of the progression of cardiovascular disease, the examination of resting autonomic and hemodynamic relationships would be beneficial in the study of the pathophysiological development of cardiovascular disease, and the identification of preclinical cardiovascular disease risk.

Multiple neural and mechanical determinants of cardiovascular regulation work jointly to maintain hemodynamic functioning within homeostatic limits (e.g., Randall, 1977). The study of the pathophysiological development of cardiovascular disease becomes complicated because of the numerous measures that can be derived to characterize hemodynamic functioning. Our hypothesis has been that abnormal autonomic mechanisms, consequent to the progression of cardiovascular disease will be present and more easily detectable by examining a weighted combination of variables rather than by examination of the variables independently. Disease-related cardiovascular dysregulation is commonly assessed during dynamic cardiovascular challenge, such as during exercise or dobutamine stress testing (Ryan, 1991; Theroux, Waters, Halphen, Debaiseux, & Mizgala, 1979). However, if disease related abnormal cardiovascular regulation is present, then this abnormal regulation should also be present and observable at rest with appropriately sensitive measures. A line of research is presented in which quantitative methods are used to develop a model of autonomic mediation of resting cardiovascular regulation and to investigate its relation with putative cardiovascular risk factors in normotensive healthy individuals and in individuals with essential hypertension.

INSULIN METABOLISM
AND CARDIOVASCULAR DISEASE

Epidemiological research has identified elevated levels of serum cholesterol, hypertension, advancing age, diabetes mellitus, cigarette smoking, and a family history of heart disease as measures for CHD risk (Kannel, McGee, & Gordon, 1976). Other measures of CHD risk have been proposed including such parameters as gender, race, levels of serum triglycerides, impaired vital capacity, obesity, abnormal glucose tolerance, hyperuricemia and gout, hypothyroidism, socio-psychological stress, certain personality behavior patterns, physical inactivity, and sedentary lifestyle (Borhani, 1977). Although CHD risk is related to blood pressure, antihypertensive medications have been less successful in reducing CHD morbidity and mortality compared to their effectiveness in reducing mortality from stroke and congestive heart failure (Collins et al., 1990). Therefore, the relation between blood pressure and CHD is not direct.

In recent years, a constellation of disorders associated with insulin resistance and hyperinsulinemia has been identified, which appears to be associated with the risk of CHD. This constellation has had several names—among the earliest being glucose intolerance-obesity-hypertension

(GOH) syndrome (Modan et al., 1985), "syndrome X" (Reaven, 1988), and the "deadly quartet" (Kaplan, 1989). The members of the quartet include upper-body obesity, glucose intolerance, hypertriglyceridemia, and hypertension. More recently, these disorders have been referred to as the insulin metabolic syndrome, which includes tendencies toward hyperglycemia, dyslipidemia (hypertriglyceridemia, hyperlipidemia, and low concentration of high density lipoprotein), and atherosclerosis in addition to the above described disorders (Schneiderman & Skyler, 1996).

Schneiderman and Skyler (1996) proposed a pathway of CHD pathogenesis that is based on an interactive relation among insulin resistance, hyperinsulinemia, and increased sympathetic tone. According to this conception, behavioral and related factors, for example, emotional stressors (including unstable environments), poor dietary practices (including alcohol abuse and excess ingestion of fats and sugar), and a sedentary lifestyle, together with genetic and nonmodifiable factors (e.g., race, age) can combine and interact to promote the development of cardiovascular disease. It is insulin metabolism and the activation of the sympathetic nervous system that play an integral role in their model in mediating the relationships between measures of CHD risk and CHD morbidity and mortality; hyperinsulinemia stimulates sympathetic nervous system activity, which can lead to further insulin resistance. Once the physiological chain is set in motion, it may behave like a positive feedback loop. Subsequently, increased lipid mobilization, cardiac hypertrophy, diminished left ventricular function, and increased blood pressure are associated with vascular injury and atherogenesis.

Insulin resistance is associated with increased insulin concentration; in insulin resistant individuals, normal concentrations of insulin elicit a less than normal biological response with decreased insulin, binding to cellular receptors. Thus, diminished glucose utilization results in the centrally-mediated overproduction of insulin by the pancreas to improve glucose uptake. A significant correlation between hyperinsulinemia and mortality from CHD has been reported (Ducimetière et al., 1980; Pyörälä, 1972; Welborn & Wearne, 1979). In a series of experiments, Baron and colleagues (Baron, 1993; Baron, Brechtel-Hook, Johnson, & Hardin,1993) have demonstrated that insulin has profound effects of increasing blood flow and decreasing vascular resistance.

Our studies have also demonstrated that there is an inverse correlation between insulin sensitivity and blood pressure (Marks et al., 1991; Skyler, Marks, & Schneiderman, 1995; Hurwitz & Schneiderman, 1998); in addition, on induction of hyperinsulinemia in healthy individuals using the euglycemic insulin clamp under resting conditions, those who were more insulin sensitive displayed larger changes in norepinephrine, systolic blood pressure (SBP) and cardiac output than those who were more insulin resistant. These findings suggest that the effect of insulin in insulin-sensitive individuals is to promote increased sympathetic myocardial drive. In addition, we have observed that insulin resistance is associated with underlying cardiac mechanisms that support blood pressure elevations (Hurwitz & Schneiderman, 1998). In this study in both normotensive and hypertensive individuals, higher insulin resistance was associated with greater contribution of cardiac output than total peripheral resistance (TPR) responsiveness to the blood pressure increase during stressful behavioral challenge. These observations are consistent with the notions that (a) resting blood pressure elevation arises as a consequence of resistance to the action of insulin as mediated by vasodilatation, and (b) greater cardiac contribution to the blood pressure response to challenge is a consequence of the inability to vasodilate. Whether insulin resistance per se and not hyperinsulinemia represents the primary defect, or whether it is secondary to increased sympathetic drive, the progressive development of insulin metabolic syndrome may provide a marker for the pathogenesis of the constellation of disorders that impacts negatively on cardiovascular functioning.

SYMPATHETIC NERVOUS SYSTEM
AND CARDIOVASCULAR DISEASE

Chronic sympathetic nervous system hyperactivity can cause hemodynamic and structural changes (i.e., smooth muscle cell hypertrophy and vascular rarefaction) that may reduce insulin sensitivity by reducing glucose delivery to skeletal muscle (Julius, Gubdrandsson, Jamerson, Shahab, & Andersson, 1991). Sympathetic nervous system activation has been postulated as a mediating factor in the insulin-induced elevated blood pressure. Only a few studies have examined the direct effects of insulin on adrenergic activity. Acute insulin infusion has been reported to increase muscle sympathetic nerve discharge and elevate plasma norepinephrine concentration (Anderson, Balon, Hoffman, Sinkey, & Mark, 1992; Anderson, Hoffman, Balon, Sinkey, & Mark, 1991; Christensen, Hilsted, Hegedus, & Madsbad, 1984; Fagius, Niklasson, & Berne, 1986; Liang et al., 1982; Rowe, Young, Monaker, et al., 1981) and blockade of adrenergic activity has been reported to attenuate the rise in blood pressure observed with insulin infusion (Pereda, Eckstein, & Abboud, 1962). Results from the Normative Aging Study of Men, ranging from 43 to 85 years of age, demonstrated higher urinary norepinephrine excretion in subjects classified as hyperinsulinemic (Troisi et al., 1991). Direct effects of adrenergic activity on insulin resistance were also documented; acute insulin resistance was induced by infusions of epinephrine in healthy subjects (Diebert & DeFronzo,

1980). In addition, the induced insulin resistance was mediated by beta-adrenergic effects because blockade with propranolol reinstated normative glucose uptake levels.

Two mechanisms whereby chronically enhanced central sympathetic drive may lead to insulin resistance have been proposed. Both are based on the fact that the site of the majority of glucose uptake is the skeletal muscle, which is also the site of insulin resistance in hypertensive and non-insulin dependent diabetic individuals (DeFronzo, Gunnarsson, Bjorkman, Olsson, & Wahren, 1985: Reaven, 1995). One potential mechanism is derived from evidence that hypertensives display increased proportions of fast-twitch muscle fibers and that chronically increased sympathetic drive can induce a switch from slow-twitch insulin-sensitive muscle fibers to fast-twitch insulin-resistant muscle fibers in animals (Karlsson & Smith, 1984; Juhlin-Dannfelt, Frisk-Holmberg, Jarlsson, & Tesch, 1979). The second mechanism suggests that due to the progression of vascular hypertrophy in hypertension, which is associated with a decrease in small blood vessels penetrating skeletal muscle, the diffusion distance for glucose is increased, thereby promoting insulin resistance (Julius, Gubdrandsson, Jamerson, & Andersson, 1992; Julius et al., 1991).

Indeed, in experimental studies of psychological stress, many of the pathophysiological states implicated in the atherogenic process and the precipitation of clinically detectable CHD have been observed in conjunction with increased sympathetic adrenal–medullary or pituitary adrenal–cortical activity. For example, research from animal and human studies has demonstrated that exposure to acute and chronic uncontrollable stress may augment resting sympathetic tone and enhance sympathetic reactivity to acute, novel stressors (see Anderson et al., 1991). Biochemical changes such as increased levels of catecholamines, cortisol, and serum cholesterol, and hemodynamic effects such as elevated heart rate and blood pressure are produced in animals under prolonged or severe stress and have been observed in acute and chronic studies of humans (Frankenhaeuser, 1975; Henry, 1983; Herd, 1981; Januszewicz, Sznajderman, Wocial, Fettynowski, & Klonowicz, 1979; Mason, 1975; Schneiderman, 1983). These stress related changes are mitigated by beta-adrenoreceptor blockade (Hirsch, Maksem, & Gagen, 1984; Kaplan, Manuck, Adams, & Clarkson, 1987; Kaplan, Manuck, Adams, Weingand, & Clarkson, 1987; Kaplan, Manuck, Clarkson, Lusso, & Taub, 1982; Strawn et al., 1991). Evidence linking exaggerated sympathetic nervous system activity with a variety of pathophysiologic changes in predisposed organisms includes vascular and endothelial damage (Hallbäck, 1975; Hirsch et al., 1984; Gordon, Guyton, & Karnovsky, 1981), lipid mobilization (Dimsdale, Herd, & Hartley, 1983), conduction disturbances (Matta, Lawler, & Lown, 1976), altered ventricular function

(Rozanski et al., 1988), clotting abnormalities (Levine et al., 1985), platelet aggregation (Canizares, Vivar, & Herdoiza, 1994; Guivernau, Meza, Barja, & Roman, 1994; Jamieson et al., 1992), and coronary thrombosis (Ardlie, Glew, & Schwartz, 1966).

In a series of studies, Julius and colleagues (Julius, 1988; Julius et al., 1991, 1992) examined the association between hypertension and the sympathetic nervous system. Julius (1988) postulated that activation of negative feedback from the central nervous system underlies the rate of progression of the blood pressure elevation in the course of hypertension. During hypertension development, an initial hyperkinetic circulatory state, in which plasma norepinephrine, cardiac output and heart rate are elevated, progressively changes to a low-flow circulation that is characterized by an elevated vascular resistance and reduced cardiac output (Julius et al., 1991). The mechanisms that underlie the transition from a high cardiac output to the high-resistance state in the progression toward borderline hypertension are not entirely established. The increased sympathetic cardiac input, however, leads to a functional down-regulation of beta-adrenergic responsiveness, contributing to a decline in heart rate toward normal values. This change in chronotropic responsiveness evolves in parallel with a gradual decrease in stroke volume during the course of hypertension. The responsiveness of cardiac output to both sympathetic stimulation and venous filling decreases. Low cardiac output, at rest or in response to physical exertion, dobutamine infusion, or stressful behavioral challenge, characterizes heart failure occurring in most forms of heart disease (i.e., hypertensive, congenital, valvular, rheumatic, cardiomyopathic, and coronary; Braunwald & Grossman, 1992). Thus, a similar hemodynamic transition to a low-flow circulatory state may also be involved in CHD pathogenesis.

In parallel with the cardiac and autonomic changes that result in decreased cardiac output, there is an alteration of vascular anatomy and function in the course of hypertension that yields a steady increase of vascular resistance. As hypertension advances, the prolonged pressure load causes hypertrophy of the medial layer of the major resistance vessels. In such hypertrophic vessels, the contraction of vascular smooth muscle causes a larger encroachment of the thick wall into the lumen, that in turn, produces an increase in vascular resistance (Folkow, 1977). When exposed to the same constrictor stimulus, a hypertrophic arteriole responds with a much steeper increase of resistance than a normal blood vessel. Thus, the increased vascular reactivity acts as positive feedback; hypertrophic vessels offer larger resistance and the higher resistance, leads to higher pressures, that in turn, further favor an increase in the wall thickness. Higher pressures are consequently established that do not require increased sympathetic drive to maintain. Thus, Julius (1988) suggested that the transition from a hyperkinetic state to one of increased vascular resistance and elevated blood pressure involves a gradual decrement in sympathetic tone along with accompanying cardiac and vascular structural alterations. In addition to the role of the sympathetic nervous system, reduced parasympathetic control may be involved in hypertension pathophysiology. This is supported by findings that hypertensives exhibit decreased respiratory sinus arrhythmia amplitude (a measure of vagal cardiac input) at rest and in response to challenge (Drummond, 1990; Grossman, Brinkman, & de Vries, 1992).

SYMPATHETIC NERVOUS SYSTEM: RELATIONSHIP WITH SELECTED MEASURES OF CARDIOVASCULAR DISEASE RISK

The previous discussion emphasizes the importance of the sympathetic nervous system and its role in cardiovascular disease pathogenesis. To further elucidate this path, the following describes in more detail the association between the sympathetic nervous system on the one hand and selected modifiable and nonmodifiable measures of cardiovascular disease risk on the other.

Age

Men and women 65 years and older represent one of the most rapidly growing segments of our population, and CHD is the leading cause of death in this age group (U.S. Department of Health and Human Services, 1994). Every major prospective epidemiological investigation carried out in the United States over the past several decades has shown a marked increase in the risk of CHD with increasing age. The question of whether parasympathetic, sympathetic, or total autonomic system reactivity declines with age, has been controversial. Most evidence supports the view that an increase in relative dominance of the sympathetic nervous system occurs with age (Sato et al., 1981). For example, a gradual increase in resting muscle sympathetic activity in humans (Sundlof & Wallin, 1978) and an increase in plasma catecholamine concentration, both at rest and in response to static exercise and postural stress, have been reported with increasing age (Julius, Amery, Whitlock, & Conway, 1967; Lakatta, 1979; McDermott, Stekiel, Barboriak, Kloth, & Smith, 1974; McDermott, Tristani, Ebert, Porth & Smith, 1980; Pfeifer et al., 1983; Tuck, 1992; Ziegler, Lake, & Kopin, 1976). In addition, numerous studies report that parasympathetic cardiac input decreases with age, as evidenced by decreased respiratory sinus arrhythmia with increasing age (Hrushesky, 1992; Murata, Landrigan, & Araki, 1992;

Pfeifer et al., 1983; Shannon, Carley, & Benson, 1987; Waddington, MacCulloch, & Sambrooks, 1978).

In addition, aging is associated with a significant increase in maximum SBP and resting blood pressure (Astrand & Rodahl, 1970; Brandfonbrener, Landowne, & Shock, 1955; Julius et al., 1967; Landowne, Brandfonbrener, & Shock, 1955; Marshall & Shepherd, 1968; Pfeifer et al., 1983; Tuck, 1992). The changes in the hemodynamic pattern underlying the age-related increase in blood pressure are similar to those underlying hypertension; increased age is associated with a decline in cardiac output (1% per year), predominantly caused by a decrease in stroke volume that is not completely compensated by an increase in heart rate, and consequently, a concomitant increase in TPR is observed (Astrand & Rodahl, 1970; Brandfonbrener et al., 1955; Ebert, Hughes, Tristani, Barney & Smith, 1982; Fleg, 1986; Julius et al., 1967; Landowne et al., 1955; Luisada, Bhat, & Bioeng, 1980; Marshall & Shepherd, 1968; Miyamura & Honda, 1973; Pfeifer et al., 1983; Rodeheffer et al., 1984; Strandell, 1964; Tuck, 1992). Thus, with increasing age there is a decline in cardiac output and a progression toward a low-flow circulatory state that is accompanied by diminished cardiac parasympathetic input and increased sympathetic input to the vasculature.

Obesity

In studies that use a comparison of body weight relative to a desirable standard or body mass index (BMI), obesity has been shown to be associated with various measures of CHD risk. For example, obesity measures were positively related to levels of serum cholesterol and to blood pressure in a continuous and graded manner, as well as to categorical definitions of hypertension and hypercholesterolemia (Barrett-Connor, 1985; Hubert, 1986; National Institutes of Health Consensus Development Panel on the Health Implications of Obesity, 1985). In addition, weight change among adults studied in Framingham was associated with a corresponding change in CHD risk factors (Ashley & Kannel, 1974). More specifically, others have found that central body obesity is associated with atherosclerosis (Vague, 1956). At least three prospective studies have demonstrated that body fat distribution is associated with subsequent CHD, even after adjustment for differences in BMI (Ducimetière, Richard, Cambien, Avons, & Jacqueson, 1985; Lapidus et al., 1984; Larsson et al., 1984).

Sympathetic function is influenced by dietary patterns; activation of the sympathetic nervous system is suppressed by caloric restriction and stimulated by overfeeding (Young & Landsberg, 1977a, 1977b). Studies using norepinephrine turnover in rodents to assess sympathetic activity, for example, have shown that overfeeding in rats increases sympathetic activity

(Young, Saville, Rothwell, Stock, & Landsberg, 1982). Similarly, increased BMI and caloric intake have each been associated with elevated urinary norepinephrine excretion in humans (Troisi et al., 1991). In addition, evidence has shown that plasma norepinephrine levels are increased in hypertensive, obese patients, and are decreased following weight reduction (Dornfeld, Maxwell, Waks, & Tuck, 1987; Krieger & Landsberg, 1988; Reisin et al, 1978; Reisin, Frohlich, & Messerli, 1983; Rocchini et al., 1989; Sowers et al., 1982; Troisi et al., 1991; Tuck, Sowers, Dornfield, Whitfield, & Maxwell, 1983).

The underlying mechanisms of cardiovascular control appear to relate differently to obesity being a function of hypertensive status. In hypertensive individuals, obesity, as measured by BMI, was found to be positively correlated with hyperkinetic forearm circulation and to have an increase in cardiac output (Alexander, 1964; Jern, Bergbrant, Bjorntorp, & Hansson, 1992; Licata, Scaglione, Capuana, et al., 1990; Messerli, Christie, DeCarvalho et al, 1981; Messerli, Sundgaard-Riise, Reisin, et al., 1983; Raison, Safar, Cambien, & London, 1988). In contrast, in normotensive subjects, central distribution of body fat, as measured by waist-to-hip ratio, was associated with lower cardiac output and stroke volume and higher systemic vascular resistance, the hemodynamic pattern reflecting the low-flow circulatory state (Jern et al., 1992).

Ethnicity

One of the most consistent findings in cardiovascular epidemiological literature is the higher resting blood pressure and greater prevalence of essential hypertension among Black Americans compared with White Americans (Folkow, 1982, 1987; U.S. Department of Health and Human Services, 1994). Higher rates of hypertension-related mortality from CHD, cerebral vascular disease, and renal disease among Black Americans have been documented (Fray, 1993). For over a decade, researchers have addressed the extent to which prevalence differences in essential hypertension between Black Americans and White-Americans parallel group-related differences in factors involved in blood pressure regulation. This line of investigation has largely been pursued by evaluating the mechanisms involved in the blood pressure regulation of Black Americans and White Americans (Fray & Douglas, 1993) in response to stressful behavioral challenges (Saab et al., 1992; Anderson & McNeilly, 1993).

Although conflicting evidence is available (e.g., Anderson, Lane, Taguchi, & Williams, 1989; Anderson, Lane, Taguchi, Williams, & Houseworth, 1989; Calhoun, Mutinga, Wyss, & Oparil, 1994), the data generally support the view that normotensive Blacks and Whites differ in their physiological responses to some laboratory challenges. The research that includes healthy normotensive adults provides evidence that Blacks and Whites are differentially responsive to active coping (characterized by increases in myocardial indices) and to inhibitory passive coping (characterized by increases in vascular indices) challenges. Specifically, some studies demonstrated that Whites typically respond with greater challenge-induced heart rate (Anderson, Lane, Monou, Williams, & Houseworth, 1988; Falkner & Kushner, 1989; Light, Turner, Hinderliter, & Sherwood, 1993; Saab et al., 1997), with greater SBP reactivity (Anderson et al., 1988; McAdoo, Weinberger, Miller, Fineberg, & Grim, 1990; Nelesen, Dimsdale, Mills, & Ziegler, 1995; Saab et al., 1997), with greater diastolic blood pressure (DBP) response (Anderson et al., 1988; Nelesen et al., 1995) and with greater cardiac output response (Light et al., 1993; Saab et al., 1997) for tasks that involve active coping (e.g., math, competitive reaction time, speaking, video games, interviews, and bicycle ergometry challenges). Other studies reported that Blacks displayed greater blood pressure responsivity to active coping challenges than White Americans and have attributed these differences to systemic vascular mechanisms (Light et al., 1993; Light & Sherwood, 1989; Tischenkel, Saab, Schneiderman, et al., 1989).

An investigation from our laboratory found that normotensive Black American and White American men were relatively indistinguishable in terms of their blood pressure and heart rate responses to a series of active coping and inhibitory–passive coping challenges (Saab et al., 1992). However, the results also indicated that the processes underlying these responses differed for Black Americans and White Americans. Black American men responded with vascular mechanisms (i.e., with greater TPR) to both active and passive coping challenges, whereas White Americans responded with cardiac mechanisms (i.e., with greater cardiac output) to active coping challenges and responded with vascular mechanisms to passive coping challenges. These findings are consistent with other reported observations in adults and children that Black American normotensives react with increased TPR responsivity to active coping challenges known to stimulate cardiac output activity in Whites (Arensman, Treiber, Gruber, & Strong, 1989; Dysart, Treiber, Pflieger, Davis, & Strong, 1994; Light et al., 1993; Light & Sherwood, 1989).

Heightened sympathetic activity has been proposed to explain the racial reactivity differences. In the study by Light and colleagues (Light, Turner, Hinderliter, Girdler, & Sherwood, 1994), Black American subjects as a whole demonstrated greater increases in plasma norepinephrine levels to the majority of the stressors than White American subjects. Heightened vascular (alpha-adrenergic) receptor sensitivity has also been suggested to explain the apparent differences between Black American and White

American reactivity. Reports that Black American hypertensives showed enhanced alpha–adrenergic receptor sensitivity to agonist infusions relative to their White American counterparts supports this conclusion (Dimsdale, Graham, Ziegler, Zusman, & Berry, 1987; Sherwood & Hinderliter, 1993). This evidence is consistent with research showing that beta-blockers alone are not effective in lowering blood pressure in Black Americans, whereas labetolol, an alpha- and beta-antagonist, is more effective (Flamenbaum et al., 1985; Veterans Administration Cooperative Study Group on Antihypertensive Drugs, 1982, 1983). More recently, healthy Black American men and women matched with White American men and women on age and ambulatory blood pressure, demonstrated a blunted maximal vasodilatory capacity suggestive of early structural change in the vasculature (Hinderliter et al., 1996). That the stressor-response profile observed in the normotensive Black American subjects (cf. Saab et al., 1992) parallels the profiles observed by others in borderline hypertensive patients (Julius, Pascual, Sannerstedt, & Mitchell, 1971) suggests that Black Americans may be transitioning to a low-flow–high-resistance circulatory state earlier than White Americans.

The ethnicity differences in cardiovascular reactivity may also be related to the expression of social, environmental, and psychological concomitants of ethnicity roles. A contextual model, incorporating social, environmental, and psychological factors together with biological predispositions, has been proposed (Anderson & McNeilly, 1993). It was postulated that because Black Americans are exposed to a wider array of chronic stressors (e.g., unemployment, poverty, low social status, residential crowding) than are their White counterparts, these chronic stressors interact with biological (e.g., heightened vascular sensitivity), behavioral (e.g., suppressed anger and hostility), and psychological (e.g., "John Henryism") risk factors to increase sympathetic nervous system activity. This, in turn, leads to the release of neuroendocrine substances, including norepinephrine and adrenocorticotropin, thereby augmenting sodium retention, enhancing vasoconstriction, and with vascular structural alteration, blood pressure levels increase, and vascular reactivity to challenge is heightened.

Reactivity to Stressful Behavioral Challenge

It has been hypothesized that persons who exhibit sympathoadrenal or hemodynamic responses in greatest magnitude (i.e., individuals who exhibit a characteristic cardiovascular "hyper-reactivity" to stressful behavioral challenges (Eliot, Buell, & Dembroski, 1982; Falkner, Onesti, Angelakos, Fernandes, & Langman, 1979) are at a higher risk for cardiovascular disease (Manuck, Kaplan, & Matthews, 1986). However, the current trend in cardiovascular reactivity research is to study subgroups of reactors that may vary in the propensity to display cardiac or vascular patterns of response during stress. The notion is that the different patterns of response will have different implications for disease. For example, vascular reactors that display large pressor responses to multiple stressors associated primarily with an increase in TPR in the absence of any notable increase in cardiac output (e.g., Light et al., 1994) may have heightened sympathetic nerve input to peripheral vascular alpha-receptors or increased responsivity of these receptors. In addition, although not yet hypertensive, these individuals may already have structural changes in their blood vessels that limit vasodilatory responses and potentiate vasoconstrictive influences (Korner, Bobik, Jennings, Angus, & Anderson, 1991; Lever, 1986; Rizzoni, Castellano, Porteri, et al., 1994). The association between increased vascular reactivity and disease state is demonstrated in a study (Hurwitz & Schneiderman, 1998) in which hypertensive relative to normotensive men and women displayed elevated resting blood pressure, accompanied by elevated TPR, diminished stroke volume, and cardiac output, reflecting a low-flow circulatory state; they also displayed diminished respiratory sinus arrhythmia estimates of cardiac vagal input. This resting cardiovascular profile of the hypertensive individuals was similar to the low-flow circulatory profile previously observed in insulin-dependent diabetic subjects (Hurwitz, Quillian, Marks, et al., 1994), in borderline hypertensive individuals (Lund-Johansen, 1980), and among individuals with a family history of hypertension (Tafil-Klawe, Trzebski, Klawe, & Polko, 1985). The same profile was observed in another study of cardiovascular responses to the cold pressor test in normotensive young adult men, where we observed that hyper-reactors to the cold pressor test were further distinguished by relatively elevated baseline resting levels of systemic vascular resistance and reduced cardiac output (Peckerman et al., 1994). These findings underscore the link between a low-flow circulatory state at rest and heightened cardiovascular responsiveness to stressful behavioral challenge.

A MODEL OF RESTING AUTONOMIC MEDIATION OF CARDIOVASCULAR REGULATION

To study the association among measures of autonomic mediation of cardiovascular regulation and measures of cardiovascular disease risk, a quantitative approach was used, similar to that employed decades ago (Wenger, 1941, 1942, 1948). A quantitative model of autonomic mediation of resting cardiovascular regulation was developed based on the interrelations of the autonomic and cardiovascular parameters. Because there was a prespecified theoretical model, confirmatory factor analysis was used and applied to data previously collected. This methodology has a number of advantages that lend themselves to the present objectives. In confirmatory factor analysis, one can specify which variable will define specific factors, test the fit of the model, and test one nested model against another until the model that best fits the data is derived (Bollen, 1989; Gorsuch, 1983).

The data used in this analysis were derived from 206 healthy normotensive White ($n = 159$) and African-American ($n = 47$) men, aged 18 to 55 years (mean age 30.5 11.2), who participated in six research protocols with similar methodology[1] (Hurwitz, Nelesen et al., 1993; Hurwitz et al., 1994; Peckerman et al., 1994; Saab et al., 1992; Saab et al., 1993; Saab et al., 1997). Eligible subjects were free of medication, displayed resting blood pressure less than 140/90 mmHg, were affirmed healthy on a physical examination by physician, reported no history of cardiopulmonary abnormality, and showed no evidence of ventricular arrhythmias other than premature ventricular contractions on 12-lead electrocardiogram evaluation. No age or body mass differences were present for White and Black American groups. Mean age for White men was 29.7 ± 12 years and for Black American men was 33.3 ± 8 years. Mean body mass index for White men was 25.4 ± 4 kg/m^2 and for Black American men was 24.8 ± 4 kg/m^2.

For each of the research protocols, subjects were instructed that preceding the testing session they were to eat a light meal, and to abstain from coffee or other substances containing caffeine for at least 2 hours, aspirin or other medication for at least 12 hours, smoking or nicotine use for at least 2 hours, strenuous physical exercise for 2 hours, and alcohol for at least 12

---

[1]Prior to performing the confirmatory factor analysis, intercorrelations were examined to ensure that the relations among the autonomic and cardiovascular variables did not differ as a function of methodological differences among the six studies where these data were recruited. Although all of the studies examined the subjects when they were seated, two of the six studies used a chair with a back-rest that put the subjects in a somewhat more reclined (about 15°–20°) posture. Therefore, the correlations among all variables were examined as a function of posture (seated vs. partially reclined seated) and ethnicity (White, Black). In addition, in the present analysis, subjects from two studies ($N = 96$) were fitted with an half-band impedance cardiography electrode configuration, whereas subjects from the remaining studies ($N = 110$) were fitted with a full-band electrode configuration. The use of the half-band impedance cardiography configuration has been compared favorably to the full-band configuration for measuring stroke volume (Watanabe, Kamide, Torii, & Ochiai, 1981). However, preliminary data from our laboratory suggest that the half-band configuration may produce a larger mean thoracic impedance by approximately three ohms relative to the full-band configuration. This may artificially reduce stroke volume values by about 24% uniformly across subjects, without influencing dZ/dt max, which is used to calculate stroke volume and contractility indices. The intercorrelations among the autonomic and cardiovascular variables did not appear to systematically differ as a function of the subjects ethnicity, seated posture, or electrode configuration. Of the significant intercorrelations, there was no evidence of specific variables or combinations of variables that were over-represented among the significant correlations. Thus, the subjects were combined across the different studies for the confirmatory factor analysis.

hours prior to the reactivity session. On the day of the session an intravenous catheter was inserted into an antecubital vein to measure hematocrit from a sample of blood withdrawn at the same time as the blood pressure determinations. In a subset of the subjects, only a finger stick was performed to measure hematocrit for the determination of stroke volume. The baseline measurements were taken at least 30 minutes following the needle stick or catheter insertion. Blood pressure, electrocardiogram, phonocardiogram, respiration, and impedance cardiogram signals were measured. These procedures and other details concerning electrode placement, signal acquisition, signal processing and data collection have been reported previously (Hurwitz, Nelesen et al., 1993; Hurwitz et al., 1994; Peckerman et al., 1994; Saab et al., 1992; Saab et al., 1993; Saab et al., 1997).

The final three blood pressure determinations and the corresponding physiological signals of the first resting period were derived for each parameter and averaged for use in the confirmatory factor analysis. Twenty-one indices of autonomic and cardiovascular function were assessed in the analysis that could be characterized as reflecting autonomic input to the myocardium or reflecting cardiovascular performance. Indices of cardiovascular performance included SBP, DBP, MAP, cardiac output, stroke volume (using the Kubicek formula; Kubicek, Witsoe, Patterson, & From, 1969), and TPR. Indices of myocardial contractility that were examined included acceleration index (ACI), pre-ejection period (PEP), left ventricular ejection time (LVET), ratio of PEP to LVET, Heather index, electrical systole (QT), electromechanical systole (EMS), and ratio of QT to EMS. These indices were included because of the extensive literature demonstrating that they reflect inotropy and indirectly sympathetic cardiac input (e.g., Hurwitz, Nelesen et al., 1993; Larsen, Schneiderman, & Pasin, 1986; Lewis, Rittgers, Forester, & Boudoulas, 1977; Weissler, 1977).

Indices of parasympathetic function were derived by examining the relationship of heart rate with respiration because parasympathetic cardiac input is gated by respiration and the amplitude of the consequent oscillation of heart rate, that is, respiratory sinus arrhythmia (RSA), is a function of the magnitude of this input (see review Berntson, Cacioppo, & Quigley, 1993). To derive the RSA, an adaptive filtering technique previously reported was used (Han, Nagel, Hurwitz, & Schneiderman, 1991; Nagel, Han, Hurwitz, & Schneiderman, 1993), which decomposes the heart rate signal that is most highly correlated with respiration. In addition, indices of parasympathetic cardiac input included the mean heart rate, heart rate variance (HRV) and the difference between the maximum and minimum heart rate (HRmax-min). Although RSA, as derived using the adaptive filtering method, is free of linear trends in the heart rate signal, variance measures of heart rate (e.g., HRV, HRmax-min) are not free of this potential source of error but have also been shown to reflect parasympathetic influence (Ewing, Borsey, Bellavere, & Clarke, 1981; Genovely & Pfeifer, 1988).

A factor analytic model was developed based on the specification of the three autonomic/cardiovascular influences previously described (i.e., blood pressure/vascular, cardiac parasympathetic, and cardiac sympathetic/inotropy) using the average of the three resting measures from the first baseline period for each parameter (Hurwitz, Massie, Llabre, & Schneiderman, 1993; Massie, 1994). Confirmatory factor analysis examines the extent to which various specifications about the factor pattern underlying a data matrix (constraints) are consistent with the observed covariances (e.g., Bentler & Bonnett, 1980). Confirmatory factor analysis was performed using a structural equation modeling procedure with maximum likelihood estimation (LISREL version 7.0; Joreskog & Sorbom, 1989). To avoid an underidentification problem each indicator was allowed to define one and only one factor as previously detailed. Three, rather than two indicators per factor, are preferred due to model identification problems, although two indicators may be acceptable (Bollen, 1989). To determine the indicators to be used for the factor definition from the 21 available parameters, preliminary exploratory techniques were used. The most highly intercorrelated parameters for each of the three predicted factors (i.e., cardiac sympathetic/inotropy, cardiac parasympathetic, blood pressure/vascular) were included in the model. The following factor structure was predicted on the basis of the exploratory analysis, which satisfied convergent criteria for defining a model. Factor 1, the cardiac parasympathetic factor (PNS), was defined by RSA, HRmax-min, and HRV. Factor 2, the blood pressure/vascular factor (VAS), was defined by DBP, TPR, and stroke volume. Stroke volume was included because it is strongly influenced by afterload and because it had higher correlations with TPR and DBP than SBP or cardiac output. Factor 3, the cardiac sympathetic/inotropy factor (SNS), was defined by PEP and ACI, reflecting pre-ejection and ejection phase influences.

In assessing the fit of the model, the test statistic is a chi-square; the null hypothesis in confirmatory factor analysis is that all the population covariance has been extracted by the hypothesized number of factors. If the chi-square is significant then the residual matrix still has significant covariance in it. Thus, a nonsignificant chi-square reflects a minimal departure of the predicted model from the data, indicating that the model fits the data. The chi-square of the proposed three-factor model with 17 degrees of freedom was 17.90 ($p = 0.395$), indicating a good fit of the model to the data. Two additional overall indices of fit were evaluated, the adjusted goodness-of-fit index (AGFI) and the root mean square residual (RMR). The AGFI is a ratio between the fit function after the model has been fitted and the fit function before the model has been fitted. The AGFI is adjusted for the degrees of freedom and can have a value from zero to one, with values closer to one indicating a better fit. The RMR is a measure of the average of the fitted residuals. Ideally, the RMR should be near zero for a good fit (Jöreskog & Sorbom, 1989).

For the three-factor model, the AGFI was 0.954 and the RMR was 0.034. All factor loadings, standard errors, squared multiple correlations, and t-values are presented in Table 4.1. Standard errors and squared multiple correlations of the factor loadings were within an acceptable range. The t-values indicated that all indicators loaded significantly on the respective factors. This final three-factor model was thus properly estimated. Notably, no other parameters of the 21 available measures yielded a model that fit the data better than this one. In summary, this model met the rules for identification and estimation and could be said to be parsimonious and interpretable.[2]

Examination of the phi matrix for this final model indicated that the PNS and SNS factors correlated positively, $r = 0.20$. This small positive correlation reflects the homeostatic relation of the two branches of the autonomic nervous system, where changes in the parasympathetic branch are accompanied by similar changes in the sympathetic branch, despite having reciprocal effects on the cardiovascular system (Berne & Levy, 1992; Randall, 1977). The SNS and VAS factors were inversely correlated, $r = -0.71$. This correlation, for example, implies that for those individuals with increased resting afterload or systemic vascular resistance, myocardial contractility or inotropy was diminished. The PNS and VAS factors inversely correlated, $r = -0.31$, reflecting that with increased cardiac parasympathetic input, the decreased heart rate permits increased left ventricular filling time resulting in greater stroke volume and greater cardiac output and, consequently, less systemic vascular resistance and blood pressure. The dynamic interplay among the three factors of the model reflect commonly accepted reflex

---

[2]There are methodological issues that deserve attention. First, to generate a sample large enough to perform the confirmatory factor analysis, it was necessary to aggregate subjects across several studies. The large percentage of similar correlations between seated, and partially reclined but seated, men, and between Black and White men and the random pattern among the significant correlations were used as justification for combining subjects across the protocols. However, combining subjects across protocols might have increased the error variability and examining this model on a different, more homogenous, sample is indeed desirable and has been performed more recently in our laboratory (Goldstein, Llabre, Donahue, et al., 1997). Second, the variables used to define each of the factors in this study were derived conceptually. Variables that have been more extensively researched and reported in the literature and variables with well established reliability and validity were chosen. However, although variables that are a linear combination of other variables were not included in the analysis, some variables are inherently related to other variables in the model (e.g., TPR = (heart rate x stroke volume)/MAP/16.7). Nevertheless, the final model resulted in a fully proper solution.

TABLE 4.1

Factor Loadings, Squared Multiple Correlations, Standard Errors, t-values and Goodness-of-Fit Indices for the Three-Factor Model of Autonomic Mediation of Resting Cardiovascular Regulation[a]

Factor Loadings

PNS Factor		VAS Factor		SNS Factor	
RSA	0.82	DBP	0.69	PEP	0.40
HRV	0.91	TPR	0.95	ACI	0.86
HRmax-min	0.91	SV	-0.84		

Squared Multiple Correlations

PNS Factor		VAS Factor		SNS Factor	
RSA	0.67	DBP	0.48	PEP	0.16
HRV	0.82	TPR	0.90	ACI	0.73
HRmax-min	0.84	SV	0.71		

Standard Errors

PNS Factor		VAS Factor		SNS Factor	
RSA	0.06	DBP	0.06	PEP	0.08
HRV	0.06	TPR	0.06	ACI	0.11
HRmax-min	0.06	SV	0.06		

*t-values**

PNS Factor		VAS Factor		SNS Factor	
RSA	13.94	DBP	10.97	PEP	5.02
HRV	16.28	TPR	17.18	ACI	8.14
HRmax-min	16.46	SV	-14.37		

Goodness of Fit Indices

(2 (17)	17.9, $p = 0.395$
AGFI	0.954
RMR	0.034

[a]abbreviations are as follows: PNS = cardiac parasympathetic nervous system; VAS = vascular; SNS = cardiac sympathetic nervous system; RSA = respiratory sinus arrhythmia; HRV = heart rate variance; HRmax-min = difference between heart rate maximum and heart rate minimum; DBP = diastolic blood pressure; TPR = total peripheral resistance; SV = stroke volume; PEP = pre-ejection period; ACI = acceleration index; AGFI = Adjusted Goodness-of-Fit Index; RMR = Root Mean Square Residual.

homeostatic relationships underlying blood pressure regulation (Berne & Levy, 1992) and could not be captured in a unidimensional model.

Other investigations have used multivariate techniques to examine the association among many cardiovascular performance variables (e.g., Albright, Andreassi, & Steiner, 1988; Allen, Boquet, & Shelley, 1991; Fahrenberg & Foerster, 1991; Grossman et al., 1992; Kasprowicz, Manuck, Malkoff, & Krantz, 1990), but only one outside of our laboratory has attempted to derive latent factors based on the associations among observed variables (Kamarck, Jennings, Pogue-Geile, & Manuck, 1994). This latter study (Kamarck et al., 1994) examined the factor structure for five noninvasive measures of stress-related cardiovascular reactivity in a sample of university adult employees and a sample of young adult twins. Consistent with the three-factor model, a two-factor model was developed with one vascular factor and one cardiac factor. Similar to the VAS factor of the three-factor model, DBP and stroke volume loaded primarily on their vascular factor (factor loadings were 0.42 and -0.36, respectively). In addition, similar to the SNS factor of the three-factor model, PEP was important in the definition of their cardiac factor (factor loading was -0.81). Thus, both cardiovascular regulation at rest and cardiovascular reactivity to stressful behavioral challenge may be characterized in terms of vascular and cardiac components. The similarity in the derived models between reactivity and resting cardiovascular hemodynamics suggests that the same underlying factors may be operating, both under challenge and at rest. Moreover, it concluded that the same, potentially pathogenic, processes that are postulated to be revealed during cardiovascular challenge may be observable at rest given sensitive and appropriate methodology. This suggestion is consistent with Porges' (1992) notion that the state of the autonomic nervous system at rest may provide an index of the patient's vulnerability to stress

THE THREE-FACTOR MODEL, AGE, AND BODY MASS

Changes in autonomic and cardiovascular function have been documented with increasing age and body mass, and the epidemiological literature indicates that they strongly reflect risk for development of hypertension and CHD. To study the association between model and measures reflecting cardiovascular risk, factor scores were calculated. The factor scores option in LISREL was used to estimate regression weights for each indicator. The regression equation for the PNS factor was: $X^{PNS} = 0.192^{RSA} + 0.400^{HRV} + 0.432^{HRmax-min}$. The regression equation for the VAS factor was: $X^{VAS} = 0.094^{DBP} + 0.676^{TPR} - 0.207^{STROKE\ VOLUME}$. The regression equation for the SNS factor was: $X^{SNS} = 0.099^{PEP} + 0.671^{ACI}$. The coefficients represent the estimated univariate regression weights when the latent variable was regressed on the observed variables. The observed variables were standardized before being multiplied by these regression weights. In this way, factor scores were calculated for each subject. The factor scores were multiplied by 15, and then 100 was added, giving each factor a mean of 100 and a standard deviation of 15.

Age correlated negatively with PNS ($r = -0.43$, $p < .01$) and SNS ($r = -0.46$, $p < .01$) factor scores and positively with VAS ($r = 0.68$, $p < .01$) factor scores. In summary, the increase in age-related blood pressure ($r^{SBP} = 0.17$, $r^{DBP} = 0.68$, $p < .01$) was associated with decreased contractility ($r^{PEP} = -0.50$, $p < .01$, $r^{ACI} = -0.42$, $p < .01$), diminished cardiac output and stroke volume $r^{cardiac\ output} = -0.61$, $p < .01$, $r^{stroke\ volume} = -0.68$, $p < .01$), and increased vascular resistance ($r^{TPR} = 0.63$, $p < .01$). These relations illustrate that with increasing age, there is a transition toward greater vascular and less cardiac contribution to blood pressure regulation. As noted previously, age was also associated with decreased parasympathetic cardiac input ($r^{HR} = 0.41$, $p < .01$, $r^{RSA} = -0.38$, $p < .01$, $r^{HRV} = -0.38$, $p < .01$, $r^{HRmax-min} = -0.43$, $p < .01$), which is consistent with the previously reported decline in the baroreflex sensitivity with age (Pfeifer et al., 1983). These hemodynamic relations with age are similar to the hemodynamic transition that occurs in the progression of hypertension, as described previously, and is consistent with a large literature assessing cardiovascular regulation in aging (Astrand & Rodahl, 1970; Brandfonbrener et al., 1955; Ebert et al., 1982; Fleg, 1986; Hrushesky, 1992; Julius et al., 1967; Landowne et al., 1955; Luisada et al., 1980; Marshall & Shepherd, 1968; Miyamura & Honda, 1973; Murata et al., 1992; Pfeifer et al., 1983; Rodeheffer et al., 1984; Shannon et al., 1987; Strandell, 1964; Tuck, 1992; Waddington et al., 1978).

Similar to age, BMI correlated negatively with PNS ($r = -0.10$) and with SNS ($r = -0.42$, $p < .01$) factor scores but was positively correlated with VAS ($r = 0.38$, $p < .01$) factor scores. Similar to the age-related increases in blood pressure, the increase in weight-related blood pressure ($r^{SBP} = 0.22$, $p < .05$, $r^{DBP} = 0.24$, $p < .05$) was associated with decreased contractility ($r^{PEP} = -0.25$, $p < .05$, $r^{ACI} = -0.41$, $p < .01$), diminished cardiac output and stroke volume ($r^{cardiac\ output} = -0.33$, $p < .01$, $r^{stroke\ volume} = -0.34$, $p < .01$), and increased vascular resistance ($r^{TPR} = 0.38$, $p < .01$). A positive relation of BMI with heart rate was also observed ($r_{HR} = 0.22$, $p < .05$). These findings are consistent with reports that a central distribution of body fat (i.e., measured as waist-to-hip ratio [WHR]) is associated with lower cardiac output and stroke volume and also higher TPR, reflecting the tendency for the development of a low-flow circulatory state in individuals with increased central body mass (Jern et al., 1992).

THE THREE-FACTOR MODEL
AND ETHNICITY

Differences between the factor scores as a function of ethnicity (non-Hispanic White vs. African American) were examined with a series of one-way analyses of covariance. Ethnicity was used as the grouping variable, and age and BMI were used as covariates. In this manner, comparisons could be made independent of age and BMI. The assumption of homogeneity of regression slopes was met ($ps > 0.11$). Although no significant ethnicity differences in SNS factor scores were observed, Black men had higher VAS factor scores than White men [$F(1,114) = 4.31, p = 0.04$]. Adjusted VAS factor score means were 111.1 and 105.6, respectively, for Black and White men. This finding is consistent with the literature demonstrating that Black normotensive men react with increased peripheral resistance responsivity to active coping challenges known to stimulate beta-adrenergic receptor activity in White normotensive men (Arensman et al., 1989; Dysart et al., 1994; Light et al., 1993; Light & Sherwood, 1989; Saab et al., 1992). However, the groups in our study did not significantly differ on DBP or on TPR, although the TPR values approached significance. In addition, after controlling for the effects of age and BMI, Black men tended to display lower parasympathetic cardiac input, as reflected by PNS factor scores, compared to White men [$F(1,114) = 3.70, p = 0.057$]. Adjusted PNS factor score means were 92.9 and 96.8, respectively, for Black and White men. Examination of the individual variables revealed that HRV and HRmax-min, but not RSA, differed between Black and White men. In summary, for both the VAS and PNS factor scores, the examination of a weighted combination of variables provided information that was not contained in individual variables and uncovered ethnicity differences that were not pronounced when examining component variables independently. Multivariate analysis may therefore be of greatest importance when differences between groups cannot be documented using single variables. Previously, the use of individual variables may have been related to the failure to detect differences in resting blood pressure and systemic vascular resistance between White and Black normotensive subjects in several studies (e.g., Anderson et al., 1988; Fredrikson, 1986; Light, Obrist, Sherwood, Jones, & Strogatz, 1987; Saab et al., 1993). An advantage of using multivariate analysis may be in its increased reliability as documented recently, in which measures were ultimately required to provide the stability of a two-factor pattern (Kamarck et al., 1994).

PREDICTING CARDIOVASCULAR REACTIVITY
TO STRESSFUL BEHAVIORAL CHALLENGE

In psychophysiological research of cardiovascular regulation, it is well established that stereotypically different patterns of underlying hemodynamic responses (i.e., cardiac output, TPR, or mixed) supporting the induced blood pressure increases, are produced by tasks with different behavioral demands, which has been termed situational stereotypy (Ax, 1953; Lacey, Bateman, & Van Lehn, 1953; see review Schneiderman & McCabe, 1989). In contrast, individual differences in reactivity to stressful behavioral challenge have been assessed by examining the consistency of response patterning across different stressors, which has been termed individual response specificity (Engel, 1972; Sternbach, 1966). A great deal of effort in psychophysiological research has been placed into characterizing stressors- as to their psychological composition (e.g., active coping vs. inhibitional coping) and the propensity to induce specific patterns of behavioral and cardiovascular response (Schneiderman & McCabe, 1989). Some investigators have speculated that there may be subgroups of reactors that may vary in their propensity to display consistently cardiac or vascular patterns in response to all stressful challenges (e.g., Allen et al., 1991; Kasprowicz et al., 1990; Manuck, 1994). Although it is well accepted in the physiological literature that the cardiovascular system is regulated within the context of the homeostasis of the organism (Guyton, 1981), little of the psychophysiological endeavor has focused on whether individual differences in cardiovascular reactivity is accounted for by the individuals' physiological status prior to the onset of the stressor (i.e., baseline). Usually baseline differences are considered an experimental confound or problem (i.e., Berntson, Uchino, & Cacioppo, 1994) rather than a source of explanation of individual differences. The examination of the hypothesis that cardiovascular reactivity is a marker of cardiovascular disease risk has yet to reveal what physiological variables might be related to both reactivity and cardiovascular disease. The multidimensional approach to assessing autonomic mediation of cardiovascular regulation may assist in the detection of underlying mechanisms that are both more reliable and valid as physiological-homeostatic processes than the cardiovascular measures, which they influence and may provide information that was previously obscured by the study of individual variables.

Therefore, as presented earlier, an examination of a subset of the data on which the three-factor model was derived was undertaken. Assessed was whether the three-factor model would reveal individual differences in resting cardiovascular functioning, and individual differences in cardiovascular reactivity to stressful behavioral challenge. Subjects ($N = 96$) were pooled from two of the studies (Saab et al., 1992; Saab et al., 1997) in which the same stressor paradigm and experimental methodology were used. The response patterning of the stressors (i.e., speech preparation and mirror tracing) have been characterized previously (Hurwitz, Nelesen et al., 1993) as inducing an active coping–cardiac output response pattern and an inhibitory coping–vascular resistance response pattern, respectively; the delivery of the speech (i.e., speech talk) typically induces a mixed cardiac and vascular response pattern. The stressors were preceded by a 20-minute baseline resting period on which the reactivity scores (change relative to baseline) were calculated. Of these subjects, 58 were White men, and 38 were African-American men, ranging in ages from 25 to 54 years, with the mean age of 38.6 ± 2 years and mean BMI of 25.8 ± 3 kg/m^2. Men in the top quartile (HI) and bottom quartile (LO) of factor scores were compared within each factor. Figure 4.1 displays the mean baseline MAP, cardiac output, and TPR for these groups. Inspection of this figure reveals that the resting cardiovascular profiles were distinguished as a function of the SNS and VAS factors. No difference in cardiovascular profile was observed between HI and LO groups on the PNS factor. However, those individuals who were low in SNS factor scores or high in VAS factor scores exhibited diminished cardiac output [HI vs. LO SNS, $F(1,45) = 14.6, p < .001$; HI vs. LO VAS, $F(1,46) = 177.2, p < .001$], elevated TPR [HI vs. LO SNS, $F(1,45) = 14.6, p < .001$; HI vs. LO VAS, $F(1,46) = 177.2, p < .001$], and elevated MAP levels [HI vs. LO SNS, $F(1,45) = 14.6, p < .001$; HI vs. LO VAS, $F(1,46) = 177.2, p < .001$], relative to their counterpart factor score groups; these hemodynamic resting profiles are characteristic of a low-flow circulatory state, with cardiac outputs below normal levels. The similarity in resting profiles in both the LO SNS and HI VAS groups would suggest that these groups would possibly have the same or similar group membership. However, only 50% of the LO SNS group were also members of the HI VAS group.

Blood pressure and heart rate reactivity did not differ as a function of PNS or VAS factor HI or LO grouping. However, compared with the HI SNS group, men displaying low SNS factor scores exhibited significantly greater SBP [$F(1,45) = 4.3, p < .05$], MAP [$F(1,45) = 4.4, p < .05$] and heart rate [$F(1,45) = 7.4, p < .01$] reactivity. The LO SNS group also displayed greater DBP reactivity but only during the mirror tracing task [$t(45) = 2.19, p < .05$]. Figure 4.2 depicts the HI and LO SNS factor groups mean change $\pm$ stand error (SE) from prestressor baselines in SBP, heart rate, cardiac output, and TPR. Although no significant difference between HI and LO SNS group was observed in cardiac output reactivity across all three stressors, the difference in SBP between groups may be accounted for by the

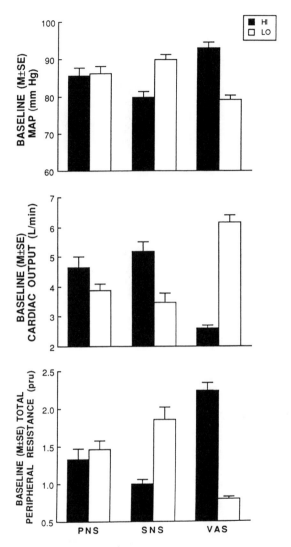

FIG. 4.1. Depicted are the mean ± SE baseline pre-stressor mean arterial pressure (MAP), cardiac output, and total peripheral resistance levels for the top (HI) and bottom (LO) quartile of the three factors of the model: PNS or cardiac parasympathetic, SNS or cardiac sympathetic/inotropy, and VAS or vascular/afterload.

fact that the LO SNS group compared to the HI SNS group displayed greater mean differences in cardiac output during the speech task; respective mean ± SE changes in cardiac output were 0.42 ± 0.18 and 0.18 ± 0.17 L/min. The differences in blood pressure reactivity during the mirror tracing

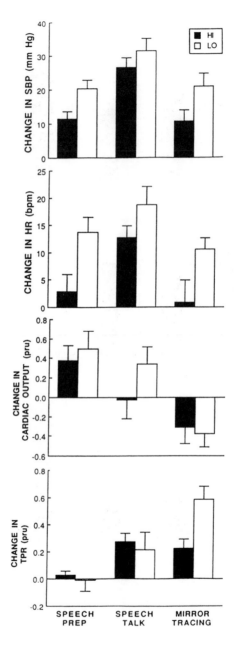

FIG. 4.2. Displayed are the mean ± SE change from baseline pre-stressor levels of the systolic blood pressure (SBP), heart rate (HR), cardiac output, and total peripheral resistance (TPR) responses during three stressor periods: speech preparation, speech delivery or talk, and mirror tracing for the subjects in the top (HI) and bottom (LO) quartile of the SNS or cardiac sympathetic/inotropy factor.

task may be accounted for by the fact that the LO SNS group produced greater TPR reactivity than the HI SNS group, with respective mean ± SE changes in TPR of 0.58 ± 0.1 and 0.22 ± 0.1 peripheral resistance units. Therefore, the LO SNS group was still capable of producing cardiac output and TPR responses and retained the typical situational stereotypy previously observed in response to these tasks. Apparently, the difference in reactivity may be accounted for by differences in the magnitude of the underlying cardiac or vascular responsiveness supporting the blood pressure response.

The presence of reactivity differences in the SNS groups, but not in the VAS, groups further indicates that, at least in terms of predicting cardiovascular reactivity, the LO SNS factor scores are conferring different information than the HI VAS factor scores, even though both groups overlap 50% in group membership, and both groups displayed a low-flow circulatory state at rest. Therefore, individuals with low-SNS factors scores, who by definition have low-resting cardiac contractility, exhibited a low-flow circulatory resting state and also exhibited heightened blood pressure and heart rate reactivity to stressful behavioral challenge. It should also be noted that these differences were observed across all of the stressors, and thus the propensity for individuals with low SNS factor scores to produce more pronounced cardiovascular reactivity occurred regardless of the tendency for the stressors to induce different underlying hemodynamic mechanisms to support the induced blood pressure elevation.

HYPERTENSION AND LOW CARDIAC CONTRACTILITY

The transition to a low-flow circulatory state in the course of the development of hypertension has been documented in longitudinal studies (Lund-Johansen, 1980). Similarities in hemodynamic functioning were observed in the LO SNS normotensive men ($n = 24$) when compared to a group of borderline and mildly hypertensive men ($n = 11$), who were untreated or treated with calcium antagonists or angiotensin converting enzyme inhibitors. The hypertensive men were significantly older than the LO SNS normotensive men, [$t(33) = 2.418, p < .05$], although the mean difference was only a few years; respectively, mean ± SE age was 50.7 ± 7 and 44.5 ± 7 years. Only the VAS factor scores significantly differed between groups, [$t(33) = 2.293, p < .05$], with the hypertensive men displaying greater systemic vascular resistance. The respective mean ± SE factor score values for the hypertensive and LO SNS groups for the SNS factor were 83.3 ± 5 and 76.2 ± 1, for the VAS were 135.0 ± 4 and 118.6 ± 4, and for the PNS factor were 96.8 ± 2 and 92.6 ± 2. Similar low-flow circulatory patterns were observed at rest for both groups, but as expected, the hypertensive men displayed significantly greater MAP, $[t(33) = 4.538, p < .01]$ and TPR, $[t(33) = 2.056, p < .05]$ than the LO SNS men; no difference in resting cardiac output was observed. The respective mean (SE values for the hypertensive and LO SNS groups for MAP were 106.6 ± 3 and 89.8 ± 1 mmHg, for TPR were 2.5 ± 0.3 and 1.9 ± 0.2 pru, and for cardiac output were 2.9 ± 0.3 and 3.5 ± 0.3 L/min. The hypertensive men participated in a protocol in which a 30-minute-baseline period preceded the speech-preparation challenge. Comparison of the blood pressure and heart rate reactivity between the LO SNS group and the hypertensive group revealed no significant differences. The respective mean $\pm$ SE values for the hypertensive and LO SNS groups for change in SBP were 21.5 ± 4 and 20.4 ± 2 mmHg, for change in DBP were 6.0 ± 1 and 7.4 ± 2 mmHg, and for change in heart rate were 12.9 ± 2 and 13.8 ± 3 bpm. Therefore, both hypertensive men and normotensive men with low SNS factor scores displayed similar factors scores, diminished contractility, low-flow circulatory state, and heightened cardiovascular reactivity.

CONCLUSION

Using noninvasive and quantitative methodology we have developed a three-factor model of resting cardiovascular regulation that appears to reflect parasympathetic, sympathetic, and vascular status. The three dimensions of the model included a cardiac sympathetic/inotropy factor, a cardiac parasympathetic factor, and a vascular factor. Replication and validation of the three-factor model is necessary to establish the model's robustness. In addition, the sample was limited to men only because insufficient numbers of women had been included in the studies where the data was drawn. There have been no studies that indicate that autonomic mediation of cardiovascular regulation is substantively different in women than men, although some differences have been noted previously (e.g., Freedman, Sabharwal & Desai, 1987; Girdler, Turner, Sherwood, & Light, 1990; Hurwitz, Nelesen et al., 1993). Therefore, the present findings need to be replicated in women.

However, the examination of a weighted combination of variables in the three factor model provided information that was not contained in individual variables. The significant associations among factors in the model with age and with body mass index, which are measures that reflect cardiovascular disease risk, and the distinctions among factor scores as a function of ethnicity contribute to the external validity of the model. In addition, more than a two-fold heightened magnitude of blood pressure and heart rate reactivity is predicted by low-SNS factor scores, suggesting that diminished resting cardiac contractility may be an important consideration when examining individual differences in cardiovascular responsiveness to stressful behavioral challenge. Moreover, diminished resting cardiac contractility accompanied by a low-flow circulatory state and heightened cardiovascular reactivity are three cardiovascular characteristics common to both hypertensive men and men with low-SNS factor scores. Thus, these findings may provide evidence of the model's predictive utility in reflecting preclinical risk of cardiovascular disease.

In conclusion, the literature shows that hemodynamic patterns of resting cardiovascular regulation may be intrinsically related to cardiovascular disease process. The transition to a low-flow circulatory state may be the hallmark of cardiovascular disease. The possibility that the transitioning of resting hemodynamic function to a low-flow circulatory state may be indicative of nonclinically detectable cardiovascular disease supports the notion that the quantitative method advanced above may be valuable in disease detection, prediction, and prevention.

ACKNOWLEDGMENT

This research was supported by research grants (HL36588, HL50183) and a training grant (T32 HL04726) from the National Heart, Lung, and Blood Institute of the National Institutes of Health.

REFERENCES

Albright, G. L., Andreassi, J. L., & Steiner, S. S. (1988). Interactive effects of Type A personality and psychological and physical stressors on human cardiovascular functions. *International Journal of Psychophysiology, 6*, 315–326.

Alexander, J. K. (1964). Obesity and cardiac performance. *American Journal of Cardiology, 14*, 860–865.

Allen, M. T., Boquet, A. J., & Shelley, K. S. (1991). Cluster analyses of cardiovascular responsivity to three laboratory stressors. *Psychosomatic Medicine, 53*, 272–288.

Anderson, E. A., Balon, T. W., Hoffman, R. P., Sinkey, C.A., & Mark, A. L. (1992). Insulin increases sympathetic activity but not blood pressure in borderline hypertensive humans. *Hypertension, 19*, 621–627.

Anderson, E. A., Hoffman, R. P., Balon, T. W., Sinkey, C. A., & Mark, A. L. (1991). Hyperinsulinemia produces both sympathetic neural activation and vasodilation in normal humans. *Journal of Clinical Investigation, 87*, 2246–2252.

Anderson, N. B., Lane, J. D., Monou, H., Williams, R. B., & Houseworth, S. J. (1988). Racial differences in cardiovascular reactivity to mental arithmetic. *International Journal of Psychophysiology, 6*, 161–164.

Anderson, N. B., Lane, J. D., Taguchi, F., & Williams, R. B. (1989). Patterns of cardiovascular responses to stress as a function of race and parental hypertension in men. *Health Psychology, 8,* 525–540.

Anderson, N. B., Lane, J. D., Taguchi, F., Williams, R. B., & Houseworth, S. J. (1989). Parental history of hypertension, and patterns of cardiovascular reactivity in women. *Psychophysiology, 26,* 39–47.

Anderson, N. B., & McNeilly, M. (1993). Autonomic reactivity and hypertension in blacks: Toward a contextual model. In J. C. S. Fray, J. G. Douglas (Eds.), *Pathophysiology of hypertension in Blacks* (pp. 107–139). New York, Oxford University Press.

Ardlie, N. G., Glew, G., & Schwartz, C. J. (1966). Influence of catecholamines on nucleotide-induced platelet aggregation. *Nature, 212,* 415–417.

Arensman, F. W., Treiber, F. A., Gruber, M. P., & Strong, W. B. (1989). Exercise induced differences in cardiac output, blood pressure and systemic vascular resistance in healthy biracial population of ten-year-olds. *American Journal of Disease in Children, 143,* 212–216.

Ashley, R. W., & Kannel, W. B. (1974). Relation of weight changes to changes in atherogenic traits. The Framingham Study. *Journal of Chronic Disease, 27,* 103–104.

Astrand, P. O., & Rodahl, K. (1970). *Textbook of work physiology.* New York: McGraw-Hill.

Ax, A. (1953). The physiological differentiation between fear and anger in humans. *Psychosomatic Medicine, 15,* 433–442.

Baron, A. D. (1993). Cardiovascular actions of insulin. *Ballieres Clinical Endocrinology and Metabolism, 7,* 961–987.

Baron, A. D., Brechtel-Hook, G., Johnson, A., & Hardin, D. (1993). Skeletal muscle blood flow: A possible link between insulin resistance and blood pressure. *Hypertension, 21,* 129–135.

Barrett-Connor, E. (1985). Obesity, atherosclerosis, and coronary artery disease. *Annals of Internal Medicine, 103,* 1010–1019.

Bentler, P. M., & Bonett, D. G. (1980). Significance tests and goodness of fit in the analysis of covariance structures. *Psychological Bulletin, 88,* 588–606.

Berne, R. M., & Levy, M. N. (1992). *Cardiovascular physiology* (6th ed.). Chicago: Mosby.

Berntson, G. G., Cacioppo, J. T., & Quigley, K.. S. (1993). Respiratory sinus arrhythmia: Autonomic origins, physiological mechanisms, and psychophysiological implications. *Psychophysiology, 30,* 183–196.

Berntson, G. G., Uchino, B. N. & Cacioppo, J. T. (1994). Origins of baseline variance and the Law of Initial Values. *Psychophysiology, 31,* 204–210.

Bollen, K. A. (1989). *Structural equations with latent variables.* New York: John Wiley and Sons.

Borhani, N. O. (1977). Epidemiology of coronary heart disease. In E. A. Amsterdam, J. H. Wilmore, & A. N. Demaria (Eds.), *Exercise in cardiovascular health and disease* (pp. 1–12). New York: Yorke Medical Books.

Brandfonbrener, M., Landowne, M., & Shock, N. (1955). Changes in cardiac output with age. *Circulation, 12,* 557–566.

Braunwald, E. & Grossman, W. (1992). Clinical aspects of heart failure. In E. Braunwald (Ed.), *Heart disease: A textbook of cardiovascular medicine* (4th ed., pp. 444–463). Philadelphia: W. B. Saunders.

Calhoun, D. A., Mutinga, M. L., Wyss, J. M., & Oparil, S. (1994). Muscle sympathetic nervous system activity in Black and Caucasian hypertensive subjects. *Journal of Hypertension, 12,* 1291–1296.

Canizares, C., Vivar, N., & Herdoiza, M. (1994). Role of the microtubular system in platelet aggregation. *Brazilian Journal of Biological Results, 27*(7), 1533–1551.

Christensen, N. J., Hilsted, J., Hegedus, L., & Madsbad, S. (1984). Effects of surgical stress and insulin on cardiovascular function and norepinephrine kinetics. *American Journal of Physiology, 247*, E29–E34.

Collins, R., Peto, R., MacMahon, S., Herbert, P., Fiebach, N. H., Eberlein, K. A., Godwin, J., Qizilbash, N., Taylor, J. O. & Hennekens, C. H. (1990). Blood pressure, stroke, and coronary heart disease: Part 2. Short-term reduction in blood pressure: Overview of randomized drug trials in their epidemiological context. *Lancet, 335*, 827–838.

DeFronzo, R. A., Gunnarsson, R., Bjorkman, O., Olsson M. & Wahren, J. (1985). Effects of insulin on peripheral and splanchnic glucose metabolism in non-insulin dependent diabetes mellitus. *Journal of Clinical Investigation, 76*, 149–155.

Diebert, D. C., & DeFronzo, R. A. (1980). Epinephrine-induced insulin resistance in man. *Journal of Clinical Investigation, 65*, 717–721.

Dimsdale, J. E., Graham, R. M., Ziegler, M. G., Zusman, R. M., & Berry, C. C. (1987). Age, race, diagnosis, and sodium effects on the pressor response to infused norepinephrine. *Hypertension, 10*, 564–569.

Dimsdale, J. E., Herd, A., & Hartley, L. H. (1983). Epinephrine mediated increases in plasma cholesterol. *Psychosomatic Medicine, 45*, 227–232.

Dornfeld, L. P., Maxwell, M. H., Waks, A., & Tuck, M. (1987). Mechanisms of hypertension in obesity. *Kidney International Supplement, 22*, S254–258.

Drummond, P. D. (1990). Parasympathetic cardiac control in mild hypertension. *Journal of Hypertension, 8*, 383–387.

Ducimetire, P., Eschwege, E., Papoz, L., Richard, J. L., Claude, J. R., & Rosselin, G. (1980). Relationship of plasma insulin levels to the incidence of myocardial infarction and coronary heart disease mortality in a middle-aged population. *Diabetologia, 19*, 205–210.

Ducimetire, P., Richard, J., Cambien, F., Avons, P., & Jacqueson, A. (1985). Relationships between adiposity measurements and the incidence of coronary heart disease in middle-aged male population—The Paris Prospective Study I. In J. Vague, P. Bjorntorp, B. Guy-Grand, M. Rebuffe-Scrive, & P. Vague (Eds.), *Metabolic complications of human obesities* (pp. 31–38). New York: Elsevier.

Dysart, J. M., Treiber, F. A., Pflieger, K., Davis, H., & Strong, W. B. (1994). Ethnic differences in the myocardial and vascular reactivity to stress in normotensive girls. *American Journal of Hypertension, 7*, 15–22.

Ebert, T. J., Hughes, C. V., Tristani, F. E., Barney, J. A., & Smith, J. J. (1982). Effect of age and coronary heart disease on the circulatory responses to graded lower body negative pressure. *Cardiovascular Research, 16*, 663–669.

Eliot, R. S., Buell, J. C., & Dembroski, T. M. (1982). Bio-behavioral perspectives on coronary heart disease, hypertension, and sudden cardiac death. *Acta Medica Scandinavica, 13* (Suppl. 606), 203–219.

Engel, B. T. (1972). Response Specificity. In N. S. Greenfield & R. A. Sternbach (Eds.), *Handbook of psychophysiology* (pp. 571–576). New York: Holt, Rinehart, & Winston.

Ewing, D. J., Borsey, D. Q., Bellavere, F., & Clarke, B. F. (1981). Cardiac autonomic neuropathy in diabetes: comparison of measure of RR-interval variation. *Diabetologia, 21*, 18.

Fagius, J., Niklasson, F., & Berne, C. (1986). Sympathetic outflow in human muscle nerves increases during hypoglycemia. *Diabetes, 35*, 1124–1129.

Fahrenberg, J., & Foerster, F. (1991). A multiparameter study of non-invasive cardiovascular assessment. *Journal of Psychophysiology, 5*, 145–158.

Falkner, B., & Kushner, H. (1989). Race differences in stress-induced reactivity in young adults. *Health Psychology, 8*, 613–627.

Falkner, B., Onesti, G., Angelakos, E. T., Fernandes, M., & Langman, C. (1979). Cardiovascular response to mental stress in normal adolescents with hypertensive parents. *Hypertension, 1*, 23–30.

Flamenbaum, W., Weber, M. A., McMahon, G., Materson, B., Albert, A., & Poland, M. (1985). Monotherapy with labetalol compared with propranolol: Differential effects by race. *Journal of Clinical Hypertension, 75*, 24–31.

Fleg, J. L. (1986). Alterations in cardiovascular structure and function with advancing age. *American Journal of Cardiology, 57*, 33C–43C.

Folkow, B. (1977). Role of vascular factors in hypertension. *Cont Nephrol, 8*, 81–94.

Folkow, B. (1982). Physiological aspects of primary hypertension. *Physiological Reviews, 62*, 347–504.

Folkow, B. (1987). Psychosocial and central nervous influences in primary hypertension. *Circulation, 76* (Suppl I), 110–119.

Frankenhaeuser, M. (1975). Sympathetic-adrenomedullary activity, behavior and the psychosocial environment. In P. H. Venables & M. Christie (Eds.), *Research in psychophysiology* (pp. 71–94). London: Wiley.

Fray, J. C. S. (1993). Hypertension in Blacks: Physiological, psychosocial, theoretical and therapeutic challenges. In J. C. S. Fray, J. G. Douglas (Eds.). *Pathophysiology of hypertension in Blacks* (pp. 3–22). New York: Oxford University Press.

Fray, J. C. S., & Douglas J. G. (1993). *Pathophysiology of hypertension in Blacks*. New York: Oxford University Press.

Fredrickson, M. (1986). Racial differences in cardiovascular reactivity to mental stress in essential hypertension. *Journal of Hypertension, 4*, 325–331.

Freedman, R. R., Sabharwal, S. C. & Desai, N. (1987). Sex differences in peripheral vascular adrenergic receptors. *Circulation Research, 61*, 581–585.

Genovely, H., & Pfeifer, M. A. (1988). R-R variation: The autonomic test of choice in diabetes. *Diabetes/Metabolism Reviews, 4*, 255–271.

Girdler, S. S., Turner, J. R., Sherwood, A., & Light, K. C. (1990). Gender differences in blood pressure control during a variety of behavioral stressors. *Psychosomatic Medicine, 52*, 571–591.

Goldstein, R., Llabre, M. M., Donahue, R. P., Schneiderman, N., Prineas, R. J. & Hurwitz, B. E. (1997). A model of autonomic regulation of cardiovascular function in White, Black, and Cuban Men. *Eighteenth Annual Proceedings of the Society for Behavioral Medicine* (p. S156) San Francisco: Society of Behavioral Medicine.

Gordon, D., Guyton, J. R., & Karnovsky, M. J. (1981). Intimal alterations in rat aorta induced by stressful stimuli. *Laboratory Investigation, 45*, 14–27.

Gorsuch, R. L. (1983). *Factor analysis* (2nd ed.). Hillsdale, NJ: Lawrence Erlbaum Associates.

Grossman, P., Brinkman, A., & de Vries, J. (1992). Cardiac autonomic mechanisms associated with borderline hypertension under varying behavioral demands: Evidence for attenuated parasympathetic tone but not for enhanced beta-adrenergic activity. *Psychophysiology, 29*, 698–711.

Guivernau, M., Meza, N., Barja, P., & Roman, O. (1994). Clinical and experimental study on the long-term effect of dietary gamma-linolenic acid on plasma lipids, platelet aggregation, thromboxane formation, and prostacyclin production. *Prostaglandis Leikot Essent Fatty Acids, 51*(5), 311–316.

Guyton, A. G. (1981). *Textbook of medical physiology*. Philadelphia: Saunders.

Hallback, M. (1975). Consequences of social isolation on blood pressure, cardiovascular reactivity in design in spontaneously hypertensive rats. *Acta Physiologica Scandinavica, 93*, 455–465.

Han, K., Nagel, J. H., Hurwitz, B. E., & Schneiderman, N. (1991). Decomposition of heart rate variability by adaptive filtering for estimation of cardiac vagal tone. *Annual International Conference of the IEEE Engineering in Medicine and Biology Society, 13*, 660–661.

Henry, J. P. (1983). Coronary heart disease and arousal of the adrenal cortical axis. In T. M. Dembroski, T. H. Schmidt, & G. Blumchen (Eds.), *Biobehavioral bases of coronary heart disease* (pp. 365–381). Basel, Switzerland: Karger.

Herd, J. A. (1981). Behavioral factors in the physiologic mechanisms of cardiovascular disease. In S. M. Weiss, J. A. Herd, & B. H. Fox (Eds.), *Perspectives on behavioral medicine* (pp. 55–66). New York: Academic Press.

Hinderliter, A. L., Sager, A. R., Sherwood, A., Light, K. C., Girdler, S. S. & Willis, P. W., IV. (1996). Ethnic differences in forearm vasodilator capacity. *American Journal of Cardiology, 78*, 208–211.

Hirsch, E. Z., Maksem, J. A., & Gagen, D. (1984). Effects of stress and propranolol on the aortic intima of rats. *Arteriosclerosis, 4*, 526.

Hrushesky, W. J. M. (1992). Quantitative respiratory sinus arrhythmia analysis: A simple, noninvasive, reimbursable measure of cardiac wellness and dysfunction. *Annals of the New York Academy of Sciences, 618*, 67–101.

Hubert, H. B. (1986). The importance of obesity in the development of coronary risk factors and disease: The epidemiologic evidence. *Annals of the Review of Public Health, 7*, 493–502.

Hurwitz, B. E., Massie, C. A., Llabre, M. M. & Schneiderman, N. (1993). Autonomic Balance: A factor analysis of resting cardiovascular regulation reveals high risk cardiovascular profiles. *Psychophysiology, 30*, S36.

Hurwitz, B. E., Nelesen, R. A., Saab, P. G., Nagel, J. H., Spitzer, S. B., Gellman, M. D., McCabe, P. M., Phillips, D. J., & Schneiderman, N. (1993). Differential patterns of dynamic cardiovascular regulation as a function of task. *Biological Psychology, 36*, 75–95.

Hurwitz, B. E., Quillian, R. E., Marks, J. B., Agramonte, R., Freeman, C. R., LaGreca, A. M., Schneiderman, N., & Skyler, J. S. (1994). Resting parasympathetic status and cardiovascular response to orthostatic and psychological challenge in Type I insulin-dependent diabetes mellitus. *International Journal of Behavioral Medicine, 1*, 137–162.

Hurwitz, B.E. & Schneiderman, N. (1998). Cardiovascular reactivity and its relation to cardiovascular disease. In D. Krantz & A. Baum (Eds.), *Technology and methodology in behavioral medicine* (pp. 245–273). Mahwah, NJ: Lawrence Erlbaum Associates.

Jamieson, G. A., Agrawal, A. K., Greco, N. J., Tenner, T. E., Jones, G. D., Rice, K. C., Jacobson, A. E., White, J. G., & Tandon, N. N. (1992). Phencyclidine binds to blood platelets with high affinity and specifically inhibits their activation by adrenaline. *Biomechanical Journal, 285*, 35–39.

Januszewicz, W., Sznajderman, M., Wocial, B., Feltynowski, T. & Klonowicz, T. (1979). The effect of mental stress on catecholamines, their metabolites and plasma renin activity in patients with essential hypertension and in healthy subjects. *Clinical Science, 57* (Suppl. 5), 229–231.

Jern, S., Bergbrant, A., Bjontorp, P., & Hansson, L. (1992). Relation of central hemodynamics to obesity and body fat distribution. *Hypertension, 19*, 520–527.

Joreskog K. G., & Sorbom, D. (1989). *LISREL 7: A guide to the program and applications* (2nd ed.). Chicago: SPSS, Inc.

Juhlin-Dannfelt, A., Frisk-Holmberg, F., Jarlsson, J., & Tesch, P. (1979). Central and peripheral circulation in relation to muscle-fibre composition in normo- and hyper-tensive man. *Clinical Science, 56*, 335–340.

Julius, S. (1988). The blood pressure seeking properties of the central nervous system: Editorial review. *Journal of Hypertension, 6*, 177–185.

Julius, S., Amery, A., Whitlock, L. S., & Conway, J. (1967). Influence of age on the hemodynamic response to exercise. *Circulation, 36,* 222–230.

Julius, S., Gubdrandsson, T., Jamerson, K., & Andersson, O. (1992). The interconnection between sympathetics, microcirculation, and insulin resistance in hypertension. *Blood Pressure, 1,* 9–19.

Julius, S., Gubdrandsson, T., Jamerson, K., Shahab, S. T., & Andersson, O. (1991). Hypothesis: The hemodynamic link between insulin resistance and hypertension. *Journal of Hypertension, 9,* 983–986.

Julius, S., Pascual, A. V., Sannerstedt, R., & Mitchell, C. (1971). Relationship between cardiac output and peripheral resistance in borderline hypertension. *Circulation, 43,* 382–390.

Kamarck, T. W., Jennings, J. R., Pogue-Geile, M., & Manuck, S. B. (1994). A multidimensional measurement model for cardiovascular reactivity: Stability and cross-validation in two adults samples. *Health Psychology, 13*(6), 471–478.

Kannel, W. B., McGee, D., & Gordon, T. (1976). A general cardiovascular risk profile: The Framingham Study. *American Journal of Cardiology, 38,* 46–51.

Kaplan, N. M. (1989). The deadly quartet: Upper-body obesity, glucose intolerance, hypertriglyceridemia and hypertension. *Archives of Internal Medicine, 149,* 1514–1520.

Kaplan, J. R., Manuck, S. B., Adams, M. R., & Clarkson, T. B. (1987). The effects of beta-adrenergic blocking agents on atherosclerosis and its complications. *European Heart Journal, 8,* 928–944.

Kaplan, J. R., Manuck, S. B., Adams, M. R., Weingand, K. W., & Clarkson, T. B. (1987). Inhibition of coronary atherosclerosis by propranolol in behaviorally predisposed monkeys fed an atherogenic diet. *Circulation, 76,* 1364–1372.

Kaplan, J. R., Manuck, S. B., Clarkson, T. B., Lusso, F., & Taub, D. M. (1982). Social status, environment, and atherosclerosis in cynomolgus monkeys. *Arteriosclerosis, 2,* 359–368.

Karlsson, J., & Smith, H. J. (1984). Muscle fibers in human skeletal muscle and their metabolic and circulatory significance. In S. Hunyor, J. Ludbrook, J. Shaw, & M. McGrath (Eds), *The peripheral circulation* (pp. 67–77). Amsterdam: Elsevier Science.

Kasprowicz, A. L., Manuck, S. B., Malkoff, S. B., & Krantz, D. S. (1990). Individual differences in behaviorally evoked cardiovascular response: Temporal stability and hemodynamic patterning. *Psychophysiology, 27,* 605–619.

Korner, P. I., Bobik, A., Jennings, G. L., Angus, J. A., & Anderson, W. P. (1991). Significance of cardiovascular hypertrophy in the development and maintenance of hypertension. *Journal of Cardiovascular Pharmacology, 17* (Suppl. 2), 25–32.

Krieger, D. R., & Landsberg, L. (1988). Mechanisms in obesity-related hypertension: Role of insulin and catecholamines. *American Journal of Hypertension, 1,* 84–90.

Kubicek, W. G., Witsoe, D. A., Patterson, R. P., & From, A. H. L. (1969). *Development and evaluation of an impedance cardiographic system to measure cardiac output and other cardiac parameters* (NASA-CR-101965). Houston, TX: National Aeronautics and Space Administration.

Lacey, J. I., Bateman, D. E., & VanLehn, R. (1953). Autonomic response specificity: An experimental study. *Psychosomatic Medicine, 15,* 8–21.

Lakatta, E. G. (1979). Alterations in the cardiovascular system that occur in advanced age. *Fed Proc, 38,* 163–167.

Landowne, M., Brandfonbrener, M., & Shock, N. W. (1955). The relation of age to certain measures of performance of the heart and the circulation. *Circulation, 12,* 567–576.

Lapidus, L., Bengtsson, C., Larsson, B., Pennert, K., Rybo, E., & Sjostrom, L. (1984). Distribution of adipose tissue and risk of cardiovascular disease and death: A 12-year follow up of participants in the population study of women in Gothenburg, Sweden. *British Medical Journal, 289,* 1257–1261.

Larsen, P. B., Schneiderman, N., & Pasin, R. D. (1986). Physiological bases of cardiovascular psychophysiology. In M. G. H. Coles, E. Donchin, and S. W. Porges (Eds.). *Psychophysiology: Systems, processes, and applications* (pp. 122–165). New York: Guilford.

Larsson, B., Svardsudd, K., Welin, L., Wilhelmsen, L., Bjorntorp, P., & Tibblin, G. (1984). Abdominal adipose tissue distribution, obesity, and risk of cardiovascular disease and death: 13 year follow up to participants in the study of men born in 1913. *British Medical Journal, 288,* 1401–1404.

Lever, A. F. (1986). Slow pressor mechanisms in hypertension: Role for hypertrophy of resistance vessels? *Journal of Hypertension, 4,* 515–524.

Levine, S. P., Towell, B. L., Suarez, A. M., Knieriem, L. K., Harris, M. M., & George, J. N. (1985). Platelet activation and secretion associated with emotional stress. *Circulation, 71,* 1129–1134.

Lewis, R. P., Rittgers, S. E., Forester, W. F., & Boudoulas, H. (1977). A critical review of the systolic time intervals. *Circulation, 56,* 146–158.

Liang, C. S., Doherty, J. V., Faillace, R., Mackawa, K., Arnold, S., Gavias, H., & Hood, W. B., Jr. (1982). Insulin infusion in conscious dogs: Effects on systemic and coronary hemodynamics, regional blood flows and plasma catecholamines. *Journal of Clinical Investigation, 69,* 1321–1336.

Licata, G., Scaglione, R., Capuana, G., Parrinello, G., Di Vicenzo, D., & Mazzola, G. (1990). Hypertension in obese subjects: Distinct hypertensive subgroup. *Journal of Human Hypertension, 4,* 3741.

Light, K. C., Obrist, P. A., Sherwood, A., James, S. A., & Strogatz, D. S. (1987). Effects of race and marginally elevated blood pressure on response to stress. *Hypertension, 10,* 555–563.

Light, K. C., & Sherwood, A. (1989). Race, borderline hypertension, and hemodynamic responses to behavioral stress before and after beta-adrenergic blockade. *Health Psychology, 8,* 577–595.

Light, K. C., Turner, J. R., Hinderliter, A., Girdler, S. S., & Sherwood, A. (1994). Comparison of cardiac versus vascular reactors and ethnic groups in plasma epinephrine and norepinephrine responses to stress. *International Journal of Behavioral Medicine, 1*(3), 229–246.

Light, K. C., Turner, J. R., Hinderliter, A., & Sherwood, A. (1993). Race and gender comparisons: I. Hemodynamic responses to a series of stressors. *Health Psychology, 12*(5), 354–365.

Luisada, A. A., Bhat, P. K., & Bioeng, V. K. (1980). Changes of cardiac output caused by aging: An impedance cardiographic study. *Angiology, 31*(2), 75–81.

Lund-Johansen, P. (1980). Haemodynamics in essential hypertension. *Clinical Science, 59,* 343–354.

Manuck, S. B. (1994). Cardiovascular reactivity in cardiovascular disease: "Once more unto the breach." *International Journal of Behavioral Medicine, 1,* 4–31.

Manuck, S. B., Kaplan, J. R., & Matthews, K. A. (1986). Behavioral antecedents of coronary heart disease and atherosclerosis. *Atherosclerosis, 6,* 2–14.

Marks, J. B., Hurwitz, B. E., Ansley, J., Quillian, R. E., Thompson, N. E., Olsson-Istel, G. M., Spitzer, S., Schneiderman, N., & Skyler, J. S. (1991). Effects of induced hyperinsulinemia on blood pressure and sympathetic tone in healthy volunteers. *Diabetes, 40,* (Suppl. 1), 367A.

Marshall, R. J., & Shepherd, J. T. (1968). *Cardiac function in health and disease.* Saunders, Philadelphia-London-Toronto.

Mason, J. W. (1975). A historical view of the stress field: Part II. *Journal of Human Stress, 1*(2), 22–36.

Massie, C.A., (1994). Cardiac, autonomic balance: A confirmatory factor analysis of estimates of autonomic mediation of cardiovascular function in African-American and White men at rest. *Dissertation Abstracts International: Section B: The sciences & Engineering, 54, (11-B),* 5948.

Matta, R. J., Lawler, J. E., & Lown, B. (1976). Ventricular electrical instability in the conscious dog. *The American Journal of Cardiology, 38,* 594–598.

McAdoo, W. G., Weinberger, M. H., Miller, J. Z., Fineberg, N. S., & Grim, C. E. (1990). Race and gender influence hemodynamic responses to psychological and physical stimuli. *Journal of Hypertension, 8,* 961–967.

McDermott, D. J., Stekiel, W. J., Barboriak, J. J., Kloth, L. C., & Smith, J. J. (1974). Effect of age on hemodynamic and metabolic response to static exercise. *Journal of Applied Physiology, 37,* 923–926.

McDermott, D. J., Tristani, F. E., Ebert, T. J., Porth, C. J., & Smith J. J. (1980). Age-related changes in cardiovascular responses to diverse circulatory stresses. In P. Sleight (Ed.), *Arterial baroreceptors and hypertension* (pp. 361–364). Oxford: Oxford University Press.

Messerli, F. H., De Carvalho, J. G. R., Christie, B., & Frolich, E. D. (1978). Systemic and regional hemodynamics in low, normal and high cardiac output borderline hypertension. *Circulation, 58,* 441–448.

Messerli, F. H., Christie, B., DeCarvalho, J. G. R., Aristimuno, G. G., Suarez, D. H., Dreslinski, G. R., & Frohlich, E. D. (1981). Obesity and essential hypertension. *Archives of Internal Medicine, 141,* 81–85.

Messerli, F. H., Sundgaard-Riise, K., Reisin, E., Dreslinski, G., Dunn, F. G., & Frohlich, E. (1983). Disparate cardiovascular effects of obesity and arterial hypertension. *American Journal of Medicine, 74,* 808–812.

Miyamura, M., & Honda, Y. (1973). Maximum cardiac output related to sex and age. *Japanese Journal of Physiology, 23,* 645–656.

Modan, M., Halkin, H., Almog, S., Lusky, A., Eshkol, A., Shefi, M., Shitrit, A., & Fuchs, Z. (1985). Hyperinsulinemia: A link between hypertension, obesity and glucose intolerance. *Journal of Clinical Investigation, 75,* 809–817.

Murata, K., Landrigan, P. J., & Araki, S. (1992). Effects of age, heart rate, gender, tobacco, and alcohol ingestion on R-R interval variability in human ECG. *Journal of the Autonomic Nervous System, 37,* 199–206.

Nagel, J. H., Han, K., Hurwitz, B. E., & Schneiderman, N. (1993). Assessment and diagnostic applications of heart rate variability. *Biomedical Engineering-Applications, Basis, & Communications, 5,* 147–158.

National Institutes of Health Consensus Development Panel on the Health Implications of Obesity. (1985). Health implications of obesity. *Annals of Internal Medicine, 103,* 1073–1077.

Nelesen, R. A., Dimsdale, J. E., Mills, P. J., & Ziegler, M. G. (1995). Relationship of insulin, race, and hypertension with hemodynamic reactivity to a behavioral challenge. *American Journal of Hypertension, 8,* 12–19.

Peckerman, A., Hurwitz, B. E., Saab, P. G., Llabre, M. M., McCabe, P. M., & Schneiderman, N. (1994). Stimulus dimensions of the cold pressor test and the associated patterns of cardiovascular response. *Psychophysiology, 31,* 282–290.

Pereda, S. A., Eckstein, J. W., & Abboud, F. M. (1962). Cardiovascular responses to insulin in the absence of hypoglycemia. *American Journal of Physiology, 202,* 249–252.

Pfeifer, M. A., Weinberg, C. R., Cook, D., Best, J. D., Reenan, A., & Halter, J. B. (1983). Differential changes of autonomic nervous system function with age in man. *The American Journal of Medicine, 75*, 249–258.

Porges, S. W. (1992). Vagal tone: A physiological marker for stress vulnerability. *Pediatrics, 90*, 498–504.

Pyorala, K. (1972). Relationship of glucose tolerance and plasma insulin to the incidence of coronary heart disease: Results from two population studies in Finland. *Diabetes Care, 2*, 131–141.

Raison, I. M., Safar, M. E., Cambien, F. A., & London, G. M. (1988). Forearm hemodynamics in obese normotensive and hypertensive subjects. *Journal of Hypertension, 6*, 299–303.

Randall, W. C. (Ed.). (1977). *Neural regulation of the heart.* New York: Oxford University Press.

Reaven, G. M. (1988). Role of insulin resistance in human disease: Banting lecture. *Diabetes, 37*, 1595–1607.

Reaven, G. M. (1995). Pathophysiology of insulin resistance in human disease. *Physiological Review, 75*, 473–486.

Reisin, E., Abel, R., Modan, M., Silverberg, D. S., Eliahow, H. E., & Modan, B. (1978). Effect of weight loss without salt restriction in the reduction of blood pressure. *New England Journal of Medicine, 298*, 1–6.

Reisin, E., Frohlich, E. D., & Messerli, F. H. (1983). Cardiovascular changes in obesity after weight reduction. *Annals of Internal Medicine, 98*, 315–319.

Rizzoni, D., Castellano, M., Porteri, E., Bettoni, G., Muiesan, M. L., & Agabiti-Rosei, E. (1994). Vascular structural and functional alterations before and after the development of hypertension in SHR. *American Journal of Hypertension, 7*, 193–200.

Rocchini, A. P., Key, J., Bordie, D., Chico, R., Moorehead, C., Katch, V., & Martin, M. (1989). The effect of weight loss on the sensitivity of blood pressure to sodium in obese adolescents. *North England Journal of Medicine, 321*, 580–585.

Rodeheffer, R. J., Gerstenblith, G., Becker, L. C., Fleg, J. L., Weisfeldt, M. L. & Lakatta, E. G. (1984). Exercise cardiac output is maintained with advancing age in healthy human subjects: Cardiac dilatation and increased stroke volume compensate for a diminished heart rate. *Circulation, 69*, 203–213.

Rowe, J. W., Young, J. B., Monaker, K. L., Stevens, A. L., Pallotta, J., & Landsberg, L. (1981). Effect of insulin and glucose infusions on sympathetic nervous system activity in normal man. *Diabetes, 30*, 219225.

Rozanski, A., Bairey, C. N., Krantz, D. S., Friedman, J., Resser, K. J., Morell, M., Hilton-Chalfen, S., Hestrin, L., Bietendorf, J., & Berman, D. S. (1988). Mental stress and the induction of silent myocardial ischemia in patients with coronary artery disease. *The New England Journal of Medicine, 318*(16), 1005–1012.

Ryan, T. (1991). Dobutamine stress echocardiography. *Coronary Artery Disease, 2*, 552–558.

Saab, P. G., Llabre, M. M., Hurwitz, B. E., Frame, C. A., Reineke, L. J., Fins, A. I., McCalla, J., Cieply, L. K., & Schneiderman, N. (1992). Myocardial and peripheral vascular responses to behavioral challenges and their stability in Black and White Americans. *Psychophysiology, 29*, 384–397.

Saab, P. G., Llabre, M. M., Hurwitz, B. E., Schneiderman, N., Durel, L. A., Wohlgelmuth, W., Massie, C. & Nagel, J. (1993). The cold pressor test: Vascular and myocardial response patterns and their stability. *Psychophysiology, 30*, 366–373.

Saab, P. G., Llabre, M. M., Schneiderman, N., Hurwitz, B. E., MacDonald, P. G., Evans, J., Wohlgemuth, W., Hayashi, P., & Klein, B. (1997). Influence of ethnicity and gender on cardiovascular responses to active coping and inhibitory-passive coping challenges. *Psychosomatic Medicine, 59*, 427–446.

Sato, I., Hasegawa, Y., Takahashi, N., Hirata, Y., Shimomura, K., & Hotta, K. (1981). Age-related changes of cardiac control function in man. With special reference to heart rate control at rest and during exercise. *Journal of Gerontology, 36*(5), 564–572.

Schneiderman, N. (1983). Behavior, autonomic function and animal models of cardiovascular pathology. In T. M. Dembroski, T. H. Schmidt, & G. Blumchen (Eds.), *Biobehavioral bases of coronary heart disease* (pp. 304–364). Basel, Switzerland: Karger.

Schneiderman, N., & McCabe, P. M. (1989). Psychophysiologic strategies in laboratory research. In N. Schneiderman, S. M. Weiss, & P. G. Kaufman (Eds.), *Handbook of research methods in cardiovascular behavioral medicine* (pp. 349–364). New York: Plenum.

Schneiderman, N., & Skyler, J. S. (1996). Sympathetic system regulation, and coronary heart disease prevention. In K. Orth-Gomer, & N. Schneiderman (Eds.), *Behavioral medicine approaches to cardiovascular disease prevention* (pp. 105–134). Mahwah, NJ: Lawrence Erlbaum Associates.

Shannon, D. C., Carley, D. W., & Benson, H. (1987). Aging of modulation of heart rate. *American Journal of Physiology, 253*, 874–877.

Sherwood, A., & Hinderliter, A. L. (1993). Responsiveness to alpha- and beta-adrenergic receptor agonists: Effects of race in borderline hypertensive compared to normotensive men. *American Journal of Hypertension, 6*, 630–635.

Skyler, J. S., Marks, J. B., & Schneiderman, N. (1995). Hypertension in patients with diabetes mellitus. *American Journal of Hypertension, 8*, 100S–105S.

Sowers, J. R., Whitfield, L. A., Catania, R. A., Stern, N., Tuck, M. L., Dornfeld, L., & Maxwell, M. (1982). Role of the sympathetic nervous system in blood pressure maintenance in obesity. *Journal of Clinical Endocrinology and Metabolism, 54*, 1181–1187.

Sternbach, R. A. (1966). *Principles of Psychophysiology.* New York: Academic Press.

Strandell, T. (1964). Circulatory studies on healthy old men with special reference to the limitation of the maximal physical working capacity. *Acta Media Scandanavia, 11* (Suppl. 414), 1–44.

Strawn, W. B., Bondjers, G., Kaplan, J. R., Manuck, S. B., Schwenke, D. C., Hansson, G. K., Shively, C. A., & Clarkson, T. B. (1991). Endothelial dysfunction in response to psychosocial stress in monkeys. *Circulation Research, 68*, 1270–1279.

Sundlof, G., & Wallin, B. G. (1978). Human muscle nerve sympathetic activity at rest. Relationship to blood pressure and age. *Journal of Physiology, 274*, 621–637.

Tafil-Klawe, M., Trzebski, A., Klawe, J., & Palko, T. (1985). Augmented chemoreceptor reflex tonic drive in early human hypertension and in normotensive subjects with family background of hypertension. *Acta Physiologica Polonica, 36*(1), 51–58.

Theroux, P., Waters, D. D., Halphen, C., Debaiseux, J-C., & Mizgala, H. F. (1979). Prognostic value of exercise testing soon after myocardial infarction. *New England Journal of Medicine, 301*, 341–345.

Tischenkel, N. J., Saab, P. G., Schneiderman, N., Nelesen, R. A., DeCarlo Pasin, R., Goldstein, D. A., Spitzer, S.B., Woo-Ming, R., & Weidler, D.J. (1989). Cardiovascular and neurohumoral responses to behavioral challenge as a function of race and sex. *Health Psychology, 8*, 503–524.

Troisi, R. J., Weiss, S. T., Parker, D. R., Sparrow, D. S., Young, J. B., & Landsberg, L. (1991). Relation of obesity and diet to sympathetic nervous system activity. *Hypertension, 17*, 669–677.

Tuck, M. L. (1992). Obesity, the sympathetic nervous system, and essential hypertension. *Hypertension, 19* (Suppl. I), I67–I77.

Tuck, M. L., Sowers, J. R., Dornfield, L., Whitfield, L., & Maxwell, M. (1983). Reductions in plasma catecholamines and blood pressure during weight loss in obese subjects. *Acta Endocrinol (Copenhagen), 102*, 252–257.

U.S. Department of Health and Human Services. (1994). *National Institutes of Health: National heart, lung, and blood institute report of the task force on research in epidemiology and prevention of cardiovascular diseases.* Public Health Service.

Vague, J. (1956). The degree of masculine differentiation of obesities: A factor determining predisposition to diabetes, atherosclerosis, gout, and uric calculous disease. *American Journal of Clinical Nutrition, 4,* 20–34.

Veterans Administration Cooperative Study Group on Antihypertensive Drugs (1982). Comparison of propranolol and hydrochlorothiazide for the initial treatment of hypertension: I. Results of short-term titration with emphasis on racial differences in response. *Journal of the American Medical Association, 248,* 1996–2003.

Veterans Administration Cooperative Study Group on Antihypertensive Drugs (1983). Efficacy of nadolol alone and combined with bendroflumethiazide and hydralazine for systemic hypertension. *American Journal of Cardiology, 52,* 1230–1237.

Waddington, J. L., MacCulloch, M. J., & Sambrooks, J. E. (1978). Resting heart rate variability in man declines with age. *Experientia, 35,* 1197–1198.

Watanabe, T., Kamide, T., Torii, Y., & Ochiai, M. (1981). A convenient measurement of cardiac output by half-taped impedance cardiography. *Japanese Journal of Medical Electronics and Biological Engineering, 19,* 30–34.

Weissler, A. M. (1977). Current concepts in cardiology: Systolic–time intervals. *New England Journal of Medicine, 296,* 321–323.

Welborn, T. A., & Wearne, K. (1979). Coronary heart incidence and cardiovascular mortality in Busselton with reference to glucose and insulin concentrations. *Diabetes Care, 2,* 154–160.

Wenger, A. M. (1941). The measurement of individual differences in autonomic balance. *Psychosomatic Medicine, 3,* 427–434.

Wenger, A. M. (1942). The study of physiological factors: The autonomic nervous system and the skeletal musculature. *Human Biology, 14,* 69–84.

Wenger, A. M. (1948). Studies of autonomic balance in Army Air Force personnel. *Comparative Psychology Monographs, 19,* 240–244.

Young, J. B., & Landsberg, L. (1977a). Stimulation of the sympathetic nervous system during sucrose feeding. *Nature, 269,* 615–617.

Young, J. B., & Landsberg, L. (1977b). Suppression of sympathetic nervous system during fasting. *Science, 196,* 1473–1475.

Young, J. B., Saville, E., Rothwell, N. J., Stock, M. J., Landsberg, L. (1982). Effect of diet and cold exposure on norepinephrine turnover in brown adipose tissue in the rat. *Journal of Clinical Investigation, 69,* 1061–1071.

Ziegler, M. G., Lake, C. R., & Kopin, I. J. (1976). Plasma noradrenaline increases with age. *Nature, 261,* 333–335.

5

Blood Pressure, Appraisal, and Coping With Stressors

Ivan Nyklíček
Ad J. J. M. Vingerhoets
Guus L. Van Heck
Tilburg University, The Netherlands

Essential *hypertension,* defined as sustained high blood pressure for which there is no known physical cause (Pickering, 1990), has generally been acknowledged to be a complex multifactorial disease in which biological, behavioral, and psychosocial factors play a role in its etiology and course (e.g., Davies, 1971; Mann, 1986; Marmot, 1984; Sommers-Flanagan & Greenberg, 1989). In addition, there is accumulating evidence that hypertension and being aware of having elevated blood pressure, in its turn, may influence several psychological functions, including perception, memory, and behavior (e.g., Irvine, Garner, Olmstead, & Logan, 1989; Madden & Blumenthal, 1989), and physiological parameters, including baroreceptor sensitivity (Ditto & France, 1990; Harrell, 1980). These complex interplays imply a dynamic relation between hypertension and various psychological and physiological factors.

One research tradition in this area focuses on the association between experienced environmental stressors and hypertension. A wide range of stressors have been studied, sometimes as an independent variable, like the nuclear accident on Three Mile Island (Baum, 1990), sometimes as a dependent variable, like in studies in which hypertensive patients and normotensives were compared on the number of negative life events experienced (e.g., Myers & Miles, 1981; Osti, Trombini, & Magnani, 1980). However, the results have often been contradictory. Not only have methodological limitations been responsible for the discrepancies but the results may have also been influenced systematically by several psychological sample characteristics, which have often been neglected, like awareness of having hypertension (Nyklíček, Vingerhoets & Van Heck, 1996). Moreover, there are considerable differences among studies in the amount to which the measurements deal with subjective aspects of stressor exposure, rather than merely focusing on objectively established measures, which could account for a part of the inconsistent findings.

In this chapter a brief review is provided concerning studies on the relation between hypertension and objectively derived measures of real-life stressor exposure by comparing exposed with nonexposed groups. Then, studies concerning the relation between blood pressure and self-reports of exposure to psychosocial stressors are discussed. Possible confounders in this relation (e.g., awareness of having hypertension) are addressed. Next, a putative underlying psychological mechanism—defensive coping style—for the associations between hypertension and stressor appraisal are investigated. Evidence in favor of the model proposed is offered by our own recent data. Finally, conclusions and suggestions for future research are given.

BLOOD PRESSURE AND OBJECTIVELY ASSESSED STRESSOR EXPOSURE

In this section, a brief, selective overview is offered of investigations on the relationship between blood pressure and objectively established stressor exposure, that is, studies are discussed in which stressor exposure has been established by other means than self-reports. Included are studies of individuals exposed to acute traumatic events or to chronic stressors.

For example, Ruskin, Beard, and Schaffer (1948) studied subjects who witnessed the 1947 Texas City Explosion. Subjects who experienced this disaster showed elevated blood pressure levels for days after the event. Miasnikov (1961) reported prolonged elevations of blood pressure in Leningrad residents after heavy bombardments of the city in World War II. However, besides the methodological limitations of these early studies, the controversy remains whether such acute disastrous stressor-exposures contribute to the development of hypertension. Another dramatic event that has been studied is the Three Mile Island nuclear accident. This event also had chronic aspects, because the threat of radiation remained for a long time. Baum (1990) has summarized the Three Mile Island studies and demonstrated that, compared with a control group living near another nuclear power plant, Three Mile Island residents exhibited higher levels of blood pressure and catecholamines up to six years after the accident.

Although methodologically often limited, studies on chronic psychosocial stressors have provided evidence for an association between exposure to environmental stressors and elevated blood pressure. This evidence comes from both local and national studies (e.g., Harburg, Schull, Erfurt, & Schork, 1970; Rofé & Goldberg, 1983) and from cross-cultural studies (e.g., Cassel, 1974; Marmot, 1984). For instance, Rofé and Goldberg (1983) found that pregnant women who lived in a high-stress environment (e.g., frequent terrorist attacks) displayed higher blood pressure levels than women living in a low-stress area (e.g., no terrorist attacks). Moreover, the beginning of a war was associated with increased blood pressure in all the women, especially in those living in the high-stress area.

Other evidence of psychosocial effects on blood pressure comes from the well-known study on crowding in prisons (D'Atri, Fitzgerald, Kasl, & Ostfeld, 1981) and from research on objectively derived measures of occupational stressors, like the famous investigation on a sample of air traffic controllers by Cobb and Rose (1973) and the longitudinal study on effects of job-loss on blood pressure by Kasl and Cobb (1970). For instance, recently, Theorell et al. (1991) found that job strain, assessed by an objective job classification procedure, was significantly positively associated with diastolic blood pressure during both work and at night. In all of this, research results indicated that persons exposed to stressors had higher blood pressure levels than nonexposed individuals.

Although this brief literature overview concerning the relationship between exposure to real-life stressors and elevated blood pressure is merely illustrative, it certainly suggests that, overall, the results are in favor of a positive association between objectively established stressor exposure and blood pressure level.

Confounding Variables

When interpreting results of retrospective case-control studies based on self-reports, one should always be aware of the possible presence of biasing mechanisms, like search for meaning, socially desirable responding, denial, and so forth. In this context, two factors, namely awareness of having hypertension and treatment for the disease, which may potentiate the distortion of self-reports of affect-laden matters, are of special interest (Nyklíček et al., 1996).

For instance, in studies in which aware hypertensives have been compared to normotensives and unaware hypertensives with respect to self-reported well-being and physical and psychological symptoms, the former group often had poorer scores than the latter groups (e.g., Irvine et al., 1989; Kidson, 1973; Monk, 1980; Müller, Montoya, Schandry, & Hartl, 1994; Zonderman, Leu, & Costa, 1986). On the other hand, unaware hypertensives have been found to have better scores on these measures than normotensives (Davies, 1970; Kidson, 1973). Similar results have been found when treated hypertensives were compared to normotensives and untreated hypertensives on these measures (e.g., Comstock, & Graves, 1980; Monk, 1980; Goldberg, Tibblin & Lindström, 1972). Whether these outcomes are the result of an effect of awareness or treatment per sé, or whether a third variable is responsible for the effects—such as help-seeking behavior on the part of complainers and neurotics—is of secondary importance. Because of the statistical relationship of variables as awareness and treatment of hypertension with self-report scores, these variables should always be accounted for in studies concerning the relationship between blood pressure and self-reports of affect-laden matters, including stressor exposure.

In the next sections, the focus is on the relationship between blood pressure and three categories of self-reported stressor experiences, namely regarding life stressors, occupational stressors, and physical (painful) stressors.

Life Stressors

The results of studies in which self-reported life changes is the subject of interest, seem rather contradictory. In their classical study, Reiser et al. (1951) found that the occurrence of stressful life situations was associated with both the onset of hypertension and medical complications during the course of the disease. Unfortunately, in this study no control group was included, which is a serious limitation, preventing clear conclusions. Myers and Miles (1981) found that in a sample of low-income Blacks, individuals with borderline hypertension (a part of them was treated for the disease) reported more negative life events than normotensive Blacks. Lal, Ahuja, and Madhukar (1982) demonstrated corresponding results in India; treated hypertensives reported more negative life events than matched normotensives. Also Osti, Trombini, and Magnani (1980) found more negative life events reported by hypertensive patients, compared to a control group of patients with other cardiovascular disorders. In contrast, results from several other studies strongly suggest a negative association between blood pressure and the number of self-reported life stressors. For instance, Svensson and Theorell (1983) found that 18-year-old men with sustained blood pressure elevation reported fewer negative life events than control subjects. Theorell, Svensson, Knox, Waller, and Alvarez (1986) showed that young males with elevated blood pressure reported fewer life stressors than subjects with normal blood pressure readings. Linden and Feuerstein (1983) also showed that untreated hypertensives reported fewer interpersonal stressors and were less depressed than medicated hypertensives and normotensives.

The inconsistencies between the results of these studies may partly be due to differences between the samples of subjects used in these investigations. Studies in which positive associations were found between blood pressure level and reported life events included hypertensive patients, whereas studies in which the association was negative, the subjects were either unaware of their blood pressure (Svensson & Theorell, 1983) or were primarily untreated hypertensives (Linden & Feuerstein, 1983; Theorell et al., 1986). This may be a relevant difference between the studies in the view of the well-known caveat of retrospective bias. As previously discussed in greater detail, treatment and awareness may have an influence on reporting behavior, resulting in a bias of the results due to phenomena such as a search for meaning. The data suggest that, when treatment and awareness are absent, an inverse association is more likely to be found between blood pressure level and self-reported stressor exposure. This is in line with the results obtained in two large studies on occupational stressors in the discussion following (Jenkins, Hurst, & Rose, 1985; Winkleby, Ragland, & Syme, 1988). As Theorell (1990) has stated, persons at risk for the development of hypertension or persons being in an early stage of asymptomatic hypertension (and mostly unaware of it) may tend to have a "noncomplaining" life attitude and under-report stressors.

Occupational Stressors

Inconsistencies in regard to the relationship between blood pressure level and self-reported exposure to stressors have also been found in occupational research. On several occasions, a positive association has been found between blood pressure level and self-reported job stressors (Matthews, Cottington, Talbott, Kuller, & Siegel, 1987; Schnall et al., 1990; Theorell, Ahlberg-Hulten, Jodko, Sigala, & De la Torre, 1993; Van Egeren, 1992). For instance, Matthews et al. (1987) examined the relationship between occupational stressors and diastolic blood pressure among 288 male bluecollar workers. After controlling for a number of potentially confounding variables, it was shown that diastolic blood pressure level correlated positively with various indices of the stressfulness of work conditions, namely poor contact with co-workers, low decision latitude, and overall job dissatisfaction. Schnall et al. (1990) operationalized job strain as the combination of high workload and low-decision latitude. After controlling for confounders, they found that high blood pressure in males, from a wide range of occupations was associated with high job strain. Van Egeren (1992) and Theorell et al. (1993) found similar results using the same operationalization of job strain as Schnall et al. (1990).

In contrast, in other studies, negative associations were reported, often contrary to the expectations of the researchers. For example, Jenkins, Hurst, and Rose (1985) found in their study on 416 air traffic controllers that normotensives who developed borderline or definite hypertension during a three year follow-up reported fewer life stressors, less tension–anxiety, less depression, less burn-out, and more satisfaction with jobs and co-workers than did their colleagues who stayed normotensive. In an extensive study ($N = 1428$), conducted by Winkleby, Ragland, and Syme (1988), San Francisco bus drivers were surveyed as part of an occupational health study. An inverse association was obtained between blood pressure levels and subjects' self-reports of work-related problems. This association remained significant after adjustments for 12 potentially confounding variables. When the analysis was done using only the data of the 1,040 normotensive subjects, again an inverse association was found.

It is difficult to find proper explanations for these inconsistencies. Various sample characteristics, and interactions between them, may have influenced the self-reported rates of stressor exposure. However, there were no systematic differences in sample characteristics, such as age, sex, awareness, and treatment for hypertension, between the studies with positive and negative findings. On the other hand, an explanation may be offered by taking into account another varying factor: the assessment method used to determine the level of stressor exposure. Occupational questionnaires like the Job Content Questionnaire (used in three of the four studies in which positive associations were found (Schnall et al., 1990; Theorell et al., 1993; Van Egeren, 1992), have a strong objective component as suggested by a large interoccupation variance (Karasek & Theorell, 1990; Schnall et al., 1990). In the previous section, it was stated that when measures of stressor exposure are derived objectively, positive associations between blood pressure and stressor exposure dominate the results obtained. Therefore, Theorell et al. (1991) suggested that, in order to obtain positive associations between these variables, stressor measurement has to be as objective as possible. In contrast, as stated by Winkleby et al. (1988), when stressors are assessed via more subjective measures, null or reverse findings are often reported. This explanation is in line with a recent study conducted by Fox, Dwyer, and Ganster (1993). In a sample of 136 nurses, they linked objective and subjective measures of job stressors to blood pressure and cortisol levels. The objective measure of job stressors was the head nurse's ratings of individual nurses' work load. Subjective measures were various self-report question-naires concerning workload, perceived control, the number of stressful events at work, and overall job satisfaction. The intriguing results could be summarized as follows: (a) the objective measure of workload was positively associated with blood pressure level, both at work and at home, (b) job strain (the Karasekian interaction of high-workload and low perceived con-trol) was positively associated with blood pressure level (which is in line with the other job strain studies), (c) the subjective measure of workload did not correlate with blood pressure, and (d) the self-reported number of stressful events at work correlated negatively with diastolic blood pressure levels at home.

Physical Stressors

Evidence for a diminished appraisal of threatening stimuli in hypertensives has also been obtained from pain research. Since the 1980s, a solid body of evidence has been accumulated regarding links between blood pressure and diminished sensitivity to painful stimulation (antinociception). It has been demonstrated that individuals with high blood pressure have a higher pain threshold and pain tolerance than individuals with normal blood pressure, indicating a tendency for hypertensives to perceive these stimuli as less aversive. This has been found for electrical (Elbert, Rockstroh, Lutzenberger, Kessler, & Pietrowsky, 1988; Zamir & Shuber, 1980), thermal (Sheps et al., 1992), and finger pressure pain stimulation techniques (Bruehl, Carlson, & McCubbin, 1992). Moreover, also in normotensive samples an inverse relationship between blood pressure levels and per-ceived painfulness of physical stressors has been found (Bruehl et al., 1992). This inverse relationship has been found in both between-subjects (e.g., Zamir & Shuber, 1980) and within-subjects designs (e.g., Dworkin, Filewich, Miller, Craigmyle, & Pickering, 1979), in animal (e.g., Randich & Maixner, 1984), as well as in human studies (e.g., Sheps et al., 1992).

Evidence has been obtained for the mediation of the baroreceptors in this diminished sensitivity to pain; direct baroreceptor stimulation produced antinociception in rats (e.g., Randich, 1986). It has been hypothesized that baroreceptor stimulation could have this effect via cortical inhibition, which has been found to be associated with diminished pain sensitivity in in-dividuals with elevated blood pressure (e.g., Elbert et al., 1988). These au-thors demonstrated that in students with elevated blood pressure, baroreceptor stimulation elevated their pain threshold, whereas the same procedure had the opposite effect in normotensives. Additionally, the au-thors found a positive shift in negative cortical slow waves during baroreceptor stimulation, suggesting cortical inhibition. This positive shift was related to resting blood pressure, indicating differences in cortical activity during pain between normotensives and hypertensives. The findings of France, Ditto, and Adler (1991) suggest that this hyposensitivity to painful stimuli might be associated with a risk for hypertension. They found that healthy males with a parental history of hypertension showed reduced pain sensitivity to a constrictive thigh-cuff pressure stimulus compared to males without a parental history of hypertension but with the same resting blood pressure values.

Only Rau et al. (1994) found less clear results. As in earlier studies, hypertensives exhibited higher pain thresholds for thermal pain than normotensives. However, for pressure pain this effect was not found. The authors suggested that this might be due to the fact that, unlike in other studies, the pain stimulus was not as inescapable in this study; the subjects could terminate the pain before it became too uncomfortable.

In conclusion, although some inconsistencies have been found regarding results that involved different pain modalities, overall, a good body of evidence exists in support of an association between blood pressure and antinociception, which seems to be mediated by the baroreceptors. Thus, individuals with elevated blood pressure appear to have an altered appraisal of physical aversive stimuli.

Conclusions

The studies using self-reports of stressor exposure in the psychosocial domain show conflicting results. However, when report biasing factors, in particular awareness and treatment, are absent, and the questionnaires are subjective rather than objective, results are more in favor of an inverse association between blood pressure and stressor exposure (Nyklíček et al., 1996). With respect to the appraisal of physical stressors, this inverse association seems well established.

This conclusion contrasts the outcome of the review of the literature based on objectively established stressor exposure in which positive associations predominate. An example of the discrepancy between objective and subjective stress measures in relation to blood pressure is, besides the aforementioned investigation of Fox et al. (1993), the study of Harburg et al. (1970). An objectively established index of stressfulness, namely the area in which the subjects lived, was associated with a higher proportion of hypertension. In contrast, the persons with high blood pressure who were actually living in high-stress areas were more satisfied with their neighborhood than their normotensive counterparts in the same tract, consequently, they judged their area as less stressful than the normotensives.

The discrepancy between results of studies based on objectively established measures of stressor exposure and those of studies using subjective measures needs clarification. Whereas objectively measured psychosocial stressors might contribute to blood pressure elevations, other factors may be responsible for underreporting subjective stress in hypertensive subjects. One explanation for the underreporting by hypertensives may be a repressive–defensive coping style (Nyklíček, Vingerhoets, & Van Heck, 1998). In the next section whether in literature evidence can be found for an association between repressive–defensive coping styles and hypertension is discussed.

In that section, the relationship is investigated between blood pressure levels and defensive coping styles, which may have an influence on the reporting behavior of hypertensives, often via altered appraisal of threatening situations. These coping styles include constructs such as repression, defensiveness, and nondisclosure.

There is much conceptual confusion concerning these constructs. Some researchers have used them as synonyms (e.g., Sommers-Flanagan & Greenberg, 1989), while others have attempted to make theoretical distinctions between them, which however are often mutually incongruous (Paulhus & Reid, 1991; Sackheim, 1988; Tomaka, Blascovich, & Kelsey, 1992). For example, repression is said to be both independent of self-deception (Tomaka et al., 1992), but is also described as a form of self-deception (Paulhus & Reid, 1991; Sackheim, 1988). The Marlowe-Crowne Social Desirability Scale (Crowne & Marlowe, 1964), assessing social desirability, is sometimes called defensiveness and is also used as a part of an operationalization of repression (e.g., Warrenburg et al., 1989). Moreover, this construct was found to reflect both self-deception and impression management (the tendency to give favorable self-descriptions to others; Paulhus & Reid, 1991) but has also been claimed to be independent of self-deception (Tomaka et al., 1992).

Trying to disentangle the various constructs conceptually is beyond the scope of this chapter. The interest here is a common feature that is shared by these defensive coping styles: deception of the self or the other in order to prevent problems or to put the self (in front of others) or the external world (in front of the self) in a more favorable light, regardless of whether the subject is aware or unaware of this. This implies that an individual using these coping styles tends to trivialize negative experiences and not to express negative emotions. In this way, defensive coping might be responsible for distortions of self-reports of stressor exposure.

In the literature on emotional repression and hypertension, many studies have traditionally dealt with the repression of anger and hostility (Ewart, 1991).

Some studies found no relation between repressed hostility and hypertension (e.g., Cochrane, 1973). Other, more recent studies (e.g., Boutelle, Epstein, & Ruddy, 1987; Netter & Neuhäuser-Metternich, 1991) demonstrate that hypertensive patients score higher on repressed aggression than normotensives. As stated previously, however, studies based on patient samples always contain the danger of biases due to awareness, treatment, and self-selection.

In screening studies conducted in general populations, hypertensive samples consist of subjects with high blood pressure, who have just been labeled hypertensive, instead of hypertensive patients. This implies that biases due to treatment or self-selection do not apply here. Thomas and Kirkcaldy (1988) found diminished aggressiveness, dominance, and openness to expression (and depression among females) in young individuals who were just diagnosed as hypertensives in such a screening study. In contrast, Mann (1984) found no evidence for repressed hostility in unaware hypertensives in comparison with normotensives. However, the subjects consisted predominantly of individuals who responded positively to the General Health Questionnaire (Goldberg, 1972), thus admitting having psychological difficulties. Such persons may not have a tendency to repress emotions, including anger. Therefore, the sample may have been too specific to permit any conclusions concerning the general population. Finally, Cottington, Matthews, Talbott, and Kuller (1986) found that among hourly workers, those who suppressed their anger, and reported more uncertain job futures, and dissatisfaction with co-workers had more often elevated blood pressure.

Cardiovascular hyperreactivity has been suggested to be a risk factor for the development of hypertension in two recent prospective studies (Light, Dolan, Davis, & Sherwood, 1992; Menkes et al., 1989). Jorgensen and Houston (1988) investigated whether this risk factor for hypertension could be associated with repression of aggressive feelings. They compared normotensive subjects with a positive family history of hypertension (also a risk factor for hypertension) with normotensive subjects with no family history of hypertension. It was found that systolic blood pressure reactivity was associated with repressed hostility in subjects with a family history of hypertension. These results suggest that repressing of aggression may be associated with a risk factor for hypertension. A similar association has been suggested for repression or denial in general; repressors and individuals with a family history of hypertension who were characterized by denial have been found to be more cardiovascularly reactive than nonrepressors (Jamner & Schwartz, 1986a; Jorgensen & Houston, 1986; Weinberger, Schwartz, & Davidson, 1979).

This section evolves to studies concerning repression (and related concepts) in general (see Table 5.1).

In his review of the literature, Davies (1971) concluded that the relationship between blood pressure and psychosocial factors has often been obscured by self-selection bias and inaccurate measurement methods. According to this author, results from several studies have suggested that high blood pres-

TABLE 5.1

Blood Pressure and Repression

Studies	N^a	Independent Variables[b]	Measurements[c]	Results[d]
		Blood Pressure as Independent Variable		
Davies, 1971	review	HTs vs. Nts	BP; self-report, interview	HTs: emotional inhibition ←
Sapira et al., 1971	34 (m + f)	HT patients vs. NT patients	BP; interview	HTs: emotional denial ←
Tibblin and Lindström, 1972	622 (m)	untreated HTs vs. NTs	BP; a 10-item scale	HTs: emotional denial ←
Sommers-Flanagan and Greenberg, 1989	review	HTs vs. Nts	BP; self-report, interview	HTs: repression ←

(continues)

TABLE 5.1 (continued)

Studies	N^a	Independent Variables[b]	Measurements[c]	Results[d]
		Blood Pressure as Dependent Variable		
Cottington et al., 1985	402 (m + f)	emotional suppression	BP, an 8-item scale	DBP ↑
Jamner and Schwartz, 1986	534 (?)	repression	BP, MC-SDS, WAS	BP-reactivity ↑
Jorgensen and Houston, 1986	122 (m + f)	denial + FH+	BP, MMPI-DS	BP-reactivity ↑
King et al., 1990	120 (m + f)	repression	BP, MC-SDS, TMAS	SBP + SBP-reactivity ↑
Warrenburg et al., 1989	45 (m)	defensiveness	BP, MC-SDS	SBP + SBP-reactivity ↑

[a]The number of subjects in the study, m = male, f = female, review = review article, based on several studies with unknown total number of subjects.

[b]HTs = hypertensives (systolic blood pressure ≥ 140 mmHg and/or diastolic blood pressure ≥ 90 mmHg), NTs = normotensives (systolic blood pressure < 140 mmHg and diastolic blood pressure < 90 mmHg), FH + = normotensives with a family history of hypertension.

[c]BP = blood pressure, MC-SDS = Marlowe-Crowne Social Desirability Scale, MMPI-DS = Denial Scale of the Minnesota Multiphasic Personality Inventory, TMAS = Taylor Manifest Anxiety Scale.

[d]When groups were compared: scores of the first group (mentioned under 'Independent variables') compared to the second group (HTs = hypertensives, SBP = systolic blood pressure, DBP = diastolic blood pressure, BP = blood pressure [systolic and diastolic], HR = heart rate, ↑ higher).

Note. Table reprinted with permission by Overseas Publishers Association.

sure may indeed be related to emotional inhibition when not suffering from these methodological drawbacks. Also, in a more recent review (Sommers-Flanagan & Greenberg, 1989), support was reported in favor of an association between hypertension and the use of psychologically inhibiting mechanisms (i.e., denial and repression), both in patient samples and in samples of unaware hypertensives. For example, Sapira, Scheib, Moriarty, and Shapiro (1971) examined hospitalized patients with hypertension, who were watching two movies about doctor–patient interactions. In one film the doctor was rough and not interested in the patient (the bad doctor), in the other one the doctor was gentle and considerate (the good doctor). Blood pressure and pulse rate were measured during the two films and during an interview thereafter. Hypertensives showed significantly greater pressor and pulse rate responses during the films and during the interview. The most important finding, however, was that the hypertensives tended to deny seeing any differences in behavior between the two doctors (which were clearly seen by the normotensive controls). Thus, hypertensive patients seemed to perceive noxious information less clearly. As Lacey and Lacey (1970) have suggested, cardiovascular pressor responses—which are stronger in hypertensives—may go along with rejection of or nonresponsiveness to the external environment. It is tempting to speculate whether this could concern a causal relationship and, if so, in what direction.

Tibblin and Lindström (1972) found that untreated hypertensives reported less physical and psychological symptoms compared to normotensive controls and treated hypertensives. Moreover, for most symptoms a gradient was found: The higher the blood pressure, the lower the reported frequency of symptoms. These authors therefore concluded that hypertensives "are denying or suppressing their feelings" (p. 139).

In contrast with the studies discussed previously, in several investigations the blood pressure level was the dependent variable. However, the direction of the associations found was not different from those obtained in the former studies. For instance, in an epidemiological study in Michigan (Cottington, Brock, House, & Hawthorne, 1985), suppressed emotion was associated with higher blood pressure in both males and females undiagnosed and untreated for hypertension. Finally, several recent studies (King, Taylor, Albright, & Haskell, 1990; Warrenburg et al., 1989) have demonstrated that repressive individuals have higher resting systolic blood pressure levels and higher systolic blood pressure reactivity in response to a mental challenge than nonrepressive individuals.

Results from the studies concerning the relationship between blood pressure and coping or reporting style reviewed, generally suggest that individuals with elevated blood pressure tend to minimize aversiveness, in particular, concerning their negative emotions and experiences or, to put it differently, tend to be defensive. The issue of causality cannot be resolved from these cross-sectional studies. However, apart from the question, whether the association is a causal one and, if so, what the direction of this causality might be, the importance of the association between blood pressure and defensiveness is that it may explain the observed diminished stressor report rates by an altered appraisal of threatening stimuli or by hiding negative information. To what extent the underreporting may be attributed to one or more of the defensive constructs mentioned in this review (repression, self-deception, denial, etc.) remains unclear, partly due to the definitional confusion. Therefore, elucidating the theoretical and statistical relationship between these constructs, in addition to directly examining the association of these constructs with self-reported stressor exposure, seems desirable in order to be able to construct a design that could discriminate between the various possible hypotheses regarding the role of defensive coping in the underreporting tendency of hypertensives.

In the next section, briefly described is our recent study that provides more direct support for defensive coping as being a potential explanation for underreporting stressors and problems in general in individuals with elevated blood pressure.

DEFENSIVENESS, HASSLE REPORTS, AND BLOOD PRESSURE

We have investigated the relationship between blood pressure, defensive coping, and the amount of self-reported daily hassles. The purposes of this study were to examine the hypothesis that high-defensive people would simultaneously report less daily hassles and demonstrate higher resting blood pressure levels than low-defensive people, when controlling for awareness and other possible confounders.

The subjects were 115 male and 26 female employees from a wide range of occupations, with a mean age of 47.2 years, who volunteered to participate in a periodic (once every 3 years) medical screening. Before their medical examination, the subjects filled out, among other things the following questionnaires: (a) Everyday Problems Checklist (EPCL; Vingerhoets & Van Tilburg, 1994), a checklist assessing the number and impact of all kinds of daily hassles experienced in the past two months; we used a 49-item version; (b) Repressive Defensiveness (RD) subscale (11 items) of the shortened version of the Weinberger Adjustment Inventory (WAI, Weinberger, 1989); and (c) a questionnaire to assess various control variables, such as sex, age, education, smoking, and alcohol consumption. The medical data consisted of systolic and diastolic blood pressure (SBP and DBP), serum cholesterol level, and body mass index (BMI). Analyses of covariance were performed on data of two groups obtained as a result of a median-split procedure on the RD scores: a high-RD group ($N = 70$; 57 males and 13 females), and a low-RD group ($N = 71$; 58 males and 13 females).

A 2 (group) by 2 (sex) analysis of covariance revealed that, after controlling for nine potentially confounding variables, namely BMI, age, level of education, smoking, consumption of coffee and alcohol, exercise, having a physically demanding job, and being labeled as hypertensive, the groups differed significantly with respect to self-reports of everyday problems (F [1, 118] $= 4.24$, $p < .05$) and SBP (F [1, 118] $= 4.47$, $p < .05$), with the high-RD group reporting the fewest daily hassles while displaying the highest SBP (see Figs. 5.1 and 5.2). There were no significant group by sex interactions, indicating that the group main effects were similar for both sexes. No differences between the groups were found with respect to DBP.

These results support the notion that repressive–defensive individuals tend to underreport problems while exhibiting elevated resting blood pressures and, thus, may be considered as further evidence for the notion that defensiveness may be (partly) responsible for the inverse association found between blood pressure level and self-reported stressor exposure.

CONCLUSIONS

Rather than to provide an exhaustive review of the literature, the primary objective of this chapter is to search for possible psychological mechanisms (e.g., appraisal and coping styles) underlying discrepancies found in the literature concerning the relationship between blood pressure and stressor ex-

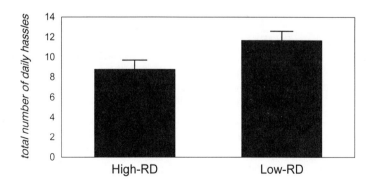

FIG. 5.1.   Means and standard errors of the number of daily hassles reported by the high-defensive (High-RD) and low-defensive (Low-RD) groups.

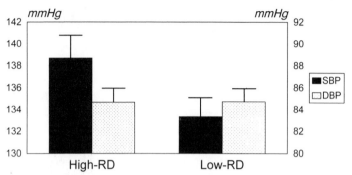

FIG. 5.2.   Means and standard errors of the systolic and diastolic blood pressures (SBP and (DBP) of high-defensive (High-RD) and low-defensive (Low-RD) groups.

posure. Studies concerning this relationship have been reviewed, and possible explanations for the discrepancies found have been offered. Especially the results of studies based on self-reported stressor exposure have often been contradictory, partly because of differences in operationalizations of the concepts studied, and partly because of the confounding effect of awareness of having hypertension and being treated for the disease. Therefore, it has been argued that these variables should always be accounted for in studies concerning the relationship between blood pressure and psychosocial variables. Nevertheless, overall, some striking tendencies in the results were observed.

A discrepancy has been found between the results of studies based on objectively established measures of stressor exposure and those of studies using more subjective measures. Whereas the former studies often showed a positive association between stressor exposure and blood pressure, the results of research based on self-reported psychosocial stressors with a low objectivity level tended to more often yield negative associations between reported stressors and blood pressure levels (Nyklíček et al., 1996). These negative associations have also been frequently demonstrated in studies on self-reported pain as a result of exposure to laboratory physical stressors, such as electric shock and the cold pressor test. A possible explanation is that, whereas objectively measured psychosocial stressors might contribute to blood pressure elevations, other factors related to hypertension may be responsible for the negative associations between blood pressure and self-reported stressor exposure and distress. For the possible role of defensive coping styles (e.g., repression) in the inverse associations previously described, support has been obtained in recent literature. Because of the confusion between the various defensive coping concepts (and related reporting tendencies), it would be desirable to perform studies aiming at elucidating the relationships between constructs such as repression, denial, defensiveness, social desirability, and so forth, in order to develop more specific hypotheses regarding the role of defensive coping in hypertension (Nyklíček et al., 1998) .

The association of high blood pressure with antinociception has frequently been found to be mediated by the activation of the baroreceptors. It might be speculated that CNS inhibition, brought about by baroreceptor activation and possibly opioid mediated, is linked to defensive coping styles. Indirect support for this notion has been offered by studies, in which repression has been found to be related to antinociception (e.g., Jamner & Schwartz, 1986b). The baroreceptor stimulation mediated antinociception has been suggested to play a role in the development of hypertension by a conditioning mechanism. Blood pressure elevation in stressful situations may be learned because it results in baroreceptor activity, mediated CNS-inhibition and subsequently an altered appraisal of the stressor (which becomes less aversive). In this way, frequent exposure to such stressors may potentiate the development of sustained blood pressure elevation in individuals sensitive to the baroreceptor mediated antinociception (Dworkin et al., 1979; Elbert et al., 1988; Randich & Maixner, 1984). If this operant conditioning hypothesis of hypertension would be found to be correct, this could have considerable consequences for hypertension treatment. A behavioral therapy treatment of hypertension, based on simultaneous extinction of the learned blood pressure elevation under stress, together with establishing and reinforcing other aversiveness reducing responses, for instance, by a relaxation technique, may prove to be fruitful (Dworkin, 1988). This treatment could also be applied as prevention in persons at high risk for the development of hypertension.

In future research, it would be desirable to perform research in which blood pressure levels are studied in relation to simultaneously established objective as well as self-reported stressor exposure, appraisal of, and coping with the stressor, as well as simultaneously obtained measures of different defensive coping styles. Furthermore, studies are necessary in which self-reported stressor exposure is directly related to appraisal, defensive coping styles, pain sensitivity, baroreceptor activity, and CNS-inhibition. Preferably subjects who have not yet elevated blood pressure but who are at risk for hypertension—like persons having a family history of hypertension—should be included in future investigations. Needless to say that particularly in all such cross-sectional research potential confounders, like the awareness of having elevated blood pressure, should be controlled for. Finally, besides cross-sectional studies, prospective studies should receive much attention in order to be able to obtain more insight into causal associations.

REFERENCES

Baum, A. (1990). Stress, intrusive imagery, and chronic distress. *Health Psychology, 2,* 653–675.

Boutelle, R. C., Epstein, S., & Ruddy, M. C. (1987). The relation of essential hypertension to feelings of anxiety, depression and anger. *Psychiatry, 50,* 206–217.

Bruehl, S., Carlson, C. R., & McCubbin, J. A. (1992). The relationship between pain sensitivity and blood pressure in normotensives. *Pain, 48,* 463–467.

Cassel, J. (1974). Hypertension and cardiovascular disease in migrants: A potential source of clues? *International Journal of Epidemiology, 3,* 204–205.

Cobb, S., & Rose, R. (1973). Hypertension, peptic ulcers, and diabetes in air traffic controllers. *Journal of the American Medical Association, 224,* 489–492.

Cochrane, R. (1973). Hostility and neuroticism among unselected essential hypertensives. *Journal of Psychosomatic Research, 17,* 215–218.

Cottington, E. M., Brock, B. M., House, J. S., & Hawthorne, V. M. (1985). Psychosocial factors and blood pressure in the Michigan statewide blood pressure survey. *American Journal of Epidemiology, 121,* 515–529.

Cottington, E. M., Matthews, K. A., Talbott, E., & Kuller, L. H. (1986). Occupational stress, suppressed anger, and hypertension. *Psychosomatic Medicine, 48,* 249–260.

Crowne, D. P., & Marlowe, D. (1964). *The approval motive.* New York: Wiley.

D'Atri, D. A., Fitzgerald, E. F., Kasl, S. V., & Ostfeld, A. M. (1981). Crowding in prison: The relationship between changes in housing mode and blood pressure. *Psychosomatic Medicine, 43,* 95–105.

Davies, M. H. (1970). Blood pressure and personality. *Journal of Psychosomatic Research, 14,* 89–104.

Davies, M. H. (1971). Is high blood pressure a psychosomatic disorder? *Journal of Chronic Disease, 24,* 239–258.

Ditto, B., & France, C. (1990). Carotid baroreflex sensitivity at rest and during psychological stress in offspring of hypertensive and non-twin sibling pairs. *Psychosomatic Medicine, 52,* 610–620.

Dworkin, B. (1988). Hypertension as a learned response: The baroreceptor reinforcement hypothesis. In T. Elbert, W. Langosch, A. Steptoe, & D. Vaitl (Eds.), *Behavioural medicine in cardiovascular disorders* (pp. 17–48). Chichester, England: Wiley.

Dworkin, B. R., Filewich, R., Miller, N., Craigmyle, N., & Pickering, T. (1979). Baroreceptor activation reduces reactivity to noxious stimulation: Implications for hypertension. *Science, 205,* 1299–1301.

Elbert, T., Rockstroh, B., Lutzenberger, W., Kessler, M., & Pietrowsky, R. (1988). Baroreceptor stimulation alters pain sensation depending on tonic blood pressure. *Psychophysiology, 25,* 25–29.

Ewart, C. K. (1991). Familial transmission of essential hypertension: Genes, environments, and chronic anger. *Annals of Behavioral Medicine, 13,* 40–47.

Fox, M. L., Dwyer, D. J., & Ganster, D. C. (1993). Effects of stressful job demands and control on physiological and attitudinal outcomes in a hospital setting. *Academy of Management Journal, 36,* 289–318.

France, C., Ditto, B., & Adler, P. S. (1991). Pain sensitivity in offspring of hypertensives at rest and during baroreflex stimulation. *Journal of Behavioral Medicine, 14,* 513–525.

Goldberg, D. P. (1972). *The detection of psychiatric illness by questionnaire* (Maudsley Monograph No. 22). Oxford, England: Oxford University Press.

Goldberg, E. L., Comstock, G. W., & Graves, C. G. (1980). Psychosocial factors and blood pressure. *Psychological Medicine, 10,* 243–255.

Harburg, E., Schull, W. J., Erfurt, J. C., & Schork, M. A. (1970). A family set method for estimating heredity and stress-1. *Journal of Chronic Disease, 23,* 69–81.

Harrell, J. P. (1980). Psychological factors and hypertension: A status report. *Psychological Bulletin, 87,* 482–501.

Irvine, M. J., Garner, D. M., Olmstead, M. P., & Logan, A. G. (1989). Personality differences between hypertensive and normotensive individuals: Influence of knowledge of hypertension status. *Psychosomatic Medicine, 51,* 537–549.

Jamner, L. D., & Schwartz, G. E. (1986a). Integration of self-report and physiological indices of affect: Interactions with repressive coping strategies [abstract]. *Psychophysiology, 23,* 444.

Jamner, L. D., & Schwartz, G. E. (1986b). Self-deception predicts self-report and endurance of pain. *Psychosomatic Medicine, 48,* 211–223.

Jenkins, C. D., Hurst, M. W., & Rose, R. M. (1985). Biomedical and psychosocial predictors of hypertension in air traffic controllers. In C. D. Spielberger & I. G. Sarason (Eds.), *Stress and anxiety* (Vol. 9, pp. 231–238). Washington, DC: Hemisphere.

Jorgensen, R. S., & Houston, B. K. (1986). Family history of hypertension, personality patterns, and cardiovascular reactivity to stress. *Psychosomatic Medicine, 48,* 102–117.

Jorgensen, R. S., & Houston, B. K. (1988). Cardiovascular reactivity, hostility, and family history of hypertension. *Psychotherapy and Psychosomatics, 50,* 216–222.

Karasek, R., & Theorell, T. (1990). *Healthy work: Stress, productivity, and the reconstruction of working life.* New York: Basic Books.

Kasl, S. V., & Cobb, S. (1970). Blood pressure changes in men undergoing job loss: A preliminary report. *Psychosomatic Medicine , 32,* 19–38.

Kidson, M. A. (1973). Personality and hypertension. *Journal of Psychosomatic Research, 17,* 35–41.

King, A. C., Taylor, C. B., Albright, C. A., & Haskell, W. L. (1990). The relationship between repressive and defensive coping styles and blood pressure responses in healthy, middle-aged men and women. *Journal of Psychosomatic Research 34,* 461–471.

Lacey, J. I., & Lacey, B. C. (1970). Some autonomic-central nervous system interrelationships. In P. Black (Ed.), *Physiological correlates of emotion* (pp. 205–227). New York: Academic Press.

Lal, N., Ahuja, R. C., & Madhukar, (1982). Life events in hypertensive patients. *Journal of Psychosomatic Research, 26,* 441–445.

Light, K. C., Dolan, C. A., Davis, M. R., & Sherwood, A. (1992). Cardiovascular responses to an active coping challenge as predictors of blood pressure patterns 10 to 15 years later. *Psychosomatic Medicine, 54,* 217–230.

Linden, W., & Feuerstein, M. (1983). Essential hypertension and social coping behavior: Experimental findings. *Journal of Human Stress, 9,* 22–31.

Madden, D. J., & Blumenthal, J. A. (1989). Slowing of memory-search performance in men with mild hypertension. *Health Psychology, 8,* 131–142.

Mann, A. (1984). Hypertension: Psychological aspects and diagnostic impact in a clinical trial. *Psychological Medicine, 5,* 1–35.

Mann, A. H. (1986). Invited review: The psychological aspects of essential hypertension. *Journal of Psychosomatic Research, 30,* 527–541.

Marmot, M. G. (1984). Geography of blood pressure and hypertension. *British Medical Bulletin, 40,* 380–386.

Matthews, K. A., Cottington, E. M., Talbott, E., Kuller, L. H., & Siegel, J. M. (1987). Stressful work conditions and diastolic blood pressure among blue collar factory workers. *American Journal of Epidemiology, 126,* 280–291.

Menkes, M. S., Mattheuws, K. A., Krantz, D. S., Lundberg, U., Mead, L. A., Quaqish, B., Liang, K. Y., Thomas, C. B., & Pearson, T. A. (1989). Cardiovascular reactivity to the cold pressor test as a predictor of hypertension. *Hypertension, 14,* 524–530.

Miasnikov, A. L. (1961). The significance of disturbances of higher nervous activity in the pathogenesis of hypertensive disease. In J. H. Cort, V. Fencl, Z. Hejl, & J. Jirka (Eds.), *The pathogenesis of essential hypertension* (pp. 153–161). Prague: State Medical Publishing House.

Monk, M. (1980). Psychological status and hypertension. *American Journal of Epidemiology, 112,* 200–208.

Müller, A., Montoya, P., Schandry, R., & Hartl, L. (1994). Changes in physical symptoms, blood pressure, and quality of life over 30 days. *Behaviour Research and Therapy, 32,* 593–603.

Myers, H. F., & Miles, R. E. (1981). Life events stress, subjective appraisal and somatization in hypertension: A pilot study. *Journal of Human Stress, 71,* 17–27.

Netter, P., & Neuhäuser-Metternich, S. (1991). Types of aggressiveness and catecholamine response in essential hypertensives and healthy controls. *Journal of Psychosomatic Research, 35,* 409–419.

Nyklíček, I., Vingerhoets, A. J. J. M., & Van Heck, G. L. (1996). Hypertension and objective and self-reported stressor exposure: A review. *Journal of Psychosomatic Research, 40,* 585–601.

Nyklíček, I., Vingerhoets, A. J. J. M., & Van Heck, G. L. (1998). The under-reporting tendency of hypertensives: An analysis of potential psychological and physiological mechanisms. *Psychology and Health, 13,* 1–21.

Osti, R. M., Trombini, G., & Magnani, B. (1980). Stress and distress in essential hypertension. *Psychotherapy and Psychosomatics, 33,* 193–197.

Paulhus, D. L., & Reid, D. B. (1991). Enhancement and denial in socially desirable responding. *Journal of Personality and Social Psychology, 60,* 307–317.

Pickering, G. (1990). Hypertension: Definitions, natural histories, and consequences. In J. H. Laragh, & B. M. Brenner (Eds.), *Hypertension: Pathophysiology, diagnosis, and management* (pp. 3–16). New York: Raven Press.

Randich, A. (1986). Volume loading hypoalgesia in SHR, WKY and F-sub- I offspring of a SHR x WKY cross. *Brain Research, 363,* 178–182.

Randich, A., & Maixner, W. (1984). Interactions between cardiovascular and pain regulatory systems. *Neuroscience and Biobehavioral Reviews, 8,* 343–369.

Rau, H., Brody, S., Larbig, W., Pauli, P., Whringer, M., Harsch, B., Kröling, P., & Birbaumer, N. (1994). Effects of PRES baroreceptor stimulation on thermal and mechanical pain threshold in borderline hypertensives and normotensives. *Psychophysiology, 31,* 480–485.

Reiser, M. F., Brust, A. A., Ferris, E. B., Shapiro, A. P., Baker, H. M., & Ransohoff, W. (1951). Life situations, emotions, and the course of patients with arterial hypertension. *Psychosomatic Medicine, 13,* 133–139.

Rofé, Y., & Goldberg, J. (1983). Prolonged exposure to a war environment and its effects on the blood pressure of pregnant women. *British Journal of Medical Psychology, 56,* 305–311.

Ruskin, A., Beard, O. W., & Schaffer, R. L. (1948). "Blast Hypertension." Elevated arterial pressures in the victims of the Texas City Disaster. *American Journal of Medicine, 4,* 228–236.

Sackheim, H. A. (1988). Self-deception: A synthesis. In J. S. Lockard & D. L. Paulhus (Eds.), *Self-deception: An adaptive mechanism?* (pp. 146–163). Englewood Cliffs, NJ: Prentice-Hall.

Sapira, J. D., Scheib, E. T., Moriarty, R., & Shapiro, A. P. (1971). Differences in perception between hypertensive and normotensive populations. *Psychosomatic Medicine, 33,* 239–250.

Schnall, P. L., Pieper, C., Schwartz, J. E., Karasek, R. A., Schlussel, Y., Devereux, R. B., Ganau, A., Alderman, M., Warren, K., & Pickering, T. G. (1990). The relationship between "job strain", workplace diastolic blood pressure, and left ventricular mass index. *Journal of the American Medical Association, 263,* 1929–1935.

Sheps, D. S., Bragdon, E. E., Gray, T. F., Ballenger, M., Usedom, J. E., & Maixner, W. (1992). Relation between systemic hypertension and pain perception. *The American Journal Of Cardiology, 70,* 3f–5f.

Sommers-Flanagan, J., & Greenberg, R. P. (1989). Psychosocial variables and hypertension: A new look at an old controversy. *Journal of Nervous and Mental Disease, 177,* 15–24.

Svensson, J., & Theorell, T. (1983). Life events and elevated blood pressure in young men. *Journal of Psychosomatic Research, 27,* 445–456.

Theorell, T. (1990). Family history of hypertension—an individual trait interacting with spontaneously occurring job stressors. *Scandinavian Journal of Work Environment and Health, 16,* 74–79.

Theorell, T., de Faire, U., Johnson, J., Hall, E., Perski, A., & Stewart, W. (1991). Job strain and ambulatory blood pressure profiles. *Scandinavian Journal of Work Environment and Health, 17,* 380–385.

Theorell, T., Svensson, J., Knox, S., Waller, D., & Alvarez, M. (1986). Young men with high blood pressure report few recent life events. *Journal of Psychosomatic Research, 30,* 243–249.

Theorell, T., Ahlberg-Hulten, G., Jodko, M., Sigala, F., & De la Torre, B. (1993). Influence of job strain and emotion on blood pressure in female hospital personnel during workhours. *Scandinavian Journal of Work Environment and Health, 19,* 313–318.

Thomas, W., & Kirkcaldy, B. D. (1998). Personality profiles of adolescent hypertensives. *Personality and Individual Differences, 9,* 297–305.

Tibblin, G., & Lindstrom, B. (1972). Complaints in subjects with angina pectoris and hypertension. In A. Zanchetti (Ed.), *Neural and psychological mechanisms in cardiovascular disease* (pp. 135–139). Milano: Casa Editrice 'Il Ponte.'

Tomaka, J., Blascovich, J., & Kelsey, R. M. (1992). Effects of self-deception, social desirability, and repressive coping on psychophysiological reactivity to stress. *Personality and Social Psychology Bulletin, 18,* 616–624.

Van Egeren, L. F. (1992). The relationship between job strain and blood pressure at work, at home, and during sleep. *Psychosomatic Medicine, 54,* 337–343.

Vingerhoets, A. J. J. M. & Van Tilburg, M. A. L. (1994). *Alledaagse Problemen List (APL)*; [Everyday problems checklist]. Lisse: Swets.

Warrenburg, S., Levine, J., Schwartz, G. E., Fontana, A. F., Kerns, R. D., Delaney, R., & Mattson, R. (1989). Defensive coping and blood pressure reactivity in medical patients. *Journal of Behavioral Medicine, 12,* 407–424.

Weinberger, D. A. (1989). *Social-emotional adjustment in older children and adults I: Psychometric properties of the Weinberger Adjustment Inventory.* Unpublished manuscript.

Weinberger, D. A., Schwartz, G. E., & Davidson, R. J. (1979). Low-anxious, high-anxious, and repressive coping styles: Psychometric patterns and behavioral and physiological responses to stress. *Journal of Abnormal Psychology, 88,* 369–380.

Winkleby, M. A., Ragland, D. R., & Syme, L. (1988). Self-reported stressors and hypertension: Evidence of an inverse association. *American Journal of Epidemiology, 127,* 124–134.

Zamir, N., & Shuber, E. (1980). Altered pain perception in hypertensive humans. *Brain Research, 201,* 471–474.

Zonderman, A. B., Leu, V. L., & Costa, P. T., Jr. (1986). Effects of age, hypertension history, and neuroticism on health perceptions. *Experimental Gerontology, 21,* 449–458.

6

Ethnic Differences
in Blood Pressure Regulation

Patrice G. Saab
Maria M. Llabre
Anita Fernander-Scott
Rachel Copen
Mindy Ma
Vicki DiLillo
Judith R. McCalla
Marisabel Davalos
Carol Gallaher
University of Miami

Varied hypotheses have been offered to explain the difference in hypertension prevalence among Black and White Americans. Etiological hypotheses cover the gamut and implicate such diverse factors as slavery (Wilson & Grim, 1991), evolutionary adaptation to decreased availability of dietary sodium in the regions of origin (Wilson, 1986), pathogenesis of keloid fibroblasts (Dustan, 1995), and low birth weight (Lopes & Port, 1995). Although physiological–biological, nutritional, social, behavioral, and psychological factors have been implicated to explain the Black–White differential (Anderson, Myers, Pickering, & Jackson, 1989), no single factor appears to be sufficient to account for the prevalence rates. Rather, it is likely that the basis for the difference is multifactorially determined.

At the outset, it is important to acknowledge that the following discussion of Black–White differences, as pertains to hypertension and blood pressure regulation, does not assume that group differences are attributable to genetic variation. In the course of this chapter, Black–White differences are referred to as ethnic differences, rather than as race differences. The rationale for this distinction follows from the recommendations of those who contend that the race taxonomy is relatively arbitrary and that there is considerable genetic variation within Black and White groups that may actually exceed the variation between groups (Cooper, 1984; McKenzie & Crowcroft, 1994; Senior & Bhopal, 1994). The literature describing comparisons of Black versus White Americans is considered to have involved ethnic comparisons because the nature of the investigations and the procedures described do not readily lend themselves to genetic analyses or interpretations.

This chapter reviews factors thought to influence blood pressure regulation and shown to distinguish Blacks and Whites. As background, hypertension prevalence and related comorbidities and comortalities are first considered. The impact of salt sensitivity and ethnic differences in sodium metabolism as well as insulin resistance is then reviewed. A discussion of the contributions of social, environmental, and psychological factors on blood pressure follows. Blood pressure profiles and stress-induced cardiovascular responsivity of Blacks and Whites will likewise be compared. This chapter concludes with a discussion of the response to pharmacological and nonpharmacological intervention.

PREVALENCE

Although hypertension prevalence rates among American adults have been declining since the 1960s, hypertension remains a significant health concern. Data available from Phase 1, 1988–1991, of the National Health and Nutrition Examination Survey (NHANES) III estimate the age-adjusted prevalence of hypertension in American adults at 20.4%. Blacks and Whites, however, are differentially affected as respective rates are 30.2% and 19.2%. Among both ethnic groups, age-adjusted prevalence rates are higher for men than women and increase with advancing age (Burt et al., 1995). Although some regional surveys also show higher blood pressures for Black relative to White pediatric-aged groups (e.g., Manatunga, Jones, & Pratt, 1993), this pattern is not supported by national surveys (Gillum, 1996).

Black–White hypertension disparities have also been reported in Britain. The prevalence for Blacks (from West Africa and the Caribbean) is 35% relative to 14% for Whites (Chaturverdi, McKeigue, & Marmot, 1993). Comparative data, examining Caribbean Blacks relative to their US counterparts, indicate that the hypertension rates of Caribbeans, although lower than Americans, exceed 24% across countries (Freeman et al., 1996). It is interesting to note, however, that data from Africa, show that hypertension rates for Blacks and Whites are comparable (Sigola & Adewuyi, 1992). This similarity is consistent with the view that rates in the United States are likely to be affected by social-environmental factors that are not operating in populations living in Africa.

Hypertension-related morbidity and mortality is excessive in Black Americans compared with White Americans (e.g., Eisner, 1990; Kaplan, 1994; Saunders, 1991a). This primarily manifests in cerebrovascular, renal, and cardiovascular complications. Hypertension may lead to cerebrovascular disease by contributing to hemorrhages or ruptures of the cerebral vessels (Chobanian, 1992). Blacks are more likely to incur hemmorraghic and small vessel strokes whereas Whites are more likely to have embolic and large vessel strokes (Alter, 1994). Among hypertensives, Blacks are more prone to suffer strokes than Whites (Eisner, 1990; Modan & Wagener, 1992) and to have higher stroke-related mortality (Gaines & Burke, 1995; Modan & Wagener, 1992; Saunders, 1991a). For individuals 35 to 77 years of age, stroke explains 25% of the Black–White difference in mortality (Gibaldi, 1993). Although stroke mortality rates have been declining since the 1960s across sociodemographic groups, stroke mortality is negatively related to socioeconomic status (SES) in general and for Blacks in particular (Modan & Wagener, 1992).

Although noninsulin diabetes is the most frequent cause of end-stage renal disease in Whites, end-stage renal disease as a consequence of hypertension is most common among Blacks (Agodoa, 1995; Gillum, 1996; Kaplan, 1994). From 1990 to 1992, age- and gender-adjusted Black cases outnumbered White cases by almost 8:1 (Agodoa, 1995). End-stage renal disease is responsible for most renal failure in Blacks (Kaplan, 1994). Data from the Hypertension Detection and Follow-up Program (Shulman et al., 1989) revealed that creatinine levels of hypertensive Blacks exceeded those of hypertensive Whites. Furthermore, elevated serum creatinine was associated with mortality. Inadequate blood pressure control is thought to contribute to the growing rates of end-stage renal disease in Blacks (Agodoa, 1995).

Coronary heart disease remains the leading cause of death for Blacks and Whites. Multiple cardiovascular risk factor aggregation is more common for Blacks than for Whites (Clark & Emerole, 1995). Mortality rates are comparable for Black and White men under 70 years of age but greater for Black women than White women under 85 years of age (National Heart, Lung, & Blood Institute [NHLBI] Report of the Task Force on Research in Epidemiology and Prevention of Cardiovascular Diseases, 1994). Hypertensive heart disease, as reflected by left ventricular hypertrophy, is also more prevalent in Blacks compared to Whites (Gillum, 1996; Saunders, 1991a) and predicts cardiovascular morbidity and mortality.

Left ventricular mass as well as hypertrophy (i.e., echocardiographically determined) is an independent predictor of morbidity and mortality in adults with and without diagnosed cardiovascular disease (e.g., Ghali et al., 1992; Koren, Devereux, Casale, Savage, & Laragh, 1991; Levy, Garrison, Savage, Kannel, & Castelli, 1989). Estimates of left ventricular mass using electrocardiographic techniques as well as M-mode echocardiography, the currently accepted methodology, have been made. Electrocardiographic data from such sources as the Georgia Heart Study (Arnett, Strogatz, Ephross, Hames, & Tyroler, 1992), the Chicago Heart Association Detection Project in Industry (Xie, Liu, Stamler & Stamler, 1994), and the Atherosclerosis Risk in Communities (ARIC) Study (Arnett et al., 1994) reflect greater left ventricular mass or prevalence of left ventricular hypertrophy in Blacks compared to Whites even after controlling for standard risk factors.

Research comparing electrocardiographic and echocardiographic assessments, however, conclude that the electrocardiograph magnifies Black–White differences (Gottdiener et al., 1994; Lee et al., 1992). Gottdiener and colleagues (Gottdiener et al., 1994) studied untreated and treated hypertensive Black and White men. The expected ethnic differences in electrocardiographic left ventricular hypertrophy were found. Although no echocardiographic-determined ethnic differences for left ventricular mass were obtained, the wall thickness of Blacks exceeded Whites. Other echocardiographic studies have replicated the finding for wall thickness. They also, however, document that hypertensive Blacks have greater left ventricular mass and a substantially higher prevalence of left ventricular hypertrophy than hypertensive Whites (e.g., Koren, Menash, Blake, Laragh, & Devereux, 1993; Mayet et al., 1994). In samples of healthy, young to middle-aged adults, ethnic differences for left ventricular mass adjusted for risk factors has either been absent (e.g., Hinderliter et al., 1991) or limited to men (Gardin et al., 1995).

These data show that ethnicity influences estimates of left ventricular mass, particularly among hypertensives. It is also important to acknowledge the contributions that other demographic and lifestyle factors make to estimates of left ventricular mass. For example, hypertension risk factors such as gender (e.g., Hinderliter et al., 1991), age (e.g., Hinderliter et al., 1991; Koren et al., 1993), and obesity (e.g., Gardin et al., 1995; Gottdiener et al., 1994) make independent contributions to left ventricular mass in multivariate analyses. This underscores the need to consider such factors in studies comparing Blacks and Whites.

SODIUM AND BLOOD PRESSURE

Salt sensitivity indexes variations in blood pressure as a function of variations in sodium ingestion (Wilson, Bayer, & Sica, 1996). Although salt sensitivity is an attribute of some youth (Wilson et al., 1996), it is common in adults (Luft et al., 1991). Based on laboratory studies, salt sensitivity is more prevalent among normotensive and hypertensive Black Americans than White Americans (Blaustein & Grim, 1991; Falkner, 1990; Falkner &

Kushner, 1991; Svetkey, McKeown, & Wilson, 1996), although true prevalence rates for the population are unknown (Flack et al., 1991).

The basis for the ethnic differences in salt sensitivity are unclear. Even salt sensitive normotensives who are lean are likely to exhibit insulin resistance, a condition that increases the risk of eventual cardiovascular disease (Sharma, Schorr, & Distler, 1993). Salt sensitivity is accompanied by decreased plasma renin activity (Saunders, 1991a; Weinberger, 1993). For adults as well as children, renin levels for Blacks are typically lower than for Whites across blood pressure status groups, although the mechanism for this difference has yet to be determined (Anderson, 1989; Eisner, 1990; Fray & Russo, 1990; Grim et al., 1980). Plasma renin differences are present even in situations in which excreted sodium is comparable for the two ethnic groups (Grim et al., 1980; M'Buyamba-Kabangu, Amery, & Lijnen, 1994).

Evidence suggests that, among Blacks, salt sensitivity has a heritable component (Svetkey et al., 1996). Ethnic differences in salt sensitivity do not appear to be attributable to dietary differences. Dietary studies indicate that, although Blacks consume less potassium and calcium than Whites (Langford & Watson, 1990), Blacks do not necessarily consume more sodium than Whites (Anderson, McNeilly, & Myers, 1992; M'Buyamba-Kabangu et al., 1994). Furthermore, because salt sensitivity is related to slower sodium natriuresis, Blacks are expected to excrete sodium more slowly than Whites (Weinberger, 1993).

In a series of elegant studies, Weinberger, Grim, Luft, and their colleagues (see Blaustein & Grim, 1991; Brier & Luft, 1994; Luft et al., 1991; Weinberger, 1993) have evaluated the effects of dietary and pharmacological sodium loading and depletion in Blacks and Whites. At high sodium levels, the slope of the blood pressure increase is greater for Blacks than for Whites. Moreover, for a given amount of sodium, Blacks excrete less of the sodium load during a 24-hour period than Whites, although they excrete more sodium at night. Consequently, Blacks retain more sodium for a given sodium intake. Such findings suggest possible ethnic differences in the renal handling of sodium that likely contribute to augmented renal tubule reabsorption of sodium (Blaustein & Grim, 1991; Weinberger, 1993).

Additional support for ethnic differences in renal function suggests that increased dietary sodium negatively impacts renal dynamics in hypertensive Blacks. Although hypertensive Whites and Blacks display comparable increments in blood pressure, renal blood flow, and renal plasma flow in response to a change from a low- to high-sodium diet, glomerular filtration rates increase for Blacks but do not change for Whites (Parmer, Stone, & Cervenka, 1994). Under conditions of controlled dietary intake, Light and Turner (1992) showed that normotensive Blacks were more likely than Whites (43% vs. 18%) to respond with slower natriuresis when exposed to stress. Data, however, are mixed with respect to whether sodium differentially alters cardiovascular responsivity to stress in Blacks and Whites (e.g., Ambrosioni et al., 1982; Dimsdale, Ziegler, Mills, Delchanty, & Berry, 1990; Falkner & Kushner, 1991; Falkner, Kushner, Khalsa, Canessa, & Katz, 1986; Falkner, Onesti, & Angelakos, 1981; Light & Turner, 1992). High dietary sodium, however, does increase the pressor response of hypertensive Blacks and normotensive Blacks and Whites but not hypertensive Whites to alpha agonists such as norepinephrine (Dimsdale et al., 1987). These data are consistent with the view that sodium influences blood pressure via vascular mechanisms. To the extent that enhanced vascular resistance accompanies salt sensitivity, sodium appears to act as a vasoconstrictive agent (Svetkey et al., 1996).

Black–White differences for several indices of sodium metabolism have also been documented, although the explanatory significance of these differences is not entirely clear. Concentrations of intracellular sodium of Blacks surpasses Whites (see Lijnen, M'Buyamba-Kabangu, Fagard, Staessen, & Amery, 1990; M'Buyamba-Kabangu et al., 1994; Persky et al., 1990). Although such differences are typically found for red blood cells (Cooper & Rotimi, 1995; Worthington et al., 1993), differences in platelets have also been demonstrated (Touyz, Milne, & Reinach, 1993). The greater erythrocyte sodium concentration of Blacks might be accounted for by the concomitant decrease in sodium–potassium adenosine triphosphatase (ATPase) pump activity (Lasker et al., 1985; Lijnen et al., 1990; Smith, Wade, Fineberg, & Weinberger, 1988). Data pertaining to sodium–potassium ATPase activity in platelets, however, are mixed (Cooper & Rotimi, 1995; Touyz et al. 1993).

Sodium–potassium cotransport is also reported to be lower in Blacks than Whites (Canessa, Spalvins, Adranga, & Falkner, 1984; Lijnen et al., 1990). For example, Canessa (Canessa et al., 1984) initially demonstrated that sodium–potassium cotransport is depressed in hypertensive Blacks and in normotensive Blacks at risk for hypertension by virtue of a family history of hypertension. Furthermore, erythrocyte sodium–potassium cotransport is correlated with salt sensitivity across blood pressure status in young Black adults (Canessa, Bize, Splavins, Falkner, & Katz, 1988).

Red blood cell sodium–lithium countertransport is often depressed in Blacks relative to their White counterparts (Canessa et al., 1984; Johnson, Sowers, Zemel, Luft, & Zemet, 1990; Lijnen et al., 1990; Persky et al., 1990) with some reports of increased activity in hypertensive compared to normotensive Blacks (Weinberger, Smith, Fineberg, & Luft, 1989). In a large scale study conducted by Persky and colleagues (1990), ethnicity was a significant predictor of sodium–lithium countertransport in men and women in multivariate analyses. Diabetic status may moderate

Black–White differences. Although nondiabetic hypertensive and normotensive Blacks had lower countertransport rates than the White cohort, noninsulin dependent hypertensive Blacks had somewhat higher rates than the nondiabetic Whites (Johnson et al., 1990).

The sodium-lithium countertransport functions as a marker for sodium–hydrogen antiport activity (Johnson et al., 1990). Ethnic differences in sodium–hydrogen exchange have been documented in skin fibroblasts. Sodium–hydrogen antiport activity of Blacks surpasses Whites. Hatori and colleagues (Hatori, Gardner, Tomonari, Fine, & Aviv, 1990) suggested that Blacks may have increased sodium and hydrogen turnover rates or a greater density of sodium and hydrogen carriers. In another study from their laboratory, it was demonstrated that although calcium levels of the skin fibroblasts were comparable for Blacks and Whites, the serum agonist-stimulated cytosolic free calcium response of Blacks exceeded that of Whites (Nakamura et al., 1989).

With the exception of cytosolic free calcium, the function of differences in sodium metabolism are not entirely clear. A greater cytosolic free calcium response in Blacks would be significant because an increase in cytosolic calcium contributes to vasoconstriction by stimulating vascular smooth muscle and contributes to hyperplasia and hypertrophy of the vessel walls (Blaustein & Grim, 1991; M'Buyamba-Kabangu et al., 1994; Svetkey et al., 1996). This would result in a rise in total peripheral resistance that would contribute to increases in blood pressure. Cytosolic free calcium may also suppress plasma renin activity (M'Buyamba-Kabangu et al., 1994). According to Blaustein and Grim (1991), the sodium–calcium exchanger in the plasma membrane is instrumental in regulating cytosolic free calcium. For example, inhibiting the sodium-calcium exchanger in the plasma membrane of sympathetic neurons leads to increased cytosolic free calcium which, in turn, stimulates catecholamine release, further contributing to increased vascular resistance. Anderson (Anderson et al., 1992) contends that sodium's effects on plasma norepinephrine, in particular, is critical in contributing to augmented vascular resistance.

INSULIN RESISTANCE

Noninsulin dependent diabetes comorbidity is twice as likely among hypertensive Blacks as Whites (National Diabetes Data Group, 1985). The significance of this distinction is apparent when considering that insulin resistance and the concomitant hyperinsulinemia are thought to be the link for the association of hypertension, hypertriglyceridemia, obesity, and diabetes, i.e., the metabolic syndrome (Ferrannini, Santoro, & Manicardi, 1989; Kaplan, 1989; Reaven, 1988; Schneiderman & Skyler, 1995). Blacks have a higher risk of developing hyperinsulinemia than Whites (NHLBI Report of the Task Force on Research in Epidemiology and Prevention of Cardiovascular Diseases, 1994). There are several reports suggesting that hypertension is an insulin resistant condition (e.g., Ferrannini et al., 1987; McGill et al., 1995; Modan et al., 1985; Pollare, Lithell, & Berne, 1990; Swislocki, Hoffman, & Reaven, 1989), although contrary data have also been reported (Cambein et al., 1987; Mbanya, Thomas, Wilkenson, Alberti, & Taylor, 1988). Work in normotensive nondiabetic adults shows positive associations between serum insulin concentrations and blood pressure (Bonora et al., 1987; Donahue, Orchard, Becker, Kuller, & Drash, 1987; Folsom et al., 1989; Freedman et al., 1987; Lucas, Estigarribia, Darga, & Reaven, 1985; Manolio et al., 1990; Wing, Bunker, Kuller, & Matthews, 1989; Zavaroni et al., 1989; Zavaroni et al., 1990). For example, Zavoroni's (Bonora et al., 1987; Zavaroni et al., 1989; Zavaroni et al., 1990) work in Whites suggests that abnormalities in carbohydrate and lipid metabolism are associated with blood pressure regulation, and the mechanisms linking blood pressure and insulin are present before obesity, hypertension, or impaired glucose tolerance develop. Falkner and colleagues (Falkner, Hulman, & Kushner, 1993; Falkner, Hulman, Tannenbaum, & Kushner, 1990) reported a significant relationship between insulin resistance and blood pressure in young Black nondiabetic adults with borderline elevated blood pressure. Furthermore, there is some indication that insulin may make a larger contribution to peripheral resistance for Blacks relative to Whites. Various indices of insulin resistance (including insulin-stimulated glucose utilization) indicate that borderline hypertensive Blacks are more insulin resistant than their normotensive counterparts (Falkner, Kushner, Tulenko, Sumner, & Marsh, 1995). Autopsy data from young adult Black and White men accident victims show that impaired glucose tolerance was associated with a 2.5 times higher prevalence of hypertension than normal glucose tolerance (McGill et al., 1995).

Research with children and adolescents (Berenson et al., 1981; Jiang, Srinivasan, Bao, & Berenson, 1993, 1993b; Jiang, Srinivasan, Urbina, & Berenson, 1995 ; Radhakrishnamurthy, Srinivasan, Webber, Dalferes, & Berenson, 1985; Rocchini, Katch, Schork, & Kelch, 1987; Svec et al., 1992; Voors et al., 1982) demonstrated independent associations between blood pressure and serum insulin concentrations, although these relationships may not always be apparent during periods of dramatic growth (Jiang et al., 1993a). The findings from the Bogalusa Heart Study (Jiang et al., 1993b; Radhakrishnamurthy et al., 1985) also emphasize the importance of examining the influence of ethnicity and gender on insulin–blood pressure associations in children and adolescents. In response to a 1-hour oral glucose tolerance test, the insulin levels of 5- to 17-year-old Black boys and girls exceeded those of White boys and girls with and without adjusting for age, body size, and Tanner-staged level of pubertal development (Svec et al., 1992). Thus, data from the Bogalusa Heart Study indicate that Black–White differences in glucose metabolism are apparent at an early age in nondiabetic samples, although the bases for this difference remains to be elucidated.

There are several mechanisms by which hyperinsulinemia, secondary to insulin resistance, could contribute to the development of hypertension. These include renal sodium retention, altered transport and composition of cellular electrolytes, sympathetic nervous system hyperactivity, and smooth muscle hypertrophy. Alternatively, blood pressure elevation could arise as a consequence of resistance to the action of insulin in terms of its usual effect on vasodilation (Schneiderman & Skyler, 1995). It has been suggested that Black–White differences in salt-sensitivity might be explained by differences in hyperinsulinemia contributing to enhanced renal tubular sodium reabsorption, possibly through the stimulation of the sympathetic nervous system (Flack et al., 1991). Others have hypothesized that hyperinsulinemia might contribute to hypertension via its affects on cation transport (Falkner et al., 1995; Grunfeld, Balzareti, Romo, Gimenez, & Gutman, 1994). The data, however, are equivocal on this point. For example, although Argentinean children with a positive family history of hypertension had higher insulin levels and erythrocyte sodium–lithium countertransport (as well as intracellular sodium) than the negative family history cohort, there was no association between these variables (Grunfeld et al., 1994).

Insulin has been shown to increase heart rate, cardiac output and contractility (Liang et al., 1982; Natali et al., 1990; Rowe et al., 1981). Hyperdynamic circulation is associated with increased levels of fasting insulin and triglycerides in adults and children (Jiang et al., 1995; Stern, Morales, Haffner, & Valdez, 1992) and blood pressure in children (Jiang et al., 1995). Although interactions between insulin metabolism and the sympathetic nervous system largely rule out considering either factor alone, under some circumstances, sympathetic activation may be the etiologic cause of elevated blood pressure through its actions on the vasculature and the myocardium (for a review, see Schneiderman & Skyler, 1995).

SOCIOECONOMIC AND PSYCHOSOCIAL FACTORS

A controversy exists as to whether apparent physiological differences between Blacks and Whites, as pertains to hypertension, are actually due to biological factors. Rather, the disparity appears more likely to be a function of social, environmental, or psychological factors that contribute to the physiological variations (Anderson & McNeilly, 1993; Williams, 1992;

Williams, Lavizzo-Mourey, & Warren, 1994). The contributions of SES to Black–White dissimilarities in health status certainly bears on this issue. Among Americans, 33% of Blacks versus 11% of Whites live in poverty (Williams & Collins, 1995). The negative relationship between SES and blood pressure has been well established for American Blacks and Whites and has also been described in other countries for diverse groups (Dressler, 1993; James, 1994; Myers & McClure, 1993; Williams, 1992). Controlling for SES in blood pressure studies usually eliminates or attenuates Black–White differences (Williams & Collins, 1995) supporting the contribution that social, economic, and environmental factors make to health.

Despite gains in social and economic arenas since the 1940s, the status of Black Americans remains subordinate to White Americans (Farley & Allen, 1987; Jackson, McCullough, Gurin, & Broman, 1991). For example, because the quality of primary and secondary education that blacks receive tends not to be equivalent to that of Whites, Blacks acquire fewer skills (Williams & Collins, 1995). This undereducation (Ruiz, 1990), together with access and treatment discrimination, contributes to employment concentrated in low status occupations, lower income, underemployment, and higher unemployment rates (Farley & Allen, 1987; Gottlieb & Green, 1987; Jaynes & Williams, 1989; Williams & Collins, 1995). Neighborhoods with Black concentrations also tend to be less desirable, and exposure to environmental hazards is probable (Williams, 1996; Williams & Collins, 1995). Moreover, and in part related to area of residence, Blacks generally have greater costs for goods and services than Whites (Williams, 1996). By extrapolating, it is not difficult to imagine how these social, economic, and environmental factors might have health consequences as suggested by differences in accessibility to medical care and insurance costs (Matthews, 1989). Ethnic disparities in medical treatment have been documented (Williams, 1996). Taken together, the aforementioned conditions support the view that Blacks as a whole are chronically exposed to considerable socioeconomic and psychosocial stress (e.g., Anderson & McNeilly, 1993; James, 1994; Syme, 1979; Williams & Collins, 1995).

Based on economic, social, and crime statistic indicators, high- and low-stress neighborhoods were categorized by Harburg and colleagues (Harburg et al., 1973) to evaluate their impact on blood pressure in Blacks and Whites. High socioecologic stress areas were lower SES neighborhoods with high levels of social instability. Initial reports indicated that the highest blood pressure levels and rates of hypertension were particularly characteristic of Black men under age 40, residing in high stress Detroit neighborhoods, who endorsed both guilt, concerning the expression of anger, and suppressed hostility, that is, holding anger-in. This was relative to those reporting holding their anger inwardly, without guilt (anger-in) and to those contending that they expressed anger outwardly (anger-out) in response to hypothetical scenarios (Harburg et al., 1973). Reanalyses of data, including Black and White men and women, revealed that greater rates of hypertension prevalence was associated with holding anger-in, being Black, male gender, and residing in a high-stress area (Gentry, Chesney, Gary, Hall, & Harburg, 1982). Additional work addressing coping with an angry boss revealed that anger-out responses were associated with greater blood pressure for Black men and White women relative to the other two sociodemographic groups. Furthermore, reported use of a reflective coping style by lower SES Black men to handle an angry boss was associated with lower diastolic blood pressure than anger-in or anger-out styles (Harburg, Blakelock, & Roeper, 1979). Subsequent work with Black and White men residing in Buffalo found significant associations between blood pressure levels and anger-out but not anger-in for Black and White men 40 years of age and older and young white men (Harburg, Gleiberman, Russell, & Cooper, 1991).

This seminal work of Harburg and colleagues (e.g., Harburg et al., 1973) spurred interest in investigating the relationship between blood pressure and coping with stress among Blacks and Whites (e.g., Dressler, 1993; James, 1994; Krieger, 1990). The relevance of SES to coping style is further illustrated by James' (1994) research on John Henryism. John Henryism, a construct reflecting "effortful active coping" with challenging environmental and psychosocial stressors was initially proposed and evaluated to explain the excess prevalence rates of hypertension in Black Americans (James, 1994). Intrinsic to this construct is the view that low SES individuals, in general, and low SES Blacks, in particular, are inveterately confronted by stressors (see Syme, 1979). In a series of studies, James demonstrates that excess hypertension prevalence was related to effortful active coping among low SES Blacks but not Whites. Blacks endorsing low John Henryism across high and low SES groups show comparable hypertension rates. However, the combination of low SES with high John Henryism is associated with excess cases of hypertension, exceeding the rates of the high SES with high John Henryism group by three-fold. The findings are similar for men and women and suggest that effortful active coping may be pathogenic under circumstances of chronic stress but protective under better economic conditions. It is interesting to note, however, that the SES distinctions were relatively small, such that the high SES Blacks were blue collar with at least some high school education. It is plausible that more marked differences would be obtained comparing more divergent education groups.

Dressler (1985) examined the associations among the mode of coping, persistent economic stressors, and psychological and psychosomatic symptoms in Black men and Black women. The use of active coping, operationalized as the belief in one's personal ability to cope with stress, was associated with positive health benefits in women but negative health effects for men in the face of increased economic stressors. In contrast, emotional control, a coping style involving detachment and behavioral disengagement (i.e., inhibitory-passive coping) from stressors, yields the opposite pattern for Black men and Black women. In a recent paper (Saab et al., 1997), Black men reported a more passive, detached, or uninvolved approach to coping. In addition, Black men endorsed more hostility and pessimism, and less tangible social support than Black women and Whites. Taken together, these findings are consistent with the position that some Black men employ a strategy of emotional and behavioral disengagement to cope with threats to self-esteem and the consequent negative emotions they may experience because of their relatively disadvantaged situation in society (Myers & McClure, 1993).

In addition to coping with stress, behavior has measurable effects on blood pressure. Unhealthy lifestyle behaviors are implicated in the excess morbidity and mortality of Blacks (Gottlieb & Green, 1987; Secretary's Task Force, 1986; Williams & Collins, 1995). At least three lifestyle factors related to SES distinguish Blacks and Whites and have implications for blood pressure: nutrition, alcohol consumption, and weight (Myers & McClure, 1993; Shea et al., 1991; Strogatz et al., 1991; Williams, 1992). Unhealthy lifestyle behaviors may potentiate the negative effects of chronic stress (McEwen, 1998). Although sodium consumption is comparable for Blacks and Whites, epidemiological data indicate that the two ethnic groups vary on potassium and calcium consumption, nutrients that affect blood pressure (e.g., Langford & Watson, 1990; McCarron, 1983; M'Buyamba-Kabangu et al., 1994; Saunders, 1991a). Decreased potassium consumption leads to increased sodium retention and a higher sodium to potassium ratio, whereas decreased calcium intake is hypothesized to contribute to increased vascular responsivity in Blacks (M'Buyamba-Kabangu et al., 1994; Saunders, 1991a). In the case of calcium, differential consumption is thought to be a function of a higher proportion of lactose deficiency in Blacks; potassium differences are attributed to traditional cooking and the costs associated with obtaining fresh foods (Melnyk & Weinstein, 1994; Williams, 1992).

Blood pressure is positively associated with alcohol consumption, particularly for individuals who consume alcohol regularly (Klatsky, Friedman, Siegelaub, & Gerard, 1977). In most studies, blood pressure levels are greater at moderate levels of consumption than at low levels (Gordon & Kannel, 1985; Witteman et al., 1990). According to Williams (1992, 1996), although Black women are likely to be nondrinkers, alcohol abuse is common among Black men. It has been documented that Blacks have been targeted by manufacturers and that alcohol availability is high in Black neighborhoods. Blacks also spend more money to acquire alcohol than Whites. Because drinkers often use alcohol as a coping strategy, the high alcohol consumption of Black men may be a technique to deal with their disadvantaged position.

Obesity and blood pressure also show a strong positive association (Berenson et al., 1989; Clarke, Woolson, & Lauer, 1986; Webber, Wattigney, Srinivasan, & Berenson, 1995). Rates of obesity, though comparable in Black and White men, are twice as high in Black women than White women (Williams, 1992). After controlling for the influence of age, body mass index predicts systolic blood pressure for Black American women and systolic and diastolic blood pressure in White American women (Adams-Campbell et al., 1988). From 1970 to 1990, Black women showed the largest gain in the proportion of those considered obese (Stern, 1995). Abdominal obesity, which constitutes a critical risk for the development of the metabolic syndrome, is more prevalent in Black women than White women (Clark & Emerole, 1995). Increased weight in black women appears to be a function of decreased physical activity rather than caloric consumption. Data from the NHANES III found that women had lower rates of leisure-time physical activity than men, and Black women had the lowest rates of all sociodemographic groups examined (Crespo, Keteyian, Heath, & Sempos, 1996). Similar findings have been reported in other large-scale surveys (e.g., Gottlieb & Green, 1987; Washburn, Kline, Lackland, & Wheeler, 1992). Although the bases for Black women's low levels of physical activity is not entirely clear, it has been hypothesized that social and economic factors (e.g., attitudes toward exercise and access to facilities) may act in concert to deter women from exercising and losing weight (Clark, 1995; Heath & Smith, 1994; Melnyk & Weinstein, 1994; Washburn et al., 1992; Williams, 1992).

The literature examining socioeconomic and psychosocial factors is consistent with Cooper's (1984) view that purported differences in health outcomes between Blacks and Whites are more likely to reflect environmental and social differences that are indicative of cultural or ethnic differences rather than genetically determined physiological differences.

AMBULATORY BLOOD PRESSURE MONITORING

Regulatory disorders such as hypertension have traditionally been assessed under basal conditions at one or a few points in time. Although assessment under resting conditions provides valuable information, it is limited insofar as it does not address regulatory adjustments that operate in a behaving individual (Saab & Schneiderman, 1993). Ambulatory blood pressure monitoring provides an index of blood pressure fluctuations in the environment.

Furthermore, evidence suggests that ambulatory values are a better prognostic indicator of cardiovascular and other systemic complications than casual blood pressure (e.g., Devereaux et al., 1983; Perloff, Sokolow, & Cowan, 1983). Furthermore, ambulatory blood pressure monitoring can be informative about blood pressure profiles of Blacks and Whites.

Studies have been conducted comparing Blacks with Whites in samples comprised of either normotensives, hypertensives, or both blood pressure status groups. Although data reflecting Black–White similarities are available (e.g., Prisant, Thompson, Bottini, Carr, & Rhodes, 1991; Rowlands et al., 1982), the emergent pattern indicates that Blacks have a blunted nocturnal decline in blood pressure, that is, their blood pressure dips less during sleep than Whites (e.g., Fumo et al., 1992; Gretler, Fumo, Nelson, & Murphy, 1994; Harshfield et al., 1989; Harshfield, Hwang, & Grim, 1990; Harshfield, Pulliam, Somes, & Alpert, 1993; Murphy, Fumo, Gretler, Nelson, & Lang, 1991; Treiber et al., 1994). When wake blood pressures are actually reported and group differences tested, the literature indicates that the blood pressure of Blacks is either comparable (e.g., Harshfield et al., 1989; Murphy, Fumo, et al., 1991) or exceeds that of Whites (e.g., Treiber et al., 1994). Overall, relative to Whites, Blacks are characterized by higher blood pressures during sleep and/or smaller differences between average wake and sleep blood pressures (Fumo et al., 1992; Gretler et al., 1994; Harshfield et al., 1989; Harshfield, Pulliam et al., 1993; Murphy, Fumo et al., 1991; Treiber et al., 1994). These relationships have been obtained in youth as well as adults (e.g., Harshfield et al., 1989; Harshfield, Pulliam et al., 1993).

The significance of the blunted nocturnal decline for Blacks is not entirely clear. One hypothesis is that this phenomenon may explain the more extensive target organ damage that afflicts Blacks (Chaturvedi, Athanassopoulos, McKeigue, Marmot, & Nihoyannopoulos, 1994; Gretler et al., 1994; Schneiderman, 1992; Vaughan & Murphy, 1994). Gretler (Gretler et al., 1994) contends that the 24-hr blood pressure profile of Blacks reflects that they are under a greater blood pressure load than Whites, which may account for ethnic differences in hypertension-related morbidity. Blood pressure load alone, however, is unlikely to provide an adequate explanation for the group differences in morbidity.

Fumo (Fumo et al., 1992) demonstrated that though the 24-hr blood pressure profiles of unmedicated American White and South African Black normals were functionally equivalent; the left ventricular mass of the former exceeded the latter. In that same study, American Blacks had a smaller nocturnal blood pressure dip than the aforementioned comparison groups as well as a significantly greater left ventricular mass. Although the greater sleep blood pressure may have contributed to the increase in left ventricular mass in American Blacks, the relationship among these parameters was not evaluated. The associations for ambulatory blood pressure and left ventricular mass were replicated in a sample of hypertensive Black and White Americans by Murphy (Murphy, Fumo et al., 1991). Likewise, in a sample of over 1,100 normotensive and hypertensive Black and White men and women living in Britain, Chaturvedi and colleagues (Chaturvedi et al., 1994) demonstrated that left ventricular hypertrophy, as indexed by wall thickness, was greater in Blacks than Whites across blood pressure status groups and between blood pressure status groups. Although the wall thickness of Blacks surpassed that of Whites at comparable casual and ambulatory blood pressure levels, the prediction of left ventricular hypertrophy by the blood pressure assessment procedures was not enhanced for Blacks.

Also requiring clarification is what accounts for the ethnic differences in the blood pressure profiles. Although the potential contribution of sodium handling has been proposed, equivocal results have been obtained. For example, Harshfield and colleagues (Harshfield, Alpert et al., 1991) demonstrated associations for excreted sodium with wake and sleep systolic blood pressure and casual systolic blood pressure in Black youth but not White youth. In contrast, Fumo (Fumo et al., 1992) reported that excreted sodium was similar for Black and White Americans during day and during night periods. It is noteworthy, however, that salt sensitivity is associated with a blunted nocturnal blood pressure fall in hypertensives of other ethnic groups (e.g., Uzu et al., 1996). This implies that it may be of value to examine the impact of salt sensitivity on sleep blood pressure in American Blacks and Whites. Given ethnic differences in salt sensitivity, it is possible that salt sensitivity may account for the Black–White differences in ambulatory blood pressure profiles, implicating differences in the renal handling of sodium as the mechanism as suggested by Calhoun and Oparil (1995).

Pickering (1994) identified three factors that may affect 24-hr blood pressure. The factors included the consumption of substances such as tobacco, caffeine, and alcohol, the quality of sleep, and the daytime activity level. Although nicotine, caffeine, and alcohol have known cardiovascular effects, their influence has not been systematically studied during ambulatory monitoring (Pickering & Blank, 1989). Furthermore, information about these variables has not typically been reported in studies of ethnic differences. Gretler (Gretler et al., 1994) collected self-reported quality of sleep for the night that the ambulatory monitor was worn as well as a control night on approximately 20% of his cohort. Although sleep quality was rated better for the control night than the ambulatory night, the ratings by Blacks and Whites were equivalent for both assessments and would not explain the nocturnal blunting in Blacks.

With respect to activity level, the physical activity levels of Blacks and Whites have not been methodically evaluated to determine whether differences exist and if such dissimilarities explain the smaller nocturnal decline characteristic of Blacks. Because physical activity is associated with cardiovascular changes, it would be expected that Blacks would be less physically active during the ambulatory period, although this is yet to be demonstrated. In fact, studies that reported that Blacks had higher wake blood pressures than Whites would not support this expectation (e.g., Treiber et al., 1994). Low activity level, however, might explain the Black–White similarities reported by Rowlands (Rowlands et al., 1982), who completed intra-arterial blood pressure monitoring with hospitalized patients. When the influence of alterations in activity level and environmental factors are decreased, the variability of wake blood pressure is attenuated, and sleep blood pressure is estimated to drop 20% (Pickering & Blank, 1989).

The potential contribution of environmental factors to explain Black–White differences in nocturnal blood pressure decline is underscored by the work of Fumo and colleagues (Fumo et al., 1992). Black South Africans and White Americans displayed the same decrease in sleep blood pressure, which exceeded the nocturnal dip of Black Americans. Williams et al. (1994) suggested that high levels of physiological arousal stimulated by chronic exposure to socioecological stressors is likely to contribute to the attenuated fall in sleep blood pressure of Black Americans.

STRESS AND BLOOD PRESSURE REGULATION

The psychosocial perspective discussed previously suggests that exposure to stress affects blood pressure regulation. It is well established that exposure to stressors may have negative cardiovascular as well as metabolic, nervous system, and immune effects (McEwen, 1998). A now classic body of literature shows that stressful living environments (Gentry, Chesney, Hall, & Harburg, 1982; Harburg et al., 1973), life threatening events (Ruskin, Beard, & Schaeffer, 1948), and combat conditions (Ehrstrom, 1945; Graham, 1945), as well as being employed in certain high demand occupations may be associated with hypertension or prolonged chronic elevations in blood pressure (Cobb & Rose, 1973; Rose, Jenkins, & Hurst, 1978). Results from the few available longitudinal studies indicates that blood pressure typically returns to normal levels during the period following the termination of the stressor (e.g., Graham, 1945; Ruskin et al., 1948).

Several theories regarding causal processes have been proposed to address the role of stress in the development of hypertension (e.g., Folkow, 1978; Julius & Esler, 1975; Obrist, 1981). The sympathoadrenomedullary axis figures prominently in most theories. Although not the sole factor, it is known to assume a critical function in increasing cardiovascular as well as metabolic activity during stress (Schneiderman, 1983). Although sympathetic activation can be adaptive in stressful situations, if the challenge is too severe, chronic, or frequently repeated, or if the individual has marked organ or tissue pathology, sympathetic activation could exacerbate existing disorders or initiate new ones.

Folkow (1978) hypothesized that cardiovascular smooth muscle hypertrophy is due to an adaptive process (over a period of months) resulting from exposure to functional trigger elements, such as environmental alerting stimuli (i.e., stressors). Trigger influences, however, are not necessarily apparent during resting conditions. Furthermore, continuous exposure to the triggers are not a prerequisite for arteriolar structural changes. Rather, it is sufficient for exposure to occur repeatedly and periodically over a fixed interval, as suggested by Manuck and Krantz's (1986) model of recurrent activation. Thus, repeated excitatory influences would result in recurrent hyperreactive pressor episodes that ultimately contribute to adaptations leading to hypertension.

Julius (1987; Julius & Esler, 1975; Julius, Weder, & Hinderliter, 1986) suggested that, for those individuals with neurogenic borderline hypertension, hypertension may be due to behavioral factors. Behavioral factors may, in part, result in sympathoadrenomedullary activity, which contributes to the secretion of renin and increases in cardiac output, leading to myocardial changes (e.g., down regulation of beta-adrenergic receptors) and greater peripheral resistance (Esler et al., 1977). Behavioral factors are presumed to exert their influence via a defect in CNS integration of autonomic control of the cardiovascular system (Julius & Esler, 1975), such that greater sympathetic influences co-occur with decreased parasympathetic influences (Julius et al., 1986).

The hypotheses of Folkow (1978) and Julius (1987; Julius & Esler, 1975; Julius et al., 1986) offered a framework for studying blood pressure regulation and hypertension in terms of the differential effects proposed for peripheral resistance and cardiac output. Obrist (1981), like Folkow (1978), suggested that recurrent episodes of stress-induced sympathetic activation can contribute to hypertension in vulnerable individuals. However, cardiac output responses in excess of metabolic demands, as well as arteriolar hypertrophy, are implicated in Obrist's model.

The reactivity protocol is a laboratory strategy that psychophysiologists have employed to examine the influence of stress-induced sympathetic activity on blood pressure regulation. Although comparisons of Black and White groups comprised of hypertensive and normotensives have found Whites exhibiting a greater pressor response to active coping stressors (those that stimulate beta-adrenergic activity, e.g., mental arithmetic and the evaluated speaking task) than Blacks (e.g., Dimsdale et al., 1990; Saab et al., 1991), Blacks and Whites typically respond similarly to inhibitory-passive coping (those that stimulate alpha-adrenergic activity, e.g., the cold pressor test and mirror tracing task) stressors (e.g., Dimsdale et al., 1990; Mills et al., 1993; Saab et al., 1991). When the comparison has been restricted to hypertensives, Blacks display greater systolic (Nelesen et al., 1995) and diastolic blood pressure responsivity (Nelesen et al., 1995; Saab et al., 1991) than Whites to active coping stressors but not to inhibitory-passive coping stressors (Calhoun et al., 1993).

Most efforts utilizing the reactivity strategy, however, have investigated normotensive individuals. Studies of normotensives provide information as to whether alterations in physiology occur in response to a disturbance of the system in presumably healthy individuals prior to any manifestation of the disease. Ethnic differences in responsivity to stress are apparent early in life. The literature supports the position that Blacks are characterized by increased blood pressure reactivity to laboratory stimuli at a young age (Alpert, Dover, Booker, Martin, & Strong, 1981; Hohn et al., 1983; Murphy, Alpert, Moes, & Somes, 1986; Murphy, Alpert et al., 1988; Treiber et al., 1993; Voors, Webber, & Berenson, 1980), although differences are sometimes limited to high risk groups such as those with a family history of hypertension (e.g., Hohn et al., 1983) or those with higher resting blood pressure (e.g., Voors et al, 1980). Enhanced reactivity to active coping tasks as well as inhibitory passive coping tasks has been shown to characterize black youth (Arensman, Treiber, Gruber, & Strong, 1989; Dysart, Treiber, Pflieger, Davis, & Strong, 1994; Murphy et al., 1986; Murphy et al., 1988; Murphy, Alpert, & Walker, 1992; Murphy, Alpert et al., 1991; Treiber et al., 1990; Treiber et al., 1993).

Ethnic differences reported for inhibitory-passive coping stressors showed that Black adults, relative to their White counterparts, are also generally more responsive (Anderson, Lane, Muranaka, Williams, & Houseworth, 1988; Fredrickson, 1986; Light, Turner, Hinderliter, & Sherwood, 1993; McAdoo, Weinberg, Miller, Fineberg, & Grim, 1990; Saab et al. 1992). Unlike that observed for children, the data reveal that when adults are studied and Black–White differences are reported for stressors that involve active coping, Whites are typically more responsive than Blacks (Anderson, et al., 1988; Calhoun et al., 1993; Dimsdale et al., 1990; Falkner & Kushner, 1989; Fredrickson, 1986; Light et al., 1993; McAdoo et al., 1990; Mills et al., 1993; Saab et al. 1992; Tischenkel et al., 1989). Accounts of Black adults displaying heightened responsivity to active coping tasks have been primarily limited to measures of vascular function, such as total peripheral resistance (Light & Sherwood, 1989; Light et al, 1993; Saab et al., 1992).

Saab and colleagues (Saab et al., 1992) showed that Blacks responded vascularly with greater total peripheral resistance, whereas Whites responded myocardially with greater cardiac output to a series of active coping and inhibitory-passive coping laboratory stressors. Furthermore, evidence of sympathetic drive on the myocardium was diminished in Blacks relative to Whites. To the extent that hypertension appears to be, in large measure, a disorder of peripheral resistance, the finding that Blacks, who, relative to Whites, are at greater risk for hypertension, primarily respond to a variety of stressors with an increase in peripheral resistance, even while normotensive, is of considerable interest.

The notion that Black–White differences in cardiovascular reactivity reported by Saab (Saab et al. 1992) may have limited generalizability to women was suggested by Light (Light et al. 1993), and Dysart (Dysart et al. 1994), and supported in a recent study by Saab (Saab et al. 1997). Whereas the association of Blacks with vascular responsivity and Whites with myocardial responsivity was replicated in a study of young girls conducted by Dysart (Dysart et al. 1994), Light (Light et al. 1993) replicated the associations for adult men but not for adult women. Likewise, Saab (Saab et al., 1997) reported that for parameters reflecting increased myocardial responsivity during an active coping stressor (the evaluated speaking task), Black men responded differently than White men, Black women, and White women, who did not differ from each other. Taken together, the data are consistent with the position that among adults, Black–White differences in cardiovascular reactivity to social-evaluative, active coping challenges are not in large part attributable to genetic–constitutional factors. Rather, under such circumstances, it is possible that cardiovascular responsivity differences may be related to the expression of social, environmental, and psychological concomitants of ethnicity and gender roles.

Anderson (Anderson et al., 1992), following the work of others (e.g., Syme, 1979), suggested that chronic exposure to stressors by Blacks may stimulate sympathetic nervous system activity contributing to the different pattern of cardiovascular responsivity for Black and White men. Anderson contended that increased sympathetic nervous system activity, together with sodium, contributes to the increased vascular reactivity that is thought to be a hallmark of Blacks. The extent to which the blood pressure of Blacks is regulated through vascular mechanisms and the blood pressure of Whites is controlled by myocardial factors have implications for blood pressure control, which will be reviewed in the following section.

INTERVENTION

The argument has been made that the efficacy of antihypertensive agents differs for Blacks and Whites (e.g., Hypertension Detection and Follow-up Program Cooperative Group, 1979). It has been suggested that this may relate to the varying hemodynamic profiles of Blacks and Whites (Saunders, 1990). More specifically, the increased prevalence of low renin hypertension among blacks may explain the effectiveness of diuretics as a monotherapy for Blacks because diuretics raise renin levels (Moser, 1990; Saunders, 1990). Diuretics represent a good first step in drug treatment because they reduce hypertension-related morbidity and mortality in Blacks in addition to Whites (Rutledge, 1994). Calcium channel blockers are also effective with low renin hypertension and are often used in lieu of diuretics (Moser, 1990; Saunders, 1990). Likewise, alpha-blockers have been effective as monotherapy and in combination with other antihypertensive agents and have positive effects on other cardiovascular risk factors in Black hypertensives (Saunders, 1991b).

In contrast, beta-blockers, as well as angiotensin converting enzyme (ACE) inhibitors, suppress renin activity and are assumed to be ineffective as a single drug therapy in Blacks. Whereas beta-blockers aggravate insulin resistance, the use of ACE inhibitors is associated with improvements in insulin resistance (Rutledge, 1994). The ACE inhibitors reduce peripheral resistance and increase renal blood flow, both desired outcomes. Although beta-blockers may increase peripheral resistance in some groups, younger Blacks, however, do respond well to beta-blockers (Saunders, 1990, 1991b). Moreover, whereas Whites are thought to have greater beta-adrenergic activity and/or receptor sensitivity than Blacks, research suggests that the beta-adrenergic functioning of young blacks is comparable or may exceed that of young Whites (Light & Sherwood, 1989). It should also be noted that hypertensive Blacks and Whites are equally responsive to diuretics when combined with either beta-blockers or ACE inhibitors (Moser, 1990; Saunders, 1990).

Results of a recent cooperative study on monotherapy comparing a diuretic, calcium channel blocker, beta-blocker, alpha-blocker, ACE inhibitor, centrally acting drug, and placebo, generally support the relationships described previously (Materson, Reda, & Cushman, 1995). For younger and older Blacks, diltiazem, a calcium channel blocker, was the most effective agent at the end of a one-year treatment. Hydrochlorothiazide, a diuretic, was more effective than atenolol, a beta-blocker, in older Blacks but equally effective as the beta-blocker in younger Blacks. For Whites, no efficacy differences among the classes of drugs were found for older patients. Hydrochlorothiazide, however, was the least effective active agent in controlling blood pressure for the younger White patients.

Nonpharmacologic intervention procedures (e.g., lifestyle and stress reduction) have been widely used with hypertensive adults and are typically implemented prior to prescribing drug treatment. They are recommended as a sole therapy as well as an adjunct to pharmacotherapy (Joint National

Committee, 1993). Relaxation training has an extensive and long history of use in the treatment of hypertension in adults (for a review see Rosen, Brondolo, & Kostis, 1993). The rationale for the use of relaxation training and other forms of stress reduction, such as meditation, is based on the view that excessive sympathetic activity underlies the blood pressure elevations (Julius & Esler, 1975). It is believed that relaxation training lowers blood pressure by decreasing stress-induced sympathetic arousal (Appel, 1986; Benson, Rosner, Marzetta, & Klemchuk, 1974; Glasgow, Engel, & D'Lugoff, 1989). It has been hypothesized that relaxation training lowers blood pressure by reducing cardiac output and total peripheral resistance (Glasgow et al., 1989).

In a sample of medication treated and untreated older Black men and Black women, a brief course of relaxation training was associated with a greater reduction in casual systolic and diastolic blood pressures over the 3-month follow-up than lifestyle education (Schneider et al., 1995). Transcendental meditation was more effective than abbreviated progressive muscle relaxation in lowering blood pressure assessed in the clinic and at home. Muscle relaxation was no more effective than the control condition for blood pressure measured at home.

Ewart (Ewart et al., 1987) conducted a high school-based relaxation study for Black and White students whose blood pressure was persistently at the 85th to 95th percentile. Abbreviated progressive muscle relaxation training was offered as part of a health class four times per week for 12 weeks. The training implemented social learning theory principles for skill acquisition, to maintain motivation, to increase self-efficacy and mastery, and to generalize relaxation skills to settings outside the classroom. Students were also provided with relaxation tapes, and instructions were given for home practice. Behavioral observations in the classroom indicated that students had mastered the procedures. Systolic blood pressure was significantly decreased for students randomized to treatment but not to control conditions. Students from the predominantly Black school had significantly larger drops in systolic blood pressure than students from the predominantly White school. There were, however, no group differences evident at the 4-month follow-up. The outcomes of Ewart (Ewart et al., 1987) with those from Schneider (Schneider et al., 1995) show that Blacks attain blood pressure benefits from a course of relaxation training. However, efforts need to be directed at further sustaining effects.

It is not entirely clear whether the effects of abbreviated progressive muscle relaxation and other relaxation techniques are limited to resting levels or whether they also modify sympathetic responsivity to stressors. Work examining the influence of relaxation training on cardiovascular reactivity to laboratory stressors has yielded mixed results (e.g., Albright, Andreassi, &

Brockwell, 1991; Cole, Pomerleau & Harris, 1992; Holmes & Roth, 1988; Larkin, Knowlton, & D'Alessandri, 1990). It is unknown whether this is due to the methodological features of the assessment (e.g., types of stressors selected) or the limited cardiovascular parameters (e.g., blood pressure and heart rate) sampled or the variations in interventions across studies. Recent findings with hypertensive and normotensive adults, however, show promise for further pursuing this line of work. Parker et al. (Parker et al., 1986) has argued that a need exists to devise relaxation and stress management procedures that influence cardiovascular reactivity in addition to casual blood pressure levels. Little work in this area, however, has included Black participants.

For any intervention (i.e., pharmacological or nonpharmacological) to be effective, adherence with the intervention is a prerequisite. Adherence with antihypertensive agents can be influenced by a variety of factors, including medication side effects, costs of medication and health care, as well as access to health care. The latter three may be of particular concern to economically disadvantaged Blacks (Fong, 1995; Saunders, 1990). Data from the NHANES II showed that age was a positive predictor of medication adherence among Blacks when education, gender, and smoking status were controlled (Daniels, René, & Daniels, 1994). Exposure to personal or community violence is also thought to be a barrier to adherence in the Black community (Fong, 1995). Effective pharmacologic as well as nonpharmacologic treatments require commitment and follow through on the part of the patient as well as the interventionist (Clark & Emerole, 1995).

Nonpharmacologic interventions have also raised obvious concerns regarding adherence. The demands involved in making behavior changes can pose considerable patient burden. Treatment adherence, whether with respect to attendance or following recommendations, is related to treatment outcomes (Epstein et al., 1986). Schneider and colleagues (Schneider et al., 1995) found high adherence rates for patient-reported practice of stress reduction procedures in a sample of older Black men and Black women. Likewise, Ewart et al. (1987) reported good attendance with treatment. This, however, was obviously facilitated by presenting the treatment as a component of a health class curriculum. In contrast, adherence with practice outside of the classroom was poor and not sustained at follow-up.

Taken together, the data suggest that Blacks and Whites may have differential responses to pharmacologic agents intended to control their blood pressure. In contrast, nonpharmacologic relaxation-based interventions, widely used for Whites, appear promising as a treatment for Blacks. The effect of relaxation therapies on vascular and/or myocardial factors remains to be determined.

CONCLUSION

The data available to explain the ethnic differences in hypertension prevalence suggest that the difference is likely to be multifactorially determined rather than attributable to a sole parameter. To date, the precise biobehavioral mechanisms underlying the ethnic difference remain to be elucidated. Nonetheless, several studies implicate vascular differences in blood pressure regulation. More specifically, vascular resistance appears to make a more important contribution in regulating the blood pressure of Blacks than Whites and has implications for the treatment of hypertension. To the extent that hypertension appears to be, in large measure, a disorder of vascular resistance, the finding that Blacks respond to various stressors with an increase in peripheral resistance, although normotensive, is of interest (e.g., Dysart et al., 1994; Light et al., 1993; Saab et al., 1992; Treiber et al., 1993).

Vascular resistance appears to be affected by a variety of variables. For example, the chronic exposure to stressors that confronts Blacks is likely to lead to increased sympathetic nervous system arousal. This sympathetic activation contributes to ethnic differences in renal handling of sodium and catecholamine stimulation as well as the release of cytosolic free calcium, all of which lead to enhanced vasoconstriction and increased peripheral resistance (e.g., Anderson et al., 1992; Blaustein & Grim, 1991). A body of research also relates blood pressure elevations to insulin resistance and hyperinsulinemia (e.g., Ferrannini et al., 1987). It appears that hyperinsulinemia also affects sympathetic nervous system activity and the renal handling of sodium. It is thought that increases in total peripheral resistance among Blacks may, in part, be attributable to insulin (e.g., Falkner et al., 1990). Sodium and sympathetic activation are common threads for the aforementioned associations.

Several studies examining the contributions of socioeconomic and psychosocial factors to the development of hypertension have implicated low SES (and the concomitant decreased access to health care), socioecologic stress, coping style, and unhealthy lifestyle behaviors. The precise biobehavioral mechanisms driving these variables remains to be identified. The exact manner in which coping style and unhealthy lifestyle behaviors (e.g., poor nutrition, excess alcohol consumption, and obesity) interact with the harsh environmental conditions experienced by many Black Americans is yet to be determined. Furthermore, persistent exposure to socioecological stressors is hypothesized to have an influence on the blunted nocturnal blood pressure decline that distinguishes Black from White Americans. The contribution of ethnic differences in 24-hr blood pressure profiles to ethnic differences in left ventricular mass requires additional study.

Although this chapter reviews a number of physiological characteristics that differentiated Blacks and Whites, there is little evidence that the bases for the ethnic differences is genetically determined. Rather, the differences appear to be largely influenced by social and environmental factors. Future research should be directed at understanding the bases for the ethnic differences in blood pressure regulation and hypertension prevalence. Such studies will be particularly useful in the prediction of hypertensive risk and the treatment of the disease.

ACKNOWLEDGMENT

This research was supported by National Institutes of Health grants HL36588 and HL07426.

REFERENCES

Adams-Campbell, L. L., Nwankwo, M., Ukoli, F., Omene, J., Haile, G. T., & Kuller, L. H. (1988). Body fat distribution patterns and blood pressure in black and white women. *Journal of the National Medical Association, 82*, 573–576.

Agodoa, L. (1995). Review: African American study of kidney disease and hypertension clinical trial. *Nephrology News & Issues, 9*, 18–19.

Albright, G. L., Andreassi, J. L., & Brockwell, A. L. (1991). Effects of stress management on blood pressure and other cardiovascular variables. *International Journal of Psychophysiology, 11*, 213–217.

Alpert, B. S., Dover, E. V., Booker, B. L., Martin, A. M., & Strong, W. B. (1981). Blood pressure response to dynamic exercise in healthy children—Black vs. white. *Journal of Pediatrics, 99*, 556–560.

Alter, M. (1994). Black–white differences in stroke frequency: Challenges for research. *Neuroepidemiology, 13*, 301–307.

Ambrosioni, E., Costa, F. V., Borghi, C., Montebugnoli, L., Giordani, M. F., & Magnani, B. (1982). Effects of moderate salt restriction on intralymphocytic sodium and pressor response to stress in borderline hypertension. *Hypertension, 4*, 789–794.

Anderson, N. B. (1989). Racial differences in stress-induced cardiovascular reactivity and hypertension: Current status and substantive issues. *Psychological Bulletin, 105*, 89–105.

Anderson, N. B., & McNeilly, M. (1993). Autonomic reactivity and hypertension in blacks: Toward a contextual model. In J. C. S. Fray & J. G. Douglas (Eds.), *Pathophysiology of hypertension in blacks* (pp. 107–139). New York: Oxford University Press.

Anderson, N. B., McNeilly, M., & Myers, H. (1992). Toward understanding race difference in autonomic reactivity: A proposed contextual model. In J. R. Turner, A. Sherwood & K. C. Light (Eds.), *Individual differences in cardiovascular response to stress* (pp. 125–145). New York: Plenum.

Anderson, N. B., Myers, H. F., Pickering, T., & Jackson, J. S. (1989). Hypertension in blacks: Psychosocial and biological perspectives. *Journal of Hypertension, 7*, 161–172.

Anderson, N. J., Lane, J. D., Muranaka, M., Williams, R. B., & Houseworth, S. J. (1988). Racial differences in blood pressure and forearm vascular responses to the cold face stimulus. *Psychosomatic Medicine, 50,* 57–63.

Appel, M. A. (1986). Hypertension. In K. A. Holroyd, & T. L. Creer (Eds.), *Self-management of chronic disease: Handbook of clinical interventions and research* (pp. 347–372). Orlando, FL: Academic Press.

Arensman, F. W., Treiber, F. A., Gruber, M. P., & Strong, W. B. (1989). Exercise-induced differences in cardiac output, blood pressure, and systemic vascular resistance in a healthy biracial population of 10-year-old boys. *American Journal of Disease in Children, 143,* 212–216.

Arnett, D. K., Rautaharju, P., Crow, R., Folsom, A. R., Ekelund, L. G., Hutchinson, R., Tyroler, H. A., Heiss, G., & the ARIC Investigators. (1994). Black–white differences in electrocardiographic left ventricular mass and its association with blood pressure (the ARIC Study). *American Journal of Cardiology, 74,* 247–252.

Arnett, D. K., Strogatz, D. S., Ephross, S. A., Hames, C. G., & Tyroler, H. A. (1992). Greater incidence of electrocardiographic left ventricular hyperterophy in black men than in white men in Evans County, Georgia. *Ethnicity and Disease, 2,* 10–17.

Benson, H., Rosner, B. A., Marzetta, B. R., & Klemchuk, H. P. (1974). Decreased blood pressure in borderline hypertensive subjects who practiced meditation. *Journal of Chronic Diseases, 27,* 163–169.

Berenson, G. S., Radhakrishnamurthy, B., Srinivasan, S. R., Voors, A. W., Foster, T. A., Dalferes, E. R., Jr., & Webber, L. S. (1981). Plasma glucose and insulin levels in relation to cardiovascular risk factors in children from a biracial population—The Bogalusa heart study. *Journal of Chronic Diseases, 34,* 379–391.

Berenson, G. S., Srinivasan, S. R., Wattigney, W., Webber, L. S., Newman, W. P., III, & Tracy, R. E. (1989). Insight into a bad omen for white men: Coronary artery disease—The Bogalusa heart study. *American Journal of Cardiology, 64,* 32C–39C.

Blaustein, M. P., & Grim, C. E. (1991). The pathogenesis of hypertension: Black–white differences. In W. D. Hall, E. Saunders, & N. B. Shulman (Eds.), *Cardiovascular disease in blacks* (pp. 97–114). Philadelphia: F. A. Daves.

Bonora, E., Zavaroni, I., Alpi, O., Pezzarossa, A., Bruschi, F., Dall'Aglio, E., Guerra, L., Coscelli, C., & Butturini, U. (1987). Relationship between blood pressure and plasma insulin in non-obese and obese-non-diabetic subjects. *Diabetologia, 30,* 719–723.

Brier, M. E., & Luft, F. C. (1994). Sodium kinetics in white and black normotensive subjects: Possible relevance to salt-sensitive hypertension. *American Journal of Medical Science, 307,* (Suppl. 1), 38–42.

Burt, V. L., Cutler, J. A., Higgins, M., Horan, M. J., Labarthe, D., Whelton, P., Brown, C., & Roccella, E. J. (1995). Trends in the prevalence, awareness, treatment, and control of hypertension in the adult US population. *Hypertension, 26,* 60–69.

Calhoun, D. A., & Oparil, S. (1995). Racial differences in the pathogenesis of hypertension. *American Journal of Medical Science, 310* (Suppl. 1), 86–90.

Calhoun, D. A., Mutinga, M. L., Collins, A. S., Wyss, J. M., & Oparil, S. (1993). Normotensive blacks have heightened sympathetic response to cold pressor test. *Hypertension, 22,* 801–805.

Cambien, F., Warnet, J. M., Eschwege, E., Jacqueson, A., Richard, J. L., & Rosselin, G. (1987). Body mass, blood pressure, glucose, and lipids. Does plasma insulin explain their relationships? *Atherosclerosis, 7,* 197–202.

Canessa, M., Bize, J., Spalvins, A., Falkner, B., & Katz, S. (1988). Na-K-Cl cotransport and Na pump in red cells of young blacks. *Journal of Clinical Hypertension, 2,* 101–108.

Canessa, M., Spalvins, A., Adragna, M., & Falkner, B. (1984). Red cell sodium countertransport and cotransport in normotensive and hypertensive blacks. *Hypertension*, 6, 344–351.

Chaturvedi, N., Athanassopoulos, G., McKeigue, P. M., Marmot, M. G., & Nihoyannopoulos, P. (1994). Echocardiographic measures of left ventricular structure and their relation with rest and ambulatory blood pressure in blacks and whites in the United Kingdom. *Journal of the American College of Cardiology*, 24, 1499–1505.

Chaturvedi, N., McKeigue, P. M., & Marmot, M. G. (1993). Resting and ambulatory blood pressure differences in Afro-Caribbeans and Europeans. *Hypertension*, 22, 90–96.

Chobanian, A. V. (1992). Vascular effects of systemic hypertension. *American Journal of Cardiology*, 69, 3E–7E.

Clark, D. O. (1995). Racial and educational differences in physical activity among older adults. *Gerontologist*, 35, 472–480.

Clark, L. T., & Emerole, O. (1995). Coronary heart disease in African Americans: Primary and secondary prevention. *Cleveland Clinic Journal of Medicine*, 62, 285–292.

Clarke, W. R., Woolson, R. F., & Lauer, R. M. (1986). Changes in ponderosity and blood pressure in childhood: The Muscantine study. *American Journal of Epidemiology*, 124, 195–206.

Cobb, S., & Rose, R. M. (1973). Hypertension, peptic ulcer, and diabetes in air traffic controllers. *Journal of the American Medical Association*, 224, 489–492.

Cole, P. A., Pomerleau, C. S., & Harris, J. K. (1992). The effects of nonconcurrent and concurrent relaxation training on cardiovascular reactivity to a psychological stressor. *Journal of Behavioral Medicine*, 15, 407–414.

Cooper, R. (1984). A note on the biologic concept of race and its application in epidemiologic research. *American Heart Journal*, 108, 715.

Cooper, R. S., & Rotimi, C. N. (1995). Absence of black–white differences in sodium and calcium in platelets. *American Journal of Hypertension*, 8, 558–564.

Crespo, C. J., Keteyian, S. J., Heath, G. W., & Sempos, C. T. (1996). Leisure-time physical activity among US adults. Results from the Third National Health and Nutrition Examination Survey. *Archives of Internal Medicine*, 156, 93–98.

Daniels, D. E., René, A. A., & Daniels, V. R. (1994). Race: An explanation of patient compliance—Fact or fiction? *Journal of the National Medical Association*, 86, 20–25.

Devereaux, R. B., Pickering, T. G., Harshfield, G. A., Kleinert, H. D., Denby, L., Clark, L., Pregibon, D., Jason, M., Kleiner, B., Borer, J. S., & Laragh, J. H. (1983). Left ventricular hypertrophy in patients with hypertension: Importance of blood pressure response to regularly recurring stress. *Circulation*, 68, 470–476.

Dimsdale, J. E., Graham, R. M., Ziegler, M. G., Zusman, R. M., & Berry, C. C. (1987). Age, race, diagnosis, and sodium effects on the pressor response to infused norepinephrine. *Hypertension*, 10, 564–569.

Dimsdale, J. E., Ziegler, M., Mills, P., Delehanty, S. G., & Berry, C. (1990). Effects of salt, race, and hypertension on reactivity to stressors. *Hypertension*, 16, 573–580.

Donahue, R. P., Orchard, T. J., Becker, D. J., Kuller, L. H., & Drash, A. L. (1987). Sex differences in the coronary heart disease risk profile: A possible role for insulin. The Beaver County study. *American Journal of Epidemiology*, 125, 650–657.

Dressler, W. W. (1985). The social and cultural context of coping: Action, gender and symptoms in a southern black community. *Social Science Medicine*, 21, 499–506.

Dressler, W. W. (1993). Social and cultural dimensions of hypertension in blacks: Underlying mechanisms. In J. C. S. Fray, & J. G. Douglas (Eds.), *Pathophysiology of hypertension in blacks* (pp. 69–88). New York: Oxford University Press.

Dustan, H. P. (1995). Does keloid pathogenesis hold the key to understanding black/white differences in hypertension severity? *Hypertension, 26,* 858–862.

Dysart, J. M., Treiber, F. A., Pflieger, K., Davis, H., & Strong, W. B. (1994). Ethnic differences in the myocardial and vascular reactivity to stress in normotensive girls. *American Journal of Hypertension, 7,* 15–22.

Ehrstrom, M. D. (1945). Psychogene kriegshypertonien [Psychogenic hypertension]. *Acta Medica Scandinavica, 122,* 546–570.

Eisner, G. M. (1990). Hypertension: Racial differences. *American Journal of Kidney Diseases, 16* (Suppl. 1), 35–40.

Epstein, L. H. (1984). The direct effects of compliance on health outcome. *Health Psychology, 3,* 385–393.

Esler, M., Julius, S., Zweifler, A., Randall, O., Harburg, E., Gardiner, H., & De Quattro, V. (1977). Mild high-renin essential hypertension: Neurogenic hypertension? *New England Journal of Medicine, 296,* 405–411.

Ewart, C. K., Harris, W. L., Iwata, M. M., Coates, T. J., Bullock, R., & Simon, B. (1987). Feasibility and effectiveness of school-based relaxation in lowering blood pressure. *Health Psychology, 6,* 399–416.

Falkner, B. (1990). Differences in blacks and whites with essential hypertension: Biochemistry and endocrine. *Hypertension, 15,* 681–686.

Falkner, B., & Kushner, H. (1991). Interaction of sodium sensitivity and stress in young adults. *Hypertension, 17* (Suppl. I), 162–165.

Falkner, B., & Kushner, H. (1989). Race differences in stress-induced reactivity in young adults. *Health Psychology, 8,* 613–627.

Falkner, B., Hulman, S., & Kushner, H. (1993). Insulin-stimulated glucose utilization and borderline hypertension in young adult blacks. *Hypertension, 22,* 18–25.

Falkner, B., Hulman, S., Tannenbaum, J., & Kushner, H. (1990). Insulin resistance and blood pressure in young black men. *Hypertension, 16,* 36–43.

Falkner, B., Kushner, H., Khalsa, D. K., Canessa, M., & Katz, S. (1986). Sodium sensitivity, growth and family history of hypertension in young blacks. *Journal of Hypertension, 4* (Suppl. 5), 381–383.

Falkner, B., Kushner, H., Tulenko, T., Sumner, A. E., & Marsh, J. B. (1995). Insulin sensitivity, lipids, and blood pressure in young American Blacks. *Arteriosclerosis Thrombosis and Vascular Biology, 15,* 1798–1804.

Falkner, B., Onesti, G., & Angelakos, E. (1981). Effect of salt loading on the cardiovascular response to stress in adolescents. *Hypertension, 3* (Suppl. II), 195–199.

Farley, R., & Allen, W. R. (1987). The color line and the quality of life in America. In *The population of the United States in the 1980s: A census monograph series.* New York: Russell Sage Foundation.

Ferrannini, E., Buzzigoli, G., Bonadonna, R., Giorico, M. A., Oleggini, M., Graziadei, L., Pedrinelli, R., Brandi, L., & Bevilacqua, S. (1987). Insulin resistance in essential hypertension. *New England Journal of Medicine, 317,* 350–357.

Ferrannini, E., Santoro, D., & Manicardi, V. (1989). The association of essential hypertension and diabetes. *Comprehensive Therapy, 15,* 51–58.

Flack, J. M., Ensrud, K. E., Mascioli, S., Launer, C. A., Svendsen, K., Elmer, P. J., & Grimm, R. H., Jr. (1991). Racial and ethnic modifiers of the salt–blood pressure response. *Hypertension, 17* (Suppl. I), 115–121.

Folkow, B. (1978). Cardiovascular structural adaptation: Its role in the initiation and maintenance of primary hypertension. *Clinical Science and Molecular Medicine, 55,* 3s–22s.

Folsom, A. R., Burke, G. L., Ballew, C., Jacobs, D. R., Haskell, W. L., Donahue, R. P., Liu, K. A., & Hiher, J. E. (1989). Relation of body fatness and its distribution to cardiovascular risk factors in young blacks and whites. The role of insulin. *American Journal of Epidemiology, 130*, 911–924.

Fong, R. L. (1995). Violence as a barrier to compliance for the hypertensive urban African American. *Journal of the National Medical Association, 87*, 203–207.

Fray, J. C. S., & Russo, S. M. (1990). Mechanism for low renin in blacks: Studies in hypophysectomised rat model. *Journal of Human Hypertension, 4*, 160–162.

Fredrickson, M. (1986). Racial differences in cardiovascular reactivity to mental stress in essential hypertension. *Journal of Hypertension, 4*, 325–331.

Freedman, D. S., Srinivasan, S. R., Burke, G. L.,Shear, C. L., Smoak, C. G., Harsha, D. W., Webber, L. S., & Berenson, G. S. (1987). Relation of body fat distribution to hyperinsulinemia in children and adolescents: The Bogalusa heart study. *American Journal of Clinical Nutrition, 41*, 403–410.

Freeman, V., Fraser, H., Forrester, T., Wilks, R., Cruickshank, J., Rotimi, C., & Cooper, R. (1996). Comparative study of hypertension prevalence, awareness, treatment, and control rates in St. Lucia, Jamaica and Barbados. *Journal of Hypertension, 14*, 495–501.

Fumo, M. T., Teeger, S., Lang, R. M., Bednarz, J., Sareli, P., & Murphy, M. B. (1992). Diurnal blood pressure variation and cardiac mass in American blacks and whites and South African blacks. *American Journal of Hypertension, 5*, 111–116.

Gaines, K., & Burke, G. (1995). Ethnic differences in stroke: Black–white differences in the United States population. *Neuroepidemiology, 14*, 209–239.

Gardin, J. M., Wagenknecht, L. E., Anton-Culver, H., Flack, J., Gidding, S., Kurosaki, T., Wong, N. D., & Manolio, T. A. (1995). Relationship of cardiovascular risk factors to echocardiographic left ventricular mass in healthy young black and white adult men and women. The CARDIA study. *Circulation, 92*, 380–387.

Gentry, W. D., Chesney, A. P., Gary, H. E., Hall, R. P., & Harburg, E. (1982). Habitual anger-coping styles: I. Effect on mean blood pressure and risk for essential hypertension. *Psychosomatic Medicine, 44*, 195–202.

Gibaldi, M. (1993). Ethnic differences in the assessment and treatment of disease. *Pharmacotherapy, 13*, 170–176.

Gillum, R. F. (1996). Epidemiology of hypertension in African American women. *American Heart Journal, 131*, 385–395.

Glasgow, M. S., Engel, B. T., & D'Lugoff, B. C. (1989). A controlled study of a standardized behavioral stepped treatment for hypertension. *Psychosomatic Medicine, 51*, 10–26.

Gordon, T., & Kannel, W. B. (1985). Drinking and its relation to smoking, blood pressure, blood lipids, and uric acid: The Framingham Study. *Archives of Internal Medicine, 143*, 1366–1374.

Gottdiener, J. S., Reda, D. J., Materson, B. J., Massie, B. M., Notargiacomo, A., Hamburger, R. J., Williams, D. W., & Henderson, W. G. (1994). Importance of obesity, race and age to the cardiac structural and functional effects of hypertension. *Journal of the American College of Cardiology, 24*, 1492–1498.

Gottlieb, N. H., & Green, L. W. (1987). Ethnicity and lifestyle health risk: Some possible mechanisms. *American Journal of Health Promotion, 2*, 37–51.

Graham, J. D. P. (1945). High blood pressure after battle. *Lancet, 248*, 239–240.

Gretler, D. D., Fumo, M. T., Nelson, K. S., & Murphy, M. B. (1994). Ethnic differences in circadian hemodynamic profile. *American Journal of Hypertension, 7*, 7–14.

Grim, C. E., Luft, F. C., Miller, J. Z., Meneely, G. R., Battarbee, H. D., Hames, C. G., & Dahl, L. K. (1980). Racial differences in blood pressure in Evans County, Georgia: Relationship to sodium and potassium intake and plasma renin activity. *Journal of Chronic Disease, 33*, 87–94.

Grunfeld, B., Balzareti, M., Romo, M., Gimenez, M., & Gutman, R. (1994). Hyperinsulinemia in normotensive offspring of hypertensive parents. *Hypertension, 23* (Suppl. I), 12–15.

Harburg, E., Blakelock, E. H., Jr., & Roeper, P. R. (1979). Resentful and reflective coping with arbitrary authority and blood pressure: Detroit. *Psychosomatic Medicine, 41,* 189–202.

Harburg, E., Erfurt, J., Hauenstein, L., Chape, C., Schull, W., & Schork, M. A. (1973). Socioecological stress, suppressed hostility, skin color, and black–white male blood pressure: Detroit. *Psychosomatic Medicine, 35,* 276–296.

Harburg, E., Gleiberman, L., Russell, M., & Cooper, A. (1991). Anger-coping styles and blood pressure in black and white males: Buffalo, New York. *Psychosomatic Medicine, 53,* 153–164.

Harshfield, G. A., Alpert, B. S., & Pulliam, D. A. (1993). Renin-angiotensin-aldosterone system in healthy subjects aged ten to eighteen years. *The Journal of Pediatrics, 122,* 563–567.

Harshfield, G. A., Alpert, B. S., Pulliam, D. A., Wiley, E. S., Somes, G. W., & Stapleton, F. B. (1991). Sodium excretion and racial differences in ambulatory blood pressure patterns. *Hypertension, 18,* 813–818.

Harshfield, G. A., Alpert, B. S., Wiley, E. S., Somes, G. W., Murphy, J. K., & Dupal, L. M. (1989). Race and gender influence ambulatory blood pressure patterns of adolescents. *Hypertension, 14,* 598–603.

Harshfield, G. A., Hwang, C., & Grim, C. E. (1990). Circadian variation of blood pressure in blacks: Influence of age, gender and activity. *Journal of Human Hypertension, 4,* 43–47.

Harshfield, G. A., Pulliam, D. A., Somes, G. W., & Alpert, B. S. (1993). Ambulatory blood pressure patterns in youth. *American Journal of Hypertension, 6,* 968–973.

Heath, G. W., & Smith, J. D. (1994). Physical activity patterns among adults in Georgia: Results from the 1990 Behavioral Risk Factor Surveillance System. *South Medical Journal, 87,* 435–439.

Hinderliter, A. L., Light, K. C., & Willis, P. W., IV. (1991). Left ventricular mass index and diastolic filling: Relation to blood pressure and demographic variables in a healthy biracial sample. *American Journal of Hypertension, 4,* 579–585.

Hohn, A. R., Riopel, D. A., Keil, J. E., Loadholt, C. B., Margolius, H. S., Halushka, D. V., Privitera, P. J., Webb, J. G., Medley, E. S., Schuman, S. H., Rubin, M., Pantell, R., & Braunstein, M. (1983). Childhood familial and racial differences in physiologic and biochemical factors related to hypertension. *Hypertension, 5,* 56–70.

Holmes, D. S., & Roth, D. L. (1988). Effects of aerobic exercise training and relaxation training on cardiovascular activity during psychological stress. *Journal of Psychosomatic Research, 32,* 469–474.

Hypertension Detection and Follow-Up Program Cooperative Group: Five-year findings of the hypertension detection and follow-up program. II. (1979). Mortality by race, sex and age. *Journal of the American Medical Association, 242,* 2572–2577.

Jackson, J. S., McCullough, W. R., Gurin, G., & Broman, C. L. (1991). Race identity. In J. S. Jackson (Ed.), *Life in black America* (pp. 238–253). London: Sage Publications.

James, S. A. (1994). John Henryism and the health of African-Americans. *Culture, Medicine, and Psychiatry, 18,* 163–182.

Jaynes, G. D., & Williams, R. M., Jr. (1989). *A common destiny: Blacks and American society.* Washington, DC: National Academy Press.

Jiang, X., Srinivasan, S. R., Bao, W., & Berenson, G. S. (1993a). Association of fasting insulin with blood pressure in young individuals—The Bogalusa heart study. *Archives of Internal Medicine, 153,* 323–328.

Jiang, X., Srinivasan, S. R., Bao, W., & Berenson, G. S. (1993b). Association of fasting insulin with longitudinal changes in blood pressure in children and adolescents—The Bogalusa heart study. *American Journal of Hypertension, 6,* 564–569.

Jiang, X., Srinivasan, S. R., Urbina, E., & Berenson, G. S. (1995). Hyperdynamic circulation and cardiovascular risk in children and adolescents—the Bogalusa heart study. *Circulation, 91,* 1101–1106.

Johnson, B. A. B., Sowers, J. R., Zemel, P. C., Luft, F. C., & Zemel, M. B. (1990). Increased sodium–lithium countertransport in black non-insulin-dependent diabetic hypertensives. *American Journal of Hypertension, 3,* 563–565.

Joint National Committee (1993). Fifth Report of the Joint National Committee on Detection, Evaluation and Treatment of High Blood Pressure (JNC V). *Archives of Internal Medicine, 153,* 154–186.

Julius, S. (1987). Hemodynamic, pharmacologic and epidemiologic evidence for behavioral factors in human hypertension. In S. Julius, & D. R. Basset (Eds.), *Handbook of hypertension: Vol. 9. Behavioral factors in hypertension* (pp. 59–74). Amsterdam: Elsevier Science.

Julius, S., & Esler, M. (1975). Autonomic nervous cardiovascular regulation in borderline hypertension. *American Journal of Cardiology, 36,* 685–695.

Julius, S., Weder, A. B., & Hinderliter, A. L. (1986). Does behaviorally induced blood pressure variability lead to hypertension? In K. A. Matthews, S. M. Weiss, T. Detre, T. M., Dembroski, B. Falkner, S. B. Manuck, & R. B. Williams, Jr. (Eds.), *Handbook of stress, reactivity, and cardiovascular disease* (pp. 71–82). New York: Wiley.

Kaplan, N. M. (1989). The deadly quartet. *Archives of Internal Medicine, 149,* 1514–1520.

Kaplan, N. M. (1994). Ethnic aspects of hypertension. *The Lancet, 344,* 450–452.

Klatsky, A. L., Friedman, G. D., Siegelaub, A. B., & Gerard, A. (1977). Alcohol consumption and blood pressure. *New England Journal of Medicine, 296,* 1194–1200.

Koren, M. J., Devereux, R. B., Casale, P. N., Savage, D. D., & Laragh, J. H. (1991). Relation of left ventricular mass and geometry to morbidity and mortality in uncomplicated essential hypertension. *Annals of Internal Medicine, 114,* 345–352.

Koren, M. J., Mensah, G. A., Blake, J., Laragh, J. H., & Devereux, R. B. (1993). Comparison of left ventricular mass and geometry in black and white patients with essential hypertension. *American Journal of Hypertension, 6,* 815–823.

Kreiger, N. (1990). Racial and gender discrimination: Risk factors for high blood pressure? *Social Science Medicine, 30,* 1273–1281.

Langford, H. G., & Watson, R. L. (1990). Potassium and calcium intake, excretion, and homeostasis in blacks, and their relation to blood pressure. *Cardiovascular Drugs and Therapy, 4,* 403–406.

Larkin, K. T., Knowlton, G. E., & D'Alessandri, R. (1990). Predicting treatment outcome to progressive relaxation training in essential hypertensive patients. *Journal of Behavioral Medicine, 13,* 605–618.

Lasker, N., Hopp, L., Grossman, S., Bamforth, R., & Aviv, A. (1985). Race and sex differences in erythrocyte Na^+, K^+ and Na^+, K^+-adenosine triphosphatase. *Journal of Clinical Investigations, 75,* 1813–1820.

Lee, D. K., Marantz, P. R., Devereux, R. B., Kligfield, P., & Alderman, M. H. (1992). Left ventricular hypertrophy in black and white hypertensives. Standard electrocardiographic criteria overestimate racial differences in prevalence. *Journal of the American Medical Association, 267,* 3294–3299.

Levy, D., Garrison, R. J., Savage, D. D., Kannel, W. B., & Castelli, W. P. (1989). Left ventricular mass and incidence of coronary heart disease in an elderly cohort: The Framingham Heart Study. *Annals of Internal Medicine, 110,* 101–107.

Liang, C.-S., Doherty, J. U., Faillace, R., Maekawa, K., Arnold, S., Haralambos, G., & Hood, W. B. (1982). Insulin infusion in conscious dogs: Effects on systematic and coronary hemodynamics, regional blood flows, and plasma catecholamines. *Journal of Clinical Investigation, 69,* 1321–1336.

Light, K. C., & Sherwood, A. (1989). Race, borderline hypertension, and hemodynamic responses to behavioral stress before and after beta-adrenergic blockade. *Health Psychology, 8,* 577–595.

Light, K. C., & Turner, J. R. (1992). Stress-induced changes in the rate of sodium excretion in healthy black and white men. *Journal of Psychosomatic Research, 36,* 497–508.

Light, K. C., Turner, J. R., Hinderliter, A. L., & Sherwood, A. (1993). Race and gender comparisons: I. Hemodynamic responses to a series of stressors. *Health Psychology, 12,* 354–365.

Lijnen, P., M'Buyamba-Kabangu, J., Fagard, R., Staessen, J., & Amery, A. (1990). Erythrocyte concentrations and transmembrane fluxes of sodium and potassium in essential hypertension: Role of intrinsic and environmental factors. *Cardiovascular Drugs and Therapy, 4,* 321–333.

Lopes, A. A. S., & Port, F. K. (1995). The low birth weight hypothesis as a plausible explanation for the black/white differences in hypertension, non-insulin-dependent diabetes, and end-stage renal disease. *American Journal of Kidney Diseases, 25,* 350–356.

Lucas, C. P., Estigarribia, J. A., Darga, L. L., Reaven, G. M. (1985). Insulin and blood pressure in obesity. *Hypertension, 7,* 702–706.

Luft, F. C., Miller, J. Z., Grim, C. E., Fineberg, N. S., Christian, J. C., Daugherty, S. A., & Weinberger, M. H. (1991). Salt sensitivity and resistance of blood pressure: Age and race as factors in physiological responses. *Hypertension, 17* (Suppl. I),102–108.

Manatunga, A. K., Jones, J. J., & Pratt, J. H. (1993). Longitudinal assessment of blood pressures in black and white children. *Hypertension, 22,* 84–89.

Manolio, T. A., Savage, P. J., Burke, G. L., Liu, K. A., Wagenknecht, L. E., Sidney, S., Jacobs, D. R., Jr., Roseman, J. M., Donahue, R. P., & Oberman, A. (1990). Association of fasting insulin with blood pressure and lipids in young adults: The CARDIA study. *Arteriosclerosis, 10,* 430–436.

Manuck, S. B., & Krantz, D. S. (1986). Psychophysiologic reactivity in coronary heart disease and essential hypertension. In K. A. Matthews, S. M. Weiss, T. Detre, T. M. Dembroski, B. Falkner, S. B. Manuck, & R. B. Williams, Jr. (Eds.), *Handbook of stress, reactivity, and cardiovascular disease* (pp. 11–34). New York: Wiley.

Materson, B. J., Reda, D. J., & Cushman, W. C. (1995). Department of Veterans Affairs single-drug therapy of hypertension study: Revised figures and new data. *American Journal of Hypertension, 8,* 189–192.

Matthews, K. A. (1989). Are sociodemographic variables markers for psychological determinants of health? *Health Psychology, 8,* 641–648.

Mayet, J., Shahi, M., Foale, R. A., Poulter, N. R., Sever, P. S., & McGThom, S. A. (1994). Racial differences in cardiac structure and function in essential hypertension. *British Medical Journal, 308,* 1011–1014.

Mbanya, J. C., Thomas, T. H., Wilkenson, R., Alberti, K. G., & Taylor, R. (1988). Hypertension and hyperinsulinemia: A relation in diabetes but not essential hypertension. *Lancet, 1,* 733–734.

M'Buyamba-Kabangu, J. R., Amery, A., & Lijnen, P. (1994). Differences between black and white persons in blood pressure and related biological variables. *Journal of Human Hypertension, 8,* 163–170.

McAdoo, W. G., Weinberg, M. H., Miller, J. Z., Fineberg, N. S., & Grim, C. E. (1990). Race and gender influence hemodynamic responses to psychological and physical stimuli. *Journal of Hypertension, 8*, 961–967.

McCarron, D. A. (1983). Calcium and magnesium nutrition in human hypertension. *Annals of Internal Medicine, 98*, 800–805.

McEwen, B. S. (1998). Protective and damaging effects of stress mediators. *New England Journal of Medicine, 338*, 171–179.

McGill, H. C., Jr., Strong, J. P., Tracy, R. E., McMahan, C. A., Oalmann, M. C., & the Pathobiological Determinants of Atherosclerosis in Youth (PDAY) Research Group. (1995). Relation of a postmortem renal index of hypertension to atherosclerosis in youth. *Arteriosclerosis, Thrombosis & Vascular Biology, 15*, 2222–2228.

McKenzie, K. J., & Crowcroft, N. S. (1994). Race, ethnicity, culture, and science. *British Medical Journal, 309*, 286–287.

Melnyk, M. G., & Weinstein, E. (1994). Preventing obesity in black women by targeting adolescents: A literature review. *Journal of the American Diet Association, 94*, 536–540.

Mills, P. J., Berry, C. C., Dimsdale, J. E., Nelesen, R. A., & Ziegler, M. G. (1993). Temporal stability of task-induced cardiovascular, adrenergic, and psychological responses: The effects of race and hypertension. *Psychophysiology, 30*, 197–204.

Modan, B., & Wagener, D. K. (1992). Some epidemiological aspects of stroke: Mortality/morbidity trends, age, sex, race, socioeconomic status. *Stroke, 23*, 1230–1236.

Modan, M., Halkin, H., Almog, S., Lusky, A., Eshkol, A., Shefi, M., Shitrit, A., & Fuchs, Z. (1985). Hyperinsulinemia: A link between hypertension, obesity and glucose intolerance. *Journal of Clinical Investigation, 75*, 809–817.

Moser, M. (1990). Hypertension treatment results in minority patients. *The American Journal of Medicine, 88* (Suppl. 3B), 24–31.

Murphy, J. K., Alpert, B. S., & Walker, S. S. (1992). Ethnicity, pressor reactivity, and children's blood pressure—Five years of observations. *Hypertension, 20*, 327–332.

Murphy, J. K., Alpert, B. S., Moes, D. M., & Somes, G. W. (1986). Race and cardiovascular reactivity—A neglected relationship. *Hypertension, 8*, 1075–1083.

Murphy, J. K., Alpert, B. S., Walker, S. S., & Willey, E. S. (1988). Race and cardiovascular reactivity: A replication. *Hypertension, 11*, 308–311.

Murphy, J. K., Alpert, B. S., Walker, S. S., & Willey, E. S. (1991). Children's cardiovascular reactivity: Stability of racial differences and relation to subsequent blood pressure over a one-year period. *Psychophysiology, 28*, 447–457.

Murphy, M. B., Fumo, M. T., Gretler, D. D., Nelson, K. S., & Lang, R. M. (1991). Diurnal blood pressure variation: Differences among disparate ethnic groups. *Journal of Hypertension, 9* (Suppl. 8), 45–47.

Myers, H. F., & McClure, F. H. (1993). Psychosocial factors in hypertension in blacks: The case for an interactional perspective. In J. C. S. Fray, & J. G. Douglas (Eds.), *Pathophysiology of hypertension in blacks* (pp. 90–106). New York: Oxford University Press.

Nakamura, A., Gardner, J., Hatori, N., Nakamura, M., Fine, B. P., & Aviv, A. (1989). Differences of Ca^{2+} regulation in skin fibroblasts from blacks and whites. *Journal of Cell Physiology, 138*, 367–374.

National Diabetes Data Group. (1985). Summary in National Diabetes data group: Diabetes in America, publication 85-1468. Washington, DC: The Department of Health and Human Services.

National Heart, Lung, and Blood Institute (1994). Report of the Task Force on Research in Epidemiology and prevention of cardiovascular diseases. Washington, DC: U.S. Department of Health and Human Services.

Nelesen, R. A., Dimsdale, J. E., Mills, P. J., & Ziegler, M. G. (1995). Relationship of insulin, race, and hypertension with hemodynamic reactivity to a behavioral challenge. *American Journal of Hypertension, 8*, 12–19.

Obrist, P. A. (1981). *Cardiovascular psychophysiology: A perspective.* New York: Plenum.

Parker, F. C., Harsha, D. W., Farris, R. P., Webber, L. S., Frank, G. C., & Berenson, G. S. (1986). Reducing the risk of cardiovascular disease in children. In K. A. Holroyd, & T. L. Creer (Eds.), *Self-management of chronic disease—Handbook of clinical interventions and research* (pp. 231–266). New York: Academic Press.

Parmer, R. J., Stone, R. A., & Cervenka, J. H. (1994). Renal hemodynamics in essential hypertension: Racial differences in response to changes in dietary sodium. *Hypertension, 24*, 752–757.

Perloff, D., Sokolow, M., & Cowan, R. (1983). The prognostic value of ambulatory blood pressures. *Journal of the American Medical Association, 249*, 2792–2798.

Persky, V., Ostrow, D., Langenberg, P., Ruby, E., Bresolin, L., & Stamler, J. (1990). Hypertension and sodium transport in 390 healthy adults in Chicago. *Journal of Hypertension, 8*, 121–128.

Pickering, T. G. (1994). What is the meaning of racial differences in diurnal blood pressure changes? *American Journal of Hypertension, 7*, 112–113.

Pickering, T. G., & Blank, S. G. (1989). The measurement of blood pressure. In N. Schneiderman, S. M. Weiss, & P. G. Kaufmann (Eds.), *Handbook of research methods in cardiovascular behavioral medicine* (pp. 69–80). New York: Plenum Press.

Pollare, T., Lithell, H., & Berne, C. (1990). Insulin resistance is a characteristic feature of primary hypertension independent of obesity. *Metabolism, 39*, 169–174.

Prisant, L. M., Thompson, W. O., Bottini, P. B., Carr, A. A., & Rhodes, R. (1991). Racial aspects of ambulatory blood pressure. *Journal of Human Hypertension, 5*, 369–373.

Radhakrishnamurthy, B., Srinivasan, R., Webber, L. S., Dalferes, E., Jr., & Berenson, G. S. (1985). Relationship of carbohydrate intolerance to serum lipoprotein profiles in childhood. The Bogalusa heart study. *Metabolism, 34*, 850–860.

Reaven, G. (1988). Role of insulin resistance in human disease. Banting Lecture 1988. *Diabetes, 37*, 1595–1607.

Rocchini, A. P., Katch, V., Schork, A., & Kelch, R. P. (1987). Insulin and blood pressure during weight loss in obese adolescents. *Hypertension, 10*, 267–273.

Rose, R., Jenkins, C., & Hurst, M. (1978). *Air traffic controller health change study.* Boston: Boston University School of Medicine.

Rosen, R. C., Brondolo, E., & Kostis, J. B. (1993). Nonpharmacological treatment of essential hypertension: Research and clinical applications. In R. J. Gatchel, & E. B. Blanchard (Eds.), *Psychophysiological Disorders* (pp. 63–110). Washington, DC: American Psychological Association.

Rowlands, D. B., De Giovanni, J., McLeay, R. A. B., Watson, R. D. S., Stallard, T. J., & Littler, W. A. (1982). Cardiovascular response in black and white hypertensives. *Hypertension, 4*, 817–820.

Ruiz, D. S. (1990). Social and economic profile of black Americans, 1989. In D. S. Ruiz (Ed.), *Handbook of mental health and mental disorder among black Americans.* New York: Greenwood Press.

Ruskin, A., Beard, O. W., & Schaffer, R. L. (1948). Blast hypertension: Elevated arterial pressure in victims of the Texas City disaster. *American Journal of Medicine, 4*, 228–236.

Rutledge, D. R. (1994). Race and hypertension. What is clinically relevant? *Drugs, 47*, 914–932.

Saab, P. G., & Schneiderman, N. (1993). Biobehavioral stressors, laboratory investigation, and the risk of hypertension. In J. Blascovich, & E. S. Katkin (Eds.), *Cardiovascular reac-*

tivity to psychological stress & disease (pp. 49–82). Washington, DC: American Psychological Association.

Saab, P. G., Llabre, M. M., Hurwitz, B. E., Frame, C., Reineke, L. J., Fins, A. I., McCalla, J., Cieply, L., & Schneiderman, N. (1992). Myocardial and peripheral vascular responses to behavioral challenges and their stability in Black and White Americans. *Psychophysiology, 29*, 384–397.

Saab, P. G., Llabre, M. M., Schneiderman, N., Hurwitz, B. E., McDonald, P. G., Evans, J., Wohlgemuth, W., Hayashi, P., & Klein, B. (1997). Influence of ethnicity and gender on cardiovascular responses to active coping and inhibitory-passive coping challenges. *Psychosomatic Medicine, 59*, 434–446.

Saab, P. G., Tischenkel, N., Spitzer, S. B., Gellman, M. D., Pasin, R. D., & Schneiderman, N. (1991). Race and blood pressure status influences cardiovascular responses to challenge. *Journal of Hypertension, 9*, 249–258.

Saunders, E. (1990). Tailoring treatment to minority patients. *The American Journal of Medicine, 88* (Suppl. 3B), 21–23.

Saunders, E. (1991a). Hypertension in blacks. *Primary Care, 18*, 607–622.

Saunders, E. (1991b). The safety and efficacy of terazosin in the treatment of essential hypertension in blacks. *American Heart Journal, 122*, 936–942.

Schneider, R. H., Staggers, F., Alexander, C. N., Sheppard, W., Rainforth, M., Kondwani, K., Smith, S., & King, C. G. (1995). A randomized controlled trial of stress reduction for hypertension in older African Americans. *Hypertension, 26*, 820–827.

Schneiderman, N. (1983). Behavior, autonomic function and animal models of cardiovascular pathology. In T. M. Dembroski, & T. H. Schmidt (Eds.), *Biobehavioral bases of coronary heart disease* (pp. 304–364). New York: Karger.

Schneiderman, N. (1992). Ethnicity and ambulatory blood pressure measurement: Relationship to clinic and laboratory measurements. *Journal of Clinical Pharmacology, 32*, 604–609.

Schneiderman, N., & Skyler, J. S. (1995). Insulin metabolism, sympathetic nervous system regulation, and coronary heart disease prevention. In K. Orth-Gomér, & N. Schneiderman (Eds.), *Behavioral medicine approaches to cardiovascular disease prevention* (pp. 105–133). Mahwah, NJ: Lawrence Erlbaum Associates.

Secretary's Task Force. (1986). *Report of the Secretary's Task Force on Black & Minority Health: Vol. 4: Cardiovascular and cerebrovascular disease* (pp. 1–288). U. S. Department of Health and Human Services. Washington, DC: U. S. Government Printing Office.

Senior, P. A., & Bhopal, R. (1994). Ethnicity as a variable in epidemiological research. *British Medical Journal, 309*, 327–330.

Sharma, A. M., Schorr, U., & Distler, A. (1993). Insulin resistance in young salt-sensitive normotensive subjects. *Hypertension, 21*, 273–279.

Shea, S., Stein, A. D., Basch, C. E., Lantigua, R., Maylahn, C., Strogatz, D. S., & Novick, L. (1991). Independent associations of educational attainment and ethnicity with behavioral risk factors for cardiovascular disease. *American Journal of Epidemiology, 134*, 567–582.

Shulman, N., Ford, C. D., Hall, W. D., Blaufox, D., Simon, D., Langford, H. G., & Schneider, K. A. (1989). Prognostic value of serum creatinine and effect of treatment of hypertension on renal function: Results from the Hypertension Detection and Follow-up Program. *Hypertension, 13*, (Suppl. I), 80–83.

Sigola, L. B., & Adewuyi, J. O. (1992). Ethnicity, haemostasis and cardiovascular disease: The evidence from Africa. *Central African Journal of Medicine, 38*, 385–391.

Smith, J. B., Wade, M. B., Finberg, N. S., Weinberger, M. H. (1988). Influence of race, sex and blood pressure on erythrocyte sodium transport in humans. *Hypertension, 12*, 251–258.

Stern, M. (1995). Epidemiology of obesity and its link to heart disease. *Metabolism, 44*, (Suppl. 3), 1–3.

Stern, M. P., Morales, P. A., Haffner, S. M., & Valdez, R. A. (1992). Hyperdynamic circulation and the insulin resistance syndrome ("Syndrome X"). *Hypertension, 20*, 802–808.

Strogatz, D. S., James, S. A., Haines, P. S., Elmer, P. J., Gerber, A. M., Browning, S. R., Ammerman, A. S., & Keenan, N. L. (1991). Alcohol consumption and blood pressure in black adults: The Pitt County study. *American Journal of Epidemiology, 133*, 442–450.

Svec, F., Nastasi, K., Hilton, C., Bao, W., Srinivasan, S. R., & Berenson, G. S. (1992). Black–white contrasts in insulin levels during pubertal development—The Bogalusa heart study. *Diabetes, 41*, 313–317.

Svetkey, L. P., McKeown, S. P., & Wilson, A. F. (1996). Heritability of salt sensitivity in black Americans. *Hypertension, 28*, 854–858.

Swislocki, A. L. M., Hoffman, B. B., & Reaven, G. M. (1989). Insulin resistance, glucose intolerance and hyperinsulinemia in patients with hypertension. *American Journal of Hypertension, 2*, 419–423.

Syme, S. L. (1979). Psychosocial determinants of hypertension. In E. Oresti, & C. Klint (Eds.), *Hypertension determinants, complications and intervention* (pp. 95–98). New York: Grune and Stratton.

Tischenkel, N. J., Saab, P. G., Schneiderman, N., Nelesen, R. A., Pasin, R. D., Goldstein, D. A., Spitzer, S. B., Woo-Ming, R., & Weidler, D. J. (1989). Cardiovascular and neurohumoral responses to behavioral challenge as a function of race and sex. *Health Psychology, 8*, 503–524.

Touyz, R. M., Milne, F. J., & Reinach, S. G. (1993). Racial differences in cell membrane ATPases and cellular cation content in urban South African normotensive and hypertensive subjects. *American Journal of Hypertension, 6*, 693–700.

Treiber, F. A., McCaffrey F., Pflieger, K., Raunikar, A., Strong, W. B., & Davis, H. (1993). Determinants of left ventricular mass in normotensive children. *American Journal of Hypertension, 6*, 505–513.

Treiber, F. A., Murphy, J. K., Davis, H., Raunikar, R. A., Pflieger, K., & Strong, W. B. (1994). Pressor reactivity, ethnicity, and 24-hour ambulatory monitoring in children from hypertensive families. *Behavioral Medicine, 20*, 133–142.

Treiber, F. A., Musante, L., Braden, D., Arensman, F., Strong, W. B., Levy, M., & Leverett, S. (1990). Racial differences in hemodynamic responses to the cold face stimulus in children and adults. *Psychosomatic Medicine, 52*, 286–296.

Uzu, T., Kazembe, F. S., Ishikawa, K., Nakamura, S., Inenaga, T., & Kimura, G. (1996). High sodium sensitivity implicates nocturnal hypertension in essential hypertension. *Hypertension, 28*, 139–142.

Vaughan, C. J., & Murphy, M. B. (1994). The use of ambulatory blood pressure monitoring in the evaluation of racial differences in blood pressure. *Journal of Cardiovascular Risk, 1*, 132–135.

Voors, A. W., Harsha, D. W., Webber, L. S., Radhakrishnamurthy, B., Srinivasan, S. R., & Berenson, G. S. (1982). Clustering of anthropometric parameters, glucose tolerance, and serum lipids in children with high and low β- and pre-β-lipoproteins—Bogalusa heart study. *Arteriosclerosis, 2*, 346–355.

Voors, A. W., Webber, L. S., & Berenson, G. S. (1980). Racial contrasts in cardiovascular response tests for children from a total community. *Hypertension, 2*, 686–694.

Washburn, R. A., Kline, G., Lackland, D. T., & Wheller, F. C. (1992). Leisure time physical activity: Are there black/white differences? *Preventive Medicine, 21*, 127–135.

Webber, L. S., Wattigney, W. A., Srinivasan, S. R., & Berenson, G. S. (1995). Obesity studies in Bogalusa. *The American Journal of the Medical Sciences, 310*, S53–S61.

Weinberger, M. H. (1993). Racial differences in renal sodium excretion: Relationship to hypertension. *American Journal of Kidney Diseases, 21* (Suppl. 1), 41–45.

Weinberger, M. H., Smith, J. B., Fineberg, N. S., & Luft, F. C. (1989). Red-cell sodium–lithium countertransport and fractional excretion of lithium in normal and hypertensive humans. *Hypertension, 13,* 206–212.

Williams, D. R. (1992). Black–white differences in blood pressure: The role of social factors. *Ethnicity & Disease, 2,* 126–141.

Williams, D. R. (1996). The health of the African American population. In S. Pedraza, & Rumbaut, R. G. (Eds.), *Origins and destinies: Immigration, race, and ethnicity in America* (pp. 404–416). Belmont, CA: Wadsworth.

Williams, D. R., & Collins, C. (1995). US socioeconomic and racial differences in health: Patterns and explanations. *Annual Review of Sociology, 21,* 349–386.

Williams. D. R., Lavizzo-Mourey, R., & Warren, R. C. (1994). The concept of race and health status in American. *Public Health Reports, 109,* 26–41.

Wilson, D. K., Bayer, L., & Sica, D. A. (1996). Variability in salt sensitivity classifications in black male versus female adolescents. *Hypertension, 28,* 250–255.

Wilson, T. W. (1986). History of salt supplies in West Africa and blood pressures today. *Lancet, 1,* 784–786.

Wilson, T. W., & Grim, C. E. (1991). Biohistory of slavery and blood pressure differences in blacks today: A hypothesis. *Hypertension, 17* (Suppl. I), 122–128.

Wing, R., Bunker, C. H., Kuller, L. H., & Matthews, K. A. (1989). Insulin, body mass index, and cardiovascular risk factors in premenopausal women. *Atherosclerosis, 9,* 479–484.

Witteman, J. M., Willett, W. C., Stampfer, M. J., Colditz, G. A., Kok, F. J., Sacks, F. M., Speizer, F. E., Rosner, B., & Hennekens, C. H. (1990). Relation of moderate alcohol consumption and risk of systemic hypertension in women. *American Journal of Cardiology, 65,* 633–637.

Worthington, M. G., Wendt, M. C. , & Opie, L. H. (1993). Sodium transport in hypertension: Assessment of membrane-associated defects in South African black and white hypertensives. *Journal of Human Hypertension, 7,* 291–297.

Zavaroni, I., Bonora, E., Massimo, P., Dall'Aglio, E., Luchetti, L., Buonanno, G., Bonati, P. A., Bergonzani, M., Gnudi, L., Passeri, M., & Reaven, G. (1989). Risk factors for coronary artery disease in healthy persons with hyperinsulinemia and normal glucose tolerance. *New England Journal of Medicine, 320,* 702–706.

Zavaroni, I., Mazza, S., Luchetti, L., Buonanno, G., Bonati, P. A., Bergonzani, M., Passeri, M., & Reaven, G. M. (1990). High plasma insulin and triglyceride concentrations and blood pressure in offspring of people with impaired glucose tolerance. *Diabetic Medicine, 7,* 494–498.

7

Cardiovascular Reactivity as an Indicator of Risk for Future Hypertension

Neil Schneiderman
Marc Gellman
Arnold Peckerman
Barry Hurwitz
Patrice Saab
Maria Llabre
Gail Ironson
Lynn Durel
Jay Skyler
Philip M. McCabe
University of Miami

During the past several years, investigating cardiovascular reactivity in the laboratory as a means of studying the pathobiology of cardiovascular diseases has been the subject of some debate. On one hand, several investigators have argued that there is sufficient evidence of a relationship between cardiovascular reactivity and hypertension to warrant further study (Fredrikson & Matthews, 1990; Manuck, 1994). On the other hand, others have concluded that laboratory reactivity studies have made little, if any, contribution to the understanding of hypertension (Pickering & Gerin, 1990; Ravogli et al., 1990) and have questioned the conceptual underpinnings of the proposed association (Julius, Wedner, & Hinderleiter, 1986; Parati et al., 1991). The purposes of the chapter are to review briefly the literature suggesting that cardiovascular reactivity may be a potential risk factor for hypertension and to discuss some of the conceptual and methodological issues surrounding the potential association.

At the outset of the discussion it would be useful to define our use of the term *cardiovascular reactivity*. *Reactivity* is a *reliable* response, or response pattern involving the autonomic nervous system, to a well-defined class of *psychologically challenging* stimuli, which involves a change from a baseline or

control level. The *reliability* of responses in the definition has been emphasized because reactivity is conceived of as being a dispositional attribute.
Consistency of response differences among individuals is therefore essential
to the concept. The term *psychologically challenging* is also emphasized because it implies that processes involving the CNS (e.g., perception and appraisal) are important mediators between the sensory stimulus and the
physiological responses. This, of course, distinguishes the type of reactivity
referred to in the definition from end-organ responses to purely physical
stimuli, such as agonist infusions.

Before turning to the discussion of cardiovascular reactivity as a potential
risk factor for hypertension, two methodological issues are discussed. One of
these issues involves the type of tasks used in reactivity experiments. The
second involves the test–retest reliability of these tasks. Following the review of cardiovascular reactivity as a potential risk factor for hypertension,
the nature of the so-called reactivity hypothesis and the potential utility of
using laboratory studies of reactivity to understand important aspects of the
pathobiology of cardiovascular disease are discussed.

TASK CONSIDERATIONS

Since 1980, several longitudinal studies have demonstrated a significant relationship between cardiovascular responses to laboratory challenges and
subsequent hypertension or changes in resting blood pressure. In two of
these investigations, initially normotensive individuals who exhibited elevated blood pressure reactions to the cold pressor test were subsequently
shown to be at risk for hypertension when evaluated at follow-up intervals
of 20 to 45 years (Menkes et al., 1989; Wood, Sheps, Elveback, & Scherger,
1984). In several other longitudinal studies, blood pressure reactivity to the
cold pressor test (Treiber et al., 1993; Treiber et al., 1994) and a variety of
purely psychological challenges (e.g., video games, serial subtraction, mirror-image tracing, reaction time) predicted subsequent blood pressure levels (Light, Dolan, Davis, & Sherwood, 1992; Matthews, Woodall, & Allen,
1993; Murphy, Alpert, & Walker, 1992; Treiber et al., 1993). Although several longitudinal studies have convincingly demonstrated a significant relationship between cardiovascular responses to laboratory challenges and
subsequent hypertension or changes in resting blood pressure, questions
have arisen concerning whether blood pressure responses to psychologically stressful stimuli actually predict hypertension. It has been argued, for
example, that the cold pressor stimulus, on which the reactivity–hypertension association is based, is a physical, as opposed to a psychological, stimulus (Parati et al., 1991). Recently, however, our research group has provided

strong evidence that large magnitude increases in blood pressure response to the cold pressor test are meaningfully related to the magnitude of perceived pain (Peckerman, Hurwitz, Saab et al., 1994), which is an important psychological attribute.

Briefly, we assumed that the increase in blood pressure during the cold pressor test is a compound response, partially stimulated by cold and partially by pain (Peckerman et al., 1994). We, therefore, analyzed the pain- and nonpain-related increases in blood pressure as residual effects of concurrent changes in total peripheral resistance and cardiac output, which are important determinants of blood pressure. The identified partial relationships indicated that the response pattern associated with pain included positive changes in both cardiac output and in total peripheral resistance. In contrast, the nonpain-related response was limited to an increase in total peripheral resistance. Analyses of individual differences in cardiovascular responses to pain further indicated that pain-related increments in blood pressure were mediated by a steeper rise in total peripheral resistance, an increase in heart rate, and an apparent increase in preload.

The results indicate that the cardiovascular response to the cold pressor test is an aggregate of several basic activities, including arterial vasoconstriction, stimulated jointly by cold and pain on the one hand, and increased heart rate and venous return stimulated by pain on the other (Peckerman et al., 1994). With the response to cold viewed as constant, differences among subjects in the blood pressure increase to the cold pressor test seem to be largely a function of the response to pain. In the absence of a significant pain reaction, the increase in afterload due to cold-related vasoconstriction reflexively reduces stroke volume and cardiac output, resulting in a relatively moderate increase in blood pressure. When perceived pain is substantial, however, the reflex reduction in cardiac output appears to be counteracted by increased heart rate and enhanced venous return, contributing to a relatively large increase in blood pressure. In the Peckerman et al. (1994) study, ratings of pain correlated positively with changes in mean arterial pressure to the foot cold pressor test, $r = 0.79, p <$ .0001. Thus, it would appear that the elevated blood pressure response to the cold pressor test is essentially due to the psychological properties of the task.

Another challenge to the hypothesis that reactivity to psychological stressors may be a potential risk factor for elevations in blood pressure and hypertension is based on the argument that reactivity as an individual characteristic does not generalize across a wide variety of tasks (Pickering & Gerin, 1990). Thus, for example, Parati et al. (1991) reviewed data in which they found a strong correlation between the response to mental arithmetic and mirror-image drawing but not with isometric exercise or the cold pressor test (Parati et al., 1988). Similarly, McKinney et al. (1985) found a strong correlation between blood pressure responses to a video game and a reaction time task, but only a weak correlation between these tasks and the cold pressor test.

The issues raised by Pickering and Gerin (1990) and by Parati et al. (1991) are interesting and important but do not really challenge the psychological reactivity–hypertension association. Instead, they tend to provide an important caution, which is that different psychological stressors may elicit different patterns of autonomic response. In general, blood pressure increases to psychological stressors are associated with either of two patterns of autonomic response although mixtures of these patterns have also been observed (Schneiderman, 1978; Schneiderman & McCabe, 1989). One of these patterns, which has been associated with the defense reaction in animal studies and with active coping in human reactivity studies, is characterized by an increase in skeletal muscle vasodilation, cardiac output and β_1 adrenergic activity. In contrast, the other autonomic response pattern, which is associated with aversive vigilance in animal studies and with inhibitory coping in the human laboratory, is characterized by an increase in skeletal muscle vasoconstriction, total peripheral resistance and adrenergic activity.

A study conducted in our laboratory suggests that both situational stereotypy and response stereotypy may be important in characterizing autonomic responses to psychological challenges (Saab et al., 1992). In a comparison of the cardiovascular responses of Black versus White men to an evaluative speech stressor, a mirror-image tracing task and a cold pressor test, we found that, in White men, preparation for speech elicited an increase in cardiac contractility and cardiac output. In contrast, the blood pressure increase to the mirror tracing and cold pressor test was due solely to an increase in total peripheral resistance. The difference found among White men to the speech stressor on the one hand and to the cold pressor test and mirror tracing task on the other, provides an example of task or situational stereotypy. In contrast to the White men, the Black men increased blood pressure on all tasks by increasing total peripheral resistance. This provides an example of response stereotypy.

In terms of the epidemiological findings by Menkes et al. (1989) and Wood et al. (1984), it would appear that a task primarily eliciting an increase in total peripheral resistance (i.e., cold pressor test) is appropriate for detecting the relationship between psychological reactivity at a young age and hypertension assessed 20 to 45 years later. The central role of total peripheral resistance, with regard to cardiovascular regulation during the cold pressor test, has been confirmed in several other studies (Peckerman et al., 1994; Saab et al., 1993).

In our definition of psychological reactivity, the *reliability* of responses is emphasized because reactivity is conceived of as being a dispositional attribute. Thus, if reactivity of a particular task (e.g., cold pressor test) is predictive of subsequent hypertension, it would be expected that individuals who show reactivity to this task at one point in time would show comparable reliability at a subsequent point in time. In terms of the cold pressor test, we have observed two week test–retest reliabilities ranging from 0.86 to 0.92 for systolic blood-pressure, diastolic blood pressure, and total peripheral resistance reactivity scores (deltas) for the head, hand, and foot versions of the cold pressor test (Saab et al., 1993). Similarly, test–retest reliabilities ranging from 0.64 to 0.88 have been found for cardiac output, total peripheral resistance, heart rate and systolic blood-pressure reactivity scores (deltas) for the speech stressor and mirror-image tracing tasks. Manuck (1994) has also shown that test–retest reliabilities greater than 0.8 can be obtained for heart rate and systolic and diastolic blood pressure reactivity measures when responses are aggregated over similar multiple psychological tasks across sessions. It would, thus, appear that cardiovascular responses to psychological stressors can be meaningfully assessed as dispositional attributes.

REACTIVITY AS A RISK FACTOR
FOR HYPERTENSION

In 1934, 300 boys and girls aged 7 to 17 years were given the cold pressor test (Wood et al., 1984). In 1961, 151 of the original subjects were again given the cold pressor test. The Mayo Clinic records of the 151 subjects who had been given cold pressor tests in 1934 and 1961 were reviewed in 1979 without knowledge of the test responses.

The cold pressor test consisted of having the subject immerse one hand to just above the wrist in ice water. During the period of ice-water immersion, blood pressure readings were taken in the opposite arm at 15-second intervals. The highest of these readings was designated as the peak blood pressure response. Subjects were classified as hyperreactors when they responded to the cold pressor test with an increase in blood pressure of at least 25 mmHg systolic or 20 mmHg diastolic blood pressure. Subjects with increases in blood pressure less than 25 mmHg systolic and 20 mmHg diastolic blood pressure were classified as normoreactors. The subsequent incidence of hypertension among the two groups was compared in an effort to determine whether the cold pressor test had served as a useful indicator of future hypertension.

All children in the original cohort studied in 1934 were normotensive, and 10% of the children were hyperreactors. Of the 151 subjects who received the cold pressor test in 1934 and 1961, data were available concerning hypertensive status for 142 subjects (94%) in 1979. Among the 142 subjects for whom data were available, the mean age of the 94 subjects who had been normoreactors in 1934 was 11 years, and the mean age of those who were hyperreactors in 1934 was 11.5 years. In 1961, 29 of the original group of 31 hyperreactors were similarly classified, and an additional 21 patients who had previously been normoreactors had become hyperreactors.

Wood et al. (1984) found that hypertension occurred in 71% of those who were hyperreactors to the cold pressor test in 1934 and/or 1961 but in only 19% of those who were normoreactors in both 1934 and 1961. Furthermore, stepwise linear regression determined that the response to the cold pressor test was the most powerful predictor of hypertension in 1979 and that a family history of hypertension, casual systolic blood pressure in 1934 or 1961, or casual diastolic blood pressure recorded in 1961 were less powerful predictors.

Although the report by Wood et al. (1984) suggested that hyperreactivity to the cold pressor test predicted subsequent hypertension 20 to 45 years later, an accompanying editorial by Horwitz (1984) pointed out important limitations of the study. First, more than half of the inception cohort was lost to follow-up by 1979. Second, because some subjects were first classified as hyperreactors in 1961 after being normotensive and normoreactors in 1934, it is possible that hyperreactivity in these subjects could have been a consequence rather than a precursor of elevated blood presure.

Although the fact that only 151 of 300 subjects were identified and brought back to the laboratory for the cold pressor test in 1961 leaves some concern regarding selection bias, this does not appear to be a fatal flaw in the study. First, because most of the subjects in 1961 were less than 40 years of age it seems unlikely that the loss to follow-up was meaningfully related to cardiovascular disease. Second, there is little theoretical basis for believing that being a hyperreactor or normoreactor to the cold pressor test would be related to selection bias. Third, and most important, it was possible to analyze separately the 1934 predictor and 1979 outcome data on 142 of the 151 subjects (94%) recalled in both 1961 and 1979.

The issue of classifying subjects as hyperreactors by their responses in either 1934 or 1961 could be potentially more damaging because the hyperreactivity in 1961 could have been a consequence rather than a precursor of hypertension. Fortunately, enough data were presented by Wood et al. (1984) to permit examination of the results after deletion of data from the 17 subjects who were normoreactors in 1934 but hyperreactors in 1961. After making this adjustment, we found that 21 of 31 subjects (68%) who were classified as normotensive and hyperreactors in 1934 became hypertensive by 1979. In contrast, only 18 of 94 subjects (19%) who were normotensive and normoreactors in 1934 became hypertensive across the same time period. It would therefore appear that the evidence indicating that hyperreactivity to the cold pressor test in normotensive children can predict subsequent hypertension 45 years later is quite substantial.

Another major epidemiological study has also indicated that cardiovascular reactivity to the cold pressor test is a significant predictor of subsequent hypertension (Menkes et al., 1989). In this study the cold pressor test was given to 910 of 1,130 eligible White male medical students enrolled in the 1948 to 1964 graduating classes of the Johns Hopkins Medical School; hypertensive status was ascertained by annual questionnaires during a 20- to 36-year follow-up period. Mean age of the cohort at the initial examination was 23 years. By the end of the follow-up period in 1984, 105 of the 910 study subjects reported being treated for hypertension.

A major finding of the Menkes et al. (1989) study was that systolic blood pressure reactivity to the cold pressor test predicted hypertension 20 to 36 years later, after adjustment for age at study entry, obesity, resting systolic blood pressure at study entry, cigarette smoking, and maternal and paternal history of hypertension prior to 65 years of age. The excess risk associated with systolic blood pressure reactivity was not apparent until the study sample aged some 20 years and was most apparent among those in whom hypertension developed before the age of 45 years. It would, thus, appear that the two epidemiological investigations that enrolled a large number of relatively young subjects and followed them for 20 years or more each provided reasonable evidence that cardiovascular reactivity to the cold pressor test is a potential indicator of risk for hypertension.

REACTIVITY AS A PREDICTOR
OF SUBSEQUENT BLOOD PRESSURE LEVEL

In addition to the Wood et al. (1984) and Menkes et al. (1989) studies, which demonstrated a relationship between cardiovascular reactivity and hypertension, several studies, which have been initiated in more recent years and have examined subjects over a shorter period of time, have also found that cardiovascular reactivity in the laboratory successfully predicts subsequent blood pressure. In part, these studies are noteworthy because they used psychological challenges other than the cold pressor test. In a study conducted on borderline hypertensive subjects, for example, it was found that subjects who revealed stable hypertension 5 years later, were characterized by an exaggerated diastolic blood pressure response to mental arithmetic, increased blood pressure recovery time after the task, and a higher intralymphocytic Na+ content (Borghi, Costa, Boschi et al., 1986).

In another study, Light et al. (1992) recruited 30 men from a pool of 204 men who had been subjected to a reaction-time task involving threat of shock 10 to 15 years before. The investigators found that those men who had shown high heart rate reactivity (task minus baseline) 10–15 years previously, subsequently showed higher heart rate and systolic and diastolic blood pressure levels at follow-up than low heart rate reactors, although their baseline blood pressures had not differed at initial testing. Similarly, men with high systolic blood pressure reactivity initially revealed higher diastolic blood pressure at follow-up than low systolic blood pressure reactors. Multiple regression analyses also demonstrated that heart rate, as well as systolic and diastolic blood pressure reactivity, improved prediction of follow-up blood pressure when added to models, including standard risk factors, resting blood pressure at study entry and parental history of hypertension.

Although the findings reported by Light et al. (1992) are interesting and informative, they are more provocative than definitive because only a small proportion of the original cohort was followed up and outcome data were obtained for only a small number of subjects. The results, however, are consistent with the findings of Matthews et al. (1993), who found that cardiovascular reactivity to psychological stressors predicted resting blood pressure level 6.5 years later in 206 middle-aged adults.

Matthews et al. (1993) subjected the 206 middle aged adults as well as their 164 elementary through high-school age children, to two psychological (i.e., serial subtraction and mirror-image tracing) and a physical (isometric handgrip exercise) stressor. The investigators found that even when statistically controlling for isometric exercise, age, obesity, sex, and entry level blood pressure, the diastolic blood pressure change to serial subtraction and mirror-image tracing in adults independently predicted diastolic blood pressure level 6.5 years later. Also, among adults, the systolic blood pressure change in response to serial subtraction—although not as strong a predictor as diastolic blood pressure—tended to predict subsequent systolic blood pressure status ($p < .07$) after controlling for systolic blood pressure change during isometric exercise and the other covariates. Among boys, but not girls, the systolic blood pressure response to serial subtraction at study entry was a significant predictor of subsequent systolic blood pressure, even after statistical controls were introduced for responses to isometric exercise, age, obesity, and resting systolic and diastolic blood pressure at study entry. The study conducted by Matthews et al. (1993) therefore suggests that cardiovascular reactivity in men, women, and boys can reliably predict subsequent blood pressure levels even after a period as short as 6.5 years.

Another study, which examined cardiovascular reactivity as a predictor of blood pressure in children several years later, was reported by Murphy,

Alpert, and Walker (1992). They measured blood pressure reactivity to a video-game challenge in 292 White and 46 Black third graders and then used this and other data to predict resting blood pressure (systolic and diastolic) levels 5 years later. Reactivity changes and resting levels of heart rate and (systolic and diastolic) blood pressure as well as obesity and age at entry into the study were predictors; blood pressure levels in the seventh grade, 5 years later, were the outcome variables.

Regression analyses indicated that among Black children, systolic and diastolic blood pressure reactivity was a stronger predictor of blood pressure levels 5 years later than was resting blood pressure at study entry (Murphy et al., 1992). In contrast, among White children, resting blood pressure at study entry was the best predictor of blood pressure level 5 years later. For the White children, video-game measurements enhanced the prediction of future systolic blood pressure but not future diastolic blood pressure. When resting blood pressure, resting heart rate, obesity, and age were entered as the first four variables in regression models, the video game measurements continued to be significant predictors of subsequent blood pressure in both White and Black children.

DISCUSSION

The two epidemiological studies that initially enrolled large cohorts of relatively young normotensive subjects and then followed them for 20 or more years have provided reasonable evidence that cardiovascular reactivity to the cold pressor test is a potential indicator of risk for hypertension (Menkes et al., 1989; Wood et al., 1984). The findings that high test–retest reliabilities can occur for systolic blood pressure, diastolic blood pressure, and total peripheral resistance responses (deltas) to the cold pressor test indicate that the cardiovascular response to the task is a dispositional attribute (Saab et al., 1993). Observation by Peckerman et al. (1994) that changes in blood pressure to the cold pressor test are strongly related to pain perception, indicate that an elevated pressor response to this challenge is closely related to its psychological properties. It would thus appear that an excessive pressor response to the cold pressor test by a normotensive adolescent or young adult is a predictor of risk for subsequent hypertension.

The generality of cardiovascular reactivity as a risk factor is still unknown, but the findings from a number of studies that have documented relationships between reactivity to psychological tasks and subsequent blood pressure levels suggest that the quest is promising. Among the issues that need to be resolved are the extent to which type of task, subject age during reactivity testing, sociodemographic variables, and initial blood-pressure level influences the reactivity relationship. Thus far, tasks as diverse as reaction time, serial subtraction, mirror-image tracing, and video games have been used as reactivity stressors that predict subsequent increases in blood pressure level (Borghi et al., 1986; Light et al., 1992; Matthews et al., 1993; Murphy et al., 1992). The study by Borghi et al. (1986) suggests that reactivity tasks in young borderline-hypertensive subjects can be used to predict stable hypertension several years later. And results from a variety of studies indicate that the relationship between reactivity and subsequent blood pressure level can be documented based upon responses to challenge in children (Murphy et al., 1992), young adults (Light et al., 1992) and mature middle aged individuals (Matthews et al., 1993).

Pathobiology

The processes underlying the reactivity–hypertension relationship are largely unknown. On the one hand, reactivity may represent a marker for another variable or process, which gives rise to both the hyperreactivity and hypertension. On the other hand, exaggerated hemodynamic responses to environmental stressors may be causally related to the development of hypertension. In the first instance, for example, reactivity could be a marker for increased sympathetic nervous system tone, which at an early stage is evidenced by exaggerated reactivity and at a later stage by increased blood pressure level. In the second instance, either tonic or recurrent intermittent psychological stressors may be associated with changes in sympathetic nervous system arousal that presumably could lead to hypertension (Manuck & Krantz, 1986).

There is currently scant evidence to suggest that behavioral stressors alone can produce chronic hypertension. Several reports based on battlefield, siege, or disaster conditions have suggested that such situations can increase the incidence of elevated blood pressure, but the increased incidence tends to diminish subsequently (Ehrstrom, 1945; Graham, 1945; Myasnikov, 1962; Ruskin, Beard, & Schaffer, 1948). Similarly, when restrained baboons received food delivery and shock avoidance contingent on increases in diastolic blood pressure, training sessions of 12 hours per day for many months led to substantial increases in blood pressure, but these returned to normal once experimental procedures were discontinued (Harris, Gilliam, & Brady, 1976; Harris, Gilliam, Findley, & Brady, 1973).

Although behavioral stressors alone do not appear to lead to hypertension, there is evidence to suggest that genetic factors may interact with behavioral variables to influence the development of hypertension. According to Page's (1949) mosaic theory, the hereditary factors underlying human hypertension consist of a spectrum of variants more or less randomly mixed in the genetic coding of human reproduction. The development of selectively bred strains of rats has provided some insight into putative genetic variants that might contribute to human hypertension and the manner in which these variants are influenced by environmental factors.

The spontaneously hypertensive rat (SHR) developed by Okamoto and Aoki (1963) has provided a widely used model for studying neurogenic hypertension. During the early accelerating phase of their hypertension, young SHRs like borderline hypertensive humans, display a hyperkinetic circulation with increased cardiac output related to enhanced sympathetic discharge. In contrast, older SHR, like chronic hypertensive humans, have a normal or subnormal cardiac output, but a high peripheral resistance.

Young SHRs show greater increases in sympathetic nervous system activity, plasma catecholamines, and cardiovascular reactivity than normotensive control rats when subjected to footshock, flashing lights, loud noises, vibrations cold temperatures, or physical restraint (Hallbäck & Folkow, 1974; McCarty, Chiveh, & Kopin, 1978; McCarty, Kvenantsky, Lake, Thoa, & Kopin, 1978; Yamori, Matsumoto, Yamabe, & Okamoto, 1969). In contrast, when blood was sampled from chronic-indwelling catheters in undisturbed SHRs and age-matched controls while in their home cages, no strain differences in plasma catecholamine levels were observed.

In order to determine the role that environmental stimulation plays in the development of hypertension in SHRs, Hallbäck (1975) socially isolated SHRs at weaning until 7 months of age. She found that the social isolates exhibited significantly lower resting blood pressure levels than group-reared SHRs, although both groups revealed similar cardiovascular responses to acute aversive stimulation. Similarly, when SHR pups were either cross-fostered to Wystar-Kyoto (WKY) mothers or infostered to SHR mothers, those SHR fostered to the WKY mothers had lower resting blood pressure levels in adulthood (Cierpial, Konarska, & McCarty, 1988). Reactivity testing to acute stressors, however, indicated that the cross-fostered SHRs retained the strain's adrenergic hyperresponsivity to stress. This suggests that, in some individuals, acute stressors may elicit cardiovascular hyperreactivity but if evoked infrequently, may not lead to hypertension.

The studies conducted on the SHR indicate that a genetic predisposition to hypertension can be modified by environmental history. These findings are consistent with those reported by Lawler and colleagues (Lawler, Barker, Hubbard, & Allen, 1980) who developed and studied the genetically borderline hypertensive rat (BHR) model. The BHR is a first generation cross between the SHR and the WKY rat. When either chronically stressed or fed a high-sodium diet, the BHR develops frank hypertension (Lawler, Cox,

Sanders, & Mitchell, 1988). The stress-induced hypertension can be blocked by exercise (Cox, Hubbard, Lawler, Sanders, & Mitchell, 1985).

The findings observed in SHRs (e.g., Cierpial et al., 1988; Hallbäck, 1975) and BHRs (e.g., Lawler et al., 1988) describe circumstances in which genetics and environment can interact to produce essential hypertension. They suggest that, although genetic predisposition might be a necessary condition to produce hypertension, it may not always be sufficient. The findings are consistent with the observation of Julius and Esler (1975) that not all borderline hypertensive individuals develop frank hypertension. These findings are also consistent with the observations of Wood et al. (1984) that 21 of 31 subjects, rather than all subjects who were normotensive but hyperreactors in 1934, became hypertensive by 1979.

One of the dilemmas in science is that different paradigms often lend themselves to addressing only partial aspects of the same question. Thus, for example, well-designed cohort studies may establish the strength of a prospective association between a putative risk factor and the development of a disorder, but may tell little about causality. The studies that we have reviewed relating cardiovascular hyperreactivity to subsequent increases in blood pressure level suggest that such an association exists, but tell us little about causality. Conversely, experiments conducted on the SHR and BHR are informative concerning causality, but lack generality. Intervention studies conducted on human subjects at risk for hypertension could be informative, but have not yet been carried out within the context of the reactivity–hypertension hypothesis. Presently, additional studies are needed to better assess the strength of association between hyperreactivity and the development of hypertension and to examine the generality and mechanisms underlying that relationship.

Psychophysiology

Hypertensive individuals show greater reactivity to standard laboratory challenges than do normotensive individuals (Brod, Fencl, Hejl, Jirkan, & Ulrich, 1962; see Schneiderman, Ironson, & McCabe, 1987, for review). Interpretation of the studies conducted on hypertensives, however, have been fraught with conceptual and methodological problems. Because most of these studies have been retrospective, it has not been possible to determine whether the increased reactivity is an antecedent or a consequence of the hypertension. As hypertension develops, both the arterioles and the heart display hypertrophy (Folkow, 1990). Because of these changes, a given amount of sympathetic nervous system stimulation gives risk to greater cardiovascular responsivity in hypertensives. In an attempt to circumvent some of these problems, some investigators have focused their attention on borderline hypertensives, presumably because the vasculature of such individuals is less likely to be hypertrophic.

Early research conducted on borderline hypertensive individuals identified a hyperkinetic circulatory state in which blood pressure was elevated due to a high cardiac output (Julius & Conway, 1968; Lund-Johansen, 1967; Sannerstedt, 1966). Subsequently, longitudinal studies have reported that the hemodynamic profile changes across time, and the high cardiac output normal peripheral resistance patterns seen in the hyperkinetic circulation gives rise to a pattern in which normal or low cardiac output is associated with high systemic vascular resistance (Lund-Johansen, 1986). As might be expected, the blood pressure hyperreactivity seen in borderline hypertensive subjects is associated with greater increases in cardiac output than those seen in normotensive individuals (Schulte, Rüddel, Jacobs, & von Eiff, 1986; Sherwood, Hinderliter, & Light, 1995).

Although the exact reasons why the change from borderline to frank hypertension is associated with a change from a high cardiac output–normal peripheral resistance pattern to a normal or low cardiac output–high peripheral resistance pattern are unknown, some attention has focused on the down regulation of beta-adrenergic receptors. Thus, during the progression of hypertension, beta-adrenergic receptors tend to become progressively down regulated (Bertel, Buhler, Kiowski, & Lutold, 1980) due to the high level of sympathetic nervous system stimulation (Trimarco et al., 1983).

To the extent that morbid structural adaptations may precede hypertension (Folkow & Hallbäck, 1977; Treiber et al., 1993), normotensive offspring of hypertensive individuals would appear to be ideal subjects for studying the relationship between cardiovascular reactivity and the genetic predisposition for human hypertension. Many such studies have been published; Muldoon, Terrell, Bunker, and Manuck (1993) have reviewed 51 published studies that contrasted cardiovascular reactivity in subjects with and without a family history of hypertension. The studies predominantly sampled White men. Muldoon et al. found that those individuals with a family history of hypertension had greater systolic (37% of studies) and diastolic (32% of studies) blood pressure reactivity. Because no studies reported the converse, it is clear that family history is important. The finding that two-thirds of the studies did not find a significant difference between groups, however, suggests that the situation is complex.

There are several reasons why the cardiovascular reactivity–family history relationship has not been found in all studies. First, of course, is the obvious problem posed by the failure of most investigators to confirm hypertension or its absence in first-degree relatives. A second reason is the failure of investigators to specify the strength of relationship in terms of one versus two parents, siblings, and so forth. The third reason why the reactivity–family history relationship may not have been found in all studies is be-cause of the different ages at which offspring have been tested; parental age has varied widely across studies, and hypertension prevalence varies with age. A fourth reason is that different studies have used different protocols. Still a fifth reason that could obscure the reactivity–family history of hyper-tension relationship is the possibility of an interaction between genetics and environment needing to occur in order for hypertension to manifest itself (Cierpial et al., 1988). Finally, a sixth reason is that factors underlying hu-man hypertension appear to consist of a spectrum of variants (Page, 1949), and not all individuals or groups may be sensitive to the same reactivity pro-tocol. Thus, for example, nearly all studies comparing reactivity in Black Americans have failed to find differences in terms of family history of hyper-tension (e.g., Anderson, Lane, Taguchi, & Williams, 1989; Anderson, Lane, Taguchi, Williams, & Houseworth, 1989; Johnson, 1989; Johnson, Nazzaro, & Gilbert, 1991). It would thus appear that the relationship be-tween reactivity and family history of hypertension occurs with a greater probability than would be expected by chance, but the need exists to unconfound studies in the area from a plethora of variables that can obscure the relationship.

One of the major problems obscuring study of the reactivity–hyperten-sion relationship has been the assumption that a single pathogenic reactiv-ity pattern underlies the relationship. Consistent with Page's (1949) mosaic theory, however, several different patterns of cardiovascular reactivity may actually be related to the pathogenesis of human hypertension.

Early studies conducted on borderline hypertensive patients described a hyperkinetic circulatory state in which the elevation in blood pressure level was due to elevated cardiac output (Julius & Conway, 1968; Lund-Johansen, 1967; Sannerstedt, 1966). Laboratory reactivity tests fur-ther determined that borderline hypertensive subjects demonstrate greater blood pressure responses than normotensive subjects to active coping tasks and that the differences are primarily mediated by cardiac output reactivity (Schulte et al., 1986; Sherwood & Hinderliter, 1993; Sherwood et al., 1995). The hyperreactivity seen in these experiments may be a marker for subsequent sustained hypertension, or they may reflect a causal mechanism.

According to the *recurrent activation model* the development of hyperten-sion may be related to the frequency and magnitude of cardiovascular or stress-hormone responses elicited in daily life, which resemble subject's physiologic reactivity to laboratory stressors (Manuck & Krantz, 1986). Al-ternatively, according to a *prevailing state model*, the heightened blood pres-sure and cardiac output observed in the laboratory may be predictive in daily life of physiologic responses to the environment prevalent throughout the day (Manuck & Krantz, 1986). To the extent that a variable such as hypervigilance may be involved, effects may be observed during the night as well as during the day (Schneiderman, 1992).

Although increased cardiovascular reactivity related to elevated cardiac output has been identified as a precursor of hypertension in White Americans, the situation may be somewhat different in Black Americans. It is well known, of course, that Black Americans have a greater prevalence of essential hypertension than Whites (Hypertension Detection and Follow-up Program Cooperative Group, 1978; Report of the Secretary's Task Force on Black and Minority Health, 1986). Interestingly, increases in forearm vascular resistance have been reported to be greater in young Black than young White men to a cold pressor test (Anderson, Lane, Muranake, Williams, & Houseworth, 1988). Similarly, Black boys and young adults have shown greater increases in total peripheral resistance to the cold pressor test than White boys and young adults (Treiber, Musante, Branden et al., 1990). In our laboratory we have observed that Black men showed greater increases in total peripheral resistance than White men to an evaluative-speech stressor and a mirror-star tracing task as well as to the cold pressor task (Saab et al., 1992). Whereas White men tended to increase blood pressure in anticipation of presenting a speech by elevating cardiac output, Black men increased their blood pressure by means of vasoconstriction.

The findings that Black youths reveal greater increases in systemic peripheral resistance than White youths (Treiber et al., 1990; Treiber et al., 1994) is of particular interest given findings that peripheral resistance to the cold pressor task is a significant and independent predictor of left ventricular mass in children (Treiber et al., 1993). Interestingly, even when controls are instituted for blood pressure, left ventricular hypertrophy is more than twice as prevalent in Blacks than in Whites (Beaglehole et al., 1975; Hammond, Alderman, Devereaux, Lucas, & Laragh, 1984). It is also worthy of note that among Black children, blood pressure reactivity is a stronger predictor of blood pressure level 5 years later than is resting blood pressure at study entry (Murphy et al., 1992).

In one of our studies of cardiovascular responses to the cold pressor test in normal young adult men, we observed that, in addition to being more reactive during the cold pressor test, high reactors were also distinguished by relatively elevated baseline levels of systemic vascular resistance and reduced cardiac output (Peckerman et al., 1994). These men thus manifested, in relative terms, a low-flow circulatory state (Messerli, Carvalho, Christie, & Frolich, 1978). A similar hemodynamic profile was previously observed in some borderline hypertensive individuals (Lund-Johansen, 1980) and among individuals with a family history of hypertension (Tafil-Klawe, Trzebski, Klawe, & Palko, 1985). Also, among high reactors in the Peckerman et al. (1994) study, baseline vascular resistance was positively related to the vasoconstrictive response to the cold pressor stimulus. In contrast, among low reactors the correlation was negative. Changes in cardiac output were also related to baseline cardiac output among high but not among low reactors. Although a negative correlation between parameters measured at baseline and during reactivity could in part reflect a statistical artifact (Weigel & Narvaez, 1991), the positive relationship suggests a common physiological basis (e.g., Conway, 1984).

In terms of an explanatory model, the pronounced increase in systemic vascular resistance among high reactors in the Peckerman et al. (1994) cold pressor study was not accompanied by a reflexive reduction in cardiac output. This resulted in a large blood pressure elevation. These findings suggest that reflex homeostatic adjustments were prevented, resulting in the parallel activation of blood pressure. In contrast, during the baseline period, the relatively low level of stroke volume and cardiac output observed among high reactors was associated with a high level of systemic vascular resistance, resulting in a normal blood pressure level. Thus, it was the lack of reciprocity between changes in vascular resistance and cardiac output, not simply their level of increase, which seems to have determined blood pressure reactivity.

The lack of reciprocity between cardiac output and total peripheral resistance has also been linked to the development of essential hypertension (Tsuyusaki, Yabata, Endo, & Kikawada, 1975). Hejl (1957) noted that a parallel rise in vascular resistance and cardiac output during stimulation characterized hypertensive but not normotensive subjects. This led him to conclude that such unregulated circulation constituted a basic disturbance in hypertension. A pattern of simultaneous increase in cardiac output and systemic vascular resistance during the cold pressor test has also been observed after vagal blockade with atropine in subjects with borderline (Cuddy, Smulyan, Keighley, Markason, & Eich, 1966; Murakami, Hiwada, & Kokubu, 1980) and essential (Murakami et al., 1980) hypertension, implicating parasympathetic involvement in some cases in which output–resistance reciprocity is not observed. This is of particular interest with regard to the Peckerman et al. (1994) study that related pain perception to reactivity because vagal pathways play an important role in mediation of nociceptive cardiovascular reflexes (Randich, Ren, & Gebhart, 1990).

The findings by Peckerman et al. (1994) suggest that in many instances an understanding of cardiovascular hyperreactivity requires information about the determinants of blood pressure as well as about blood pressure per se. In addition, the data by Peckerman and colleagues suggest that an understanding of cardiovascular hyperreactivity may also need to take into account hemodynamic regulation during resting conditions. This would appear also to be the case in understanding the relationship between reactivity and aerobic fitness. One of the consequences of aerobic-exercise training is a reduction in resting heart rate and blood pressure (Fox & Matthews, 1981).

In previous research, we observed that, in response to the Type A structured interview, sedentary subjects showed greater blood pressure increases than fit subjects (Lake, Suarez, Schneiderman, & Tocci, 1985). In contrast, during two competitive card games, physically fit Type As showed reliably greater blood pressure increases than either sedentary As, sedentary Bs, or fit Bs. Because the physically fit subjects were almost exclusively varsity athletes and the sedentary subjects were college students who reported following a sedentary lifestyle, the differences between sedentary and fit groups may have been due to differences in aerobic fitness or to the improved ability of competitive athletes or those engaged in fitness training to match arousal level to task requirements.

More recently, the relationship between exercise training and reactivity has been studied in rats with varying family histories of hypertension (Lawler, Naylor, Wang, & Cox, 1995). Rats with either no (WKY), one (BHR) or two (SHR) hypertensive parents received exercise training (i.e., swimming) or were placed in a control condition. Exercise training reduced resting blood pressure, especially in those rats with a positive family history who were exercised for the longest duration. In contrast, reactivity to stress was significantly enhanced in trained rats. In findings reminiscent of those observed in the trained athletes placed in a competitive situation (Lake et al., 1985), the rats appeared to muster a regulatory reserve when challenged with a stressful tail shock. The findings by Lawler and colleagues (Lawler et al., 1995), in particular, provide a caution that, although reactivity in certain cases may predict future hypertension, it is necessary to specify the circumstances under which the reactivity is assessed as well as the state of the circulatory system on which it is being imposed.

CONCLUSIONS

The major conclusion of this chapter is that cardiovascular reactivity to the cold pressor test is a strong candidate risk factor for essential hypertension. Epidemiological studies have provided reasonable evidence that blood pressure hyperreactivity to the cold pressor test by a normotensive White child or young adult man is predictive of hypertension 20 or more years later (Menkes et al., 1989; Wood et al., 1984). Additional data indicate that the cardiovascular response to the cold pressor test is a dispositional attribute (Saab et al., 1993), and the magnitude of the blood pressure response is closely related to its psychological properties (Peckerman et al., 1994). Important caveats surround the cold pressor reactivity–hypertension relationship, however, because it is not known how well the findings will generalize to various subpopulations (e.g., African Americans) nor the boundary ages for successful testing and retesting.

The generality of the cardiovascular reactivity–hypertension risk factor relationship is presently unknown, but thus far tasks as diverse as reaction time, serial subtraction, mirror image tracing, and competitive video games have successfully been used as reactivity stressors that predict subsequent increases in blood pressure level (Borghi et al., 1986; Light et al., 1992; Matthews et al., 1993; Murphy et al., 1992). These studies further indicate that the relationship between reactivity and subsequent blood pressure level are observable in response to challenge by children (Murphy et al., 1992), young adults (Light et al., 1992), and mature middle-aged individuals (Matthews et al., 1993). In view of the successful and promising research that has been carried out thus far, studies that can establish the generality of the reactivity–hypertension association and establish boundary conditions should be vigorously encouraged.

One of the major strengths of laboratory research investigating the reactivity–hypertension relationship is that it can focus on the determinants of blood pressure reactivity rather than measuring blood pressure alone. Thus, although early studies of the reactivity–hypertension relationship focused on the recurrent activation and prevailing state models (Manuck & Krantz, 1986), more recent models have tended to look at the determinants of the blood pressure baseline as well as the determinants of the blood pressure response to challenge (Peckerman et al., 1994). In addition, laboratory-stress protocols have shown themselves to be amenable to studies relating cardiovascular reactivity to variables, such as changes in left ventricular hypertrophy (Treiber et al., 1993), which can further elucidate reactivity–hypertension relationships. In summary, the laboratory stress paradigm has begun to provide evidence of an association between reactivity and subsequent hypertension and has also begun to provide insight into the processes underlying the relationship.

REFERENCES

Anderson, N. B., Lane, J. D., Muranaka, M., Williams, R. B., & Houseworth, S. J. (1988). Racial differences in blood pressure and forearm vascular responses to the cold face stimulus. *Psychosomatic Medicine, 50,* 57–63.

Anderson, N. B., Lane, J. D., Taguchi, F., & Williams, R. B. (1989). Patterns of cardiovascular responses to stress as a function of race and parental hypertension in men. *Health Psychology, 8,* 525–540.

Anderson, N. B., Lane, J. D., Taguchi, F., Williams, R. B., & Houseworth, S. J. (1989). Parental history of hypertension, and patterns of cardiovascular reactivity in women. *Psychophysiology, 26,* 39–47.

Beaglehole, R., Tyroler, H. A., Cassel, J. C., Duebner, D. C., Bartel, A., & Hames, C. G. (1975). An epidemiological study of left ventricular hypertrophy in a biracial population in Evans County, Georgia. *Journal of Chronic Diseases, 28,* 554–559.

Bertel, O., Buhler, F. R., Kiowski, W., & Lutold, B. E. (1980). Decreased beta-adrenoceptor responsiveness as related to age, blood pressure, and plasma catecholamines in patients with essential hypertension. *Hypertension, 2,* 130–138.

Borghi, C., Costa, F. V., Boschi, S., Mussi, A., & Ambrosioni, E. (1986). Predictors of stable hypertension in young borderline subjects: A five-year follow-up study. *Journal of Cardiovascular Pharmacology, 8,* S138–S141.

Brod, J., Fencl, V., Hejl, Z., Jirka, J., & Ulrych, M. (1962). General and regional hemodynamic pattern underlying essential hypertension. *Clinical Science, 23,* 339–347.

Cierpial, M. A., Konarska, M., & McCarty, R. (1988). Maternal effects on the development of spontaneous hypertension. *Health Psychology, 7,* 125–135.

Conway, J. (1984). The role of cardiac output in the control of blood pressure. *Journal of Hypertension, 7* (Suppl. 6), 3–7.

Cox, R. H., Hubbard, J. W., Lawler, J. E., Sanders, B. J., & Mitchell, V. P. (1985). Exercise training attenuates stress-induced hypertension in the rat. *Hypertension, 7,* 747–751.

Cuddy, R. P., Smulyan, H., Keighley, J. F., Markason, C. R., & Eich, R. H. (1966). Hemodynamic and catecholamine changes during a standard cold pressor test. *American Heart Journal, 71,* 446–454.

Ehrstrom, M. D. (1945). Psychogene Kriegshypertonien (Psychogenic hypertension of war). *Acta Medica Scandanavica, 122,* 546–570.

Folkow, B. (1990). "Structural factor" in primary and secondary hypertension. *Hypertension, 16,* 89–101.

Folkow, B., & Hallbäck, M. (1977). *Physiopathology of spontaneous hypertension in rats.* New York: McGraw-Hill.

Fox, E. L., & Matthews, D. K. (1981). *The physiological basis of physical education and athletics.* Philadelphia: Saunders.

Fredrikson, M., & Matthews, K. A. (1990). Cardiovascular responses to behavioral stress and hypertension: A meta-analytic review. *Annals of Behavioral Medicine, 12,* 30–39.

Graham, J. D. P. (1945). High blood pressure after battle. *Lancet, 248,* 239–240.

Hallbäck, M. (1975). Consequences of social isolation on blood pressure, cardiovascular reactivity and design in spontaneously hypertensive rat. *Acta Physiology Scandanavia, 93,* 455–465.

Hallbäck, M., &. Folkow, B. (1974). Cardiovascular response to acute mental 'stress' in spontaneously hypertensive rats. *Acta Physiology Scandanavia, 90,* 684–693.

Hammond, I. W., Alderman, M. H., Devereux, R. B., Lutas, E. M., & Laragh, J. H. (1984). Contrast in cardiac anatomy and function in black and white patients with hypertension. *Journal of National Medical Association, 76,* 247–255.

Harris, A. H., Gilliam, W. J., & Brady, J. V. (1976). Operant conditioning of large magnitude, 12-hour duration, heart rate elevations in the baboon. *Pavlovian Journal of Biological Science, 11,* 86–92.

Harris, A. H., Gilliam, W. J., Findley, J. D., & Brady, J. V. (1973). Instrumental conditioning of large-magnitude, daily, 12-hour blood pressure elevations in the baboon. *Science, 182,* 175–177.

Hejl, Z. (1957). Changes in cardiac output and peripheral resistance during simple stimuli influencing blood pressure. *Cardiologia, 31,* 375–382.

Horwitz, R. I. (1984). Methodologic standards and the clinical usefulness of the cold pressor test. *Hypertension, 6,* 295–296.

Hypertension Detection and Follow-up Cooperative Group (1978). Sex and race differences in end organ damage among 10,940 hypertensives. *American Journal of Cardiology, 41,* 402–410.

Johnson, E. H. (1989). Cardiovascular reactivity, emotional factors, and home blood pressures in black males and without a parental history of hypertension. *Psychosomatic Medicine, 51,* 390–403.

Johnson, E. H., Nazzaro, P., & Gilbert, D. C. (1991). Cardiovascular reactivity to stress in black male offspring of hypertensive parents. *Psychosomatic Medicine, 53,* 420–432.

Julius, S., & Conway, J. (1968). Hemodynamic studies in patients with borderline blood pressure elevation. *Circulation, 38,* 282–288.

Julius, S., & Esler, M. (1975). *The nervous system in arterial hypertension.* Springfield, IL: Charles C. Thomas.

Julius, S., Weder, A. B., & Hinderliter, A. L. (1986). *Does behaviorally induced blood pressure variability lead to hypertension?* New York: Wiley.

Lake, B. W., Suarez, E. C., Schneiderman, N., & Tocci, N. (1985). The Type A behavior pattern, physical fitness, and psychophysiological reactivity. *Health Psychology, 4,* 169–187.

Lawler, J. E., Barker, G. F., Hubbard, J. W., & Allen, M. T. (1980). The effects of conflict on tonic levels of blood pressure in the genetically borderline hypertensive rat. *Psychophysiology, 17,* 363–370.

Lawler, J. E., Cox, R. H., Sanders, B. J., & Mitchell, V. P. (1988). The borderline hypertensive rat: A model for studying the mechanisms of environmentally induced hypertension. *Health Psychology, 7,* 137–147.

Lawler, J. E., Naylor, S. K., Wang, C. H., & Cox, R. H. (1995). Family history of hypertension, exercise training and reactivity to stress: A study in rats. *International Journal of Behavioral Medicine, 2,* 233–251.

Light, K. C., Dolan, C. A., Davis, M. R., & Sherwood, A. (1992). Cardiovascular responses to an active coping challenge as predictors of blood pressure patterns 10 to 15 years later. *Psychosomatic Medicine, 54,* 217–230.

Lund-Johansen, P. (1967). Hemodynamics in early essential hypertension. *Acta Medica Scandanavica, 182*(482), 8–101.

Lund-Johansen, P. (1980). Hemodynamics in essential hypertension. *Clinical Science, 59,* 343s–354s.

Lund-Johansen, P. (1986). Hemodynamic patterns in the natural history of borderline hypertension. *Journal of Cardiovascular Pharmacology, 8* (Suppl. 5), 8–14.

Manuck, S. B. (1994). Cardiovascular reactivity in cardiovascular disease: "Once more unto the breach." *International Journal of Behavioral Medicine, 1,* 4–31.

Manuck, S. B., & Krantz, D. S. (1986). Psychophysiologic reactivity in coronary heart disease and essential hypertension. In K. A. Matthews, S. M. Weiss, T. Detre, T. M. Dembroski, B. Falkner, S. B. Manuck, & R. B. Williams, Jr. (Eds.), *Handbook of stress, reactivity and cardiovascular disease* (pp. 11–34). New York: Wiley.

Matthews, K. A., Woodall, K. L., & Allen, M. T. (1993). Cardiovascular reactivity to stress predicts future blood pressure status. *Hypertension, 22,* 479–485.

McCarty, R., Chiveh, C. C., & Kopin, I. J. (1978). Spontaneously hypertensive rats: Adrenergic hyper-reactivity to anticipation of electric shock. *Behavioral Biology, 23,* 180.

McCarty, R., Kvenantsky, R., Lake, C. R., Thoa, N. B., & Kopin, I. J. (1978). Sympathoadrenal activity of SHR and WKY rats during recovery from forced immobilization. *Physiology and Behavior, 21,* 951.

McKinney, M. E., Miner, M. H., Rüddel, H., McIlvain, H. E., Witte, H., Buell, J. C., Elliot, R. S., & Grant, L. B. (1985). The standardized mental stress protocol: Test–retest reliability and comparison with ambulatory blood pressure monitoring. *Psychophysiology, 22,* 453–463.

Menkes, M. S., Matthews, K. A., Krantz, D. S., Lundberg, U., Mead, L. A., Qagish, B., Liang, K. Y., Thomas, C. B., & Pearson, T. A. (1989). Cardiovascular reactivity to the cold pressure test as a predictor of hypertension. *Hypertension, 14,* 524–530.

Messerli, F. H., Carvalho, J. G. R., Christie, B., & Frolich, E. D. (1978). Systemic and regional hemodynamics in low, normal and high cardiac output borderline hypertension. *Circulation, 58,* 441–448.

Muldoon, M. F., Terrell, D. F., Bunker, C. H., & Manuck, S. B. (1993). Family history studies in hypertension research: Review of the literature. *American Journal of Hypertension, 6,* 76–88.

Murakami, E., Hiwada, K., & Kokubu, T. (1980). Pathophysiological characteristics of labile hypertensive patients determined by the cold pressor test. *Japanese Circulation Journal, 44,* 438–442.

Murphy, J. K., Alpert, B. S., & Walker, S. S. (1992). Ethnicity, pressor reactivity, and children's blood pressure: Five years of observations. *Hypertension, 20,* 327–332.

Myasnikov, A. L. (1962). *Significance of disturbances in higher nervous activity in the pathogenesis of hypertensive disease.* New York: Pergamon.

Okamoto, K., & Aoki, K. (1963). Development of a strain of spontaneously hypertensive rat. *Japanese Circulation Journal, 27,* 282–293.

Page, I. H. (1949). Pathogenesis of arterial hypertension. *Journal of the American Medical Association, 140,* 451–458.

Parati, G., Trazzi, S., Ravogli, A., Casadei, R., Omboni, S., & Mancia, G. (1991). Methodological problems in evaluation of cardiovascular effects of stress in humans. *Hypertension, 17* (Suppl. III), 50–55.

Peckerman, A., Huwritz, B. E., Saab, P. G., Llabre, M. M., McCabe, P. M., & Schneiderman, N. (1994). Stimulus dimensions of the cold pressor test and the associated patterns of cardiovascular response. *Psychophysiology, 31,* 282–290.

Pickering, T. G., & Gerin, W. (1990). Cardiovascular reactivity in the laboratory and the role of behavioral factors in hypertension. *Annals of Behavioral Medicine, 12,* 3–16.

Randich, A., Ren, K., & Gebhart, G. F. (1990). Electrical stimulation of cervical vagal afferents. II. Central relays for behavioral antionociception and arterial blood pressure decreases. *Journal of Neurophysiology, 64,* 1115–1124.

Ravogli, A., Trazzi, S., Villani, A., Mutti, E., Cuspidi, C., Sampieri, L., DeAmbroggi, L., Parati, G., Zanchetti, A., & Mancia, G. (1990). Early 24 hour blood pressure in normotensive subjects with parental hypertension. *Hypertension, 16,* 491–497.

Report of the Secretary's Task Force on Black and Minority Health (1986). *Volume IV: Cardiovascular and cerebrovascular disease, Part I.* Washington, DC: U.S. Department of Health and Human Services.

Ruskin, A., Beard, O. W., & Schaffer, R. L. (1948). Blast hypertension: Elevated arterial pressure in victims of the Texas City disaster. *American Journal of Medicine, 4,* 228–236.

Saab, P. G., Llabre, M. M., Hurwitz, B. E., Frame, C. A., Reineke, L. J., Fins, A. I., McCalla, J., Cieply, L. K., & Schneiderman, N. (1992). Myocardial and peripheral vascular responses to behavioral challenges and their stability in black and white Americans. *Psychophysiology, 29,* 384–397.

Saab, P. G., Llabre, M. M., Hurwitz, B. E., Schneiderman, N., Wohlgemuth, W., Durel, L. A., Massie, C., & Nagel, J. (1993). The cold pressor test: Vascular and myocardial response patterns and their stability. *Psychophysiology, 30,* 366–373.

Sannerstedt, R. (1966). Haemodynamic response to exercise in patients with arterial hypertension. *Acta Medica Scandanavica, 180*(458), 1–83.

Schneiderman, N. (1978). Animal models relating behavioral stress and cardiovascular pathology. In T. Dembroski, S. Weiss, J. Shields, S. Haynes, M. Feinleib (Eds.), *Coronary-prone behavior.* New York: Springer.

Schneiderman, N. (1992). Ethnicity and ambulatory blood pressure measurement: Relationship to clinical and laboratory measurements. *Journal of Clinical Pharmacology, 32,* 604–609.

Schneiderman, N., Ironson, G., & McCabe, P. M. (1987). *Physiology of behavior and blood pressure regulation in humans.* Amsterdam: Elsevier.

Schneiderman, N., & McCabe, P. M. (1989). Psychophysiologic strategies in laboratory research. In N. Schneiderman, S. M. Weiss, & P. G. Kaufmann (Eds.), *Handbook of research methods in cardiovascular behavioral medicine* (pp. 349–364). New York: Plenum.

Schulte, W. Ruddel, H., Jacobs, U., & von Eiff, W. (1986). Hemodynamic abnormalities in borderline hypertension during mental stress. *Journal of Cardiovascular Pharmacology, 8* (Suppl. 5), 128–130.

Sherwood, A., & Hinderliter, A. L. (1993). Responsiveness to a- and b-adrenergic receptor agonists: Effects of race in borderline hypertensive compared to normotensive men. *American Journal of Hypertension, 6,* 630–635.

Sherwood, A., Hinderliter, A. L., & Light, K. C. (1995). Physiological determinants of hyperreactivity to stress in borderline hypertension. *Hypertension, 25,* 384–390.

Tafil-Klawe, M., Trzebski, A., Klawe, J., & Palko, T. (1985). Augmented chemoreceptor reflex tonic drive in early human hypertension and in normotensive subjects with family background of hypertension. *Acta Physiologica Polonica, 36*(1), 51–58.

Treiber, F. A., McCaffrey, F., Pflieger, K., Rauniker, R. A., Strong, W. B., & Davis, H. (1993). Determinants of left ventricular mass in normotensive children. *American Journal of Hypertension, 6,* 505–513.

Treiber, F. A., Musante, L., Braden, D., Arensman, F., Strong, W. B., Levy, M., & Leverett, S. (1990). Racial differences in hemodynamic responses to the cold face stimulus in children and adults. *Psychosomatic Medicine, 52,* 281–296.

Treiber, F. A., Rauniker, R. A., Davis, H., Fernandez, T., Levy, M., & Strong, W. B. (1994). One year stability and prediction of cardiovascular functioning at rest and during laboratory stressors in youth with family histories of essential hypertension. *International Journal of Behavioral Medicine, 1,* 335–353.

Trimarco, B., Volpe, M., Ricciardelli, B., Picotti, G. B., Galva, M. D., Petracca, R., & Condorelli, M. (1983). Studies of the mechanisms underlying impairment of beta-adrenoceptor-mediated effects in human hypertension. *Hypertension, 5,* 584–590.

Tsuyusaki, T., Yabata, Y., Endo, K., & Kikawada, R. (1975). Stress as a causative factor of essential hypertension and its influence on the cardiovascular system. *Japanese Circulation Journal, 39,* 571–575.

Weigel, R. M., & Narvaez, M. (1991). Multiple regression analysis of differential response to treatment in randomized controlled clinical trials. *Controlled Clinical Trials, 12,* 378–394.

Wood, D. L., Sheps, S. G., Elveback, L. R., & Scherger, A. (1984). Cold pressor test as a predictor of hypertension. *Hypertension, 6,* 301–306.

Yamori, Y., Matsumoto, M., Yamabe, H., & Okamoto, K. (1969). Augmentation of spontaneous hypertension by chronic stress in rats. *Japanese Circulation Journal, 33,* 399–409.

8

The Prognostic Importance of Depression, Anxiety, Anger, and Social Support Following Myocardial Infarction: Opportunities for Improving Survival

Nancy Frasure-Smith
François Lespérance
The Montreal Heart Institute Research Center
McGill University
University of Montreal
Mario Talajic
The Montreal Heart Institute Research Center
University of Montreal

Since the 1980s, there has been increasing evidence that psychosocial factors influence prognosis after a heart attack. Life stress (Ruberman, Weinblatt, Goldberg, & Chaudhary, 1984), psychological distress (Frasure-Smith, 1991), anxiety (Follick et al., 1988), depressive symptoms (Ahern et al., 1990), some aspect of type A behavior, hostility, or anger (Booth-Kewley & Friedman, 1987), and social support or its absence in the form of social isolation and loneliness (Case, Moss, Case, McDermott, & Eberly, 1992; Ruberman et al., 1984) have all been linked to poor outcomes following myocardial infarction (MI). For example, we carried out a study examining the long-term prognostic consequences of high levels of psychological distress in hospitals soon after an MI (Frasure-Smith, 1991). During hospitalization, 229 male patients responded to a standardized measure of psychological distress symptoms, the General Health Questionnaire or GHQ (Goldberg, 1972). Patients who reported 5 or more of the 20 GHQ symptoms were about 2.5 times as likely to die of cardiac causes over the subsequent 5 years as other patients ($p = 0.0003$). This increase in risk remained even after controlling for other prognostic factors in the data set including history of coronary artery disease (CAD), ag, and the need for diamorphine for pain relief. Ahern and colleagues (1990) analysed data from the Cardiac Arrhythmia Pilot Study and found that scores on the Beck Depression Inventory (Beck, Ward, Mendelson, Mock, & Erbaugh, 1961), administered within 60 days after an MI, predicted 1-year cardiac death–arrest rates in a sample of 351 patients with significant arrhythmias at baseline. In Germany, data from 560 males involved in the Post-Infarction Late Potential Study showed that high degrees of depressive symptomatology in the hospital predicted cardiac deaths in the first 6 months following MI (Ladwig, Kieser, König, Breithardt, & Borggrefe, 1991).

Despite the apparent consistency of these results, a number of considerations have limited medical acceptance of the importance of psychological factors following MI. First, all of the evidence is based on secondary analysis of data sets collected to test other hypotheses in special subgroups of MI patients (e.g., patients with significant arrhythmias, males, patients under age 65). Second, despite the risks associated with different psychological factors, treatment implications are not clear because there are no recognized interventions for life stress, psychological distress, and social isolation. Third, the relative importance of these different psychological factors is unknown. Are they all measures of some common underlying dimension of negative emotions or demoralization (Dohrenwend, Shrout, Egri, & Mendelsohn, 1980), or is there evidence of independent impact? Finally, the degree to which psychosocial factors interact with measures of disease severity to influence prognosis remains unclear.

In this context, we undertook the Emotions and Prognosis Post-Infarction Project (EPPI), a prospective study designed to examine the relative prognostic importance of a variety of psychological and social factors including major depression following MI. More specifically, we focused on the following questions:

- How common is major depression in the hospital following MI?
- Does depression in the hospital predict post-MI prognosis?
- Do other negative emotions (anxiety, anger) in the hospital predict post-MI prognosis?
- What is the role of social support in predicting post-MI prognosis?
- Is the impact of psychosocial factors explained by disease severity?

METHODS

Sample

The research was conducted as an ancillary study of the Canadian Signal-Averaged Electrocardiogram (ECG) Trial (Rouleau et al., 1994). Patients admitted to the Montreal Heart Institute with a diagnosis of acute MI between July, 1991 and June, 1992 were eligible for study participation if they met two of three research criteria for MI (typical chest pain lasting 20 or more minutes, elevated cardiac enzymes, and the presence of new Q waves on the electrocardiogram). They also had to be stable enough to complete an hour-long baseline interview while hospitalized between 5 and 15 days post-MI and could not have any other life threatening conditions. There were no limits on sample inclusion in terms of age or gender.

Procedures

The baseline interview included the following standardized measures: a modified version of the National Institute of Mental Health (NIMH) Diagnostic Interview Schedule (DIS; Robins, Helzer, Croughan, & Ratcliff, 1981) for assessing major depression; the 21-item Beck Depression Inventory (BDI; Beck et al., 1961) to assess depressive symptomatology; the state scale of Spielberger's State Trait Anxiety Inventory (STAI; Spielberger, Gorsuch, Lushene, Vagg, & Jacobs, 1983); Spielberger's Anger Expression Scale (AX) including subscales for anger-in (the tendency to avoid expressing anger, even when appropriate) and anger-out (the tendency to express anger by directing it outwards towards other people or objects; AX; Spielberger, Krasner, & Solomon, 1988); and Zimet's Perceived Social Support Scale (PSSS; Blumenthal, Burg, Barefoot, Williams, Haney & Zimet, 1987).

The modifications, which were made to the DIS for current depression, have been described in detail in previous publications (Frasure-Smith, Lespérance, & Talajic, 1993, 1995). In brief, the DSM–III–R (American Psychiatric Association, Committee on Nomenclature and Statistics, 1987) duration and impairment criteria for major depression were not used. Patients were asked only about the occurrence of depression symptoms since admission (on average 7 days and, in most cases, less than the 2 weeks required by Diagnostic and Statistical Manual of Mental Disorders [3rd ed., rev., DSM–III–R]) and because of difficulties in judging impairment in daily activities while hospitalized, impairment from symptoms was not assessed. Patients also responded to questions about medical history, smoking behavior, and social and demographic characteristics.

Data on patients' medical condition was obtained from hospital charts and included Killip class (Killip & Kimball, 1967), left ventricular ejection fraction ($n = 220$), and prescription at discharge of beta-blockers and ACE inhibitors. The 4-point Killip class is a clinical assessment of the degree of left ventricular dysfunction based on a chest x-ray, heart and lung sounds, and signs of shock. Patients with higher Killip class ratings have greater cardiac dysfunction. Holter monitoring for cardiac arrhythmias over 18 to 24 hours during hospitalization was available for 197 patients. These patients did not differ from patients without Holters on any baseline variables.

All patients or their family members were contacted at 6, 12, and 18 months after the MI to assess patient survival status.

Statistical Analysis

Statistical analyses were carried out with SPSS for Windows (version 6.0; Norusis, 1993) using two-tailed tests. Multiple logistic regression analysis and the chi-square statistic were used to assess the odds ratio for mortality in various subgroups of patients. As suggested by Beck and Steer (1987) patients with BDI scores of 10 or greater in the hospital were considered to show at least moderate symptoms of depression. To select other variables related to prognosis, we followed procedures that were outlined by Hosmer and Lemeshow (1989). Baseline measures were dichotomized at points suggested in the literature, and the odds ratio for each pair of groups was assessed using logistic regression and the chi-square statistic. Because dichotomization points were unclear for the psychosocial measures other than the modified DIS and the BDI, splits were made at the upper quartile (lower quartile for social support). Those baseline variables other than depression that were significantly related ($p \leq .05$) to mortality in the bivariate analyses were entered into backwards-stepwise logistic-regression analyses to predict mortality at each time point. The resulting models were confirmed with forward analysis. Criteria for entry and removal were based on the likelihood ratio test with enter and remove limits set at $p \leq .05$ and $p \geq .10$.

RESULTS

How Common is Major Depression in Hospital Following MI?

About one in six patients (15.8%) met the modified *DSM-III-R* criteria for major depression at the time of the baseline interview. Another one in six reported elevated numbers of depressive symptoms (BDI ≥ 10) without meeting the criteria for major depression. This is similar to the results of other studies conducted in the early postinfarct period. Schleifer and colleagues (1989) administered the Schedule for Affective Disorders to 283 patients 8 to 10 days after an MI and found that 18% met Research Diagnostic Criteria for major depressive disorder, and another 27% had minor depressive disorder. More recently, German researchers evaluated the level of depression 17 to 21 days after an MI in a sample of 560 male patients 65 years of age or younger (Ladwig et al., 1991). They found that 14.5% had extreme depression according to their scale with another 22.3% exhibiting mild depression. Thus, estimates for the percentage of patients affected by some degree of depression in the hospital following MI range from about 33% to 45% depending on the sample's gender and age composition and the measure of depression used.

Does Depression in Hospital Predict Post-MI Prognosis?

Over the full 18 months of follow-up, 21 patients died (9.5%), including 19 from cardiac causes and 2 from cancer. Twelve of the 19 cardiac deaths took place during the first 6 months after discharge, and 5 occurred between 6 and 12 months. Table 8.1 shows the odds ratios associated with major depression at the end of the 6-, 12-, and 18-month follow-up periods. Major

TABLE 8.1

Odds Ratios (95% Confidence Intervals) for 6-, 12-, and 18-Month Cardiac Mortality Associated With Baseline Psychosocial Measures

	6 Months	12 Months	18 Months
Major Depression (DIS)	6.2 (1.9 - 20.7) $p = .0041$**	4.4 (1.6 - 12.6) $p = .0083$**	3.6 (1.3 - 10.0) $p = .018$*
Depressive Symptoms (BDI ≥10)	5.6 (1.4 - 22.5) $p = .0098$**	7.0 (2.2 - 23.0) $p = .0005$**	7.8 (2.4 - 25.3) $p = .0002$**
Anxiety (STAI ≥ 40)	4.5 (1.2 - 16.6) $p = .023$*	2.6 (0.9 - 5.1) $p = .084$	2.3 (0.8 - 6.5) $p = .12$
Anger-In (AXIN ≥ 19)	3.9 (1.0 - 15.1) $p = .051$	3.2 (1.1 - 9.6) $p = .042$*	2.8 (1.0 - 8.1) $p = .067$
Anger-Out (AXOUT ≥ 17)	2.7 (0.7 - 10.3) $p = .15$	1.1 (0.4 - 3.6) $p = .81$	1.4 (0.5 - 4.1) $p = .55$
Perceived Social Support (PSSS ≤ 66)	3.5 (1.0 - 2.7) $p = .061$	4.3 (1.5 - 12.4) $p = .009$**	3.7 (1.3 - 10.4) $p = .016$*

*p ≤ .05; **p ≤ .01

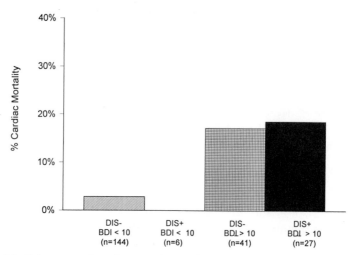

FIG. 8.1. Eighteen-month cardiac mortality in relation to depression as measured by the modified DIS and the Beck Depression Inventory (BDI).

depression significantly increased the risk of mortality at all three time points. However, its impact was largely during the first 6 months.

There were two measures of depression in the data set: major depression assessed with the modified DIS using *DSM–III–R* criteria and severity of depressive symptoms measured with the BDI dichotomized at 10. As expected, there was considerable overlap between the two approaches to measuring depression, with 78.4% of patients classified in the same way by the two measures. However, an additional 18.8% of patients had high BDI scores but did not meet the *DSM-III-R* criteria for major depression. Finally, there were six patients who were classified as depressed, according to the modified DIS, but whose BDI scores were less than 10. The mortality in each of the four groups defined by the DIS and the BDI is shown in Fig. 8.1.

Although none of the patients who were positive on the DIS and who had low BDI scores died, suggesting they may have been falsely positive on the DIS, the DIS-negative patients with elevated BDI scores were as likely to die as the DIS-positive patients. Thus, there is an increase in risk for mortality associated with elevated BDI scores independent of whether patients meet *DSM–III–R* criteria for depression. The major difference between the BDI and the DIS is that to be classified as depressed on the basis of the *DSM–III–R* criteria operationalized in the DIS, patients must report either sadness or loss of interest. Without at least one of these key symptoms, patients are not considered to be depressed regardless of how many other symptoms of depression are reported. In contrast, patients can score 10 or higher on the BDI and be classified as mildly to moderately depressed without reporting either sadness or loss of interest. Thus, patients with elevated BDI scores who do not meet *DSM–III–R* criteria for major depression may represent a group of more mildly depressed individuals. These patients may develop major depression after discharge and die subsequent to this later depression. However, it is also possible that there is a risk associated with the more minor form of depression, which is similar to the risk conveyed by major depression and does not depend on the development of major depression to have an impact. Finally, there is the possibility that differences between the modified DIS and the BDI are related to the different ways in which the questions are asked on the two scales. The differences may, in fact, reflect methodological problems related to symptom-reporting tendencies with the two formats.

Do Other Negative Emotions (Anxiety, Anger) in Hospital Predict Post-MI Prognosis?

The data set included the STAI and the AX including both anger-in and anger-out subscales, as well as the two measures of depression and the PSSS. Because these self-report measures all tap interrelated concepts, their degree of overlap was examined using Pearson's product moment correlation coefficients. The highest correlation was between BDI scores and scores on the STAI($r = 0.43; p \leq .01; n = 218$). All other coefficients were below 0.30, indicating modest correlations among the measures, but little evidence of collinearity.

Table 8.1 shows the odds ratios associated with each of the psychosocial variables at the end of the 6-, 12-, and 18-month follow-up periods. It is apparent that, although psychosocial variables are important predictors of outcomes at each time point, the pattern of prognostic variables changes somewhat with time. Baseline measures of major depression, anxiety, and anger-in are more important in the first few months following infarct, with depressive symptoms and social support becoming more important later in the follow-up period.

Because of the degree of interrelationship among the measures, the independent impact of the significant psychosocial predictors was assessed at each time point using backward stepwise multiple logistic regression analysis with forward confirmation of models. Enter and remove limits were set at 0.05 and 0.10 respectively.

At 6 months, with only 12 deaths and three significant psychosocial predictors (DIS major depression, BDI score, and state anxiety score), it is not surprising that only one variable, major depression, was retained in the final multivariate model. The 12-month model, derived from major depression,

BDI score, anger-in score, and PSSS included two variables: BDI score and social support, each of which had an independent impact. After control for BDI score and social support, major depression did not improve the 12-month model ($p = 0.30$). The 18-month data resulted in the same two variable psychosocial model including BDI score and social support. Again, after control for these variables, major depression did not improve the model ($p = 0.95$). Table 8.2 (see pages 212–213) shows the odds ratios associated with BDI score and social support, each after controlling for the other. In essence, both depressive symptomatology and perceived social support had an independent impact on mortality at both 12 and 18 months post-MI, and control for these variables totally eliminated the risk associated with major depression per se.

What is the Role of Social Support in Predicting Post-MI Prognosis?

Because of the importance of both depressive symptoms and low-perceived social support in predicting both 12-month and 18-month mortality, we also explored the joint impact of the two factors. The literature linking social support and disease outcomes makes a distinction between the stress-buffering and main-effect models (e.g., Cohen, 1988). In the main-effect model, social support is seen as having an impact on disease outcomes regardless of the level of other psychosocial risks. In the stress-buffering model, social support is viewed as beneficial primarily in the face of high stress or high psychosocial risk. If we consider depression to be a high stress situation, the two models of social support can be evaluated by examining the interrelationship between baseline social support and depression symptoms in terms of predicting subsequent cardiac mortality. This relationship appears in Fig. 8.2. Among the depressed (BDI $\geq$ 10), the risk of mortality decreases with each increase in the quartile of perceived social support, but among the nondepressed, there is no discernible relationship between social support and mortality. This is a clear demonstration of the buffering model of social support and suggests that one potentially useful approach for treating post-MI depression may involve interventions to change perceptions of support. However, it is also possible that perceived social support varies with severity of depression. Perceiving that one has little support may in fact be a type of depressive symptom itself (Henderson, 1984). Thus, Fig. 8.2 may simply illustrate an increasing risk of mortality associated with increased severity of depression. We examined this hypothesis several ways. First, we looked at the mean BDI scores among the depressed patients in each quartile of social support. Although the depressed patients in the lowest quartile of social support had the highest mean BDI score

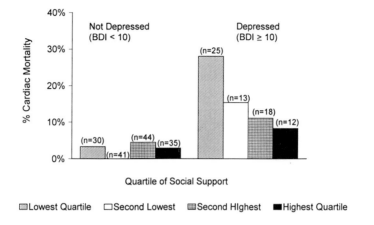

FIG. 8.2. Eighteen-month cardiac mortality in relation to social support and depression (BDI).

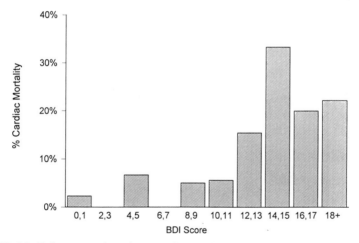

FIG. 8.3. Eighteen-month cardiac mortality in relation to BDI score in the hospital.

(19.2), there was no pattern among the depressed in the other three quartiles of social support (13.3, 14.7, and 15.1, going from lowest to highest social support). We also looked at mortality in relation to the level of the BDI score. As shown in Fig. 8.3, this data suggests that although there is an increase in risk of mortality beginning with BDI scores of around 12, after that the relationship between BDI scores and death is not linear. Thus, there is little evidence in our data to indicate that scores on the PSSS are really a proxy measure for the severity of depression.

TABLE 8.2
Comparison of Multivariate Psychosocial and Clinical Models for Predicting Cardiac Mortality at 6, 12, and 18 Months Post-MI

	6 Months		12 Months		18 Months	
	Variable	Adjusted Odds Ratio (95% CI)	Variable	Adjusted Odds Ratio (95% CI)	Variable	Adjusted Odds Ratio (95% CI)
Multivariate Psychosocial Model	Major Depression (DIS)	6.2 (1.9–20.7)	Depressive Symptoms (BDI ≥ 10)	6.0 (1.8–19.9)	Depressive Symptoms (BDI ≥ 10)	6.8 (2.1–22.2)
			Perceived Social Support (PSSS ≤ 66)	3.3 (1.1–9.9)	Perceived Social Support (PSSS ≤ 66)	2.8 (0.9–8.3)
	Model χ^2 (1 df) = 8.2 (p = .0041**)		Model χ^2 (2 df) = 16.5 (p = .0003**)		Model χ^2 (2 df) = 17.5 (p = .0002**)	
Multivariate Clinical Model	Previous MI	6.1 (1.2–30.2)	Previous MI	4.2 (1.2–14.2)	Previous MI	5.2 (1.5–9.8)
	Killip Class ≥ 2	3.7 (1.0–13.7)	Killip Class ≥ 2	4.4 (1.4–13.7)	Killip Class ≥ 2	6.2 (2.0–18.8)
	PVCs ≥ 10	4.9 (1.3–18.8)	PVCs ≥ 10	5.2 (1.6–16.7)	PVCs ≥ 10	6.1 (1.9–19.4)
	Model χ^2 (3 df) = 18.0 (p = .0004**)		Model χ^2 (3 df) = 23.7 (p < .00001**)		Model χ^2 (3 df) = 32.1 (p < .00001**)	

Pyschosocial Model's Improvement Over Clinical Model	χ^2 (1 df) = 4.3 (p = .039*)	P^2 (2 df) = 11.1 (p = .0040**)	χ^2 (2 df) = 11.7 (p = .0029**)
Clinical Model's Improvement Over Psychosocial Model	χ^2 (3 df) = 17.2 (p = .0006)	χ^2 (3 df) = 14.9 (p = .0019)	χ^2 (3 df) = 20.6 (p = .0001)
Combined Psychosocial and Clinical Model	Major Depression (DIS) OR = 4.6 (1.1–18.7)	Depressive Symptoms (BDI ≥ 10) OR = 4.0 (1.1–15.3)	Depressive Symptoms (BDI ≥ 10) OR = 5.2 (1.3–20.6)
	Previous MI OR = 5.4 (1.1–27.1)	Perceived Social Support (PSSS ≤ 66) OR = 3.6 (1.0–13.0)	Perceived Social Support (PSSS ≤ 66) OR = 3.0 (0.8–10.8)
	Killip Class ≥ 2 OR = 3.6 (0.9–14.3)	Previous MI OR = 3.7 (1.0–13.8)	Previous MI OR = 4.4 (1.2–17.1)
	PVCs ≥ 10 OR = 5.9 (1.4–24.7)	Killip Class ≥ 2 OR = 3.3 (0.9–11.8)	Killip Class ≥ 2 OR = 4.2 (1.2–15.1)
		PVCs ≥ 10 OR = 4.9 (1.3–19.2)	PVCs ≥ 10 OR = 7.3 (1.9–28.8)
	Model χ^2 (4 df) = 22.3 (p = .0002**)	Model χ^2 (5 df) = 29.1 (p < .00001**)	Model χ^2 (5 df) = 25.3 (p < .00001**)

* $p \leq .05$ ** $p \leq .01$

213

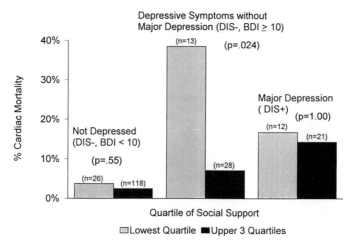

FIG. 8.4. Eighteen-month cardiac mortality in relation to social support and measure of depression.

The role of social support in relation to the DIS-positive patients and the DIS-negative patients with high BDI scores who were discussed previously was also examined. Because the cell sizes become quite small when all four quartiles of social support are examined, we compared the lowest quartile of social support in relation to the other three quartiles. The results, shown in Fig. 8.4, indicate that in our data, the buffering role of social support is mostly limited to the patients with high BDI scores who did not meet DSM–III–R criteria for major depression in hospital. This supports the interpretation that social support may have prevented these patients from going on to develop major depression after discharge, and dying subsequent to a later depression. It is also interesting to note that social support does not appear to be as important for the patients who already had major depression in hospital, or for those with no indication of depression on either measure. This suggests that treatment strategies for patients with elevated BDI scores who do not have major depression might focus on social support while patients with major depression may need a different approach involving medications or more intensive therapy.

Is the Impact of Psychosocial Factors Explained by Disease Severity?

As important as depression and social support seem to be in post-MI prognosis, they are obviously not the only prognostic factors. There is a large, well-established literature linking post-MI outcomes with traditional clinical measures of cardiac disease severity including previous MI, left ejection fraction, and arrhythmias (e.g. Bigger, Fleiss, Kleiger, Miller, & Rolnitsky, 1984; Connolly, Cairns, & Huang, 1989; Moss, 1984; Wong, Cupples, Ostfeld, Levy, & Kannel, 1989). Because it seems reasonable to argue that sicker patients have every reason to be depressed, depression and low social support may simply be proxy measures of disease severity. It is entirely possible that what has been observed as risks associated with psychosocial variables are really risks associated with poor cardiac function. In order to assess this possibility we took several steps. First, multiple logistic regression analysis and the chi^2 statistic were used to compare all baseline variables for the patients with positive DIS ratings (major depression) with those of patients who were negative on the DIS. Similarly, patients were compared with BDI scores greater than or equal to 10 with those with lower scores, and those in the lowest quartile of social support with those in the other three quartiles. The results of these analyses appear in Table 8.3.

Patients with major depression, according to the modified DIS, did not differ on any measures of disease severity from other patients. They were, however, less likely to say that they had any close friends. Also, not surprisingly, they were more likely to have elevated BDI scores and to score in the upper quartiles of anxiety, anger-in and anger-out.

We observed that patients with high BDI scores were more likely to be women, to live alone, to have a Killip class greater than or equal to 2, and to not have been prescribed beta-blockers at discharge. In addition, they were more likely to meet *DSM–III–R* criteria for major depression, to score in the upper quartiles of anxiety and anger-in, and to be in the lowest quartile of perceived social support. Thus, although most of the differences between patients with elevated BDI scores and other patients were on psychosocial variables, their higher Killip class, suggestive of poorer cardiac function, and less frequent prescription of beta-blockade indicates that patients with high BDI scores may have been sicker patients. In order to control for this possibility we carried out logistic regression analysis for 12- and 18-month mortality in which the variables of Killip class and beta-blockade were forced into the equation first, followed by BDI score. At both time periods the impact of BDI scores remained significant after controlling for the baseline differences in variables related to disease severity. At 12 months the adjusted odds ratio associated with the BDI was 5.4 (95% confidence interval (CI) = 1.6 to 18.1; $p = 0.0070$), and at 18 months it was 5.9 (95% CI = 1.8 to 19.9; $p = 0.0040$). In summary, the impact of elevated BDI scores on mortality remained even after controlling for baseline imbalances on variables possibly related to disease severity. Thus, there is little evidence to support the notion that BDI scores were proxy measures for disease severity or that the impact of BDI scores on outcome was due to the fact that depressed patients were more severely compromised in terms of cardiac status.

TABLE 8.3

Baseline Characteristics Associated With Major Depression, Depressive Symptoms and Low Perceived Social Support

Characteristic	Category	Major Depression % DIS+ (n)	p	Depressive Symptoms % BDI ≥ 10 (n)	p	Social Support % PSSS ≤ 66 (n)	p
Age	≥ 65 yrs	13.5 (74)	.51	31.0 (71)	.96	23.9 (71)	.89
	< 65 yrs	16.9 (148)		31.3 (147)		23.1 (147)	
Sex	Female	24.5 (49)	.069	48.9 (47)	.0030**	21.3 (47)	.70
	Male	13.3 (173)		26.3 (171)		24.0 (171)	
Education	≤ 8 yrs	19.4 (67)	.57	40.0 (65)	.071	23.1 (65)	.94
	> 8 yrs	14.2 (155)		27.5 (153)		23.5 (153)	
Living Alone	Yes	16.7 (42)	.63	48.7 (41)	.0091**	43.9 (41)	.0011**
	No	15.6 (180)		27.4 (177)		18.6 (177)	
Close Friends	Yes	13.3 (181)	.041*	28.8 (177)	.12	19.8 (177)	.012*
	No	26.8 (41)		41.5 (41)		39.0 (41)	
Daily Smoker	Yes	15.9 (88)	.96	27.1 (85)	.29	32.9 (85)	.0084
	No	15.7 (134)		33.8 (133)		17.3 (133)	
Previous MI	Yes	19.5 (82)	.25	34.2 (79)	.47	25.3 (79)	.61
	No	13.6 (140)		29.5 (139)		22.3 (139)	
Left Ventricular Ejection Fraction	≤ 35%	20.3 (64)	.39	34.9 (63)	.43	21.3 (61)	.62
	> 35%	14.1 (156)		24.9 (153)		24.5 (155)	
Killip Class	≥ 2	21.3 (47)	.26	45.5 (44)	.022*	27.3 (44)	.50
	1	14.3 (175)		27.6 (174)		22.4 (174)	

Variable	Category						
PVCs	≥ 10/hr	18.5 (27)	.84	38.5 (26)	.61	30.8 (26)	.34
	< 10/hr	17.0 (171)		33.3 (168)		22.0 (168)	
Rx B-blockers at discharge	Yes	15.0 (140)	.68	25.7 (136)	.025*	23.5 (136)	.95
	No	17.1 (82)		40.2 (82)		23.2 (82)	
Rx ACE inhibitors at discharge	Yes	22.2 (63)	.11	40.3 (62)	.067	22.6 (62)	.86
	No	13.2 (159)		27.6 (156)		23.7 (156)	
Major Depression (DIS)	Yes	NA		81.8 (33)	< .0001**	36.4 (33)	.067
	No			22.2 (185)		20.1 (185)	
Depressive Symptoms	BDI ≥ 10	39.7 (68)	< .0001**	NA		33.8 (68)	.016*
	BDI < 10	4.0 (150)				18.7 (150)	
State Anxiety	STAI ≥ 40	37.9 (58)	< .0001**	60.3 (58)	< .0001**	39.7 (58)	.0010**
	STAI < 40	6.9 (160)		20.6 (160)		17.5 (160)	
Anger-In	AX-In ≥ 19	26.4 (53)	.015*	54.7 (53)	< .0001**	35.8 (53)	.014*
	AX-In < 19	11.7 (154)		22.1 (154)		18.8 (154)	
Anger-Out	AX-Out ≥ 17	23.2 (69)	.042*	36.2 (69)	.21	23.2 (69)	.97
	AX-Out < 17	12.1 (141)		27.7 (141)		23.4 (141)	
Perceived Social Support	PSSS ≤ 66	23.5 (51)	.067	45.1 (51)	.016*	NA	
	PSSS > 66	12.6 (167)		26.9 (167)			

*$p \leq .05.$ **$p \leq .01$

Comparisons of the patients in the two social support groups showed that patients in the lowest quartile of social support were more likely to live alone, to say they had no close friends, and to have been daily smokers at the time of admission. Although they did not differ significantly from patients with higher social support in terms of major depression, patients with low perceived social support were more likely to have BDI scores 10 or higher and to score in the upper quartiles of anxiety and anger-in. Thus, there were no baseline differences in cardiac disease severity associated with perceived social support. However, because smoking is an established cardiac risk factor, we assessed the impact of social support at 12 and 18 months after controlling for smoking using logistic regression analysis. The 12-month odds ratio for perceived social support adjusted for smoking was 4.2 (95% CI = 1.4 to 12.5; p = 0.010). At 18 months the adjusted value was 3.7 (95% CI = 1.3 to 10.8; p = 0.015). Thus, as with major depression and BDI scores, there was little evidence that the impact of perceived social support on mortality was related to baseline imbalances in measures of disease severity.

In addition to controlling for baseline imbalances in cardiac measures as a way of assessing the importance of cardiac disease severity in explaining the impact of psychosocial variables, we compared the prognostic importance of clinical and psychosocial models. The same approach was used for multivariate model-building with the clinical variables that was taken with the psychosocial variables. That is, we assessed the bivariate predictive importance of various disease severity measures at each time point and then derived multivariate models using backward stepwise multiple regression analysis confirmed with forward stepping. The baseline variables with significant bivariate odds ratios for the clinical variables at all three time points included previous MI, Killip class, left ventricular ejection fraction, and PVCs. In addition, at 12 and 18 months, prescription of beta-blockade and ACE inhibitors at baseline were also significant. The multivariate models for all three time points were identical and included previous MI, PVCs, and Killip class (see Table 8.2).

In order to evaluate the relative importance of the psychosocial and clinical models at each time point, we assessed the improvement in prediction when each model was added to the other. For example, at 6 months we began by forcing in the psychosocial variable (major depression) and then evaluated the improvement in the model by adding the three multivariate clinical predictors. The opposite was also done. That is, we forced in the three multivariate clinical variables and assessed the improvement in the model when major depression was added. The results of these analyses appear in Table 8.2.

The major conclusion is that both psychosocial and clinical factors are important in post-MI prognosis. At all three time periods the uniquely clinical models were significantly improved by the inclusion of psychosocial variables. Similarly, the psychosocial models were all improved by considering the clinical measures. Further, the odds ratios associated with depression and social support were of the same order as the odds ratios associated with previous MI, advanced Killip class, and frequent PVCs. In addition, the impact of both clinical and psychosocial variables remained largely unaffected by control for the other type of variable.

DISCUSSION

Although heart attack patients and their families have long been convinced of the close ties between their emotions and their hearts, it has only been in the last 15 years that a significant body of evidence has begun to accumulate, showing that the brain and the heart interact to influence post-MI prognosis. In understanding the link between psychosocial factors and post-MI prognosis it is necessary to consider both behavioral and physiological mechanisms.

Potential Behavioral Mechanisms

Although unstudied in post-MI patients, anxiety and depression have been related to reduced compliance with other types of treatment (Blumenthal, Williams, Wallace, Williams, Jr., & Needles, 1982; Richardson et al., 1987; Surridge et al., 1984). A recent study of coronary artery disease patients aged 65 and over found that patients with major depression complied with a prescription of aspirin twice a day on only 45% of days in comparison to 69% among the nondepressed ($p \leq 0.02$); (Carney, Freedland, Eisen, Rich, & Jaffe, 1995). Although, the clinical implications of this level of noncompliance are unknown, it is conceivable that the worse outcomes observed in depressed patients may have resulted from their failure to adhere to physicians' recommendations about lifestyle changes or medications. On the other hand, depression and anxiety are often associated with multiple physical complaints. Because of its impact on autonomic arousal, depression may cause amplification of pain and other physical symptoms, leading to earlier or more frequent use of medical care (Katon, 1988). In fact, studies of patients without cardiac disease have found higher rates of health care system use among the depressed (Katon, Berg, Robins, & Risse, 1986; Weissman, Myers, & Thompson, 1981). Thus, although depressed patients may be less compliant, they may also visit physicians more often and may seek care earlier for relatively minor problems. The ways in which patient behavior may link depression and outcome are likely to be quite complex. These complexities may also be compounded by changes in physician's treatment behavior in response to patients with depressed affect and other psychological symptoms. For example, there have been some suggestions in the literature that beta-blockers are related to depression (Avorn, Everitt, & Weiss, 1986), although there have been no controlled studies that support this. Beta-blockade is known to improve post-MI survival (Beta Blocker Heart Attack Trial, 1982), but it is not known how often physicians remove beta-blockade from post-MI patients who repeatedly complain of depression.

How social support plays a part in the potential behavioral mechanisms linking depression and cardiac mortality is also uncertain. It may facilitate compliance or encourage patients to seek medical care earlier for their symptoms. It is also possible that adequate social support acts to cushion the physiological impact of depression or to speed recovery preventing death. Our results indicate that among patients recovering from MI, social support is related to prognosis primarily among patients with elevated BDI scores, that is, it either acts as a buffer between depression symptoms and mortality, or it is a proxy index for the severity of depression among the depressed. Further, the buffering role of perceived social support around the time of the MI appears to be primarily important in preventing mortality after the first 6 months. This suggests that whatever it is about social support which prevents mortality, it takes a while to have an impact and does not really fit in with the interpretation that depressed patients with low-perceived social support are more severely depressed.

Potential Physiological Mechanisms

The potential physiological mechanisms linking depression and other negative emotions with post-MI mortality are likely to be at least as complicated as the behavioral ones. Two major mechanisms are thought to be involved in post-MI deaths: ventricular arrhythmias and recurrent acute MIs. In reviewing the research on depression and the probable physiological mechanisms involved in precipitating ventricular arrhythmias and recurrent MIs, two main hypotheses can be formulated: (a) Post-MI patients with high levels of depressive symptomatology or major depression have an increase in sympathetic nervous system activity compared to nondepressed patients; and (b) In depressed post-MI patients in comparison to nondepressed patients there is an activation of platelet aggregation that can lead to acute thrombus formation.

Although direct data is lacking in depressed post-MI patients, indirect evidence from basic animal research, as well as studies in some human samples, supports the idea that depressed patients have a chronic increase in sympathic nervous activity. By itself this increase could also increase the risk of a fatal ventricular arrhythmic event. Animal research has demonstrated that when the heart is vulnerable following an MI, increased sympathetic activity significantly increases the risk of ventricular fibrillation (Schwartz, Billman, & Stone, 1984). In this model, beta-blocking medication, left stellate ganglion blockade, and increased vagal tone all act to protect against fatal arrhythmias (de Ferrari & Schwartz, 1990; Podrid, Fuchs, & Candinas, 1990). It has also been demonstrated that increased sympathetic activity has a strong negative impact in post-MI patients with left ventricular dysfunction (Rouleau, Packer et al., 1994). Furthermore, the cardioprotective effect of beta-blocking medication in post-MI patients is mainly evidenced by a reduction in sudden death, particularly in patients with poor ventricular function (Chadda, Goldstein, Byington, & Curb, 1986). Bigger's team (Cook et al., 1991) also found that a beta-blocker, atenolol, increases heart rate variability in humans. Heart rate variability is measured through the electrocardiogram (ECG). More variability between individual heart beats means more vagal activity or less sympathetic activity directed to the heart through the autonomic nervous system. In addition, there is indirect evidence based on increases in heart rate variability that ACE inhibitors increase vagal tone after an MI in patients with congestive heart failure (Binkley et al., 1993; Bonaduce et al., 1994). In conclusion, post-MI patients seem to be protected if the deleterious effect of sympathetic nervous activity (beta-blockers, left stellate ganglion blockade) is decreased or the beneficial effect of vagal tone (beta-blockers, ACE inhibitors) is increased (Coats et al., 1992; Verrier, Calvert, & Lown, 1975).

An overall increase in sympathetic nervous system activity is well-documented in depressed patients. The basal heart rate is increased (Lahmeyer & Bellur, 1987; Carney et al., 1988; Veith et al., 1993), there is an increase in plasma norepinephrine levels (Lake et al., 1982), and it has been suggested that most of this is secondary to an increase in sympathetic outflow (Veith et al., 1993). Carney et al. (1988) found indirect evidence of this increase in sympathetic activity in depressed cardiac patients. They reported that there is a reduction in heart rate variability associated with depression in patients with established CHD.

Cardiac status as well as depression influences sympathetic nervous system outfow. Although reduced pump function induces an increase in sympathetic activity as an adaptive mechanism to maintain adequate cardiac outflow, patients with more pronounced neurohormone activation, including norepinephrine activity, have a poorer prognosis (Rouleau et al., 1994).

Meredith, Broughton, Jennings, and Esler (1991) found that patients admitted for sustained ventricular arrhythmias had an increased cardiac production of norepinephrine in comparison to coronary patients without arrhythmias. In fact, our results showed that most of the impact of high BDI scores on mortality was in those with low ejection fractions and frequent premature ventricular contractions (PVCs), (Frasure-Smith et al., 1995). Further, all of the patients with depression, low ejection fraction and PVCs ($n = 6$) died by 18 months—five of the six because of fatal arrythmias. It is possible that these patients were at especially high risk because of the impact of increases in sympathetic activity associated with depression, low ejection fraction, and PVCs. Although, to date, research has indicated that the increases in norepinephrine activity among patients suffering a major depression are restricted to those with melancholic features (Roy, Linnoila, & Potter, 1985), it is possible that, in our study, the patients who had high BDI scores, frequent PVCs, and low ejection fractions had particularly high sympathetic drive. Although the hypothesis of increased sympathetic nervous system activity in depressed post-MI patients is supported by existing literature, it remains to be documented in a well-designed study of depression following MI.

It is widely accepted that, in addition to deaths from fatal arrhythmias, post-MI deaths frequently involve recurrent MIs (Cairns et al., 1989). Platelet aggregation is a major player in this recurrent thrombogenic process that may be related to depression. Because platelets are assumed to be a peripheral model of the neuroregulation of norepinephrine and serotonin in the brain, they have been extensively studied in relation to emotional states, particularly in relation to major depression (Garcia-Sevilla, Padro, Giralt, Guimon, & Areso, 1990; Meltzer & Arora, 1991). Although the clinical impact has not been assessed in coronary patients, recent data suggest that there may be an increase in platelet reactivity to serotonin and epinephrine in patients with major depression. *Serotonin* is a $5\text{-}HT_2$ receptor agonist that weakly induces platelet aggregation in a direct fashion. However, it also amplifies platelets' reactions to other agonists like adenosine diphosphate (ADP) and thrombin (Badimon, Lacily, Badimon, & Faster, 1990; Vanhoutte, 1991). Many studies have found increased $5\text{-}HT_2$ binding (Bmax) in depressed patients compared to normal controls (Meltzer & Lowy, 1987; Arora & Meltzer, 1989; Meltzer & Arora, 1991). This increase in $5\text{-}HT_2$ binding in depressed patients has also been documented using measures of receptor function based on phosphoinositide turnover (Mikuni, Kagaya, Takahashi, & Meltzer, 1992), intracellular platelet calcium mobilization (Kusumi, Koyama, & Yamashita, 1991), and $5\text{-}HT_2$ induced platelet aggregation (Brusov et al., 1989), suggesting an upregulation of the $5\text{-}HT_2$ receptors in depressed patients. Therefore, although none of these measures of platelet serotonin function have been evaluated in depressed patients with cardiac disease, there is some data to suggest more reactive platelet aggregation in major depression. If this is also true in depressed post-MI patients, they would be more likely to have a recurrent thrombogenic event.

In summary, although the literature supports two major physiological links between depression and post-MI mortality, increased sympathetic nervous system function and changes in platelet aggregability, additional direct data is needed to establish the precise mechanisms.

Limitations

As all research, our study has limitations. First, although the sample size of 222 patients is large in comparison to many studies in health psychology, the number of deaths, even by the 18-month follow-up point, is small. This limits the ability to control for multiple variables, and, as indicated by the wide-confidence intervals observed, means that the stability of our multivariate models is in question. Thus, although we can be fairly confident about the bivariate relationships between baseline variables and mortality, the degree to which these relationships are robust to control for measures of disease severity requires further evaluation. In addition, it must be remembered that our consideration of potential mechanisms is at this point purely speculative and based on two types of assumptions, which may or may not be true. First, it has been assumed that factors thought to be involved in post-MI prognosis, which were measured during the index admission, are stable after discharge. For example, it was assumed that patients with low left ejection fractions at the time of the index MI continued to have reduced ventricular function over the follow-up period. Similarly, it was assumed that patients with high BDI scores remained depressed or at least experienced a relapse in depression prior to the terminal event. It is not known if this was the case. Second, it was assumed that the pathophysiology of depressed patients, which has mostly been documented in psychiatric populations without significant medical illness, is similar to the pathophysiology of depressed post-MI patients. Again, additional evidence is needed on this question.

Future Directions

Our research points in several directions. First, it is necessary to explore the behavioral and physiological mechanisms linking psychosocial variables with post-MI mortality. Knowledge about mechanisms could help guide treatment as well as shed light on other diseases in which psychosocial factors may play an important role. Second, it is necessary to test the link between psychosocial variables and mortality in an experimental context. That is, it is necessary to determine whether changing psychosocial factors will influence mortality. The medical literature is full of examples in which interventions designed to alter established prognostic factors had an unexpected negative or null impact on prognosis (e.g. The Cardiac Arrhythmia Suppression Trial [CAST] Investigators, 1989). Of course, research examining the impact of changing psychosocial factors assumes that we know how to change depression and social support in a post-MI population. Currently, this is far from the case. Although there are well-established medical and psychological treatments for depression, no research has yet evaluated the efficacy and safety of these approaches following a heart attack. In addition, while work is ongoing in the context of the National Heart, Lung, and Blood Institute sponsored Enhancing Recovery in Coronary Heart Disease Patients (ENRICHD) trial, interventions for improving social support remain to be designed and evaluated.

ACKNOWLEDGMENTS

This study was supported by grants from the Joint Research Grant Program in Mental Health of the Fonds de la recherche en santé du Québec (FRSQ) and the Quebec Council of Social Research (CQRS), the Medical Research Council (MRC) of Canada, and the Montreal Heart Institute Research Fund.

The contributions of Drs. Duncan Stewart and Jean-Lucien Rouleau (who served on the committee to judge causes of death), and of Nicole Gélinas, Annick Girard, Danielle Beaudoin, RN, Louise Girard, Denise Pagé, RN, and Doris Morissette, RN (who participated in data collection and coding), are gratefully acknowledged.

REFERENCES

Ahern, D. K., Gorkin, L., Anderson, J. L., Tierney, C., Hallstrom, A., Ewart, C., Capone, R. J., Schron, E., Kornfeld, D., Herd, J. A., Richardson, D. W., & Follick, M. J. (1990). Biobehavioral variables and mortality or cardiac arrest in the Cardiac Arrhythmia Pilot Study (CAPS). *The American Journal of Cardiology, 66,* 59–62.

American Psychiatric Association, Committee on Nomenclature and Statistics. (1987). *Diagnostic and statistical manual of mental disorders, revised* (3rd ed.) Washington, DC: American Psychiatric Association.

Arora, R. C., & Meltzer, H. Y. (1989). Increased serotonin$_2$ (5-HT$_2$) receptor binding as measured by ^{3}H-lysergic acid diethylamide (^{3}H-LSD) in the blood platelets of depressed patients. *Life Sciences, 44,* 725–734.

Avorn, J., Everitt, D. E., & Weiss, S. (1986) Increased antidepressant use in patients prescribed β-blockers. *Journal of the American Medical Association, 66,* 59–62.

Badimon, L., Lassila, R., Badimon, J., & Fuster, V. (1990). An acute surge of epinephrine stimulates platelet deposition to severely damaged vascular wall [Abstract]. *Journal of American College of Cardiology, 15,* 181A.

Beck, A. T., & Steer, R. A. (1987). *Beck Depression Inventory Manual.* San Antonio, TX: The Psychological Corporation, Harcourt Brace Jovanavich.

Beck, A. T., Ward, C. H., Mendelson, M., Mock, J., & Erbaugh, J. (1961). An inventory for measuring depression. *Archives of General Psychiatry, 4,* 561–571.

Beta Blocker Heart Attack Trial. (1982). A randomized trial of propranolol in patients with acute myocardial infarction. I. Mortality results. *Journal of the American Medical Association, 147,* 1707–1714.

Bigger, J. T., Jr., Fleiss, J. L., Kleiger, R., Miller, J. P., Rolnitzky, L. M., & Multicenter Post-Infarction Research Group. (1984). The relationships among ventricular arrhythmias, left ventricular dysfunction, and mortality in the 2 years after myocardial infarction. *Circulation, 69,* 250–258.

Binkley, P. E., Haas, G. J., Starling, R. C., Nunziata, E., Hatton, P. A., Leier, C. V., & Cody, R. J. (1993). Sustained augmentation of parasympathetic tone with angiotensin-converting enzyme inhibition in patients with congestive heart failure. *Journal of the American College of Cardiology, 21,* 655–661.

Blumenthal, J. A., Burg, M. M., Barefoot, J., Williams, R. B., Haney, T., & Zimet, G. (1987). Social support, type A behavior, and coronary artery disease. *Psychosomatic Medicine, 49,* 331–340.

Blumenthal, J. A., Williams, R. S., Wallace, A. G., Williams, R. B., Jr., & Needles, T. L. (1982). Physiological and psychological variables predict compliance to prescribed exercise therapy in patients recovering from myocardial infarction. *Psychosomatic Medicine, 44,* 519–527.

Bonaduce, D., Marciano, F., Petretta, M., Migaux, M. L., Morgano, G., Bianchi, V., Salemme, L., Valva, G., & Condorelli, M. (1994). Effects of converting enzyme inhibition on heart period variability in patients with acute myocardial infarction. *Circulation, 90,* 108–113.

Booth-Kewley, S. & Friedman, H. S. (1987). Psychological predictors of heart disease: A quantitative review. *Psychological Bulletin, 101,* 343–362.

Brusov, O. S., Beliaev, B. S., Katasonov, A. B., Zlobina, G. P., Factor, M. I., & Lideman, R. R. (1989). Does platelet serotonin receptor supersensitivity accompany endogenous depression? *Biological Psychiatry, 25,* 375–381.

Cairns, J. A., Singer, J., Gent, M., Holder, D. A., Rogers, D., Sackett, D. L., Sealey, B., Tanser, P., & Vandervoort, M. (1989). One year mortality outcomes of all coronary and intensive care unit patients with acute myocardial infarction, unstable angina or other chest pain in Hamilton, Ontario, a city of 375,000 people. *Canadian Journal of Cardiology, 5,* 239–245.

Carney, R. M., Freedland, K. E., Eisen, S. A., Rich, M. W., & Jaffe, A. S. (1995). Major depression and medication adherence in elderly patients with coronar artery disease. *Health Psychology, 14,* 88–90.

Carney, R. M., Rich, M. W., teVelde, A., Saini, J., Clark, K., & Freedland, K. E. (1988). The relationship between heart rate, heart rate variability and depression in patients with coronary artery disease. *Journal of Psychosomatic Research, 32,* 159–164.

Case, R. B., Moss, A. J., Case, N., McDermott, M., & Eberly, S. (1992). Living alone after myocardial infarction: Impact on Prognosis. *Journal of the American Medical Association, 267,* 515–519.

Chadda, K., Goldstein, S., Byington, R., & Curb, J. D. (1986). Effect of propranolol after acute myocardial infarction in patients with congestive heart failure. *Circulation, 73,* 503–510.

Coats, A. S., Adamopoulos, S., Radaelli, A., McCance, A., Meyer, T., Bernardi, L., Solda, P., Davey, P., Ormerod, O., Forfar, C., Conway, J., & Sleight, P. (1992). Controlled trial of physical training in chronic heart failure: Exercise performance, hemodynamics, ventilation, and autonomic function. *Circulation, 85,* 2119–2131.

Cohen, S. (1988). Psychosocial models of the role of social support in the etiology of physical disease. *Health Psychology, 7,* 269–297.

Connolly, S. J., Cairns, J. A., & Huang, Y. (1989). Predictors of one year mortality after acute myocardial infarction: analysis of a complete community experience 1986–1987 [Abstract]. *Circulation, 80* (Suppl. 4), 11–47.

Cook, J. R., Bigger, J. T., Jr., Kleiger, R. E., Fleiss, J. L., Steinman, R. C., & Rolnitzky, L. M. (1991). Effect of atenolol and diltiazem on heart period variability in normal persons. *Journal of American College of Cardiology, 17,* 480–484.

de Ferrari, G. M., & Schwartz, P. J. (1990). Autonomic nervous system and arrhythmias. *Annals New York Academy of Sciences, 601,* 247–262.

Dohrenwend, B. P., Shrout, P. E., Ergi, G., & Mendelsohn, F. S. (1980). Nonspecific psychological distress and other dimensions of psychopathology: Measures for use in the general population. *Archives of General Psychology, 37,* 1229–1236.

Follick, M. J., Gorkin, L., Capone, R. J., Smith, T. W., Ahern, D. K., Stablein, D., Niaura, R., & Visco, J. (1988). Psychological distress as predictor of ventricular arrhythmias in a post-myocardial infarction population. *American Heart Journal, 116,* 32–36.

Frasure-Smith, N. (1991). In-hospital symptoms of psychological stress as predictors of long-term outcome after acute myocardial infarction in men. *The American Journal of Cardiology, 67,* 121–127.

Frasure-Smith, N., Lespérance, F., & Talajic, M. (1993). Depression following myocardial infarction: Impact on 6-month survival. *Journal of the American Medical Association, 270,* 1819–1825.

Frasure-Smith, N., Lespérance, F., & Talajic, M. (1995). Depression and 18-month prognosis following myocardial infarction. *Circulation, 91,* 999–1005.

Garcia-Sevilla, J. A., Padró, D., Giralt, T., Guimón, J., & Areso, P. (1990). $a_{\bar{2}}$ adrenoceptor-mediated inhibition of platelet adenylate cyclase and induction of aggregation in major depression: effect of long-term cyclic antidepressant drug treatment. *Archives General Psychiatry, 47,* 125–132.

Goldberg, D. (1972). *The Detection of Psychiatric Illness by Questionnaire.* London: Oxford University Press.

Henderson, A. S. (1984). Interpreting the evidence on social support. *Social Psychiatry, 19,* 49–52.

Hosmer, D. & Lemeshow, S. (1989). *Applied Logistic Regression.* Toronto, Canada: Wiley.

Katon, W. (1988). Depression: somatization and social factors. *The Journal of Family Practice, 27,* 579–580

Katon, W., Berg, A., Robins, A. J., & Risse, S. (1986). Depression: Medical utilization and somatization. *Western Journal of Medicine, 144,* 564–568.

Killip, T., & Kimball, J. T. (1967). Treatment of myocardial infarction in a coronary care unit: a two-year experience with 250 patients. *American Journal of Cardiology, 20,* 457–464.

Kusumi, I., Koyama, T., & Yamashita, I. (1991). Serotonin-stimulated Ca^{2+} response is increased in the blood platelets of depressed patients. *Biological Psychiatry, 30,* 310–312.

Ladwig, K. H., Kieser, M., König, M., Breithardt, G., & Borggrefe, M. (1991). Affective disorders and survival after acute myocardial infarction: Results from the post-infarction late potential study. *European Heart Journal, 12,* 959–964.

Lahmeyer, H. W. & Bellur, S. N. (1987). Cardiac regulation and depression. *Journal of Psychiatric Research, 21,* 1–6.

Lake, C. R., Packar, D., Ziegler, M., Lipper, S., Slater, S., & Murphy, D. (1982). High plasma norepinephrine levels in patients with major affective disorder. *American Journal of Psychiatry, 139,* 1315–1318.

Meltzer, H. Y., & Arora, R. C. (1991). Platelet serotonin studies in affective disorders: Evidence for a serotonergic abnormality? In M. Sandler, A. Coppen, & S. Harnett (Eds.), *5-Hydroxytryptamine in psychiatry* (pp. 50–89). New York: Raven.

Meltzer, H. Y., & Lowy, M. T. (1987). The serotonin hypothesis of depression. In H. Y. Meltzer (Ed.), *Psychopharmacology: The third generation of progress* (pp. 517–526). New York: Raven Press.

Meredith, I. T., Broughton, A., Jennings, G. L., & Esler, M. D. (1991). Evidence of selective increase in cardiac sympathetic activity in patients with sustained ventricular arrhythmias. *The New England Journal of Medicine, 325,* 618–624.

Mikuni, M., Kagaya, A., Takahashi, K., & Meltzer, H. Y. (1992). Serotonin but not norepinephrine-induced calcium mobilization of platelets is enhanced in affective disorders. *Psychopharmacology, 106,* 311–314.

Moss, A. J., & Multicenter Postinfarction Research Group. (1984). Update of postinfarction-risk stratification: physiologic variables. *New York Academy of Sciences, 427,* 280–285.

Norusis, M. J. (1993). *SPSS for Windows, Release 6.0.* Chicago: SPSS.

Podrid, P. J., Fuchs, T., & Candinas, R. (1990). Role of the sympathetic nervous system in the genesis of ventricular arrhythmia. *Circulation, 82* (Suppl. I), 103–113.

Richardson, J. L., Marks, G., Johnson, C. A., Graham, J. W., Chan, K. K., Selser, J. N. et al. (1987). Path model of multidimensional compliance with cancer therapy. *Health Psychology, 6,* 183–207.

Robins, L. N., Helzer, J. E., Croughan, J., & Ratcliff, K. S. (1981). National institute of mental health diagnostic interview schedule: its history, characteristics, and validity. *Archives of General Psychiatry, 38,* 381–389.

Rouleau, J., Packer, M., Moyé, L., DeChamplain, J., Bichet, D., Klein, M., Rouleau, J., Sussex, B., Arnold, J. M., Sestier, F., Parker, J., McEwan, P., Bernstein, V., Cuddy, T. E., Lamas, G., Gottlieb, S., McCans, J., Nadeau, C., Delage, F., Chuan-Chuan, C. W., & Pfeffer, M. (1994). Prognostic value of neurohumoral activation in patients with an acute myocardial infarction: effect of captopril. *Journal of the American College of Cardiology, 24,* 583–591.

Rouleau, J. L., Talajic, M., Sussex, B., Warnica, W., Davies, R., Potvin, L., Gardner, M., Stewart, D. J., Plante, S., Dupuis, R., Lauzon, C., Ferguson, J., Mikes, E., Balnozan, V., & Savard, P. (1994). Changing patterns of patients having an acute myocardial infarction (AMI), their risk factors, risk stratification and survival [Abstract]. *Circulation, 90,* i–500.

Roy, A., Linnoila, M., & Potter, W. (1985). Plasma norepinephrine level in affective disorders: Relationship to melancholia. *Archives of General Psychiatry, 42,* 1181–1185

Ruberman, W., Weinblatt, E., Goldberg, J. D., & Chaudhary, B. S. (1984). Psychosocial influences on mortality after myocardial infarction. *The New England Journal of Medicine, 311,* 552–559.

Schleifer, S. J., Macari-Hinson, M. M., Coyle, D. A., Slater, W. R., Kahn, M., Gorlin, R., & Zucker, H. D. (1989). The nature and course of depression following myocardial infarction. *Archives of Internal Medicine, 149,* 1785–1789.

Schwartz, P. J., Billman, G. E., & Stone, H. L. (1984). Autonomic mechanisms in ventricular fibrillation induced by myocardial ischemia during exercise in dogs with healed myocardial infarction: an experimental preparation for sudden cardiac death. *Circulation, 69,* 790–800.

Spielberger, C. D., Krasner, S. S., & Solomon, E. P. (1988). The experience, expression, and control of anger. In M. P., Janisse (Ed.), *Health psychology: Individual differences and stress* (pp. 89–108). New York: Springer-Verlag.

Spielberger, C. D., Gorsuch, R. L., Lushene, R., Vagg, P. R., & Jacobs, G. A. (1983). *Manual for the state-trait anxiety inventory*. Palo Alto, CA: Consulting Psychologists Press.

Surridge, D. H., Erdahl, D. L., Lawson, J. S., Donald, M. W., Monga, T. N., Bird, C. E., & Letemedia, F. J. (1984). Psychiatric aspects of diabetes mellitus. *British Journal of Psychiatry, 145,* 269–276.

The Cardiac Arrhythmia Suppression Trial (CAST) Investigators. (1989). Preliminary report: effect of encainide and flecainide on mortality in a randomized trial of arrhythmia suppression after myocardial infarction. *The New England Journal of Medicine, 321,* 406–412.

Vanhoutte, P. M. (1991). Platelet-derived serotonin, the endothelium, and cardiovascular disease. *Journal of Cardiovascular Pharmacology, 17* (Suppl. 5), 6–12.

Veith, R. C., Lewis, N., Linares, O. A., Barnes, R. F., Raskind, M. A., Villacres, E. C., Murburg, M. M., Ashleigh, E. A., Castillo, S., Peskind, E. R., Pascualy, M., & Halter, J. B. (1993). Sympathetic nervous system major depression—basal and desipramine-induced alterations in plasma activity in norepinephrine kinetics. *Archives of General Psychiatry, 50,* 1–12.

Verrier, R. L., Calvert, A., & Lown, B. (1975). Effect of posterior hypothalamic stimulation on ventricular fibrillation threshold. *American Journal of Physiology, 228,* 923–927.

Weissman, M. M., Myers, J. K., & Thompson, W. D. (1981). Depression and its treatment in a U.S. urban community 1975–1976. *Archives of General Psychiatry, 38,* 417–421.

Wong, N. D., Cupples, L. A., Ostfeld, A. M., Levy, D., & Kannel, W. B. (1989). Risk factors for long-term coronary prognosis after initial myocardial infarction: The Framingham Study. *American Journal of Epidemiology, 130,* 469–480.

9

Stress and Social Support in Relation to Cardiovascular Health

Kristina Orth-Gomér
Karolinska Institute, Stockholm, Sweden

THE STRESS CONCEPT

The study of positive factors that enhance and promote cardiovascular health and have the capacity to counteract or even prevent the harmful effects of psychosocial stress has only recently become a research area on its own. It has become clear that in order to examine and understand the health effects of stress, several components of the stress–disease process need to be included. Selye's (1960) original definition of stress was concerned with the physiological fight or flight reaction in response to a threat or a challenge from the environment. Thus, his definition involved only the individual physiological response. Later on a strong interest arose in stressors or stimuli that arise from the environment of an individual. Investigators focused on life events, the major stressful experiences that occurred in an individual's life. Work by Rahe and others (1998) demonstrated that an accumulation of *life events* was harmful to health. These effects, however, were mostly shown in retrospective studies. To confirm the findings in relation to development and clinical expression of major chronic diseases like CHD have proven to be more difficult.

In the 1970s, another idea was introduced into the theoretical framework—the concept of vulnerability of the individual exposed to stressful stimuli. Cassel (1976) hypothesized that *host* resistance was a crucial factor in the impact of stress on health. The fact that host resistance had not been accounted for in many studies might explain why so many inconsistent and contradictory results had been obtained in studies of health effects of stress.

According to Cassel (1976) two factors were essential in determining the degree of an individual's host resistance: capacity for *coping* and *social supports*.

Today's definition of stress has come to include considerably more than the physiological, stress by Selye (1960). Both the social environmental effects as expressed by stressful life events and the resistance or vulnerability of the individual exposed to the life events are considered in conjunction with the individual physiological responses to them.

MODELS FOR HEALTH EFFECTS
OF SOCIAL SUPPORTS

In our group of investigators at the Karolinska Institute in Stockholm, recent research has been focused on factors that promote host resistance. We have hypothesized that these factors include the health promoting effects of well-functioning social networks and social support.

Two models explaining the effects of social support have been proposed. According to the buffer effect hypothesis, social supports are only relevant to health when the individual is exposed to severe stress. The support from the social-network members will help the individual to deal with the stress in many ways. Network members may help the individual to better recognize and evaluate stressors and they may help in the identification of solutions to overcome the stressor. Network members may also provide emotional support that may counteract the individual's feelings of loneliness and hopelessness and thus help the person to deal more efficiently with problems. Supportive actions may also aim at relieving stress effects in reducing tension and anxiety and counteract depressive reactions.

According to the buffer hypothesis, however, the health effects of social support can only be demonstrated when stress is present. In contrast, the main effect hypothesis claims that social contacts and social supports are among our most basic human needs. Absence or lack of social support leads to social isolation. This may create damages to health, which are similar to or analogous to the effects of stress. As seen from the following empirical evidence, both of these hypotheses are applicable. It is most probable that social support may both act as a stress buffer against harmful health effects and enhance health and well-being by itself. The issue of demonstrating health effects on cardiovascular health in empirical studies has been approached on three different levels: population, patient, and physiology.

POPULATION-BASED STUDIES
OF SOCIAL SUPPORT

In cooperation with the Central Swedish Bureau of Statistics we were able to evaluate the effects of social-network interactions on health outcome on survival in the entire Swedish population (Orth-Gomér & Johnson, 1987).

More than 17,400 men and women, representing a random sample of the adult Swedish population, responded to a questionnaire about their social ties and social networks. The questionnaire was included in two of the annual Surveys of Living Conditions in Sweden, which were designed to assess and measure the welfare of the nation in material as well as in social and psychological terms. Based on the questionnaire, we created a comprehensive social network interaction index, which included the number of members in the network and the frequency of contacts with each member. Seven sources of contacts were identified by means of factor analyses: parents, siblings, nuclear family (spouse and children), close relatives, co-workers, neighbors, distant relatives, and friends. The contacts with each source were calculated and added up to a total index score, which varied from 0 to 106.

By linkage of the Survey of Living Conditions with the Swedish National Death Register we were able to investigate the impact of the social-network interaction index on all causes and on cardiovascular mortality. Dividing the study population into tertiles according to their index score, we found that those men and women, who were in the lowest tertiles, had an invariably higher mortality risk than those who were in the middle and upper tertiles of the index score.

As indicated in Figs 9.1 and 9.2, the risk of dying if one was in the lowest tertile was four to five times higher than in the two higher tertiles (Orth-Gomér & Johnson, 1987). Many underlying and confounding factors might explain this association. Thus, for example, with increasing age, mortality risk increases and the number of social contacts decrease. Another confounding factor is cardiovascular health status at the initial examination. If one is sick and disabled from CHD, mortality risk increases, and it is also likely that the network decreases. Yet another confounding factor is social class. It is well known that cardiovascular morbidity and mortality are higher in lower social classes but also that social networks are smaller and social contacts less abundant. Thus, controlling for these and other risk factors in multivariate analyses was necessary. Using multiple-logistic-regression analyses, we obtained a final-risk estimate of 1.4 (95% confidence intervals: 1.07; 1.69) for men and women, respectively, who were in the lowest social-network interaction tertile. Thus, a 40% ex-

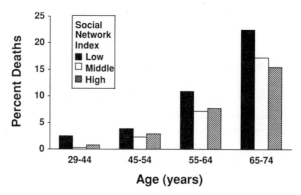

FIG. 9.1   Mortality rate in social network index tertiles for Swedish men.

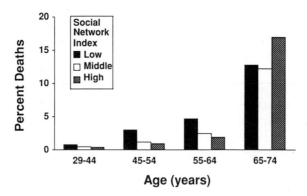

FIG. 9.2   Mortality rate in social network index tertiles for Swedish women.

cess-cardiovascular-mortality risk was associated with an impoverished social network. It is interesting to note that there was no additional
health-promoting effect for subjects who were in the highest as compared to
the middle tertile. Possibly, a great number of contacts can represent a strain
on the individual as well as protection against harmful health effects. So
without even knowing anything further about the stressors in the lives of
these men and women, we were able to confirm a cardiovascular
health-promoting main effect of social networks.

In one domain, it was possible to demonstrate an interactive effect with
stressors, namely in the work environment. For those men and women in
the population who were steadily employed, their perceived work stress was
examined and related to social support and to health outcome (Johnson,
1986). Work stress was conceptualized as the combination of high demands
and pressure at work on the one hand, with lack of control and decision lati-

tude in the work situation on the other (Karasek & Theorell, 1990). It was found that the lack of support and the lack of social interaction at work potentiated the harmful effects of work stress. Those men and women who experienced high demands, low control, and low support had the highest disease risk. Thus, an effect of lack of social ties at work was found, which increased the cardiovascular risk of psychosocial work strain.

FUNCTIONAL MODELS OF SOCIAL SUPPORT

Gradually it became clear that the quantitative concept of social-network interaction was insufficient in explaining the effects on health outcome. It was more probable that the supportive functions of the network members would be the crucial factor, not the number of contacts. Thus, we wanted to examine qualitative rather than quantitative aspects of social networks. We aimed at a more difficult investigation of social supports.

For this purpose, a suitable instrument for the assessment and measurement of social supports had to be identified. A review of methods showed that two kinds of measures could be identified. First, instruments that in quantitative terms measured social networks and social interaction were identified. These had been shown in prospective studies to affect health but were unable to describe the functions of the social contacts. Second, instruments were examined that were designed to assess quality and function of contacts, but for which the predictive capacity in studies of health outcome had not been tested. Furthermore, these measures had often been applied in small groups of patients or students. Thus they were lengthy and time consuming and not practical to use in prospective population studies.

Consequently, we developed a method that would fulfill both criteria, that is, describe function and quality as well as being easily applicable in population studies. Our method was based on the Interview Schedule for Social Interaction (ISSI), originally developed by Henderson and Byrne (Henderson, Duncan-Tores, & Byrne1980). We modified their rather lengthy questionnaire to be used as a paper and pencil test and adapted it for a Swedish study group. The details of the methodological adaptation as well as the review have been presented elsewhere (Orth-Gomér, & Undén, 1987; Undén & Orth-Gomér, 1989).

This method was used in a population study of 50-year-old men born in Gothenburg, who were also examined for cardiovascular risk factors (hypertension, hyperlidemia, smoking, diabetes, and lack of exercise, etc.). A cohort of 776 men was randomly obtained from the general population and found healthy on initial examination. They were followed for incidence of myocardial infarction and CHD mortality for 6 years.

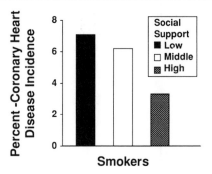

FIG. 9.3   The incidence of CHD incidence as a function of low-, medium-, or high-social support in 50-year-old male smokers in Gothenburg, Sweden.

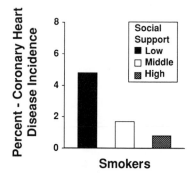

FIG. 9.4   The incidence of CHD incidence as a function of low-, medium-, or high-social support in 50-year-old male.

Lack of social support was found to be an independent predictor of CHD incidence in these previously healthy men (Orth-Gomér, Rosengren,& Wilhelmsen, 1993). The risk conveyed by lack of support was comparable in magnitude to that of smoking. Both factors had multivariate adjusted odds ratios greater than 3.0. All other risk factors, such as cholesterol, fibrinogen, blood pressure, and lack of exercise were less strong predictors of MI and sudden cardiac death. To disentangle the effects of smoking and lack of support, the analyses were conducted for smokers and nonsmokers separately. The risk gradients between men with low and high support were the same (about 3.0) with the highest incidence in smoking men without social support (7.1) and lowest incidence in nonsmoking men with high support (0.8%; Fig. 9.3, 9.4).

In this study (Rosengren, Orth-Gomér, Wedel, & Wilhelmsen, 1993) major life events were also assessed, using a short version of the PERI-scale by Dohrenwend (Dohrenwend, Kransnoff, Askenasy, & Dohrewen 1978). Only recent and serious negative-life events were included, and their effects on mortality risk were assessed in an 8-year follow-up examination. Men who had experienced three or more life events in the year prior to the examination had an almost four-fold risk of dying as compared to men who did not report life events. When the effects of social support were considered simultaneously, it was found that only in those men who lacked support, in particular, emotional support from a spouse, close relatives, or friends, were the effects of life events harmful. Men who lacked social support and had experienced several serious life events, had more than five times the mortality of men who enjoyed emotional support even when experiencing serious life events.

STUDIES OF CARDIAC PATIENTS

Another example of interactive effects was offered in a study of cardiac patients, who were examined for psychosocial factors as well as myocardial indicators of an unfavorable prognosis and then followed for a 10-year period (Orth-Gomér & Undén, 1990; Orth-Gomér, Undén, & Edwards, 1988). Psychosocial factors included the assessment of social integration and social isolation together with personality and behavior type, in particular the Type A behavior pattern. The behavior pattern was assessed using the Structured Interview procedure.

The behavior type in itself had no impact on prognosis in these patients. Some 24% of Type A men died as compared to 22% of Type B men, but when considering the interactive effects with social isolation another picture emerged. Social isolation, was assessed using a diary of activities during a regular week. The men were asked to describe and quantify anything they would engage in during the evenings and weekends of a normal week. Activities were then divided into those that involved physical exercise, those that were mainly sedentary and performed at home, and those that were performed for recreation with others. Of these activity types, lack of social recreational activity was the strongest predictor of mortality. Men who never engaged in such activities—we called them socially isolated—had about three times higher mortality risk than those who were socially active (Orth-Gomér et al., 1988). In addition, as seen in Fig. 9.5, the Type A men

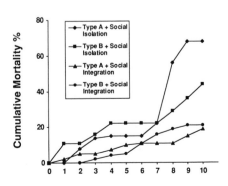

FIG. 9.5 The cumulative mortality of Type A versus Type B men as a function of social isolation and social integration in a cohort of Swedish men.

who were socially isolated, had an even higher mortality risk, than any of the other categories (Orth-Gomér & Undén, 1990).

Studies of Type A behavior patterns and their prognostic implications have yielded conflicting results. These studies typically have looked only at the effects of behavior type and disregarded characteristics of the social environment. Thus, for example, in the original Western Collaborative Group Study, the 22-year follow up of Type A versus Type B men, showed no harmful effect of the Type A behavior. In fact, Type A men lived even longer than Type B men (Ragland & Brand, 1988). On the other hand, intervention studies have shown that attenuation and modification of Type A behavior may have a beneficial prognostic effect. In the study by Friedman and colleagues (Friedman et al., 1986) of approximately 500 myocardial infarction patients, half of them were randomly submitted to Type A behavior modification. The treatment reduced the infarct recurrency rate by 50% as compared to control patients who received only cardiac counseling.

A close study of the behavior modification used in the Friedman et al. (1986) study reveals that the intervention may have had powerful effects not only on the individual behavior but also on the social environment. Some of the behavioral practices included behaviors that were directed towards the social environment, such as showing appreciation of one's co-workers or subordinates, or showing affection for one's closest family members, such as spouse and children. It is probable that the practice of these behaviors for a prolonged time also changed the behaviors and cognitions of the members of the social network and environment, so that the end result may have been an improvement of real social support. In that case, the effects on myocardial-infarction recurrence rate might be ascribed to improved support as well as to attenuated Type A behavior. The most likely explanation involves both mechanisms.

POSSIBLE PHYSIOLOGICAL MECHANISMS

Whereas, the effects of social supports on CHD seem well established and the empirical evidence is convincing, there is much less knowledge about how such effects are mediated and which pathogenetic mechanisms are involved.

One possible pathogenic pathway is via standard risk factors such as smoking, lack of exercise, and so forth. However, results concerning effects of social support mediated via standard risk factors are both incomplete and inconsistent. In no case do they explain more than a fraction of the full range of effects observed from social support (Davidson & Shumaker, 1987).

In a study of 148 working men and women, we examined the immediate physiological effects of lack of social supports on cardiovascular function

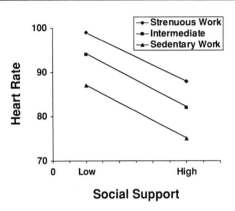

FIG. 9.6 Average heart rate at work as a function of work intensity and self-report of social support. Heart rate was assessed every 5 minutes by ambulatory monitoring and then averaged, controlling for age and sex.

(Undén, Orth-Gomér, & Elofsson, 1989). Mean heart rates were found to be significantly higher in persons reporting low-social support at work. This effect was maintained during working hours as well as during leisure time and rest. The difference in mean heart rate between subjects reporting low and high support was about 15 beats per minute (Fig. 9.6). The size of the difference was similar during work, leisure time, and sleep. There was also a significant relationship between social support and blood pressure. Subjects reporting low support, had higher systolic blood pressure. Diastolic blood pressure, smoking, alcohol consumption, and body mass index did not differ between groups.

In order to examine independent direct and indirect effects, we applied canonical correlation analysis to a model including the variables age, gender, body mass index, physical strain, smoking, alcohol consumption, demand and control, social support at work, systolic blood pressure and heart rate (Undén et al., 1989). The results confirmed a direct effect of social support on heart rate, which was not mediated by other variables in the model (Fig 9.7). Low support was strongly associated with a high strain at work (i.e., subjects who reported low support also experienced high demand and low control at work). Thus, a possible pathogenetic mechanism for the association between high demand–low control and CHD was suggested, namely, via low support and persistent elevated heart rates.

How can the effects of low-work support on average heart rates throughout the 24 hours be explained? Hypothetically, low support at work could have prolonged effects extending over a longer period of time than the work situation. Inability to unwind after work has been found to be a common effect of stress at work (Frankenhauser et al., 1989). Workers are often unable to let go of thoughts and feelings caused by a poor psychosocial environment and unsatisfactory support at work. Perhaps the effect is sufficiently strong that even the ability to relax during sleep is influenced.

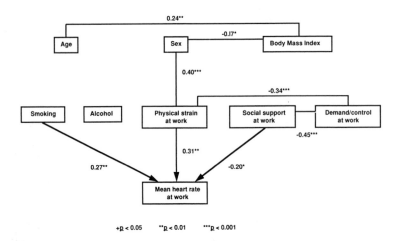

FIG. 9.7   Canonical correlations showing significant independent direct and indirect effects of personal and work-environment factors on heart rate at work.

ELEVATED HEART RATES
AND HEALTH OUTCOMES

During recent years a number of reports have been published, which indicate that elevated heart rates have long-term harmful effects. In the Framingham Heart Study, in which 5,000 men and women have been followed for more than 30 years, excess mortality rates were reported for men with heart rates over 85 beats per minute (Kannel, Kannel, Paffenbarger, & Cupples, 1987). In another population study of 9,000 men, an increased mortality was also reported in men with elevated heart rates (Dyer et al., 1980). The risk seems to be specific for CHD, and is especially high for sudden cardiac death. Thus, persistent elevated heart rates may constitute a sign of chronic autonomic arousal, which in turn may contribute to the progression of artherosclerosis as well as precipitating factors such as cardiac dysrhythmia. Similarly, in studies of patients with or without a recent heart attack, low heart rate variability was found to be related to both autonomic dysfunction and to subsequent increased mortality risk. Also, low heart rate variability was strongly associated with high persistent heart rates (Kleiger, Miller, Bigger, & Moss, 1987; Rich et al., 1988).

CONCLUSION

In conclusion, the studies reviewed in this chapter appear to demonstrate the need to consider aspects of the psychosocial environment and individual difference factors as well as physiological stress mechanisms in order to understand CHD morbidity and mortality. Only when it is attempted to describe the processes that link environmental stressors and social support to disease within this multifactorial frame work shall a proper understanding of the pathogenesis of CHD be reached.

REFERENCES

Cassel, J. (1976). The contribution of the social environment to host resistance. *American Journal of Epidemiology, 104,* 107–123.

Davidson, D. M., & Shumaker, S. A. (1987). Social support and cardiovascular disease. *Arteriosclerosis, 7,* 101–104.

Dohrenwend, B. S., Krasnoff, L., Askenasy, A. R., & Dohrenwend, B. P. (1978). Exemplification of a method for scaling life events: the PERI life events scale. *Journal of Health and Social Behavior, 19,* 5–29.

Dyer, A. R., Persky, V., Stamler, J., Oglesby, P., Shekelle, R. B., & Berkson, D. M. (1980). Heart rate as a prognostic factor for coronary heart disease and mortality: Findings in three Chicago epidemiologic studies. *American Journal of Epidemiology, 112*(6), 736–749.

Frankenhduser, M., Lundberg, U., Fredriksson, M., Melin, B., Tuomisto, M., Myrsten, A., Hedman, M., Bergman-Losman, B., & Wallin, L. (1989). Stress on and off the job as related to sex and occupational status in whitecollar workers. *Journal of Organizational Behavior, 10,* 321–346.

Friedman, M., Thoresen, C. E., Gill, J. J., Ulmer, D., Powell, L. I., Prince, V. A. et al. (1986). Alteration of type A behavior and its effect on cardiac recurrences in post myocardial infarction patients; summary results of the Recurrent Coronary Prevention Project. *American Heart Journal, 112,* 653-665.

Henderson, S., Duncan-Jones, P., & Byrne, G. (1980). Measuring social relationships. The interview schedule for social interaction. *Psychological Medicine, 10,* 723–34.

Johnson, J. V. (1986). *The impact of workplace social support, job demands and work control upon cardiovascular disease in Sweden.* Stockholm: Department of Psychology, University of Stockholm.

Kannel, W. B., Kannel, C., Paffenbarger, R. S., & Cupples, L. A. (1987). Heart rate and cardiovascular mortality: The Framingham Study. *American Heart Journal, 113*(6), 1489–1494.

Karasek, R., & Theorell, T. (1990). *Healthy work. Stress, productivity and the reconstruction of working life.* New York: Basic Books.

Kleiger, R. E., Miller, J. P., Bigger, J. T., & Moss, A. J. (1987). Decreased heart rate variability and its association with increased mortality after acute myocardial infarction. *American Journal of Cardiology, 59,* 256–262.

Orth-Gomér, K., & Johnson, J. V. (1987). Social network interaction and mortality. A six year follow-up study of a random sample of the Swedish population. *Journal of Chronic Diseases, 40*(10), 949–957.

Orth-Gomér, K., & Undén, A. L. (1987). The measurement of social support in population surveys. *Social Science and Medicine, 24*(1), 83–94.

Orth-Gomér, K., Undén, A. L., & Edwards, M. E. (1988). Social isolation and mortality in ischernic heart disease. A 10-year follow-up study of 150 middle-aged men. *Acta Medica Scandinavia, 224,* 205–215.

Orth-Gomér, K., & Undén, A. L. (1990). Type A behavior, social support and coronary risk. Interaction and significance for mortality in cardiac patients. *Psychosomatic Medicine, 52,* 59–72.

Orth-Gomér, K., Rosengren, A., & Wilhelmsen, L. (1993). Lack of social support and incidence of coronary heart disease in middle-aged Swedish men. *Psychosomatic Medicine, 55,* 37–43.

Ragland, D. R., & Brand, R. J. (1988). Type A behavior and mortality from coronary heart disease. *New England Journal of Medicine, 318,* 65–69.

Rahe, R. H. (1988). Recent life changes and coronary heart disease: 10 years' research. In S. Fisher, & J. Reason, (Eds.), *Handbook of life stress, cognition and health* (pp. 317–333). Wiley.

Rich, M. W., Saini, J. S., Kleiger, R. E., Carney, R. M., teVelde, A., & Freedland, K. E. (1988). Correlation of heart rate variability with clinical and angiographic variables and late mortality after coronary angiography. *American Journal of Cardiology 62,* 714–717.

Rosengren, A., Orth-Gomér, K., Wedel, H., & Wilhelmsen, L. (1993). Stressful life events, social support, and mortality in men born in 1933. *British Medical Journal, 307,* 1102–1105.

Selye, H. (1960). The concept of stress in experimental physiology. In J. M. Tanner (Ed.), *Stress and psychiatric disorder.* Oxford: Blackwell.

Undén, A. L., & Orth-Gomér, K. (1989). Development of a social support instrument for use in population surveys. *Social Science and Medicine, 29*(12), 1387–1392.

Undén, A. L., Orth-Gomér, K., & Elofsson, S. (1989). *Stress research report, 214. Karolinska Institute.*

Author Index

Locators annotated with *f* indicate figures.
Locators annotated with *n* indicate notes.
Locators annotated with *t* indicate tables.

A

Abbott, D. H., 74, *82*
Abboud, F. M., 88, *118*
Abel, R., 93, *119*
Abrahams, V. C., 4, 12, *38*
Abshire, V. M., 12, *38, 40*
Adamopoulos, S., 221, *226*
Adams, M. R., 72, 73, 74, *74f,* 75, 76, 77, *77f,* 78, *78f, 82, 83, 84, 89, 116*
Adams-Campbell, L. L., 157, *168*
Adewuyi, J. O., 146, *178*
Adler, P. S., 130, *140*
Adragna, M., 150, *170*
Agabiti-Rosei, E., 96, *119*
Aggleton, J. P., 36, *38*
Agodoa, L., 147, *168*
Agramonte, R., 96, 97, 98, *115*
Agrawal, A. K., 90, *115*
Ahern, D. K., 203, 204, *224, 226*
Ahlberg-Hulten, G., 127, 128, *143*
Ahuja, R. C., 126, *141*
Ahumada-Hemer, H., 72, *82*
Albert, A., 95, *114*
Alberti, K. G., 152, *175*
Albright, C. A., *134t,* 135, *141*
Albright, G. L., 102, *111,* 165, *168*
Alderman, M., 127, 128, *143*
Alderman, M. H., 148, *174,* 195, *199*
Alexander, C. N., 165, 166, *178*
Alexander, J. K., 93, *111*
Allen, M. T., 102, 105, *111,* 182, 188, 190, 191, *198, 200*
Allen, R., 3, *38*
Allen, W. R., 154, *171*

Almog, S., 87, *118,* 152, *176*
Alpert, B. S., 158, 159, 162, *168, 173, 176,* 182, 189, 190, 195, 198, *201*
Alpi, O., 152, *169*
Alter, M., 147, *168*
Alvarez, M., 126, 127, *143*
Amaral, D. G., 25, *46*
Ambrosioni, E., 150, *168,* 187, 190, 198, *199*
American Psychiatric Association Committee on Nomenclature and Statistics, 205, *224*
Amery, A., 91, 92, 103, *116,* 149, 150, 151, 156, *175*
Ammerman, A. S., 156, *179*
An, X., 15, *46*
Anderson, E. A., 88, 89, *111*
Anderson, J. L., 203, 204, *224*
Anderson, N. B., 93, 94, 95, 104, *111, 112,* 145, 149, 151, 153, 154, 163, 167, *168,* 194, 195, 198, *199*
Anderson, N. J., 162, *169*
Anderson, R. A., 29, *38*
Anderson, W. P., 96, *116*
Andersson, O., 88, 89, 90, *116*
Andreassi, J. L., 102, *111,* 165, *168*
Angelakos, E. T., 95, *114,* 150, *171*
Angus, J. A., 96, *116*
Ansley, J., 87, *117*
Anton-Culver, H., 148, *172*
Aoki, K., 191, *201*
Appel, M. A., 165, *169*
Applegate, C. D., 13, *39*
Araki, S., 91, 103, *118*
Ardlie, N.G., 90, *112*
Arensman, F., 162, *179,* 195, *202*

Engel, B. T., 60n, 105, *113*, 165, *172*
English, E., 3, *41*
Ensrud, K. E., 149, 153, *171*
Ephross, S. A., 148, *169*
Epstein, L. H., 166, *171*
Epstein, S., 131, *140*
Erbaugh, J., 204, 205, *225*
Erdahl, D. L., 219, *228*
Erfurt, J., 154, 155, 160, *173*
Erfurt, J. C., 125, 130, *141*
Ergi, G., 204, *226*
Eschwege, E., 87, *113*, 152, *169*
Eshkol, A., 87, *118*, 152, *176*
Esler, M. D., 160, 161, 165, *171*, *174*, 192, 200, 222, *227*
Estigarribia, J. A., 152, *175*
Evans, J., 94, 97, 98, 106, *119*, 156, 163, *178*
Evans, M. H., 11, *41*, *42*
Everitt, B. J., 30, *47*
Everitt, D. E., 220, *224*
Ewart, C. K., 131, *140*, 165, 166, *171*, 203, 204, *224*
Ewing, D. J., 99, *113*

F

Factor, M. I., 222, *225*
Fagard, R., 150, *175*
Fagius, J., 88, *113*
Fahrenberg, J., 102, *113*
Faillace, R., 88, *117*, 153, *175*
Falkner, B., 94, 95, *113*, *114*, 148, 149, 150, 150 *171*, 152, 153, 162, 167, *169*, *170*, *171*
Fanselow, M. S., 24, 30, *42*, *44*
Farb, C., 27, 30, *44*
Farb, C. R., *45*
Fardin, V., 14, *42*
Farley, R., 154, *171*
Farris, R. P., 166, *177*
Federoff, H. J., 74, *82*
Feinleib, M., 81, *83*
Feltynowski, T., 89, *115*
Fencl, V., 192, *199*
Ferguson, J., 204, 221, *227*
Ferin, M., 74, *83*
Fernandes, M., 95, *114*
Fernandez, T., 182, 195, *202*
Fernandez de Molina, A., 34, 36, *42*
Ferrannini, E., 151, 152, 167, *171*
Ferris, E. B., 126, *142*
Feuerstein, M., 127, *141*
Fiebach, N. H., 86, *113*
Fields, H. L., 22, *39*
Filewich, R., 129, 139, *140*
Filewich, R. J., 22, *41*, *53*, 66, *67*

Finberg, N. S., 150, *178*
Findley, J. D., 52, 68, 190, *199*
Fine, B. P., 151, *176*
Fineberg, N. S., 94, *118*, 148, 149, 150, 162, *175*, *176*, *180*
Fins, A. I., 3, 4, 47, 93, 94, 95, 97, 98, 104, 106, *119*, 162, 163, 167, *178*, 184, *201*
Fitzgerald, E. F., 125, *140*
Flack, J. M., 148, 149, 153, *171*, *172*
Flamenbaum, W., 95, *114*
Fleg, J. L., 92, 103, *114*, *119*
Fleiss, J. L., 215, 221, *225*, *226*
Flynn, J. P., 34, *41*
Foale, R. A., 148, *175*
Foerster, F., 102, *113*
Folkow, B., 90, 93, *114*, 160, 161, *171*, 191, 192, 193, *199*
Follick, M. J., 203, 204, *224*, *226*
Folsom, A. R., 148, 152, *169*, *171*
Fong, R. L., 166, *172*
Fontana, A. F., 131, 134t, 135, *143*
Ford, C. D., 147, *178*
Forest, R., 28, *45*
Forester, W. F., 98, *117*
Forfar, C., 221, *226*
Forrester, T., 146, *172*
Foster, T. A., 152, *169*
Fox, E. L., 197, *199*
Fox, M. L., 128, 130, *140*
Frame, C., 162, 163, 167, *178*
Frame, C. A., 3, 4, 47, 93, 94, 95, 97, 98, 104, 106, *119*, 184, *201*
France, C., 123, 130, *140*
Franceschi, S., 75, *83*
Frank, G. C., 166, *177*
Frankel, H. L., 52, *68*
Frankenhaeuser, M., 89, *114*, 237, *239*
Fraser, H., 146, *172*
Frasure-Smith, N., 203, 205, 222, *226*
Fray, J. C. S., 93, *114*, 149, *172*
Fredrickson, M., 104, *114*, 162, *172*
Fredrikson, M., 181, *199*
Fredriksson, M., 237, *239*
Freedland, K. E., 219, 221, *225*, 238, *240*
Freedman, D. S., 152, *172*
Freedman, R. R., 110, *114*
Freeman, C. R., 96, 97, 98, *115*
Freeman, V., 146, *172*
Friedman, G. D., 156, *174*
Friedman, H. S., 203, *225*
Friedman, J., 90, *119*
Friedman, M., 236, *239*
Frisk-Holmberg, F., 89, *115*
Frohlich, E., 93, *118*
Frohlich, E. D., 85, 93, *118*, *119*
Frolich, E. D., 195, *201*
From, A. H . L., 98, *116*

Subject Index

Locators annotated with *f* indicate figures.
Locators annotated with *n* indicate notes.
Locators annotated with *t* indicate tables.

A

Acceleration index (ACI), of myocardial contractility, 98–99, 101t
ACE, *see* Angiotensin converting enzyme
ACe, *see* Amygdala, central nucleus of
Acetylcholine, female responses to, 75
Achilles tendon reflex, barostimulation of, 55–57, 56n
ACI, *see* Acceleration index
Active coping responses, 94, 106, 155–156, 162–163
Adaptive filtering method, 98–99
Adenosine diphosphate (ADP), platelet aggregation and, 222
Adenosine triphosphatase (ATPase) pump, ethnic differences in, 150
Adherence, to intervention plans, *see* Patient compliance
Adjusted goodness-of-fit index (AGFI), in autonomic cardiovascular regulation, 99–100
ADP, *see* Adenosine diphosphate
Adrenal glands, controls of, 9, 73
Adrenergic nervous system
 blockade effects on, 89–90
 ethnic differences in, 94–95
 insulin effect on, 87–88
Aerobic exercise, hemodynamic effects of, 196–197
Affective behaviors
 in cardiovascular neurobiology research, 1–3
 conditioned, *see* Learned responses
 mediation of
  feedback signals for, 18–24

model for, 34–37
 nervous system role in, 5–7
 reflexive, *see* Unlearned responses
Afferent neurons, 5
Afferent reflexes
 blood pressure regulation by, 15–17, 51
 visceral, *see* Visceral sensory function
African-Americans, *see* Black Americans
Age
 blood pressure responses per, psychological challenges and, 185–189
 cardiovascular disease risk per, 86
  sympathetic nervous system and, 91–92
  three-factor model and, 102–103
 glucose tolerance correlation with, 152–153
 hypertension correlation with, 146–147
  drug interventions and, 164, 166
AGFI, *see* Adjusted goodness-of-fit index
Aggression, hypertension correlation with, 131–132
AL, *see* Lateral amygdaloid nucleus
Alcohol consumption, hypertension correlation with, ethnic differences in, 156–157, 159
Alpha-adrenergic activity, ethnic differences in, 94–95, 150–151, 161–162
Alpha-adrenergic agonists, ethnic differences with, 94–95, 150–151
Alpha-adrenergic blockade, ethnic differences with, 94–95, 164
Amino acids, excitatory, 12–15
Amygdala
 central nucleus of (ACe), 13, 25–26, 31f, 32
 functional anatomy of, 6, 9
 learning role of, 25–30, 31f, 32, 36–37

social isolation of females, 73, 78–79, 79f
social status incongruity of females,
79–81, 80f
cynomolgus, 71–73
macaque, 14
Mortality and morbidity factors
of coronary heart disease, 86–87, 231–236,
232f, 235f, 238
of hypertension, 147, 158, 164
of myocardial infarction, 208–211, 208f, 211f,
212t–213t, 214f, 220–224
of strokes, 147
Mosaic theory, of hypertension, 190–191
Motor system, nervous system integration with, 5
mPFC, see Medial prefrontal cortex
Multistage cognitive model, of fear conditioning,
30
Muscle fibers, insulin resistance and, 89
Muscle relaxation, progressive, hypertension applications of, 165–166
Myocardial contractility
ethnic differences in, 161–163, 195
indices of, 98–99, 101t
low, see Low-flow circulatory state
Myocardial infarction (MI)
behavioral counseling following, 235–236,
235f
mortality factors
mechanisms of, 220, 222–224
studies of, 208, 208f, 210–211, 211f,
212t–213t, 214f
prognostic factors
disease severity, 214–215, 216t–217t,
218–219
psychosocial, 204, 214–215, 216t–217t,
218–219, 224
psychosocial factors, prognostic influence of
assessment tools for, 204–206
disease severity interactions, 214–215,
216t–217t, 218–219
evidence of, 203–204
limitations of, 223
mental depression results, 206–209, 207t,
208f
multivariate models, 210, 212t–213t,
218–219
negative emotions results, 207t, 209–210
potential behavioral mechanisms,
219–220
potential physiological mechanisms,
220–223
research strategies, 223–224
social support role results, 207t, 210–214,
211f, 212t–213t, 214f
study methods, 204–206
study overview, 203–204
recurrent acute, 220, 222–223

risk factors, 203, 214–215, 216t–217t,
218–219

N

National Health and Nutrition Examination
Survey (NHANES), hypertension
results of, 146, 157, 166
Neck chamber suction, for barostimulation, 54,
56n–57n, 60
Nerves, see also specific nerve
function of, 5
Nervous systems, see also specific system
affective behavior role of, 5–7
overview of, 5
Neuronal axons (tracts), 6
Neuronal cell body clusters (nuclei), 6–7
Neuronal subsystem
defined, 5
emotional behavior role of, 5–7, 37
Neurons
function of, 5, 26
plasticity of, 26–28, 30
types of, 5, 7
NHANES, see National Health and Nutrition
Examination Survey
No-go response, 18, 19f
Nocturnal trends, in blood pressure, 158–160
Nonpharmacologic interventions, for hypertension
effectiveness of, 139, 235–236, 235f
ethnic differences with, 164–166
Noradrenergic nervous system, in stress responses, 33
Norepinephrine
ethnic differences in, 94–95, 150–151
insulin effects on, 87–88
obesity effects on, 93
post-myocardial infarction, 221–222
Nucleus ambiguus, functional anatomy of, 6–7
Nucleus of the solitary tract (NTS), functional
anatomy of, 6, 8
Nutrition, hypertension and
ethnic differences in, 149–150, 156
rat studies on, 191–192

O

Obesity
cardiovascular disease risk with, 86–88
sympathetic nervous system and, 92–93
ethnic differences in, 157
hypertension association with, 93, 157
Objective assessments, of hypertension,
124–136, 138
Occupational stress
assessment tools for, 128–129, 231, 233, 235